Carrington

Carrington

An Honourable Man

CHRISTOPHER LEE

VIKING
an imprint of
PENGUIN BOOKS

VIKING

UK | USA | Canada | Ireland | Australia
India | New Zealand | South Africa

Viking is part of the Penguin Random House group of companies
whose addresses can be found at global.penguinrandomhouse.com.

First published 2018
001

Copyright © Christopher Lee, 2018

The moral right of the author has been asserted

The portrait of Carrington on page vi is by Fiona Graham-Mackay and appears
in the book with the kind permission of Charles Carington

Picture Credits
All photographs are courtesy of Lord Carrington, except the following: 11, 31, 43, Keystone;
21, *Grimsby Evening Telegraph*; 22, 30, Australian News and Information Bureau;
23, Public Information Office, Cyprus; 27, Ian Scleater; 33, 34, *Financial Times* (Freddie Mansfield);
42, *Daily Telegraph*; 45, 46, *The Times* (Stephen Markeson)

Set in 12/14.75pt Monophoto Bembo
Typeset by Jouve (UK), Milton Keynes
Printed and bound in Great Britain by Clays Ltd, Elcograf S.p.A.

A CIP catalogue record for this book is available from the British Library

ISBN: 978-0-670-91646-7

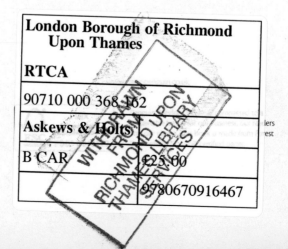

For
Christopher Sinclair-Stevenson

Contents

Preface and Acknowledgements

When Lord Carrington resigned from the Thatcher government in April 1982, it was said that he did so on a point of honour. For more than a quarter of a century, right to the moment of his obituaries, Carrington's action was described as that of an honourable man. Moreover, when the British media decided that some minister should resign but had not, then Carrington was cited as the very model of honourable behaviour. He of course became exasperated with being remembered for a long time as the last minister to resign on a point of honour. He certainly felt that he had done more for his country – he saw nothing odd in using such an expression of duty – than resign. After all, at the time of his resignation Carrington was one of the few to have served in every Tory government since and including Churchill's. He was, among other things, a celebrated Secretary-General of NATO; a successful diplomat; an international negotiator; a chairman of a bank, an auction house and a world-famous museum; an active president of VSO, and not a bad farmer. He had also been the sixth Baron Carrington and came from a long line of bankers and confidants of royalty; his 'Uncle Charlie' (who invented the allotment and horse-whipped a libeller) had been the man Queen Victoria blamed, albeit indirectly, for bringing about the death of Prince Albert.

Carrington was one of those people who seemed to be related through marriages to half the British aristocracy and who seemed to know very well the other half. There was hardly an international forum in which he was not recognized. Both President George H. W. Bush and Dr Henry Kissinger said that part of the fortune of having served in American public life was to have known Carrington. Even allowing for the standard clichés of international statesmen when saying 'nice' things, there were dozens of others who expressed similar sentiments. From all this, it may be gathered that Carrington's view of his times would have been well recorded and that record would be waiting for his biographer. His auto-biography, *Reflect on Things Past* (Collins, 1988), was a modest account of his first seventy years. The title was not a doubtful Proustian translation, but from one of Jonathan Swift's *Thoughts on Various Subjects*:

Reflect on things past, as wars, negotiations, factions, and the like; we enter so little into those interests, that we wonder how men could possibly be so busy, and concerned for things so transitory: Look on the present times, we find the same humour, yet wonder not all.

Here was prescient reference to Carrington's life. Yet his memoir told us little about the man other than that he did not much talk about himself.

I felt sure that the missing details of this life were to be found in his personal diaries. It is a common enough assumption that everyone in public life keeps his or her version of events. Car-rington never kept a diary. He said that he never thought to do so, particularly as he never believed himself likely to be of any interest. It was only shortly before his death that he started to compile, for his family and not for publication, a series of vignettes of people that he had known. We had an agreement that most of these, cer-tainly the most intimately observed, should remain 'closed books'. They will in due course go into the archive of his papers held at Churchill College, Cambridge. The lack of a diary as a springboard to events and people has made the task harder but this has been eased by the many who agreed to help. It was the distinguished Oxford historian and biographer Sir Alistair Horne who warned me that I would have to 'aim off' because everyone liked Car-rington. That was only mostly true, because there were those who did not admire him. There were those who pointed to his indiffer-ent handling of, at the time, important political events. It was partly Carrington's fault that the apparent injustice of Crichel Down in the 1950s resulted in a senior minister's resignation and Carrington's offer to Churchill to go also. Churchill said no, probably because he thought to lose two ministers was political care-lessness. Carrington's own thoughts on that event came from memory of the time. So did those on the days that led to the 1972 Bloody Sunday killings and his reaction as Secretary of State for Defence. While his achievement in bringing together most sides in the 1979 Rhodesia Agreement was largely applauded, there were some who thought it an act of surrender and even treachery. There were even those who believed Carrington most certainly deserved to lose his office over the Falklands affair. I make the points now to show two important factors: as he once said to me (and probably to others), unlike the two of us the rest of the world was imperfect and so we had best tread warily. He trod warily but also on dreams.

Secondly, Peter Carrington was a most loyal friend. He instinct-ively lived by the nineteenth-century family rule: to tell the truth and never to round on or betray a friend. I feel that the great test of any assumed friendship on my part has been to be thoroughly objective about his life and times. That was exactly what he wished. He wished also that this book should not be published in his life-time, partly so that I should not feel inhibited in preparing the manuscript. He often apologized for living on and we had an unspoken agreement that I would never ask after his health in case he suspected my motive.

Posthumous publication was an agreement of which his wife, Iona, did not entirely approve, largely I suspect because she wanted the events surrounding that resignation in 1982 clearly laid out and then to show that the Carrington reputation was not made on one incident alone. She wanted this in his lifetime and was not alone in this view. Horne was of course right in having me, in the majority of cases, aim off when talking to those who knew Carrington, who all gave me their time and guidance.

I will not mention everyone who has helped but special thanks must be to the family, especially to Lady Carrington, who entrusted me with their wartime letters, in reality their love letters, and to Rupert, their son, who offered a perspective I had entirely missed. My gratitude must also be recorded to the dozens of people who did allow me to aim off, including: Sir Anthony Acland, Mr

John Dickie, Sir Brian Fall, General Sir David Fraser, Sir Ronald Grierson, Sir Edward Heath, Professor Lord Hennessy, Sir Ludovic Kennedy, Dr Henry Kissinger, Admiral Sir Henry Leach, Sir John Leahy, Sir Roderick Lyne, Hon. Dom Mintoff, Sir John Nott, Sir Michael Palliser, Mr Paul Sizeland, Sir Kevin Tebbit and the Baroness Thatcher. Grateful thanks also to my agent and friend Christopher Sinclair-Stevenson, to whom this book is dedicated and whose interest and stoicism coaxed me through other projects while resting from *Carrington*, and, of course, to my editor Tony Lacey, who had to keep telling Penguin why the book could not be published until after the subject's death. That Peter Carrington has now freed both author and publisher of an obligation is no triumph for either.

A note on the family name

There is confusion over the family names Carrington and Carington. The explanation is simple if one is a student (no need to be a scholar) of peerage and baronetage. The original Lord Carrington's family name was Smith. He decided to change it to Carrington, claiming some descent from another family – a claim mostly thought to be doubtful. The third Lord Carrington was seemingly obsessed with the family lineage and claimed Sir Michael Carington, a standard-bearer to Richard I on his crusade, as a direct ancestor. Whatever their right to the name, the Smith family title became Carrington. In August 1839 the second Lord Carrington, until then Robert Smith, changed the family name to Carrington, to match the title. In 1880 the third Lord Carrington changed, under royal licence, the family name to Carington, with one 'r'. No one is sure why but it is assumed this was the result either of a clerical error or of Lord Carrington's hope of establishing the twelfth-century Caringtons as part of the family. The single 'r' Carington has survived. Therefore, when talking about the family after 1880, we really should use Carington for individual members, but Carrington for the barons. For example, the

Honourable Peter Carington's father was the fifth Lord Carrington, and Rupert Carington's father was the sixth Lord Carrington. This may be confusing. So, to make the name clear: if it's Carrington it refers to the sitting Lord Carrington or Lady Carrington. If it is Carington with one 'r' that person is a member of the family.

Introduction

'I've always hated the Conservative Party,' the apparently arch-Tory Lord Carrington told me towards the end of his life. 'Nothing made me hate it more than being chairman of it. Individual members all right. Collective so awful. Look at it now. Going down the plug hole.'

Why would he say something that adds up to political treason in a party that, by and large, adored him? He said it because he had always felt it, and because Carrington left political life in what became, for him, the saddest of circumstances. He had failed to convince the Thatcher Cabinet that if they did not act as he thought they should, then Britain could be at war. But to hate the party that gave him the highest office he could gain? Not at all the popular image of Peter Carrington.

The public memory of Lord Carrington is of a trim, agreeable figure in spectacles who did the honourable thing in 1982 and resigned as Foreign and Commonwealth Secretary from the Thatcher Cabinet over the Falklands debacle. A dramatic moment for one who appeared to have drifted through his political life easily and wisely, turning the base metal of public office into golden solutions as he went. So it would seem.

It is tempting to wonder how, during a time when public reputations are routinely stripped, then violated, could anyone who has held such high office, and been involved in so many national and international affairs, escape the tar-and-feathering that is a fact of public life. Maybe that generation of Tories, which included Lord (Douglas) Hurd, Lord (Geoffrey) Howe, Lord (Kenneth) Baker and Sir Edward Heath, were indeed blameless souls. Why not? The majority of politicians are sound people. It is the way of society, certainly British society, to delight in bringing down reputations. Carrington's reputation as a fair and honourable man has, by and large, survived. Some, like the late Alan Clark, had little time for Carrington, as Clark made clear with his sometimes bitter demonstration of venom (particularly, see page 381). Though he may have cut a sad figure, he was certainly not alone in his spitefulness towards Carrington.

For many in his party, Carrington was a traitor. The single issue of the Rhodesian settlement decided that. It is not true, as some in the party believed, that Carrington ignored the accusations of betrayal. He most certainly found them deeply hurtful. He was seen by others as famous and the envy of many, yet seemingly carrying the hallmark of decency smudged by some of his contemporaries.

Certainly, Carrington appeared to enjoy a charmed start to his adult life. Eton, Sandhurst with great honour and a barony before his majority. His regret was that he chose the army instead of Oxford. He joined the family regiment, the Grenadier Guards, and survived his 'good war', in which he was awarded a Military Cross. Before the war was done, he had married and started on what he called a blissful marriage to a beautiful and intelligent woman. They moved to an inherited Buckinghamshire estate and after a learning spell in the Lords, Carrington held ministerial jobs in every Conservative government from Churchill to Thatcher. He was High Commissioner in Australia (his father's birthplace); banker; chairman and company director; Secretary-General of NATO; chairman of the Trustees of the Victoria and Albert Museum and Christie's auction house; president of Voluntary Service Overseas; chairman of the European peace conference for the Balkans; Chancellor of Reading University; Knight of the Garter and Chancellor of that Order, and Companion of Honour. He appeared to regard life with an enormous sense of humour and engaged the affection of almost everyone he met. Carrington's was a fairytale life in which he achieved almost everything other than the highest political office. With few exceptions, no one begrudged him his fortune nor his right to be the last of the Whigs who saw it as their duty to rule. The blackest spot in an almost unblemished record was the savage manner of his going from the Foreign and

Commonwealth Office in April 1982 and the fact that although his resignation was thereafter regarded as a model of honourable behaviour, it was also a consequence of his failure as Foreign Secretary and his inability to ride criticism of rank-and-file Conservative Members of Parliament.

In 1999 Henry Kissinger told me Carrington was like a Mozart symphony, bright and entertaining but with a deeper quality in that he was morally and intellectually faithful to his image. He said that he considered his friendship with Carrington 'one of the genuine rewards of my public service'. In a conversation that summer Margaret Thatcher assured me that he was in her view a unique and distinguished international figure.

We would do well to remind ourselves that there has never been a saint at Westminster since the Confessor – certainly not in the Palace there. Yet there were many times when Carrington appeared to be regarded as a candidate for political canonization. It was all part of the image – surely never self-created – as one who represented a corner of public duty and honesty at a time in Britain's political history when the intrusions of the media tended to highlight and sometimes exaggerate the excesses of the personal lives of those who governed the nation.

The departure of Carrington from British politics was the symbolic exodus of the last generation to be imbued with a natural sense of public service and duty. The cynic might translate that as a euphemism for a belief in the right to govern. Whatever the definition and interpretation, in government, Peter Alexander Rupert Carington, the sixth Baron Carrington, was the last of the Whigs.[1]

So, it would seem now that all that is left for us is to add to the eulogy of a man whom John Dickie, the distinguished *Daily Mail* diplomatic correspondent, who had shadowed Carrington for many years, called very affable and agreeable.

Yet there is another view of Carrington. Might the affable personality obscure a flawed career?

1 For difference between Carington and Carrington, see Preface, pp. xii–xiii.

He resigned in 1982 because the Foreign Office had failed to grasp the significance of Argentine preparations that would lead to the invasion of the Falkland Islands in the early spring of that year. Carrington believed he had to resign. In his mind, to assume responsibility for a department meant that when something went wrong, he had also to assume the responsibility for that failure. To paraphrase the view of his friend Henry Kissinger, Carrington would not assume responsibility but then say he was not really responsible. In recent years ministerial responsibility has sometimes been self-serving and even wholly absent at Westminster and in the departments of state. Equally, we cannot point to Carrington as a blameless character who, in some style of days long gone, fell on his sword for the honour of his office and family. After all, Carrington's failure was of a serious nature and by extension had contributed to the loss of many lives. He had failed to convince his Cabinet colleagues, and most particularly Prime Minister Margaret Thatcher, of the immediate need to resolve the future of the Falkland islanders. This failure was set aside when the public judged Carrington's going as the action of an honourable man. He was, in modern parlance, carrying the can because someone had to. That the summary of the subsequent inquiry cleared him of personal responsibility, while some parts of the evidence to that inquiry did not, seemed to be irrelevant because the history of his going had already been written.[2]

However, this was not the first time that he had offered his resignation to a prime minister. He had been the junior Agricultural Minister at the time of the Crichel Down Affair[3] in 1953. Asked to assess the rights and wrongs of Crichel Down, Carrington had failed, his office was criticized and he felt the need to offer his resignation to Prime Minister Winston Churchill. Churchill refused – for political as much as moral reasons – to accept it. His second resignation offer came when he was First Lord of the Admiralty. In September 1962, William Vassall, a civil servant in

2 Franks Report, Command No. 8787. See p. 438.
3 See pp. 125–33.

the Admiralty, was charged with spying for the Soviet Union. The press called for Carrington's resignation – he had been First Lord of the Admiralty since 1959. Carrington prepared to resign, until a Committee of Inquiry chaired by Lord Radcliffe cleared him of direct responsibility.[4]

The fourth occasion when he might have resigned was not from government but from the chairmanship of the Trustees of the Victoria and Albert Museum in London. He failed to hold together the Trustees – including the sometimes acerbic Terence Conran – and the efforts to put this most famous museum on a financially sound footing, which was his immediate responsibility, ended in ignominy.[5]

And what of his great successes? For example, the resolution of the long-running Rhodesia Crisis. That never came together as he imagined it would, and he had to suffer continuous abuse from his own political colleagues, that he had 'sold out' in his enthusiasm to get a solution. His critics said he wanted any solution that would rid the government of a seemingly insoluble diplomatic situation.

Since the 1990s, no one at the top table of politics escapes public, that is, media, scrutiny. The result is not always adverse publicity. By and large, the media had Carrington as a patrician with a safe pair of hands. Most of all, Dickie's word 'agreeable' reoccurs. Even stern critics, such as the Defence Secretary at the time of the Falklands War, Sir John Nott, and Sir Roy Strong, who as director of the Victoria and Albert when Carrington was chairman of Trustees, liked Carrington. Their quarrel was not with the man. Both thought him very 'agreeable' but not nearly as efficient as would be expected of one who had, apparently, held a series of ministerial offices with considerable success.[6] Therein lies the paradox of Carrington's reputation.

4 See p. 200.
5 Sir Roy Strong, *The Roy Strong Diaries, 1967–1987*, London: Weidenfeld & Nicolson, 1997. See p. 461.
6 See pp. 457–60.

1. Pitt's Banker

To begin to understand the paradox of Carrington's reputation, we need to explore something of the history of his family. That story is a 250-year-old saga. For this is a family which took an active part in British politics from the time of Pitt the Younger in the late eighteenth century; a family which, on one side, fought for Electoral Reform in the 1830s and, on the other, defended the old order against a widening of the franchise. It is a family which, in a single generation, grew from tradesmen to confidants of the monarch, which was heaped with honours during two centuries, which used the rotten boroughs for its own ends, and championed their going. It is a family that carried its years of privilege with considerable ease.

The story of the Caringtons has every ingredient of the romantic saga: beauty, money, power, politics and the intimate detail of life at successive royal courts from Victoria to Elizabeth II. It begins in the seventeenth century.

The Caringtons were Smiths. The Smiths came from Nottingham and on 1 November 1631 in the village of Titheby the newest son, Thomas, was baptized. Thomas Smith married the daughter of Laurence Collin. Collin was the Master Gunner at Nottingham Castle and his daughter was called Fortune. They had a son called Abel. Thomas Smith did rather well for himself. He was a woolstapler, which meant he had a great deal of control over the sale of wool, its sorting into different grades and therefore its pricing. By the time he was in his fifties Smith had moved from the warehouses and auction rooms to the formalities of moneylending. He had become a banker. When he died in 1699 Thomas Smith left the banking business to his son Abel, who was rich in his own right, or rather from a good inheritance from his mother's side of the family. It was this Abel Smith's son, also called Abel (born in

1717), who was to develop the banking business and extend it to London.

Abel Smith went into partnership and set up the banking house of Smith & Payne in London with important branches at Lincoln and Hull. He had a son, Robert. It was Robert who was to become the first Lord Carrington. He was born in 1752, and the connection with politics began because his father had become an MP. Being an MP in the eighteenth and nineteenth centuries often came with business success. Abel Smith, Robert's father, had bought himself the Membership for Aldeburgh in Suffolk in 1774, and then in 1780 for St Ives in Cornwall and four years later St Germans in Devon. In 1778 Abel Smith died, leaving his son Robert to run the business and carry on the other business, politics. He became the MP for Nottingham and also one of Pitt the Younger's close financial advisers. There was a great deal of talk of Robert Smith lending Pitt money at overgenerous rates, but there is no real evidence that Smith was attempting to buy favour, nor indeed needed to. It is not clear how effective Smith was as Pitt's personal financial adviser. The twice Prime Minister certainly needed a good banker. Pitt, a sad, solitary soul, managed his private life less easily than he did the state. He died deeply in debt, so much so that Parliament raised funds to pay off creditors. So much for Smith's advice or Pitt's ability to accept it.

In 1796 Smith was raised to the peerage by Pitt. The story goes that Robert Smith was riding in his carriage with Pitt from Pall Mall to Whitehall late one night. The quickest way would have been across Horse Guards Parade, beneath the Arch and on to Whitehall. However, then, as now, only the very privileged were allowed to ride across Horse Guards. Even the Prime Minister's banking adviser had to travel the long way round. On that particular evening, Smith asked a favour of his friend. Would it be possible to get him on that very privileged list so that he too could cross Horse Guards in public? Pitt considered for a moment. He said he thought not; that would have been a favour too many. However, he could get him a peerage. As was the practice, it would have to be an Irish peerage; nevertheless it would be translated to an English barony within the year. And so Smith was ennobled.

Why not Baron Smith of, say, Nottingham? Why Lord Carrington? There is no certain answer to that. At first sight, it appears to have been an unqualified bit of social snobbery on the part of the Smiths. They would, as bankers, forever maintain the Smith surname, but socially they were also looking for a name that reflected their origins. It is a practice used by the vast majority of ennobled families (including some life peers). Thus the Seymours are the dukes of Somerset, Russell is the family name of the Bedfords, the Percys are dukes of Northumberland, and so on. The difference with the Smiths is that they eventually wanted to drop the Smith and adopt as family name the much smarter Carrington. The name came from the neighbouring county of Leicestershire. Robert Smith appears to have believed that there was a connection with an ancient family called Smith-Carrington. This connection was not so much bogus as misleading. There also seems to have been a belief that before the Smiths were Smiths they were Carringtons. Another mistake. Some of the evidence appeared indisputable but depended upon the original assumption that Thomas, the two Abels and Robert were descended from the original Carringtons. These early ennobled Carringtons were viscounts. Here is the most likely explanation of the Smith hope that they were in fact Carringtons, because Robert Smith was looking for dignity. None of this is important today, but in the nineteenth century it most certainly was; this name-changing was even more important to a family with ambitions and social opportunities that would have the son of just the second baron as a playmate and then lifelong friend of the future Edward VII.

The nineteenth century opened with the first Lord Carrington realizing that he had great commercial and social conflicts before him. The first tradesman ever to sit in the House of Lords found that he was continually snubbed by many peers. When he took his seat, they literally turned their backs on him. Smith was trade. It was as if their tailor had joined the Upper House. According to the third Lord Carrington, his ancestor was thus 'compelled to leave the banking house and he bought and inherited land in Bucks and Lincolnshire . . .'[1]

His buying spree included a house that was to become one of the most famous in Buckinghamshire, Wycombe Abbey. To become landed rather than trade, he bought Loakes Mansion House, its park and woods and three farms covering 754 acres and twelve cottages at High Wycombe from the ageing former Prime Minister Lord Shelburne. He paid Shelburne £18,900 for the lot. The house, which dated from the seventeenth century, was not in good order and Carrington rebuilt it. He then decided that Loakes Mansion was not quite what he wanted in a name for the family seat. There should be a certain dignity in a house name, especially a house in such a splendid setting. So, with a bit of research into what had once stood on the site, he took the local town name and called the house Wycombe Abbey.[2] Carrington, apart from now being a land-owner, became President of the Board of Agriculture in 1800, a post he held for three years. It was not until the twentieth century that the boards of government disappeared (the last to go was the Board of Trade) to be replaced by the title Ministry; thus Carrington's presidency of the Agricultural Board was the nineteenth-century equivalent of being the Minister of Agriculture.

Carrington now set a precedent to be followed by the next five barons Carrington. He may have had to work hard at breaking social barriers, but there was nothing wrong with his money at the other end of the social scale. Carrington became a philanthropist. This was a time in Britain's history of great hardships and the beginnings of reform and charity movements. Many of the bene-ficial societies relied on the likes of Carrington. He appears to have made little of his charitable works. Carrington simply had the money and saw that he could use some of it to the good of others.

1 The Marquess of Lincolnshire KG [the third Lord Carrington], *Recollections of My Life From Public School to Privy Seal*. Private papers, the Carrington family.
2 Wycombe Abbey was sold in 1896 with 30 acres of ground for £20,000 and became a girls' school. A new house for the then Lord Carrington was built near by at Daws Hill. Daws Hill House was perhaps one of the ugliest in the county. It certainly was thought to scar the Wycombe Abbey landscape.

No fuss and bother necessary. Perhaps his charitable epitaph is to be found in these lines of William Cowper:

> Meanwhile ye shall not want
> What conscious of your virtues we can spare,
> I mean the man, who when the distant poor
> Need help, denies them nothing but his name . . .[3]

From Thomas Smith to the first Baron Carrington the family had, like others, got their seats in Parliament with little democratic effort. In that era of rotten boroughs, patronage was not a form of corruption but simply a way of political life. A piece of marshland with no inhabitants could be a constituency – a rotten borough, an almost mythical place, hard to spot on anything but a local map, such as Old Sarum, which was a burgage borough and only populated on election day. The term rotten came from William Pitt the Elder, who said that the so-called borough representation was the 'rotten' piece of the British constitution. This was something of an irony considering that he was the MP for Old Sarum.

It was quite common for a would-be MP to attempt to buy a seat – with little pretence of ever visiting the place. All this was about to change as the movement towards parliamentary reform and the first Reform Bill, that of 1832, began. Carrington was not for reform, surprisingly, but his son, also Robert, was. Therefore in the great debate in the two or three years preceding the passing of the bill, father and son were on opposing sides. The sixth Carrington's sense of history was enough that he knew every moment of the original debate which had taken place more than a century before he took his own seat in the Lords. To the end, he was a champion of parliamentary reform. To him, the history of the debate and the progress of universal suffrage and all aspects of British parliamentary reform were intrinsic to the modern discussion. The debate from the 1960s into the present century was for him as important as it had been in the 1830s.

3 William Cowper, *The Task*, Book IV, lines 425–8.

In the nineteenth century there were three major changes to the law on who could vote. These were known as the Reform Acts (1832, 1867 and 1884). The first Reform Bill was introduced by Lord Grey's Whig government. This was not a simple idea of spreading democracy, it was far more to do with public and very vocal dissatisfaction. The bill went to the House in March 1831. The Tories – they were only now starting to be called Conservatives[4] – defeated the bill the following month. The government went to the country. In the General Election which followed they were returned. They then drafted a second bill which went through the Commons in June 1831. The House of Lords turned it down. By this time there were more than political feelings running high. The army and militia – the only source of aid to the civil authorities in those pre-police days – were called out to put down riots. In December 1831 yet another bill, the third, was put before Parliament and once more the Lords obstructed it. There was more public protest and Lord Grey's Whig government resigned. It was at this point that a British government and the monarch were forced to seriously question the power of the House of Lords. Here was a single issue which would once more arise in 1910 and 1911 and again, although to a lesser extent, at the end of the twentieth century. By 1831 Britain had had a prime ministerial form of government for more than a century which had surely

---

4 Disraeli is usually credited with giving identity to the twentieth-century concept of the Conservative Party. Although he did not get into Parliament until 1837 (the year of Victoria's accession), it was during his attempt to get into Parliament in 1832 that we have the surest Disraeli reference to Conservatives: 'I am a Conservative to preserve all that is good in our Constitution, a radical to remove all that is bad, I seek to preserve property and to respect order and I equally decry the appeal to the passions of the many of the prejudices of the few ...' Election address, 1832. Disraeli was probably taking his lead from John Wilson Croker (1780–1857), who, writing in the *Quarterly Review* in 1830, noted that the Tory Party might 'with more "propriety" be called the Conservative Party'. It was Disraeli's simple description that attracted Peter, Lord Carrington, and not that which dominated the Conservative Party after it went into opposition in 1997.

moved towards a form of parliamentary democracy that would take another hundred years or more to complete.

However, the single issue here in 1831 as in 1910 and 1911 was who governed Britain: the old aristocracy, with its origins among the earldormen of the eighth and ninth centuries, or the Elected Commoners, even though their democratic qualifications were by today's standards woefully inadequate. Grey told William IV that the only way to get reform through Parliament and therefore democracy furthered and stability restored was to create hundreds of Whig peers who would vote for the government and outvote the Tories. (The monarchy and not a few in government were mindful of the revolutionary ideals which still floated across Continental Europe.) The threat to 'load' the Upper House was sufficient. The Tories let the bill through the Lords, the 1832 Reform Bill got through and the extra peerages were not created. (The threat to do so survived into the next century, when George V was confronted with the same possibility as his government took on the Lords just before the Great War.)

The reform debate split the Caringtons. In 1832 the youthful and triumphant Robert Carrington voted as a Whig MP against his father. Robert was the first of the Carrington Whigs whereas his father's trade instinct was to be a Tory. This trait was by no means new but was long lasting in British political life. The sixth Lord Carrington was to reflect on the fact that in spite of its popular image based on aristocratic Establishment, the late twentieth-century Conservative Party was demonstrably a natural home for the small businessman, whose instincts for trading advantages and respectability could never until the end of the century allow him to vote for the idealism of the Liberal and Labour parties. Carrington believed all that was changed with the arrival of the New Labour leader, Tony Blair, who gave new respectability and therefore new public meaning to existing Tory policies.

The first Carrington Whig, although successful in the political debate which had done away with his father's rotten boroughs, would remember 1832 not for constitutional reform, but for a personal tragedy. Ten years earlier Robert Smith (they had not yet

adopted Carrington as a patronymic) had married Elizabeth, the
beautiful daughter of Lord Forester. Her elder sister was Lady
Chesterfield, the Countess of Bradford. Robert had far from married into trade but the aristocracy and Establishment could not
protect his family from the terrible disease that swept through
hovel and mansion. Cholera was rife in the Russian Baltic ports. In
1831 ships from those ports brought it to the north-east coast of
England and it became an epidemic in Sunderland. The speed at
which cholera spread through England between 1831 and 1833 was
largely to do with the lack of fundamental medical knowledge. It
had also to do with the total neglect of sanitation in English homes
and in the wretchedly cramped and dirty working conditions of a
rapidly industrializing Britain. Cholera was never slow to act
against its victims. So it was that on 22 July 1832 Elizabeth Smith
(the first Lord Carrington's daughter-in-law) went down with all
the symptoms of cholera. It was a Sunday morning. By eleven
o'clock that evening she was dead.

Robert Smith's own mother was also dead by this time and in
1836 his father the first Lord Carrington caused great kerfuffle
(then a somewhat new word) when he remarried – why should
this be so? Old Lord Carrington was not simply an ageing rake
seeking a younger wife to warm his later days. He married a widow
with six children, which severely disturbed everyone with an interest in the Carington inheritance. Carrington was advised against
the marriage and the then Lady Stanhope was sent down to Deal
in Kent, where Carrington was staying, to implore her brother to
understand that what he intended was folly for himself, for his
family and for the Carington name. As Lady Stanhope returned to
London she might well have contemplated another new expression of the nineteenth century, 'there's no fool like an old fool'.
Carrington married the widow, became stepfather to her six children and was dead within two years. He did not die in Kent but in
the rather grand Carrington House in Whitehall.[5]

By now, the Carington assets were considerable.

5 See p. 54.

With the death of the first baron in 1838, his widower son Robert became the second Lord Carrington, and eight years after the death of his beloved Elizabeth, Robert Carington remarried. His bride was Augusta Drummond-Willoughby, the second daughter of Peter, Lord Willoughby de Eresby. Her father carried one of the oldest titles in Britain, the barony having been created in 1313, and Augusta brought with her more than one hundred quarterings to the Carington coat of arms.[6] She brought also a further entrée to life at Court. In the nineteenth century many of the ancient offices of the Royal Household were hereditary. Augusta's family shared the hereditary office of Lord Great Chamberlain – so the Carington family would share this royal office right into the twenty-first century.[7]

Robert, the second Lord Carrington, inherited his title at the beginning of the Victorian era and at a time of enormous change in Britain's history. Much of what happened and what is remembered about the nineteenth century, including industrial and constitutional reform, had origins in the first thirty years of the century. Britain's pre-eminence in world trade was largely based on an early understanding by British manufacturers and investors of the potential course of the so-called Industrial Revolution. This lead was enhanced by a number of important factors: Britain exploited her natural resources, especially coal, whereas other European nations failed to; the sense of innovation and entrepreneurial ambition was seemingly greater in Britain than elsewhere; neither

6 Quarterings are the miniature coats of arms on a shield which represent the marriages into a family of the heiresses of others.

7 The Lord Great Chamberlain has jurisdiction over areas of the Palace of Westminster which are not administered by the House of Lords and House of Commons, for example, the Royal Robing Room and the Royal Gallery. In 1902 the House of Lords decided that the office should remain jointly in the families of the Marquessate of Cholmondeley, the Earldom of Ancaster and the Marquessate of Lincolnshire (the third Lord Carrington was the last holder of that office) and that the post should be held in turn for the duration of a reign. Until the end of the reign of Elizabeth II, therefore, the office is held by the seventh Marquess of Cholmondeley and his successors. On the death of the present monarch, the then Lord Carrington assumes the office.

the United States nor Germany were developed enough to pose any competition and would not be so until the opening years of the twentieth century.

The growing empire allowed Britain access to global resources. Equally important, that empire was a market for British goods. It is quite possible that at one stage of British economic development, the state finances would have struggled, even come close to foundering, without India as a ready market for British manufactures. Her geographical position meant that Britain could export easily and in her own ships – since 1805 no other nation had been able to challenge Britain's freedom to sail the seaways of any of the oceans. For much of the nineteenth century this position went unchallenged. It was in such fat and fruitful years that the Carringtons made their fortunes and continued to do so.

Equally the expectations of change had introduced to Britain certain social instabilities that could not be ignored. In 1809 Jeremy Bentham, arguing as ever that the whole reason for extending the franchise was to achieve 'the greatest happiness of the greatest number', had produced his latest catechism for parliamentary reform. The 1832 Great Reform Bill had travelled a politically rocky and sometimes physically bloody road before becoming an Act of a reforming Parliament. When Luddites, demonstrating their reasonable anxieties about the effects of industrial change, took their sledgehammers to the textile factories of Yorkshire, Derbyshire, Leicestershire and Nottinghamshire, the government feared revolution rather than simple social protest. Moreover, without a police force the authorities only had repressive systems to contain unrest. When in 1813 Luddites were executed at York no one imagined there to be an easier way of dealing with the concerns of very ordinary people about extraordinary changes in domestic and industrial life. The greatest influence on nineteenth-century life industrially and socially, the railway, had begun: the Stockton and Darlington line was opened in 1825, the same year that Telford built his Menai Bridge. London University was opened. Macadam was building his new flat-surfaced roads to replace the winter-rutted tracks that criss-crossed Britain.

Throughout this period of change, the Carington family con-
solidated its position in British commerce, politics and society.
Indeed, it literally reflected this change. Carrington House in
Whitehall, until 1820 lit by candles, was one of the first private
houses to be brightened by gaslight.[8] This house was more than a
talking point for its innovation. Carrington House, by the advent
of the Victorian Age in 1837, had become an important centre for
a society that regarded influence as the most certain of currencies.
Built by the architect of Somerset House and the founder of the
Royal Academy, Sir William Chambers, the Georgian house
became a sightseeing curiosity. Important travellers from abroad –
especially those with growing influence in their own countries, for
example, the American George Vanderbilt – believed a London
excursion had to include a visit to the Carringtons and their salon
at Carrington House.[9] It was hardly surprising therefore that the
most important man in England, the Whig Prime Minister Lord
Melbourne, was a friend of the young Carrington. It was Melbourne who was to guide the young Queen for the next three
years and who would be her mentor and most intimate friend.
Here was yet another connection for the Caringtons to the Royal
Household, one which would be unbroken even into the twenty-
first century.

This was the period of the Chartists, the political reform movement that existed more or less between 1838 and 1848. The
People's Charter of 1838, whence the name came, had appealed for
five main changes to Britain's parliamentary constitution: annual
Parliaments; equal votes for all men; the removal of property
qualification for MPs; voting by ballot; and, interestingly, payment
of MPs (something not achieved until the twentieth century). The
Chartists became focal points for everything that the Carringtons
did not represent. During that decade Chartist petitions, sometimes
carrying millions of signatures, had been dismissed by Parliament.

8 The first street gas lighting was in St Margaret's Parish around Westminster
as early as 1814.
9 George W. Vanderbilt, *1879 Travel Journal*, Biltmore Estate Archives, 1.

In April 1848 Feargus O'Connor attempted to get together the biggest mass demonstration against Parliament ever seen. The government stationed the army, including the cavalry and musketeers, around Westminster and showed a terrible determination to put down O'Connor's protest by the most brutal means. From that event, we can learn a great deal about British society and especially the Caringtons. The third Lord Carrington, who was also the Marquess of Lincolnshire, did not die until 1928. Thus the young Peter Carrington heard from a first-hand witness about one of the most famous events of nineteenth-century social and political history. The third Baron Carrington (Charlie Lincolnshire as he is still called in the Carington family) remembered as a child sitting in Carrington House as the great Chartist riot rumbled towards its beginning.

Gamekeepers sat in the hall with loaded guns between their knees. My father [the second Lord Carrington] was on duty as a Special Constable in Whitehall and a troop of the Second Life Guards under Captain Mountjoy Martin were quartered on us ... Cannon was mounted at Westminster Bridge, Buckingham Palace and at the Bank, with orders to fire if the Chartists advanced on London, given by the Duke of Wellington ... Gaunt determined-looking men marched through London with banners: this I vividly remember from the fact that I was well spanked for cheering them out of the nursery window.[10]

10 The Marquess of Lincolnshire, *Recollections of My Life*.

2. Uncle Charlie

Charlie Lincolnshire – the title coming from the family estates in that county – was the most celebrated and sometimes boisterous Carington of the nineteenth century. Uncle Charlie's boyhood memories tell us how far the family had travelled since 1796, when the first Lord Carrington had been snubbed by his fellow peers as he took his seat in the Lords.

Monday July 10, 1854
When I was 11 years old I was taken with my sister, Eva, by my mother to a children's party given by the Duchess of Gloucester at Gloucester House, Piccadilly ... Queen Victoria and Prince Albert, with the Prince of Wales, Prince Albert and the Princess Royal were there. I was presented to the Prince of Wales, and hence began a friendship which lasted to his death.[1]

Again there is an entry in his papers for 1854 which shows how close the Carringtons had become to Court and social life.

On Prince Albert we were all terrified of him. I remember tumbling off the seesaw from fright on one occasion when he suddenly appeared from behind some bushes in Buckingham Palace gardens.[2]

Charlie's friendship with the young Prince of Wales could not have taken place without Queen Victoria's and Prince Albert's approval. This approval was reflected with a certain formality, as in this note:

1 The Marquess of Lincolnshire KG [the third Lord Carrington], *Recollections of My Life from Public School to Privy Seal*. Private papers, the Carington family.
2 Ibid.

Buckingham Palace,
Saturday 15 July 1854

Mr Gibbs [the Prince's tutor] is commanded by His Royal High-
ness Prince Albert to ask Lady Carrington to allow her son to
come and play in the Palace gardens this afternoon at five and to
stay till a quarter before eight with the Prince.

In 1856 Charles Carington was sent off to Eton, a tradition
followed by every Carington boy, apart from Peter Carrington's
father, Rupert (educated in Australia), to the present day. Charles was
not over bright. He was not expected to be. He claimed to have been
badly housed and fed there and taught absolutely nothing save two
things: 'To tell the truth and never to round on or betray a friend.'
More than a century later, the sixth baron insisted that this lesson should never be forgotten however much some political
colleagues might raise an eyebrow to the first part of the homily.[3]
There is not much indication that Charles Carington was anything
but jolly at Eton apart from once being caned or 'swished'. By the
time he reached Cambridge the future third baron had developed
a lifestyle that he would pursue for the rest of his days. The Cambridge of the 1860s did not expect a great deal of its undergraduates,
especially those who showed no inclination to develop academically. The young Carington went up as a Hat Fellow Commoner:
the title for the sons of the peerage. They were easily spotted
because, as the title suggests, they wore hats and were further distinguished by their special blue and silver gowns. Carington's time
at Cambridge was a brief affair – he was there just for the two years
required to take a bachelor's degree, which was all that was necessary, if even that, to get an army commission. Instinctively, Carington
put a minimum of effort into his work and a little more into play,
as he noted with apparent pride when describing membership of
one group.

3 Conversation with the author in 2005 when reflecting on evidence to the
Bloody Sunday Inquiry.

True Blue Club, [whose members wore] old fashioned blue coats with jabots [frilly shirtfronts] and ruffles, canary waistcoats and breeches and pink silk stockings and shoes. At a member's first dinner he was required to drink a bottle of claret out of a huge glass without taking it from his lips ... During 1860 and 1861 I won the Huntingdon Cup [the University steeplechase] and also the Pony Plate and the Great Eastern Handicap Plate with my own hunter, Gorilla, pony, Fanny and hack, Chirp by Orlando – Alarm. I kept the drag with Natty Rothschild. I was also SM [stage manager] at the ADC [amateur dramatic club].[4]

Carington picked up his degree in 1863 and two years later joined the army. At that time a young man had still to buy his commission – there was no question of entry qualifications other than family and money. Accordingly his father, the second Lord Carrington, paid £1,200 for him to become a cornet, the lowest officer rank in the cavalry – in this case the Blues. To move up a rank to lieutenant, he paid another £600 and so that he could be a 'proper officer' and command a small troop of men, a further £3,400 was found.

In the same year his father bought him his commission in the Blues, Carington was elected as the Liberal MP for Wycombe in Buckinghamshire. It was regarded as the family seat. Prime Minister Lord Palmerston had died and was succeeded by John Russell (by now Earl Russell). Once more, one of the major issues of the day was parliamentary reform and again the Carringtons were deeply involved in that debate, just as Charles Carrington's father had been with his father, the first baron, in 1831 and 1832. In February 1866 Gladstone introduced a new Reform Bill. Many of the Liberals and especially Lord Sherbrooke opposed Gladstone's bill and these anti-reformists were dismissed as Adullamites.[5] Liberals to the right of that political persuasion opposed any idea of extending the franchise and, as John Bright suggested, had gathered round them all sorts of characters of different persuasions and interests.

4 Carrington family private papers.
5 I. *Samuel* XXII: 1–2.

In spite of his parliamentary seat, the young Carington was not an overtly political animal; indeed, this near indifference to political advancement was not uncommon at that time. The brief memoir of his time at Cambridge suggested more of his nature. It is not surprising therefore to find him less caught up in the intensity of the debates over Gladstone's ambitions for Home Rule than in his continuing friendship with the equally jolly Prince of Wales. When, for example, Bertie, the Prince of Wales, and Princess Alexandra went at the end of the London Season to hold court at Wiesbaden, the young Carington was invited to stay. By this time the Prince of Wales regarded him as an unofficial equerry. Two years later we find Charles Carington touring Egypt with the heir to the throne, a journey that was to last four months and that not unnaturally was somewhat tiresome. In a letter home to his recently widowed mother, Charles mentions the tedium:

We go upstairs and the Royalties are in one room and drink tea and we sit in a circle in the anti chamber [*sic*] which possesses an old volume of *Punch* which we take it in turns to look at. At 11 we are dismissed and go to bed.

None of this seems to match the young Carington's idea of fun, nor, it should be imagined, that of the Prince of Wales. But this was a very formal tour and taking place in a part of the world hardly known for its fashionable spas.

Perhaps we should not underplay his interest in politics, if only because the role of politics in fashionable life in nineteenth-century England was quite removed from that wholly professional system at Westminster and Whitehall of our time. Almost to the end of the 1940s it was still possible for the British politician to be an amateur, even in the Commons. The argument ran of course that, for the whole of the twentieth century, none other than the very committed and politically appointed was a professional politician in the House of Lords. That the Caringtons were at the centre of Victorian politics should not be a surprise considering the origins of the barony. The second Lord Carrington had pressed hard for

Parliamentary reform, just as he had in the 1830s (against his father's wishes). He was a great friend of the younger generation of Tories, including Benjamin Disraeli, who in 1866 had become Chancellor of the Exchequer. Disraeli had just become Prime Minister when the second Lord Carrington died in March 1868. Disraeli immediately wrote to the new Lord Carrington, in his celebrated flamboyant style:

Grosvenor Gate, March 18, 1868

Mr Dearest Charles

I was about to call on him! and had reproached myself for having neglecting doing so for several days.

He was a man of tender affections, and there never was a father with a more gushing heart.

I really loved him. I will say no more: all my sympathy is under your roof!

Fine and divine thoughts can alone bring solace. If I can be of any use, command me now and forever.

Your friend

D

The *Times* newspaper noted that Robert John Carrington, Baron Carrington, of Upton, county Nottingham, in the peerage of Great Britain, and Baron Carrington, of Bulcot Lodge, in the Irish peerage, Lord Lieutenant and *custos rotulorum* of Buckinghamshire, had died 'shortly after 5.0 o'clock on Tuesday, at his residence in Whitehall-Yard'.

The bells of the parish church of Wycombe rang muffled peals during the whole of Wednesday, and every mark of respect was paid to the memory of the deceased. In his earlier days a keen politician the deceased nobleman was chiefly known of late years as a kind neighbour, a staunch promoter of education, and a painstaking merciful judge when acting as Chairman of the Quarter Sessions, which office he filled for a considerable number of years.

That Disraeli had written his proper condolences was evidence enough of Carrington's standing. If any more were needed, we only have to look at the guest list when in the following year, 1869, his youngest daughter, Eva, married Charles Stanhope, the eldest son of the seventh Earl of Harrington.

The marriage was at St Martin-in-the-Fields and was conducted by the Archbishop of Armagh. The Earl of Rosebery, a future Tory Prime Minister, was the best man. At the wedding breakfast at Carrington House, the guests included the Duke and Duchess of Northumberland and those of Cleveland, the Marquis and Marchioness of Bristol and those of Queensberry, the Marquis of Lansdowne, the Earl and Countess of Bradford and those of Camarthen, and the Earl of Chesterfield. Disraeli was there and so were the Colvilles, the family whose later generation took in Peter Carrington's father when the rest of the Caringtons ostracized him. Winston Churchill's parents were there, as were the Percys and so many minor aristocrats, admirals and generals that the club tables of St James's must have been all but empty that day.

In spite of the attendance of the very great there were others who remained openly scathing of the origins of the Caringtons, of the validity of their title, and sneered that, in spite of three generations and an undoubted strong connection at Court, the Caringtons remained 'trade'. This mongering was largely based upon personal animosities. The social mores of the second half of the nineteenth century, if not exactly meritocratic, were easily able to cope with the changing aristocracy that had never been the caste system it had often imagined itself.

In June 1869 an article appeared in the *Queen's Messenger*. This was a tabloid edited by a man called Grenville Murray, a person of pretty doubtful integrity even by the often dissipated standards of Victorian journalism. Murray wrote in his newspaper what was, effectively, an attack on the origins, standards and aristocratic legitimacy of the second Lord Carrington, Charles's late father. Such an article would have wrung applause from the late eighteenth-century peers who had snubbed the first Carrington. Times had moved on and Charles, the new Lord Carrington, was incensed.

On 21 June Carrington was travelling by coach from Windsor Castle when he saw a man reading the *Queen's Messenger* and hooting with laughter. The article was headed 'Bob Coachington, Lord Jarvey', an obvious play on the names Bob Jarvey and Lord Carrington. Bob Jarvey was a term used to describe coachmen and the article suggested Carrington's position and relationship with the Prince of Wales to be akin to that of a driver. What followed was quite spectacular and gave Carrington an enormous amount of pleasure and Murray apparently very little, as Carrington's own diary shows:

June 22nd, London
As soon as I got back to London I bought a small rhinoceros hide whip at Briggs in St James's Street and waited for Mr Murray outside the Albany 'til midnight, but he never appeared. I also watched for him all next day without success, but hearing he generally went to the Conservative Club about 11 in the evening, I fortunately ran across him in St James's Street, and after asking him his name, I told him who I was, and that he had written infamous things about my father, and then I hit him with the whip across the face as hard as I could. The whip cracked like a pistol shot under his nose. He ran into the Conservative Club and I got another blow in. I followed him into the Club, gave him my name and address and said, 'if you write any more filth about any of my family I will give you the same again'.

I think I must have hurt him, as the point came off the whip – it lapped round his face just under his nose, and he jumped two feet off the ground. I then went to Pratt's Club, saw Coventry and several friends, told them what I had done and asked them to bear witness if necessary that I was neither excited nor drunk. I then went to bed happy at Whitehall.

None of this went unremarked and the gossip was not confined to Pratt's kitchen. The following day Charlie thought it best to explain himself to his mother. He told her what had happened. He was also quick to tell her that as it had taken place the previous day and Grenville Murray had not been heard of since, he was sure that the matter with 'such a low cad' was at an end. To boost his case with his mother, he quoted his brother-in-law Lord Colville of Culross and a number of his friends, including Lord Randolph Churchill. He was also much heartened by a note from Sir Christopher Teesdale, the famous lawyer:

Bless you for thrashing that scoundrel last night. If I can be of any possible service to you I need only say that you have carte blanche to command my services in any way. The man has just been kicked out of the Foreign Office as a convicted thief. Recollect that and treat him as such.

Charlie's notion that Murray would do nothing was misplaced. He went to law. Carrington's own note of the time makes almost comical reading. The defendant's solicitor, in a crowd of barristers and peers, was putting the evidence in a strongbox when there was a struggle.

Cries of Police! Police! rang through the building and the voices could not have been more urgent were murder being committed ... nothing less than a free fight was in progress. Books, papers, inkstands, and pens were scattered: hats were knocked off and smashed: and blows were freely exchanged ...

... the only persons not concerned in the scuffle were the magistrate ... the council, and the Marquess of Townshend, who at the commencement of the engagement, retired hastily, with as much dignity as circumstances would permit ... In the centre of the tumultuous crowd a terrible struggle was taking place for the possession of the strong box ... Lord Carrington, regardless of the fact that he was still nominally in custody, sprang out of the dock ... Fought his way through the throng and laid violent hands on those who sought to relieve the elderly solicitor of his charge.

Carrington then brought an action of wilful and corrupt perjury against Grenville Murray, who had denied that he was the author of the libel. It never came to court. Murray left the country and, as far as is known, never returned. Peter Carrington always seemed rather proud of the tale. He thought it a proper thing to do, he told me in 2005, and when he felt aggrieved enough to threaten the *Daily Express* with a law suit, his fingers twitched for Uncle Charlie's whip!

It was in 1868, the year before this incident with Murray, that Uncle Charlie gave up his parliamentary seat at that December's General Election.[6] Uncle Charlie's brother William became the new Liberal Member of Parliament for Wycombe, in spite of the 1832 Reform Act which had supposedly rid the electoral system of rotten boroughs. Wycombe was a family seat and no one questioned it.[7]

William (known in the family as Bill) was in the Grenadier Guards – the second battalion Grenadiers became the family regiment and the one that Peter Carrington joined from Sandhurst shortly before the Second World War. It was also to the Grenadiers that the heir to the throne, Victoria's son Bertie, was sent for a taste of what was supposed to have been military discipline. It is well documented elsewhere that the Prince of Wales was a hedonistic character. His mother wished him to have a little more purpose and structure to his life, which was not always easy for a royal prince in the nineteenth century and certainly did not reflect the history of the Hanoverian Princes of Wales. A few months before his death, Prince Albert had arranged for the Prince of Wales to 'join' the army. He would go to the Grenadier Guards for a few weeks' intensive training in Ireland. The Grenadiers were certainly not unimaginative when it came to enjoying themselves, and this was the environment to which the not always sober and responsible prince was sent and in which Bill Carington was also a junior officer. The two men became firm friends. Bill Carington was seen as quite a good influence on Bertie and certainly found

6 The election was called following the 1867 Reform Act, which extended the electoral franchise. The Liberals remained in office with 387 of the 658 seats.

7 The idea of family and estate allegiance was not something that would disappear in the nineteenth century. For example, Alec Douglas-Home may as a young man have had his political setbacks, but he represented his own constituency, Lanark & Kinross, with a not dissimilar feudal right.

favour with Queen Victoria. He became her equerry and was later Comptroller of the Household of the Prince of Wales and then Keeper of the Privy Purse. His brother Charles was quite different. He may have been a confidant of the Prince of Wales – they even shared a mistress – but he was never regarded with the same affection as Bill Carington and, as far as Victoria was concerned, for a very good reason. When the regiment went to Ireland the prince got into a little trouble when it was discovered that he had a local actress in his bed. It was widely suggested (with some conviction) that this was Uncle Charlie's doing and, worse still, it would indirectly lead to the death of the Prince Consort. The Carington version of the story of the Prince of Wales and Nellie Clifden is as reliable as any.

The truly hectic social round of a Guards officer together with the greater expectations of him as a royal prince (for example, he formally dined five nights of the week) was not the easiest of ways to fulfil the instructions of his father, Prince Albert. The Prince of Wales was expected to be trained in every officer rank and be competent to command a battalion and 'manoeuvre a Brigade in the field', all in ten weeks. An impossible task. Furthermore, the prince was humiliated by his commanding officer and made to carry out the task of the most junior of officers while dressed as a staff colonel. When the regiment came to be reviewed by the Queen, the Prince Consort and his uncle George, the Duke of Cambridge, who was commander-in-chief of the army, the young prince did not cut much of a military figure. Little wonder then that he relied on his friends to relieve his frustrations.

When Charles Carington visited his brother Bill at the Curragh, the three friends certainly relaxed. It was after a typically noisy mess night that Charles – he never denied his role – had a pretty actress by the name of Nellie Clifden slip into Bertie's bed. This was not a single moment in the cheery Nellie's life. When the prince returned to London, Nellie went too. Ever a generous man, the Prince of Wales 'shared' Nellie with his dear friend, Charles Carington – an arrangement that would last some time, and always place Charles Carington in some disfavour with the Queen.

Nellie was not a passing one-night fancy. When she came to London, the affair was so blatantly conducted that even in polite society, Nellie became known as the Princess of Wales. Although not an enemy of the prince, nor of Charles, one of the lords-in-waiting, Lord Torrington, spread the gossip through the Court so that it came to the ears of the Prince Consort, who felt it his duty to tell Victoria. There was worse to come. Nellie, it was thought, might have a child by the prince, or even claim him as the father of a child she might have by another – perhaps his close friend Carrington. The shock, and it was nothing less, was made worse when it became common knowledge that the arrangement, including Charles Carrington's part in it, was known in Continental Europe. Moreover, it was far more than gossip behind the fan. It coincided with the Queen's insistence that it was time for the prince to marry. His bride was to be Princess Alexandra of Schleswig-Holstein-Sonderburg-Glücksburg.

There is another twist to this story which brushes that of the Carrington family, or really, Uncle Charlie. It was the terrible constitutional and social dilemma over Nellie that sent an already ill Prince Consort to Cambridge to talk firmly to the prince.

November 25 1861
Prince Albert came to Cambridge to see the Prince of Wales. I drove up to the station with HRH who seemed rather nervous at the meeting. I then stood in the crowd on the platform to see the arrival. Prince Albert kissed his son when they met.[8]

His visit to Maddingly Hall is said to have worsened his condition.

December 13
The Prince left Cambridge to attend his father's deathbed.[9]

8 Diary of the third Lord Carrington, Bledlow.
9 Ibid.

Albert is believed to have died from typhoid fever. The Queen had no doubt that Bertie's behaviour was to blame for his father's death, and she did not want to have him at Windsor.[10]

The Caringtons had the notion that had not Uncle Charlie slipped Nellie between the prince's sheets, then Prince Albert would not have died from the fever. Peter Carrington told me he always believed that Victoria hated Uncle Charlie for this very reason, which was why Victoria refused to approve the third Lord Carrington's appointment as Viceroy to India. Maybe. What is certain is that Charlie Carrington's close relationship with the prince never faltered. So involved was Charles with the Prince of Wales that he found himself defending Bertie in the infamous divorce case brought by Sir Charles Mordaunt. The Caringtons, particularly Charles, knew his wife, Harriet – an attractive twenty-one-year-old woman who went to parties given by the Prince of Wales at Marlborough House. The whole thing came to a head when Harriet told her husband that she had committed adultery with quite a few people, including the prince. The prince's involvement was further complicated by letters he had written to Harriet Mordaunt. He also admitted that he had paid visits to her; however, he denied adultery.

Throughout this period, the young Lord Carrington remained at the prince's side. He travelled with him abroad for weeks on end during journeys that were chores rather than fun. Carrington's letters home were often sober. On one trip in the Mediterranean and through Suez aboard HMS *Serapis* Carrington thought the royal party behaved like thoughtful 'monks'. This was the prelude to a long tour of India, considered an enormous success and certainly one which cheered up the royal party, including Carrington, who described the prince as being a man in 100,000. 'He wins golden opinions wherever he goes ...'[11]

After that successful tour of India in the late 1870s, the prince

10 Christopher Hibbert, *Edward VII: A Portrait*, London: Allen Lane, 1976, p. 49.
11 Carrington family papers, Bledlow.

appeared quite frustrated at having to revert to a life of low-key and boring public duties. It was Charles Carrington (by now the third baron) who suggested that the prince should see for himself some of the appalling conditions lived in by so many outside his normal royal circle. Carrington, who was a member of a Royal Commission on the housing of the working classes, invited Bertie to his London house and there they disguised themselves in workmen's clothes before setting off for the London slums around St Pancras.

He, Carrington and the Chief Medical Officer of Health in the local government board ... left Carrington's house ... the Prince had wandered about the narrow streets dismayed and sickened by the appalling poverty, squalor and misery to which he was introduced, the background to many thousands of Londoners' lives. He found a shivering, half-starved woman with three ragged torpid children lying on a heap of rags in a room bereft of furniture. Asked by her landlord where her fourth child was she replied, 'I don't know. It went down into the Court some days ago and I haven't seen it since.' Distressed by her plight, the Prince took a handful of gold coins from his pocket and would have handed them over to her had not Carrington and the doctor warned him that such a display of wealth might lead to his being attacked by the woman's neighbours.[12]

By now, the prince frequently felt he could not do without the company of the young Charles Carrington. Lady Carrington, Charles's mother, was not at all flattered by the attention paid by the prince towards her son. In one letter she described the Prince of Wales as a bore for monopolizing Charles's time when he should have been visiting his own family.

Charles's mother died in July 1879. Again, it is the depth of regret revealed by the public prints that showed the undoubted station of the Caringtons. The Buckinghamshire *Telegraph* reported from its Wycombe office on 1 August:

12 Hibbert, *Edward VII*, pp. 140–41.

A fortnight ago we gave expression to the anxiety which was generally felt in Wycombe and the neighbourhood at the announcement that the dowager Lady Carrington had been attacked by a sudden and dangerous illness, which stretched her unconscious upon a bed of sickness at her residence in Barclay-square [*sic*] London. We have now the painful duty of announcing her death. Her Ladyship was taken ill about 10 o'clock in the morning of Monday, the 14th ultimo ... for a week the malady refused to yield to the unremitting care of the physicians, but on the Monday following the first seizure there was some improvement. The hopes thus raised were dashed on the next day by a relapse; and after lingering for a few days longer her Ladyship expired on Saturday, the 26th July, about 2.0pm.

... During the past few years since the death of Lord Carrington her Ladyship has resided chiefly in London, but there was fresh in the minds of Wycombe people the remembrance of her high qualities, and the delicate and considerate kindness which always marked her intercourse with those around her in the years during which she resided at Wycombe Abbey.

The remains of the late Lady Carrington were removed from the residence in Barclay-square yesterday, the 31st July, and taken by an early train to Bletchley station, and thence conveyed to the village of Moulsoe, a parish about nine miles distant, which belongs to the Carrington family ... After the usual service in the church the body was conveyed to its last resting place in a brick grave situated in an enclosed portion of the churchyard in which the late Lord Carrington was interred on March 17, 1868.

The most significant consequence of her death was that one of the great offices of the realm now passed to another family. It was this Lady Carrington who was co-heiress (with her sister, Lady Aveland) of the hereditary dignity of Lord Great Chamberlain of England – the sixth of the Great Offices of State and one that dates from Robert Malet, a knight of William the Conqueror. In the nineteenth century, the Carringtons married into the Willoughby de Eresby barony. This family had held the office since the seventeenth century even when the family title was in abeyance. In theory, the Lord Great Chamberlain holds authority over the Palace of Westminster and carries, or bears, the Sword of State at the state openings and closings of Parliament, has a say in the order of coronations and is one of the number who invests the insignia of the monarch's reign.[13] Most significantly, under the 1999 House of Lords Act, hereditary peers lost their right to sit in the Lords. But the Lord Great Chamberlain is not subject to the 1999 Act and so has a place in the Lords in order that he or she may carry on with the duties of Lord Great Chamberlain. Thus, during the reign of Queen Elizabeth II, the Cholmondeley family exercise the title. However, on the death of the monarch, a Carrington becomes Lord Great Chamberlain – in the normal course this would be the seventh Lord Carrington, Rupert. Thus, for as long as the office survives, there will be a Carrington as an hereditary peer in the Lords.

It does not take state ceremony to judge the position of a family. Peter Carrington once remarked to me that influence and opportunity was not, as is often said, a question of whom you know; it is rather a matter of who knows you. By the second half of the nineteenth century, the Caringtons were perhaps even better known than they are today. Often these acquaintances and special friendships are far more widely spread than most imagine. There is even an impression that every aristocrat is somehow related to every other aristocrat. The occasions of weddings and funerals bring out long-lost friends and guest lists of friends sometimes forgotten. There's nothing like a good funeral for all to see who really was close to the deceased and, more significantly, whom the dear departed thought close. And so it was with the friendship between Charles Carrington and Disraeli.

When the great Tory Prime Minister was weak and nearing his death, Carrington would ride over from his house at Wycombe Abbey to Hughenden, Disraeli's home, and read to him. In 1881 Disraeli died. The Prince of Wales was to travel from London to Buckinghamshire for the funeral. His Private Secretary told

13 In practice, the Sword of State is often carried by a military peer.

the Royal Household at Windsor (the Queen was rarely at
Buckingham Palace – she quite disliked it) that carriages should
be sent to Windsor railway station to take the royal party to the
funeral. The prince's Private Secretary was told that carriages
would not be made available. It is not quite clear why this should
have happened, but it seems far more likely to have been a result
of a domestic arrangement than feelings about the funeral itself.
After all, the Queen had, at last, regarded Disraeli as the finest
politician of her reign and held him in the deepest affection. Whatever the reason, the prince was to be inconvenienced if not
embarrassed. His close friend, Carrington, stepped forward and
invited the Prince of Wales to lunch at Wycombe Abbey with the
promise that he, Carrington, would take him to Hughenden.
Prince Edward was met at the station with some style by the Carington family including Colonel the Hon. William Carrington, the
Hon. Rupert Carington (Peter Carrington's grandfather) and Carrington's brother-in-law Lord Colville of Culross. Yet as Uncle
Charlie noted a little later, even that arrangement was not without
its drama.

I sent down Desabris the cook and all the servants and four carriages[;]
one of my best horses, Yeoman dropped dead going up the hill in Hughenden Park. The funeral was a wonderful sight. Lord Derby, who insisted
on walking up from the station was refused admittance into the Park by
one of the intelligent Buckinghamshire police.

An aside to that occasion is a note after the funeral in Carrington's hand. There is today a society called the Primrose League.
It is a Tory group founded in the memory of Disraeli because the
primrose is traditionally believed to have been his favourite flower.
Queen Victoria, whose affection for Disraeli seems to have been
boundless, was at her home on the Isle of Wight when Disraeli
died. She sent primroses from Osborne to be placed on his coffin,
but were they his most prized blooms? Everyone still seems to
believe so. Not according to Charles Carrington: 'The Queen ...
sent two wreaths, one of primroses bore the inscription "his

favourite flowers" an absurd fallacy invented by Mrs Blagden, wife of the vicar of Hughenden ...'

It is shortly after this that the Carington family's long association with Australia begins. In 1885 Charles Wynn-Carington, the third Lord Carrington, or Uncle Charlie as he became known, was appointed Governor of New South Wales. He and his wife Lily[14] sailed for Australia. Carrington was perfectly happy. He often said that the cleverest thing he ever did was to marry Lily, whom Lord Rosebery called 'the fairest of English lilies'. *Vanity Fair* said she was the leading factor in her husband's success as an Australian Governor. (It is interesting to note that the sixth Lord Carrington described his wife Iona as a significant factor in his success as High Commissioner to Australia in the 1950s and said that marrying her was quite the wisest thing that he had ever done.) They arrived in Australia with more than the baggage of colonial state. It would seem that the good-natured Charles Carrington assumed responsibility for his younger brother Rupert, who had also been a Member of Parliament and was to become the grandfather of Peter, the sixth Lord Carrington, who in his memoirs described his grandfather as having only one constant characteristic – extravagance.

In 1885 Rupert Carington appears to have been broke. Apart from the considerable expenses of being a Member of Parliament (they were unpaid and had to fund or have funded their always considerable election expenses), he had to keep up with his extravagant friends and his own spendthrift instinct. You had to have plenty of money to be an officer in the Grenadiers. Such a fashionable regiment spent much of its time doing very fashionable things, particularly London Duties. Even today a 'good' regiment based in London can be an expensive home for the young subaltern. In the late nineteenth century financial prudence and living within one's means was quite unfashionable.

One of the young Rupert Carington's accounts from his shirtmaker Beale & Inman around 1870 was for £900. Today that

14 Carington married the Hon. Cecilia Margaret Harbord, the daughter of the fifth Baron Suffield, in 1878.

Victorian £900 converts to close on £25,000. That is a lot of shirt money even in Jermyn Street. However, this was very much in character for the quite tall and blue-eyed youngest Carington. So, when in 1885 his elder brother Charles was appointed Governor of New South Wales, Rupert Carington thought it a good idea to put half the world between him and his creditors by going with his older brother to Australia. Six years later in 1891 Peter Carrington's grandfather believed his financial woes at an end. Rupert married Edith, the eldest daughter of perhaps the most prosperous sheep farmer in the territory, John Horsfall. The Horsfall fortune would be partly settled on the bride. It was an expensive gesture by Horsfall.

The sixth Lord Carrington records that in 1957 he met in Australia a surviving friend of John Horsfall. 'I remember old John Horsfall ... saying to me, "my daughter's going to marry Rupert Carington". I looked at him and I said, "John, that's the most expensive ram you've ever bought!"'

Horsfall could be just as full of surprises. At the age of seventy-six he married his nurse, a 'buxom young woman' of twenty-five, causing considerable consternation in the farmer's family.

It is certainly true that Rupert had a reputation as a spender of any money that came into his reach. Equally, his career was hardly undistinguished. He was born in Carrington House in Whitehall the week before Christmas 1852. His mother was the second baron's second wife Charlotte Augusta, who in turn was a Willoughby de Eresby – the holders of the office of Lord Great Chamberlain. At nineteen, Rupert Carington joined the Grenadiers and in the 1879 Zulu War was adjutant in the 24th Regiment of Foot. He failed to win Disraeli's seat in Buckinghamshire when the latter went to the Lords, although four years on, in 1880, he did become a Liberal MP for Buckinghamshire, but lost High Wycombe in the 1885 General Election. (It was also in 1880 that Rupert and his brother Charles received a royal licence to continue to use the family name Carington even though Carrington was the title of the barony.) In March 1891, at St Matthew's church at New Norfolk, Tasmania, the expensive ram married the Horsfall heiress,

Edith, and, by most accounts, proceeded to spend much of her fortune. Horsfall had arranged a £10,000 loan to help finance their partnership in the Momalong sheep station. His brother Charlie had returned to England the previous year and Rupert was on his own.

With the start of the second Anglo-African War or Boer War, Peter Carrington's grandfather resumed his military career. In 1901 he was commissioned major in the NSW Mounted Rifles and then promoted lieutenant colonel and commanded the 3rd NSW Bushmen's regiment, won the DSO and was Mentioned in Dispatches.[15] Rupert Carington returned to England after the Great War in the knowledge that because his brother's son had been killed in that conflict, he, Rupert, would become the fourth Baron Carrington – which he did in 1928 on Charlie Lincoln-shire's death. It was a short-lived title. A year later, Rupert died at his London home in Eaton Place, to be succeeded by his only son, the father of Peter Carrington.

There is a tailpiece to the potted biography of this Lord Car-rington. Peter Carrington's father (also Rupert) was not his father's only child but he was the only one born to his mother. This high-living brother of Charles Carrington fathered an illegitimate son and daughter in London, the consequence of which was that the sixth Lord Carrington's father – quite legitimate – was not immediately allowed to join the family regiment.[16] He was not in direct line to inherit the barony of Carrington. However, a great tragedy that was not theirs alone – the Great War of 1914–18 – was to redirect the inheritance.[17] But much was to happen with the existing Lord Carrington, Charles, before then.

After five years as Governor, Charles returned to England in 1890. He returned also to the company of the Prince of Wales and the Court. Some indication of the royal esteem this man was held in was shown in 1893. Seventeen years earlier, the then Prime Minister,

15 Rupert Carrington should not be confused with Sir Frederick Carrington, the CO of Carrington's Horse, an entirely different colonial regiment fighting in Africa.

16 See p. 42.

17 See p. 41.

Disraeli, had dangled before Queen Victoria the title of Empress of India, a bauble she graciously accepted. As India now had an Empress it was necessary to have someone as Viceroy to rule in her absence. For sixty years this would be the jewel of all imperial appointments. In 1893 there was great discussion with the Queen about sending Charles Carrington to India as Viceroy. This might have been something of a strange appointment inasmuch as Charles Carrington, for all his success in Australia and his gathering maturity, was still regarded in some circles as 'Champagne' Charlie. The appointment to India probably needed someone with style, which he had, but also something approaching diplomatic haughtiness, which he had not. The Viceroy really had to be seen to be above everyone, including the Indian princes. A century of aristocratic breeding in, by all accounts, a likeable and liberal baron may not have been felt to be sufficient. There was also a suggestion within the Carington family at the time that the Queen would have liked him to go but had some concern for the comfort of his family. After all, India was a very hot and sometimes dirty place; there were dozens of stories of senior colonial figures succumbing to its climate. Not that Carrington himself apparently believed this story about the Queen's consideration for his health and comfort. In August 1893 he noted in his diary: 'The Duchess of Connaught at the Queen's dinner told me that Her Majesty had told Mr Gladstone [the Prime Minister] that she wished me to go to India as Viceroy and that he was willing but was over-ruled in the Cabinet. Rosebery [Gladstone's Foreign Minister] wishing to send Elgin.'

Rosebery had his way. Lord Elgin went to India and remained there until 1898. He came from a long line of diplomatic servants, all of whom survived the weather of their postings.[18] Charles

18 His father, the eighth earl, had been Governor General of India in 1861 as well as, at other times, Governor General of Canada and Jamaica. It was Elgin's grandfather, the seventh earl, who was Ambassador to the Ottoman Sultanate at the beginning of the nineteenth century and who was responsible for bringing the sculptures from the Parthenon at Athens to England. These sculptures were later known as the Elgin Marbles.

Carrington would have rather liked to go to India but there was still plenty to do at home in public life. He was now Chamberlain to the Royal Household and, in 1895, he was created Earl Carrington. These titles did not survive him because he had no male issue.

The following year, 1896, we find a change in surnames yet again. In 1880 the surname Carrington had been confirmed by Royal Licence. In 1896 a further Royal Licence was granted to assume the surname Wynn-Carington. It is this double-barrelled name that tells a great deal about the Carrington line, which was now as noble as the original Baron Carrington, Robert Smith, had hoped it might be. The line was now as long as any and longer than most. Combining family trees meant that the Carringtons now traced their ancestors back to the sixteenth century and Katherine, Baroness Willoughby de Eresby. Through the baroness's line, Drummond's daughter was Charlotte Augusta Annabella. It was Charlotte who married, in 1840, the widower Robert, the second Baron Carrington, who thus became linked through the Drummond family to the Willoughby de Eresbys. Yet none of this explains why it was felt necessary to change the name in 1895 (confirmed in 1896). It would seem that the earldom was granted as a consequence of Charles Wynn-Carington assuming the office of Lord Great Chamberlain. As we saw earlier, through the Willoughby de Eresby family connection this office of Court was shared and the Wynn part of the name was the direct link, in heraldic terms at least. Such are the complications of the aristocracy deciding who they should be.

Thus, by his hereditary office, five years later, following Victoria's death in 1901, it was Edward VII's friend Charles, the third Baron Carrington, who carried St Edward's Staff at the Coronation.

In 1905 we find Carrington once more directly involved in national politics. In December of that year Sir Henry Campbell-Bannerman became Liberal Prime Minister. He asked Carrington to become President of the Board of Agriculture.[19] His time at the

19 See p. 10.

Board of Agriculture was apparently well spent. He did not regard it as a sinecure and his impact was almost immediate. It was Carrington who in 1908 created the idea of allotments as a legal right for everyone. He also improved the lot and legal rights of tenant farmers – much to Peter Carrington's discomfiture forty years later. Two years after his appointment, the journal *Vanity Fair* noted that

He [Carrington] makes no pretence of oratorical talent, but has got an excellent judgement and a good eye for an opportunity, and in the last two years has successfully piloted nine Agricultural Bills through the House of Lords including the Farmer's Charter which he carried through by sheer good humour and brains. He has a trick of making fun at the proper moment and the humorous man's habit of putting things at their lowest; 'this bill' he practically says 'will make no real difference': it is no use in kicking up a great deal of fuss about it; it will tend rather to do good than evil. Why bother? An opposition is disarmed and the Bill slips through, and the practical man of affairs, which Lord Carrington is, chuckles in his sleeve; he has succeeded, and that is enough for him.[20]

Carrington stayed in government until 1912. In October 1911 he was succeeded at the Board of Agriculture by Walter Runciman and he became Lord Privy Seal. In February the following year he retired from government and became the Marquess of Lincolnshire, a style to his title he took from considerable family holdings in that county. The later Carington family would always refer to the third Lord Carrington as Charlie Lincolnshire.

When the Great War began, Charlie Lincolnshire's heir was his and Lily's only son, Albert, styled Viscount Wendover and known in the family as Bob. But he was destined not to inherit the Carrington barony. In March 1915 he left for the war with the Royal Horse Guards. In his diary Charlie Lincolnshire recorded the day of Bob's departure.

20 *Vanity Fair*, 11 September 1907.

March 8 1915

Bob left for the front at 5 o'clock pm today. He was in great spirits as he has been fretting for two or three months at not having been sent out. He said goodbye to his mother in the front room . . . I saw him off at the door. I am very proud of him.[21]

On 14 May Bob Wendover was wounded in the leg and arm. The arm was amputated in the military hospital at Boulogne, to which his father had travelled in the hope of bringing him back to England. He died at 6 a.m. on 18 May 1915 and the course of the Carrington inheritance changed. If Wendover had survived, Peter Carrington would never have become Margaret Thatcher's Foreign Secretary.

21 Diary for 1915 of the third Lord Carrington, quoted by kind permission of the Hon. Rupert Carington, who became the seventh Baron Carrington.

3. Family Schism

The marquessate could only pass to a son and therefore, unless another male heir appeared, both the marquessate and the title Viscount Wendover would become extinct on Charlie Lincolnshire's death. The barony was separate and therefore Rupert Clement George Carington, Lincolnshire's brother, could expect to become the fourth Lord Carrington on Charlie Lincolnshire's death. His surviving younger son, also Rupert (Victor John), would, in his turn, succeed him and become the fifth Lord Carrington. This was the position as the Great War ended.

Considering (or perhaps because of) his father's often flamboyant and reckless nature, Rupert the younger – Peter Carrington's father – was a sober character. Unlike his father and uncle, Rupert was not sent to Eton. Instead he grew up in Australia without going to England for his education and was sent to Brighton Grammar School and Australia's equivalent of Eton, Geelong Grammar School. The school record does not show a remarkable career, for he went to GGS in February 1906, became very ill and left at Easter. He did not return to formal schooling (Melbourne Grammar School) until he was nearly eighteen. It might be that if the tragedy of the Great War had not intervened, Rupert Carrington would have spent much of his life in Australia and Peter Carrington might well have been brought up thousands of miles away from Westminster. When Rupert, in his early twenties, arrived in England shortly before the Great War, he wanted to be a professional soldier not simply for the duration of the coming conflict. But he could not join the family regiment, the Grenadiers. His father's illegitimate son had joined the Grenadiers but it was considered unacceptable and therefore unthinkable that the young man should join the same regiment as his bastard brother. So the younger Rupert Carington joined the 5th Dragoon Guards. Then the illegitimate son was killed in the war and after a suitable period of mourning, Rupert was allowed to transfer from the Dragoons to the Grenadiers.

He survived the war knowing that because Uncle Charlie had no heir, his father would become the fourth Lord Carrington and so he could expect to assume the title one day. He knew also that with the title would come the full animosity of Charlie Lincolnshire's daughters. It was their brother who had been killed in the war and he was the usurper. While they had not seemed to mind fate offering it to Charles's brother Rupert, there was little to hide the disappointment and often downright resentment of Uncle Charlie and the rest of his family towards the younger Rupert.

In these circumstances, Rupert Carington distanced himself from Charlie Lincolnshire's family. Fortunately, he was taken in by the Colvilles, relatives since 1853 through the marriage to Cecil-Katherine-Mary, the daughter of the second Lord Carrington. Lord Colville of Culross, a bony, moustached figure, was the head of the famous Scottish family that had for centuries served the Crown as sailors, soldiers and courtiers. The Scottish title dated to 1604, and the Colville who welcomed Rupert Carington to the family was the second Viscount Colville of Culross. The Colvilles were quite grand and very warm. They went out of their way to make young Rupert welcome. It was at the Colvilles' home at Godalming in Surrey that Rupert met and fell in love with the second daughter, the Hon. Sybil Marian Colville. In his memoirs Peter Carrington would describe her as 'a gentle, sweet-natured person whose character tended to soften the sternness of my father's outlook'. They married on 25 May 1916. Sybil was just eighteen – as might have been said at the time, there was a war on and who knew the future?

The following year they had a daughter, Elizabeth (Betty), and on 6 June 1919 a son, baptized Peter Alexander Rupert, who would become the sixth Baron Carrington. It was, wrote his mother, 'the happiest day of my life'.[1] The then Lord Carrington,

---

1 Carrington private papers, Bledlow.

Charlie Lincolnshire, was less than impressed. On the evening of Peter's birth, Uncle Charlie recorded in his diary that the Blues Dinner had taken place at Claridge's for the first time since 1914, that he'd done well with first, second and third in the Oaks and, in barely one line, 'Sybil Carington had a little boy this morning.' Lincolnshire's family, especially its womenfolk, could hardly bring themselves to think of losing the inheritance. Carrington and his father represented that loss.

Rupert, Peter Carrington's father, was lucky to survive the Great War. Like many of his contemporaries he was wounded – in his case twice. He stayed in the army until 1924 and then retired. Probably by then, at the age of thirty-three, he was already ill with a weakened heart.

It was now that Peter Carrington's father took the decision that showed his determination to carve out his own life away from a still not always welcoming Carington family. The death of Uncle Charlie's heir betrayed an unforgiving nature in that branch of the family. Equally, there is little evidence that they warmed to him as a person. They were not alone in finding him aloof and often uncommunicative. The feeling was so strong that in his later years Peter Carrington's father would 'spit out Aunt Lily's name'.[2] Lincolnshire's wife had the sweetest exterior and a quite different inner character.

Little wonder that instead of living in or close to London – as well he might have been expected to – Rupert Carrington was determined to live well away from the rest of the family. In this mood, in 1924 he bought Millaton House, a fine Georgian building, along with some 200 acres on the north-western edge of Dartmoor beside what was then a quiet road between Okehampton and Launceston. In White's directory of Devonshire, Millaton House was described in 1850 as 'a handsome mansion, with tasteful grounds'. The building was started in the 1600s and then restored and enlarged a hundred years later.

Carrington's father wanted comfort. He renovated the building

2 Conversation with the author, August 1998.

with central heating fed through large 'school' radiators and, most important of all, added bathrooms. Two decades later, his son was to go through the same process with the new family seat, Bledlow.

The family were definitely 'the people at the big house' and they were, by and large, a happy family well at home close to the spaces of the two great wildernesses, Dartmoor and Exmoor. Rupert Carington enjoyed their distances and depths, a reflection of his own horizons as a boy in Australia. Sybil Carington too loved the sense of space and was no stranger to the region. The Colville family had for years spent their holidays at Woolacombe and certainly Sybil Carrington always appeared happier in the West Country than anywhere else. She particularly disliked the family estates in Buckinghamshire, where she felt shut in. In those days there was still something akin to a feudal atmosphere in their part of the West Country. To the casual observer today, to live in a Georgian manor house with 200 acres and Dartmoor on the doorstep, together with servants, suggests an exceptional and privileged upbringing. In the 1920s the view was quite different. In the late 1990s Peter Carrington looked back on his childhood at Millaton as a 'conventional upbringing. Extremely isolated, few cars, few neighbours and always raining.' He and his sister Betty were very close and they often spent their days by themselves because there were few neighbours and even fewer social moments. He saw his boyhood as uneventful, even – by the standards of his contemporaries – dull. Yet he and his sister were blissfully happy in an atmosphere of country living, shooting and hunting among the often colourful people of the moors and valleys. He was eternally grateful for his quiet upbringing as a countryman. It would seem that everyone in the area was a great character, including the local doctor, a Pickwickian fellow called Hillier. The shoot was over land owned by the Bedfords at Endsleigh (now a hotel), overlooking the Tamar valley. This was the good huntin' and fishin' constituency of the Whig-cum-Liberal MP, George Lambert, although their friendship did not mean Rupert Carrington was not about to revert to the third Carrington's political persuasion. Rupert Carrington was by instinct a Tory and quickly threw himself into local Conservative politics. Whether he threw himself with the same intensity into his family life is not easy to judge. Perhaps it was the times.

The house at Millaton was presided over by the serene figure of Sybil Carrington. The discipline was her husband's. He was an uncommunicative father. He and Peter did not talk very much and father and son were not close. Again, this was not untypical of the times and of this type of family. And yet, while the nature of Peter Carrington's father remained something of a mystery within the family, it was perhaps better known outside it. It was what people said after his death in 1938 that was most revealing about his character. Inevitably, outsiders saw Carrington in roles which the family rarely witnessed, for example as an administrator and someone who became deeply involved in West Country politics.

For Peter, who never knew him beyond his teenage years, his single overwhelming memory was of an uncompromising father and a stickler for rules. The atmosphere at Millaton may have been one of space and quiet pastimes but Rupert Carrington insisted that all matters of social form should be observed. The entire family dressed for dinner, a formality that certainly extended to the two youngest: as soon as he was old enough to dine with his parents, from about eleven, every evening Peter would find his dinner jacket, stiff shirt, winged collar and black tie laid out by a footman. This formality was reflected in almost everything the family did.

The house staff were presided over by a butler by the name of Dewar. It was said that he consumed a considerable amount of the spirit 'named as himself'. Outside, Carrington had developed the formal gardens. These were no rambling parklands but, rather like Carrington himself and the style of the period, immaculate and even manicured lawns, beds and shrubbery. It took eight gardeners eight hours a day to keep the grounds in order. One of the more celebrated parts of the Carrington estate was the cricket ground. Here was an example of Carrington's apparently cold demeanour hiding an often reasonable and sociable interior. It was his idea to enlarge the cricket ground and to build a splendid pavilion. The club and ground became his own and was a regular venue for some of the most fashionable touring sides, including the MCC. In those rainy moments that are features of Test matches, the late Brian Johnston was often heard in the commentary box remembering games past of those wandering sides which paused at the Millaton ground. As a youngster, Peter Carrington had been coached well at his prep school, Sandroyd, and during his early days at Eton. He easily had a place in the side and not simply because he was Lord Carrington's heir. Even here there remained a formality to be observed. Most of the players might expect to look on the village notice board to see if they had been picked. In Carrington's case, the Hon. Sec. was expected to write formally and respectfully to Millaton House requesting that *The Hon. Peter Carrington* might play on the day.

Bridestowe Cricket Club
Millaton Lodge, Bridestowe
11.8.1935

Dear Sir,
The above cricket club would be very grateful indeed, if you could play against the Mid-Devon Ramblers Cricket Club on Tuesday August 20th.
    The match commences at 2.30pm on the Millaton ground.
    Trusting that you will be able to accept this invitation, I remain
Sir,
Your Most Obedient Servant
A. D. Dewar
(Hon. Sec.)

Inevitably in that generation the constant figure of comfort was the children's nanny, their mother's French governess who now taught them. This was the formidable figure of 'Mabbie' or, more properly, Marguerite Fleurie. Her patriotism knew few bounds. Mabbie's home was Le Havre and some of the children's earliest memories are of excursions and holidays not with their parents but with their governess to that French Channel port. They would stay, not with a grand French family and certainly not in a fine hotel. Nanny and charges would put up in a boarding house over-looking the harbour. So their memories were not of French vineyards and chateaux but of the funnels and tugs, cranes and lighters, wharves and sheds as well as the small streets, market and smells. Little wonder the young Carringtons became fluent in French.

Peter and his sister Betty loved every moment of it. The memory remained. Even in his busiest diplomatic and political life decades later, Carrington rarely passed a box hedge without remembering the smell of gardens at Le Havre. Madame Fleurie traipsed them from boarding house to boarding house in sickness and in health. She sensibly made sure that they learned her native language. Consequently, by the time Carrington went to Eton his grasp of the French language and the less complicated parts of its grammar was sound. By Sandhurst, his French was far in advance of the army instructor's – who was supposed to be fluent. Those early years, he always felt, were a great asset for a man who one day would be Foreign Secretary and then Secretary-General of NATO. It was also rather handy for the day, a few years later, when Carrington found himself in Paris – ahead of the British army.

Apart from the best way to see France, the round of boarding houses reflected the Carrington family's belief that to spend money on themselves was quite unnecessary. Money was not the question. The family was hardly badly off, although, as Carrington was later to find out when he tried to restore the manor house at Bledlow, often the wealth was tied up in properties and laying one's hands on funds was as difficult as it ever had been for the poor old aristoc-racy. Extravagance was never tolerated. Lady Carrington believed that the unnecessary spending of money was almost sinful. Even excursions to London meant a return to the low life of uncomfort-able boarding houses and grubby hotels.

So how did this vision of a footman laying out a dinner jacket for young Master Peter square with Carrington's assertion that they never spent money on themselves? For example, it was common enough for them to go to the opera in white tie and tails, but travel by bus. The answer really is in inherited wealth that was tied up in property, together with a hangover from Victorian and Edwardian times when the expression of wealth was considered unseemly (a code that even at the beginning of the very money-conscious twenty-first century has not been relaxed among older families whatever their social standing). There was in the 1920s something that had existed for many years: an enormous economic divide whereby a family did not need to have a particularly great income to live rather well. When Carrington and his family talk about a house full of servants, we might remember that this did not cost that family very much. Servants were very poorly paid.

Carrington's father drummed into his young son that if they expected the servants to do everything properly, quickly, punctually and be properly and cleanly turned out, then he, Peter, had to understand that he too should do things properly, punctually and be correctly and cleanly dressed. The discipline of prep school, Eton and most of all Sandhurst gradually reinforced these views upon the boy. To the end of his life, Peter Carrington regarded bad timekeeping as unforgivable in all but extreme circumstances. Bad manners, he would say, to waste your own time as well as other people's.

The idyllic times in Devon inevitably had to be interrupted. In 1928 Peter Carrington was sent away to his preparatory school, Sandroyd, which was then at Cobham in Surrey and run by the formidable Mr Hornby. Sandroyd (it later moved to Tollard Royal, near Cranborne Chase in Wiltshire) had a family connection for the Carringtons. His Colville uncles had been there and one of them had taught at the school. Although he was a year older than many of the new boys (a formidable gap at that age), who included Carrington's future political colleague Anthony Mayer, Peter's first day was nevertheless a daunting occasion for a boy who had been living quietly among the acres of Millaton. The night before he lodged at the Colville family home in Eridge Park, just outside Tunbridge Wells. The next morning his Colville aunt and his mother took him to school in the Colvilles' large motor car, which was then considered rather smart.[3] He was taken there and 'dumped'. The spartan French boarding houses might well have been remembered with affection. Carrington now lodged in a cold and cavernous dormitory with a dozen other boys. Each morning started with a cold bath. This Buchanesque regime continued with three or four lengths in the unheated swimming pool, 'always cold'. The boys knew the days of the week by the food they ate. Tuesdays: spotted dick. Thursdays: treacle sponge. For the first week or so, Carrington lived up to his self-proclaimed image as a very ordinary boy by being thoroughly miserable. But he seems to have quickly settled in – 'one had to' – as his letters home suggest: warm, very concerned with sporting results (although himself not over-sporty) and quite bossy.

Sandroyd, Sunday Nov 4th 1928

My Darling Betty,
Thank you ever so much for your letter and would you thank Mabbie and Mummy for theirs I wish I was at home to ride my bike with you there have been thousands of matches but we lost nearly all of them. I hope Raffles [their Sealyham terrier] is all write [sic] and not to [sic] thin I have nothing say this week so goodbye Lots of love from
Peter

There's a tinge of sadness in his sprawling fist on another missive sent home to Betty that first term. The postcard has a scene on the garden steps of Penshurst Place. There are peacocks, dreamy swathes of lavenders and grasses, and a lovely lady in a long white frock holding a basket of flowers.

Don't you think this is like mummy? Do you? Please keep it for me?
Peter

3 Carrington's schooldays were recalled in a conversation with the author, July 1999.

By Easter, Carrington's letters had moved on from the 'small-voiced' uncertainty of a boy away at school for the first time; the sprawl had been replaced by a neat, slightly backward-sloping script that he would use for the rest of his life. Also, even then, there was the evidence of common sense and an ability to make clear to others exactly what he thought of situations. It was always good to practise this authority on a sister.

Easter March 31st 1929

My Darling Betty

I enjoy your letters about the children very much But you will not need to write any more tell the twins that Marguerite as she calls herself that she can join the Alicksander gang if she likes I should not let them go on to [*sic*] long because they might get bad habits do you think so? funny there is only 4 more days not counting Friday is it not spiffing tophole . . . ?

Sandroyd was a time which Carrington thought less than important. It certainly could not assume the significance in his life that Eton was to. Yet by the time of his second term, Carrington appears to have found his feet. His headmaster and close family friend, J. Edgar Langdon, wrote to his mother:

Jan 29 1928

Dear Sybil

I thought that perhaps a line about Peter might interest you.

All goes splendidly so far and I think Peter is thoroughly enjoying life here ragging about amongst other boys – the only jar so far this term is the weather – it has been unspeakably vile and it is with great difficulty that we have got the boys out of doors at all . . . Peter has been placed rather low in work, which is not a bad thing, as he will probably get a move up for next Term in most subjects.

I get him on Tues. and Fri. for English and I found him quite useful at it, and, what is more, was delighted to find that he has a great sense of humour and a good idea of being able to concentrate on what he is doing ... I have put Peter under the charge of Micky Major, who is a capital boy ...

Did he think Carrington exceptional? Not really. He was in the first stream for French, the second for English, Latin and Mathematics. Edgar Langdon seems to have approved of Carrington's sense of humour, something that almost everyone (with the possible exception of Ian Smith, the Prime Minister of Rhodesia) who knew Carrington in later life insisted was one of his most likeable traits. If he ever gave an impression to his sister (his letters to father and mother were few) of being pleased with himself, it was at cricket.

In yesterdays game I got 3 boys out LBW and very nearly did the hat trick ... we lost 88 to 130 I took four wickets and made 3. There was a first eleven match against Westminster choir we won 27 to 88

But he never really went on to play up and win that particular game. In fact, neither Sandroyd nor Eton ever expected a great deal of him, nor, it may seem, he of them. In a letter to Betty from Sandroyd he thought the new masters amusing: '... one says "do you see" the whole time the other says em ...'

It was in 1928, Peter's first year away at school, that Uncle Charlie, the Earl and Marquis of Lincolnshire and third Lord Carrington, died. Obituaries appeared in all the national newspapers and there was hardly a regional newspaper that did not carry photographs and long articles about him, from the *Cheltenham Chronicle* to the *Grimsby Telegraph*, from the *Methodist Times* to the *Lady*. The third Lord Carrington was mourned and honoured. After all, he was the man who as Liberal Agriculture Minister had guaranteed one of the abiding scenes in British urban life – the allotment. It was also Charlie Lincolnshire who devised the legislation for smallholdings. This was the man who in an agriculture debate in the House of Lords had startled peers and shifted them on their red benches by bursting into song with the last line, 'God gave the land to the people'.

The *Daily News* called him a great Liberal. The *Bolton Evening News* said he was 'an ideal landlord'. The *Morning Post* described him as an intimate friend of King Edward. The *Manchester Evening Chronicle* said he was a friend of kings and workers. *The Times* on 14 June 1928 carried a rare photograph of him robed as Lord Great Chamberlain, and its obituary writer remarked that his death 'removes a racy and intensely English personality'.

Because his son had predeceased him, all Uncle Charlie's titles with the exception of the Carrington barony died with him. Peter Carrington's grandfather Rupert – a tall figure with a bushy white moustache and a certain reputation for free-spending – inherited the title and became the fourth Lord Carrington. The Caringtons tended towards long lives; the first baron lived until he was eighty-six, the second (his son) died when he was seventy-two, while *his* son, Uncle Charlie – whose energies and lifestyle would have been quite wearing for most men – was eighty-five when he died in 1928. Now grandfather Rupert, who had happily worked his way through his own money and much of his wife's Australian fortune, appeared to be finally set up with the Carrington inheritance. Yet he was dead within seventeen months of inheriting the title, aged seventy-seven.

In 1929 Peter Carrington's father became the fifth baron. Charlie Lincolnshire's family did not soften. Rupert was still a usurper, the person from the colonies. Their attitude was unreasonable because it was not as if there was anyone else who could have continued the line. There was no frustrated and angry male who thought he might have at least a moral right to become Lord Carrington.

The new Lord Carrington continued to assert his independence from the rest of the family and to be active in West Country politics as a serious-minded member of Tavistock Council, and a reforming member of the Devon Police Authority. These may seem mundane pastimes for anyone of his social position in the region. But Rupert Carrington did not see it that way. He was hardly a wild colonial boy brought up in the outback but he had

a strong sense of what was right and wrong. Having taken on some
public or semi-public responsibility, his sense of duty and his
awareness of the privilege of his birth meant that he put far more
into anything he took on than perhaps the average person. This
regard to duty that came with a relatively easy background was
something he impressed with uncompromising vigour on his
young son. Even before he went off to prep school Peter Carrington had taken on board this code and he was never to discard
it. Moreover, Rupert Carrington's life in the West Country was
not simply governed by an understanding of aristocratic responsibilities; he cared deeply for the region which had welcomed him
and Sybil.

Once he became the new Lord Carrington in 1929, Rupert
inherited more than the title. In spite of the reputation of his father
for spending assets, there were estates extending from Lincolnshire
to Wales and back to the Home Counties. Most were in and around
Buckinghamshire.

The one thing that was missing from all these estates was a London home. Carrington House had gone in 1885 when the Crown
Lease was up. (Uncle Charlie complained that he had been evicted
without compensation.)[4] The lack of a London home in some
ways made Rupert Carrington an even more distant figure to his
family. Apart from staying with relatives there was nowhere for
them to gather for long periods and when the fifth Lord Carrington was in London he put up at his club, the Marlborough,
once more an image of a quiet and solitary figure. It was not until
Peter Carrington was a coming man in postwar British politics
that the family had a London house,[5] by which time his mother
and father were both dead and his sister was far away in Liverpool.
He had sold Millaton and had been saddened by the decline of the
house. It became a nursing home and then a bypass bisected the

4 The government later demolished Carrington House and put in its place a
ministry that is now called the Old War Office, on the corner of Horse Guards
Avenue and Whitehall.
5 32a Ovington Square, bought in 1962.

estate. In the late 1980s a local historian, D. R. Cann, noted that the once magnificent gardens 'are not worth a mention'.[6]

The period of depression in British social and economic life in the 1920s and '30s was a constant subject of conversation in the family during Carrington's formative years. Naturally, it was a sense that not all was well rather than some precocious understanding, yet in the back of his mind there lodged a need to know more about people he did not mix with. It would be too easy to make much of this feeling. However, it is relevant to understand that a ten-year-old from a privileged background was developing the notion that his father and mother held to be important: that the recurring theme of privilege and public duty went hand in hand. It was something he would always come back to, particularly in the army, when he quickly understood that many of his soldiers had joined up because they were hungry. Time and again he made this point with some passion. The cynic could easily strip his protest to nothing more than an aristocrat justifying his hereditary position. Yet Carrington believed from childhood that one had inherited responsibilities as well as estates. It was a code that he learned in the nursery and he used throughout his life with a phrase which probably grated on the nerves of constitutional reformers: 'When in later life I wondered how to go about something, I invariably reduced it to a simple question: What would nanny have done?'[7] It was said with not a little humour and it meant that he had learned never to ignore the basic skills and codes of his earliest childhood.

By 1932 it was time for him to leave Sandroyd and follow generations of Caringtons to Eton. According to the notes of the then headmaster of Sandroyd, Eton was getting a self-confident boy with a sense of humour and yet one who seemingly believed he had no exceptional talents. Eton at that time was not always a civilized environment, especially seen through the eyes of a new

6 The house later went back to private ownership and was restored to something approaching its original state.

7 Conversation with the author, August 1999.

boy. It is also curious to an outsider that considering his family's background and history in the school, no special effort was made to introduce young Peter to the mysteries of this unique place. Therefore we see in his letters to his mother that Carrington takes it upon himself to find out how Eton works before he goes there.

Easter Sunday March 27 [1932]

My Darling Mummy
Thank you so much for your letters. That letter arrived on Saturday so it was not too late ... I am sending the usual train slip although I don't expect I shall be going that way ... the forms at Eton go Third (potty) Lower fourth, Middle Fourth, Upper Fourth Remove (scholars and highest form you can take from prep school) ...

Carrington's great friend Hugh Rocksavage committed a sartorial sin that would live with him for the rest of his life.

The Eton Society, more commonly known as Pop, was (and remains) the senior boys' self-electing body. Pop members, instead of wearing the normal Eton jacket and trousers, wore coloured waistcoats, checked spongebag trousers (the rest of the school wore black pinstripe) and braided tailcoats. The authority of these boys was never disputed – if a member of Pop told a junior boy to do something he did it.

On their first morning Carrington and Rocksavage entered the dining room for breakfast. Rocksavage had been let down by his parents. No regulation black trousers but, worse still, grey baggy Pop trousers. The howls of fury and derision 'hit us like a water cannon'. For Rocksavage there was untempered misery, but the incident revealed something in Carrington's character that was time and again to surface in his military and political career: his sense of justice. One of the people in the dining hall that morning who was noisily joining in the jeering of Carrington's friend was his Dame – the matron-cum-housekeeper at Eton College. Carrington immediately understood the 'justice' of Rocksavage being the subject of sport for the other boys; what he could not accept was this woman's noisy derision. To him it was unfair; it was wrong; he regarded her for ever with contempt. Once more a response that would be recognized in him by many of his colleagues years on.

Carrington was not an exceptional student but then, apart from the scholars, there was no need to be exceptional and, in the 1930s, there was even a sense that this was unimportant. General Sir David Fraser, sometime Vice Chief of the Defence Staff, was in his first year at Eton when Carrington was in his second. The gap between the first and second year at that age can be considerable and usually is. In Fraser's first summer he found himself unselected for his house eleven and sitting on the grass alongside Peter Carrington, who had reached a similar standard of cricket. It would have been very easy and indeed very likely for the junior boy to have been ignored. He wasn't. As Fraser remarked to me in 1989, 'His [Carrington's] easy smile and friendliness were far more important than people might imagine.' They did not immediately become firm chums but it was this friendliness and the solicitous way in which this still very junior boy could enquire with obvious sincerity whether there was anything he could do for the other that drew Fraser to Carrington's personality. Years later in the Second World War they met again. Carrington was still displaying similar charm and concern for other people's welfare – including Fraser's. The two became the closest of friends for the rest of their lives.

It is a common pastime to judge that from the earliest days a boy's character is developed enough to give a good indication of his future. Carrington's reports during his first year suggest traits that were recognizable in him during his public life. Had Sandroyd given him a better grounding in elementary Latin constructions he would have probably been good at Classics, 'but he is very willing to learn and will soon conquer the failures. His English work in History and Divinity has usually reached a high level ... he has the makings of a nice easy style which he uses to good effect ... he works hard the whole time and he never allows his attention to wander.' At the end of the Summer Half in 1932, Carrington was seventh in a class of twenty-eight. The news for Lent 1933 was not so good because Carrington could not see! His eyesight had been poor for a while but it took some time for those who could do something about it to realize the extent of the problem. He was sent to a specialist, Sir Stewart Duke-Elder, whom Carrington thought a funny man who gave him pills and told him to lie in a darkened room for six months. As Carrington remembers it, Elder was knighted and then became enormously expensive. His house-master, Cyril Butterwick, wrote to his father expressing his own doubts about the darkened room and pills treatment, which was not working.

It's dreadfully important that his eyes are not quite right, but I refuse to be as alarmist as Duke Elder & I would certainly get another opinion before any great decisions affecting Peter are arrived at.

They were about to give up on his eyesight. Meanwhile, he was desperately trying to make sense of his reading and class work, but the reports were uncompromising and unsympathetic:

Intelligent but rather confused in his thinking. His work has been very variable; often good, but sometimes he has lost his head and made mistake after mistake. Calmness would improve his work a lot.

I do not think he is very quick-witted.

Though his knowledge of the Grammar is very uncertain and his exercises feeble, I think he has learnt something.

Extremely virtuous but rather unsuccessful.

Yet beneath this was a willingness to press on – especially once he was given a pair of spectacles – as was seen in his Classical Report for Michaelmas 1933.

He has shown himself throughout the Half a keen and responsive worker, and it has been a pleasure to teach him. He is not naturally endowed with great intelligence, and can occasionally produce the most appalling Latin Prose. But there is no doubt about his will to work, and I hope he will maintain this admirable quality.

The admirable quality was evident in him for the rest of his life.

The guardian of Carrington's life at Eton was Butterwick, who became a celebrated Eton housemaster, although in the folklore of that place it may seem that all the housemasters become celebrated. Butterwick's name went far beyond the College walls. Prep schools and parents would aim their boys at housemasters rather than simply at the school. His house was not only an academic stronghold. It had a distinguished sporting reputation, especially at cricket. Carrington recalled that on one occasion, half the Eton eleven were from Butterwick's. Not surprisingly, Carrington did not appear among that number and Butterwick felt a need to write to his father explaining that his house was exceptionally blessed that year, but that his son was not so gifted even though he was no mean spinner of the ball. The mark of a fine house was to take someone like Carrington who was never to be a sporting hero nor a double first, and not to let him disappear beneath the brighter and more athletic. Carrington understood this and remembered it in almost everything he did in the future. Academically, Butterwick thought him sound but quite unexceptional. What was he trying to produce, he asked Carrington's father. 'I want a leader of men capable of doing right – rather grandly. I'd give a lot to set light to Peter.' Instead he thought Carrington a boy who would never set fire to the Thames.

It should not be imagined that Carrington's was an uneventful school career. He had not been at Eton long, when he found himself having to answer to Butterwick and to his people for behaviour that hardly suggested that the heart of a patient and pragmatic foreign secretary beat within his young breast. Carrington was in trouble – apparently for fighting. In later life he thought this very unlikely.

[Undated]

My Darling Mummy

Thank you ever so much for your letter of course I agree to your conditions and promise to keep to them especially the one about fighting. I can get off very early for Lords about 8.30 as it is a privilege for the choir to get off chapel so will you write and tell me which time you can have me. There was a holiday for Henley on Wednesday and the eight were beaten by a length as the stroke gave up halfway and they couldn't go on without him.

There is no more news
Lots of love
from Peter

In his last letter written at Eton, Carrington, as ever, was in a rush. Years on he remembered that he had never indulged in idleness. There was always in his mind a sense that he should be getting on and doing things. Even as a teenager he would gloss over his achievements and honours just as he would for the rest of his life, with an expression of surprise that anyone should think him exceptional. His final Eton letter is typical of having something important to say, casually mentioning it and then getting on quickly with the next stage of his life. He was doing the same thing in his eighties.

Wednesday [1937]

My darling Mamma

As usual I forgot your birthday but I hope the telegram arrived safely but to this day I am not sure whether your birthday is on the 20th or 21st. However you know what I meant anyway. Everything here is as much as usual and very pleasant. I have got into the House Library of which I am rather proud!

It seems rather odd to think that I have only got 6 more days at Eton and I am not very sure I like it very much. (Please don't show that to anyone as they'll think I am getting sentimental.)

I am getting a House photograph so you will be able to see what everyone looks like, after having heard their names.

I shall go by the 11 o'clock train unless you have any objections I shall have a hell of a lot of luggage so perhaps Barkwell had better come.

Lots of love

Peter

In 1937 came what was perhaps the most important turning point in Carrington's life. He did not go up to Oxford. It remained an enormous regret for the rest of his life. It could easily be argued that Eton and Butterwick failed him. His father, still a distant and sometimes difficult figure, put it to his son that he had a choice of what to do after Eton, but it seemed that the army was the natural home for someone who had not distinguished himself as a scholar.

Carrington had done rather well in the Eton Officers' Training Corps, in their heather uniform with blue facings and badges of rank. It was certainly a distinguished unit and Carrington had been one of the members who lined the route in Windsor Castle when the funeral cortege of King George V passed by with, seemingly, every monarch and prince of Europe in slow step. So Carrington rather liked the military atmosphere. His housemaster suggested banking, farming or the army. The Royal Navy was not a natural berth for Old Etonians. Carrington chose to go directly as a Gentleman Cadet to the Royal Military Academy, Sandhurst. It was not a mistake, but in time to come, a regret. If he had read History, as he later wanted to, he imagined that instead of the career for which he became famous, he would have probably joined the Foreign Office and ended his career as an agreeable ambassador in a place like Rome or Paris.

4. Carrington MC

Carrington probably went to Sandhurst because he was feeling belligerent. It was his moment of adolescent rebellion. Of course it would have been simpler to have gone up to Oxford, which in many ways Butterwick, and perhaps even his father, would have preferred him to do. At the point when he needed encouragement, he instead received advice. Rather perversely, he went against his own choice, which would have been the university. Here we have an early example of his bloody-mindedness. Carrington felt that his father was pushing him into making the sort of decision that he did not want to make. When the pressure was applied for him to make a decision between Oxford and Sandhurst, Carrington went into one of his sulks. Later in life, instead of sulking, he would often rage, it being a quicker and more practical way out of the mood. Oxford would have been three years and then into the army. Sandhurst was quicker. To Carrington it seemed also that if he was going to be a professional soldier then he really should start at the obvious place, at the Royal Military Academy. His father, who had been a professional soldier, was quietly satisfied. His attitude was simple: get in the army and get on with life. Butterwick told Carrington rather sadly that he regarded soldiering as being on a par with farming – something to go into when there was little chance of a more intellectual career. This was hardly unexpected from his housemaster who thoroughly disapproved of soldiering and had not taken part in the Great War. However, Butterwick, like all tutors, was very happy to bask in his boys' successes and celebrity. So, naturally, he was one of the first to write to Carrington's father on hearing the news that Peter Carrington had come twelfth in the entry competition.

Eton College, Windsor, October 6th 1937

My Dear Carrington

Your letter has very naturally given me a pride and a pleasure, which I appreciate more than I can possibly say. I hope and, yes, I believe that I have done a little for your dear Peter.

We missed the Sandhurst notice but Peter's place delighted us when he told us. He is a boy who always does himself rather more than justice, when the best is called for, but 12th is something better than well and he is greatly to be congratulated ...

You know I am sure that I shall always be the tutor since he will never have another[,] that all of us will always have the deepest affection for him and should any crisis ever arise in which we can be of the slightest help both my wife and I will give that help [with] open hands and full heart.

Thank you again more than I can say for a letter which I shall not destroy

Yours very sincerely

Cyril Butterwick

Peter Carrington went to Sandhurst in the autumn of 1937. He was enrolled as a Gentleman Cadet. Apart from the buildings, the parkland and the noises on and off the parade ground, the Sandhurst of 1937 is unrecognizable to cadets on today's short officer induction course. These days a would-be officer goes to the Royal Military Academy for just a few months simply of cramming before joining his or her regiment or corps. In the 1930s everything took longer. Furthermore, Sandhurst was to the vast majority of cadets their 'university'. The course was broad and included, as well as matters military, academic subjects such as History and French. As a Gentleman Cadet there were two further distinctions: the GCs were set aside from the ordinary cadets by their social standing and regimental ambitions and, most of all, by the fact that they were not really in the army. The families of Gentleman Cadets, like Carrington, had to pay for their sons to attend Sandhurst as if it were some military extension of their public school.

For all its traditions and reputation, RMA Sandhurst was not a very good officer training establishment inasmuch as it did little to prepare the students for future warfare. It is also true that many, perhaps the majority, of regiments themselves were ill prepared to go to a modern war. They hardly, if ever, studied or even gave a passing nod to those who did point out the deficiencies of the British military system. And all the while, the nation moved towards the inevitable war with Germany. There was sufficient evidence by 1937 that war was going to take place in the very near future. Yet when Carrington arrived at Sandhurst that autumn, there was seemingly not even lip service paid to the idea that the young officer cadets had to be brought up to date as quickly as possible with modern military thinking. Equally, there was very little modern military thinking. He had joined an institution that had not much moved on from the ethos of officer training of the Great War period, two decades earlier.

The first task of Sandhurst was to prepare its students physically. They learned to swim quickly, run quickly, cycle quickly and change clothes quickly. Most of all they learned to drill quickly and properly. Hour after hour, day after day, the cadets were pushed and punished by drill instructors. Even getting on and off a bicycle and cycling was done as a drill exercise. Cadets could be seen coming from the swimming pool, mounting their bicycles in unison like coordinated chorus boys, then cycling 'at the trot' in paraded lines like a cavalry troop returning from Horse Guards. In that first autumn term when the GCs weren't learning to fall in, dress right, quick march, slow march, right wheel and mark time, they spent what hours were left, between sleeping (not many) and quickly taken meals, in cleaning and polishing. They learned to clean already perfectly clean equipment and polish already gleaming kit. From tip to toe, from cap badge to boot cap, brass and leather were made to gleam so brightly that a drill sergeant could shave his craggy jaw in perfect safety in the reflection. If scabbards did not gleam as if they were varnished and bayonets glint sufficiently to reflect the sun, then the punishment was obvious – more polishing. But most of all, more drill. Polishing and drilling until even the most enthusiastic cadet learned the army's philosophy that a straight line and shiny buttons went a long way in making up for its lack of military efficiency.

There were also kit inspections, with every article displayed, gleaming and clean. One's rifle had to be stripped down to its component parts: and anyone who thinks a Lee Enfield rifle consists simply of magazine, bolt and body doesn't know much about a Lee Enfield rifle. There were more than a hundred (so I recall) tiny screws, springs and parts which had to be laid out spotless, on a sheet on one's bed for inspection. At my first such inspection the senior under Officer found a speck of dust on one part, picked up the sheet and threw the lot out of the window. It took me ages to find all the components of my rifle on the grass below.[1]

This was not at all what the eighteen-year-old Peter Carrington had in mind when he defiantly told his father and Butterwick that he preferred the idea of Sandhurst over Oxford. His first letter home, to his father, sets a very cheerful mood, and recognizes the natural command afforded by an Old Etonian tie.

RMA, Sunday

Dear Dad

All at the moment well. It was quite the most awful moment of my life arriving here, but everyone was and is very nice. There are two old Etonians (new) in the company and several very old Etonians. Also one boy who was at Sandroyd with me called Dunlop. That is rather pleasant, as one doesn't see anyone from any other company at all so far as I can see. I have a room to myself, which is very lucky, as it is potluck whether one shares or not.

I should be addressed ordinary like with no G.Cs [Gentlemen Cadets] or anything and the above address.

About money. Everyone seems to pay in to the Pocket Money

---

1 Lord Carrington, *Reflect on Things Past*, London: Collins, 1988, p. 22.

account so if you arranged about my allowance with some bank in Camberley I could cash a cheque and pay in to this footling thing.

They feed one very well here. A four course dinner and coffee and goodness knows what else. The strangeness is wearing off slightly and I don't feel quite so muddled but doubtless tomorrow it will be grim again.

It is quite astonishing what an OE tie will do in this place. People you have never seen before come up and say 'If you are in any difficulty just come and ask me'.

My section Commander comes from Harrow and is very efficient and with a good sense of humour ... Altogether at the moment it is not such a bad place as I expected.

This was the England of the 1930s. The social tapestry was finely woven, the silks of place and privilege tightly knotted. Half a century on, the term 'networking' became clearly understood and developed. At Sandhurst before the war, when a chap was from Eton and a good family, it was a natural pastime. All this is perfectly understandable and something which Carrington continued to exploit in delicate political and diplomatic situations for the next sixty years. But in his next letter home to his father, there is something else: a priggishness which at the very least confounds the popular image of the man.

Saturday [Undated, but probably late October 1937]

Dear Dad
... the adjutant and Dobson have both asked how you are, and I like the adjutant and rather dislike Dobson. He is exceedingly pompous and much more conceited.

There is a servant here called Beech who says he knew you in Turkey. He was a drummer in the regiment I believe. My company commander is a Major Davidson of some Scottish regiment and Platoon Commander is a man called Melsome from the Northamptons.

Most of the junior [cadets] seem to be most 'what the dame

would call not top drawer'. About 50% are quite shattering but probably quite nice. There is one bit of work who is unfortunately called Brown and whenever he opens his mouth puts his foot in it in broad cockney. The 50% would probably if they met you in the holidays call you sir. That may sound snobbish but is nevertheless perfectly true. They talk about serviettes and sauce instead of gravy and are always saying 'Pardon?'

Peter

But the mighty could soon fall, as an undated letter, again probably from the end of October 1937, suggests, shortly after Carrington had come off worse in a boxing match.

Dear mamma

Paramount have been filming us all week. They are making some film called the Army of Today, and apparently we come into it. They filmed the whole of the battalion parade on Saturday and of course I went and wrecked everything by saluting wrong with my sword and they had to do it all over again. They wasted endless feet of film and I got a frightful raspberry ... the general opinion amongst the officers here is that we shall fight a war sooner or later what an awful thought. I expect however that the army and Air Force will get the worst of it ...

Things here are pretty grim. Everyone seems to be getting annoyed with us and say that we are jolly slack which is absolutely untrue I can assure you.

I am beginning to dislike my section commander more than anyone I have ever met. All he does when he comes in is to say B—y you're damned idle. He comes from Harrow which may account for quite a bit. A truly horrible bit of work. I have received an Imperial Raspberry for not having my door open when some half wit shouted 'Rooms Gentlemen please' ...

My nose has nearly been broken boxing. I can't blow it for if I do it starts bleeding. My lip is cut and is all swollen and I can't shut my mouth because my jaw is cracked.

I should like to go to bed for a week. No two weeks and get some sleep, instead of which I shall probably get chased for the next two weeks like an insect.

This letter is written at 9.30PM. The room is cold the light is bad. People are yelling all round. Everything is waiting to be cleaned. NOTHING IS GOING TO BE CLEANED TO NIGHT.
Peter
PS I may feel better to-morrow but I have my doubts.

By the start of November 1937, Carrington was moved in his weekly letter to tell his mother that Sandhurst was far from a memorable social event in his young life.

Dear Mamma
. . . a day's work here is something like this

7.00	Get Up
7.25	shaving parade (to see if you are clean)
8.00	breakfast
8.25–9.30	Drill (and what drill)
9.30–12.50	work at map reading
1.00	lunch
1.30	box
2.00–4	Polish leather and steel
4.00	Change in dinner jacket
4.24–7.30	Work at tactics
8.00	Mess (best thing in day)
8.45–10.30	Polish

What a place!

I can't go as far as to say I like it, but it is not so bad. The polishing is the worst part. One just sits down and polishes polishes polishes Ugh!

I have passed the swimming test. Swim 100 yards

Peter

After a not very long time Carrington began to like the routine of bulling and drilling; to him it became a challenge. He became determined that there would not be a speck of dust. If there were a mite on a rifle barrel it meant there had to be dust not far away. That became unacceptable to him, and a point of honour that it should be unacceptable to such an extent that he and the Senior Under Officer became of a like mind. He quickly learned to enjoy the thought of being the best. It was a question in his mind of recognizing what was wanted and finding the most efficient, and at the same time satisfying, way to make that happen.

Equally he understood that others either could not or would not understand what was happening and therefore should be coaxed into getting as close as they possibly could to what was needed. Here again we find something in his make-up that he was never to abandon.

When he had gone to Sandhurst from Eton there appears to have been a certain acceptance by his elders that Carrington 'might as well go into the army'. Perhaps few had imagined that Carrington would turn out to be very good at soldiering. He had the right background inasmuch as he understood the rights and frailties of authority and how to exercise one and avoid the other. He was already a good horseman and had been since childhood, which was an advantage in a 1930s army that still relied on horsepower. He was equally comfortable with before-breakfast 'blanket' riding (i.e. bareback) as he was riding to hounds. At the end of his year, Carrington was rated in the top four Sandhurst horsemen and only narrowly missed being awarded the highest competition trophy, the Saddle, for the best equestrian in the Academy.

Carrington was also beginning to blossom in the classroom as well as in the field. His French was already better than that being taught at Sandhurst; his quick grasp of tactics and tactical appreciation exercises and his ability to analyse and summarize military information was setting him ahead of some of his contemporaries by the end of the second term, when he was promoted to corporal – a considerable achievement for any cadet.

By his last term, Carrington's ability was recognized to be high enough for him to expect a career at the top end of the army. There were four Under Officers to be appointed from the cadets. In the whole of the college there were four companies (the equivalent of school houses), each one having its Senior Under Officer whose authority, as Carrington well remembered, extended to throwing bits and pieces of rifles out of the window. Carrington became the Senior Under Officer of his company. One of the four Senior Under Officers of the Academy would be judged the best cadet and receive the Sword of Honour. Again Carrington just missed out. The person who did win was Senior Under Officer Chandos Blair, who went on to become a lieutenant general. Maybe, just maybe, there was a mild satisfaction for Carrington that when Blair became Vice Chief of the Defence Staff he had to call Carrington 'Sir', because by that time Carrington was Senior Under Officer of the sixth floor of the Ministry of Defence. He was Secretary of State.

Sandhurst should not be regarded as little more than a social interlude in Carrington's life. It introduced him to a new world. On one occasion, for example, a fellow cadet who had a motor car took him to a party in Sussex where they 'picked up' a couple of local girls. Carrington was not exactly horrified but thought them quite uncouth and was appalled at their behaviour. He continued to be amused by his contemporaries who did not come from the same background. He quickly picked up speech mannerisms of some cadets from less privileged families and in certain cases wrote to his mother and father about them like an explorer discovering a curious and hitherto unknown species. Carrington was, after all, just emerging from his teenage years, and just as people from other classes probably poked fun at his mannerisms, so he found theirs novel. Most importantly, Sandhurst was Carrington's first undisputed triumph. He had gone there after a not overly distinguished career at Eton. Yet almost from the beginning he shone at RMA. Academically he was sharper than, if not intellectually superior to, most of his contemporaries. He was, as we have seen, one of the four top horsemen, which in the 1930s British army was still a practical as well as a sporting distinction. He was good at the detail of soldiering and had developed the two most important talents for an army officer – he was lucky and he was never late for anything. So by the end of 1938 Carrington had for the first time in his short life achieved a great deal by his own talents and not simply because of his OE tie.[2]

The one important person who would not see his graduation, bedecked as Senior Under Officer as he marched with his company behind the Adjutant on his charger, was Peter Carrington's father. In November 1938, during Carrington's final term at Sandhurst, his father died and Peter Carrington became the sixth Baron Carrington.

Theirs had never been a close relationship. Only much later did Carrington learn that his father's demeanour was partly due to his natural and sometimes lonely personality, but equally to his ill health. The fifth Lord Carrington had a weakened heart, which he well knew and hid from most others. There is a moving letter in the Carrington papers from a local garage man, which tells us something of the sadness of his final hours and his determination that others, especially his wife, should not be troubled by his condition.

In the New Year, January 1939, Second Lieutenant, the Lord Carrington reported to Wellington Barracks in Birdcage Walk, London, to join the family regiment, the second battalion of the Grenadier Guards.

Carrington was born just seven months after the Armistice of the Great War. What happened in 1919 was, although few then understood so, the making of the Second World War. Interestingly, Carrington, still a teenager, had already spent much time thinking about the history of the 1920s and early 1930s and had come to the conclusion that the Keynesian analysis was probably correct.

The negotiations that led to the Treaty of Versailles might be seen as having not one, but a number of crucial agendas. First, there was the determination of France to exact the maximum revenge for the way the Germans had devastated so much of the

2 See p. 66.

country. Moreover, the French believed that if they exacted a high price in reparations, Germany would be in no position to rebuild the industrial and military infrastructure which made her such a threat in French eyes.

The major partners in the alliance, America and Great Britain, were not strong enough to argue against the French position even though they instinctively saw its dangers. Carrington had read the history and accepted at least one important element of the Keynesian wisdom: if the French plan to bleed Germany industrially and financially to death continued, where could the Germans possibly get the money to pay the reparations?

As it was, the stage payments would mean that the reparation debt would not be paid off until at least the 1960s. Also, this harsh treatment of a nation, however justifiable it may have seemed in Paris, could only lead to resentment and the inevitable movement towards nationalism.

Immediately after the war some, including John Maynard Keynes, were making this quite clear.[3] Carrington thought it obvious. Moreover, the Germans did not believe that they had lost the war and although they were forced to accept the terms of Versailles, nationally they did not – and were not forced to – behave as a vanquished nation. There was no army of occupation. The Germans still had their own army even though there were restrictions on the size of all three forces. The new republic had been declared at Weimar and the Germans got on with governing themselves, although they had lost what was left of their empire.

In Britain the war had far from resolved the problems of government. Asquith's administration in 1914 had been diverted from the events which led to the Great War by the campaigns for Irish Home Rule, and then events during the war including the 1916 Easter Rising made the so-called Troubles even more insoluble. In 1919 the Irish Republican Army, the IRA, was formed. In 1920 the seemingly terrible decision to send the infamous Black and Tans to Ireland was taken. This was the same year as the Government of

3 See J. M. Keynes, *The Economic Consequences of Peace*, 1919.

Ireland Act was passed and the following year, 1921, the Irish Free State was created. There would not be a realistic hope for peaceful coexistence in the island of Ireland until the very last days of the century.

The political tapestry during those postwar years was also changing. The domination of Lloyd George was over by 1922. For a short while, Bonar Law became Prime Minister, and then in 1923 Baldwin began his long, albeit interrupted, tenancy of 10 Downing Street. In 1924, for constitutional rather than electoral reasons, Ramsay MacDonald formed the first Labour government. It lasted only ten months, but in that short time he proved that the Labour Party could be elected as a responsible government and that the Liberal Party was no longer an alternative administration. After 1924 the Liberals were never again a great influence on the government of the British people.

Carrington had grown up in the peaceful and seemingly uneventful countryside of Devon, which appeared to have quickly reverted after the First World War to its Edwardian style of easy living. But in spite of maids and footmen along the corridors, a butler, a housekeeper, a cook and gardeners, Britain was not 'the land fit for heroes' that many imagined. By 1926 unemployment in many of the industrial regions was so great that violent industrial unrest was not at all uncommon.

This was an age of enormous social change. As a tiny child Carrington would have worn dresses, the pretty smocks worn by children of either sex especially among the gentler classes. He was dressed in sailor suits and his lifestyle in the summer was still very much that of the late Victorian and Edwardian period. There is a photograph of him and his sister in the summer of 1920 in knee-length dresses and his grandfather, Viscount Colville, relaxing in a deckchair but still wearing jacket, waistcoat and homburg. There was nothing unusual about this family scene. Yet this was the beginning of the twenties and the age of jazz, a suddenly liberated night life in London, overt promiscuity, daring homosexuality and lesbianism, young women so desperate to be seen in the latest skimpiest fashions that they took drugs and smoked heavily to suppress their appetites. Smoking among young women was so widespread that the medical profession was identifying and warning of increased cases of mouth and throat cancers. It was also the age of speed. New technologies were making cars go faster, aeroplanes sturdier. Transatlantic records were being broken.

So there was the young Carrington, brought up – by the standards of most people – in a grand manner; living in a society which learnt to dress for dinner almost as soon as its silver spoon was discarded; being quite naturally and unwittingly snobbish, even to the extent of mocking his colleagues who had serviettes but no napkins. Little wonder that with the growing authority of socialist politics, Carrington's natural habitat sometimes felt threatened.

Yet just as he was about to embark on what he called a quietly agreeable career in the Grenadiers, Britain prepared for war, a war for which he clearly believed she was ill prepared. Her political and military institutions were not ready, he said. Nor was Carrington, in spite of his military training and his claims of foresight, himself really prepared for war. The four years that he now spent in the United Kingdom, along with a vast part of the British army (for example, that which was not in the North African campaign and in the Far East), were more than a period of military adjustment, it was a political and social maturing.

It was a period during which Carrington became more politically aware. He now understood the growing demands of a nation determined to express how it wished to be governed. He reread the history of the 1832 Reform Act.

The war began with an increasing body of opinion at Westminster and in Whitehall asserting that the Prime Minister, Neville Chamberlain, had lost his authority. It is often forgotten that the party political system of government in the United Kingdom – that is, the government of the day being formed from one of the three main political parties – had been set aside in 1931 following the inability of any group to control the economy and the confidence of the electorate. Since 1931 there had been two parliaments (1931–5 and 1935–45) not of party political government, but National Government. With the forming of this first National

Government in 1931, Britain had come off the gold standard and the Royal Navy had mutinied at Invergordon. The following year, 1932, Oswald Mosley had formed the British Union of Fascists. In 1933 the Oxford Union held its famous debate and resolved that 'this House will not fight for King and Country'. It was a debate that caused other debates that sparked other debates and at Eton influenced the opinion of boys including Carrington. It was also the year that Hitler became German Chancellor.

In 1938, with Carrington nearing the end of his Sandhurst career and sure of his own impressions that war was inevitable, all political and military prejudice was confirmed in him with the infamous Munich Agreement. Then came the introduction of Air Raid Precautions and the nail which was to be driven through the heart of any oak for a peaceful Europe, the annexation of Austria by Hitler's Germany.

In 1939, when the war began and the first stages of conscription were introduced, Carrington joined his regiment – a society of traditionalists and the social elite at one hand and often the malcontent and deprived at the other. For him, there was only one immediate ambition: having now joined the Brigade of Guards, he was a professional soldier and at long last he would be let into the great secret of how this famous regiment was preparing for the conflict. It was not to be. Carrington reported to Wellington Barracks, that collection of miniature Doric temples across from Buckingham Palace, only to be told three things by his commanding officer: on no account was he to marry until he was twenty-five years old; he was never to wear a grey top hat before the June race meeting at Epsom; and, most importantly of all, he was expected to hunt two days a week in Leicestershire.

Carrington saluted and went to his quarters in the full belief that his colonel had not quite told him everything. How was it that the talk beyond Birdcage Walk was all about war? Was he missing something? Perhaps once into the swing of regimental life he would see the ruthless military efficiency that surely was at work preparing for the second German War.

The person who was not there to greet Carrington was the

officer who might have taken the moment to explain how the
regiment was to train for conflict. His company commander had
taken a house in the south of France and had no great intention of
returning to England until the summer.

For the first three or four months in his regiment, Carrington
was totally ignored. The custom of the Grenadiers in 1939 was to
totally put down a newly joined officer. No one would talk to him
and he would never be so impertinent as to even say good morning
when he entered the officers' mess. It was as if Carrington did not
exist. It was the regiment's way of making sure that every subaltern
understood his total insignificance, no matter how many trophies
and glowing reports he carried from Sandhurst and no matter how
long his family's history in the regiment and no matter what his
pedigree. The Jockey Club rated more highly than Burke's Peerage.
Between January and Easter 1939, Carrington would appear in the
mess without being spoken to, without speaking, without even a
nod of recognition. Instead he would disappear (if one who is not
there can disappear) into the anteroom, find the furthest corner and
write letters. Later in life Carrington judged that he had never written so many letters in such a short period.

How did he cope with this nonsense? What does it tell us about
the man who would one day be the political head not just of the
Grenadier Guards but of every soldier, sailor and airman of every
rank up to Chief of the Defence Staff?

First, he perfectly understood the system into which he had
arrived. Second, his whole life had been one of graduating from
station to station, starting from a childhood that really had been
based on the nursery dictum of being seen but not heard. High
chair to dinner table. Bare dormitory to Eton. Furthermore, his
background meant that he had enormous self-confidence. Someone from the lower social scales might never have had that
confidence, even in the unimaginable event of daring to apply to
join the regiment. Carrington was at home.

Inevitably, the one place he was not ignored was on the parade
ground overlooked by Birdcage Walk. Once again, the fact that
Carrington had been Senior Under Officer of his company at

Sandhurst, and by all accounts exceptionally good on the drill square, did not impress for one moment the traditional backbone of the Foot Guards, the senior NCOs.

Carrington was thrown into yet another regime of seemingly continuous 'square bashing', as the other ranks called regimental drill. He and the few other new officers drilled with the men and were respectfully humiliated. The bawled command 'Stand up straight, get those shoulders back' was always followed by 'Sir!'

The battalion might have had two options: prepare for war or prepare to be impeccably turned out for public duties. Here was a perfectly acceptable reason why the company commander could keep to his house in the south of France. Military training, apart from two useless weeks a year at Pirbright in Surrey, was never allowed to get in the way of public duties. There were guards at Buckingham Palace and the Bank of England to be mounted. There was also a seemingly endless round of mess nights, dinner parties and society balls. The poor ensign sometimes found himself struggling to attend three or four a night of the latter. None but the unimaginative young officer would complain, and no officer without imagination is recalled in Carrington's time. Thus he was inclined to remember a dilemma, not of tactical appreciation, but ceremonial procedure. He found himself confronted by not knowing the correct salute at Buckingham Palace when Princess Elizabeth and Princess Margaret were about to leave for their swimming lessons. He thought to take refuge in the excuse that he could not see them. It may seem incongruous, sixty or so years on, that someone so short-sighted as Carrington should have been allowed to join the army, never mind the fact that he could not see because he was not allowed to wear his glasses. They would not have suited his scarlet tunic and bearskin. Carrington's eyesight was appalling and it was only towards the end of the war that he actually fetched himself a pair of glasses.

There appear to be no circumstances in which the army, and certainly the battalion, could be encouraged in proper preparations for war. Warships, squadrons and battalions have a common regard for the greater military institution. A ship's company would talk about

The Navy as if it were some other organization. A squadron would talk about Them as if the RAF was quite separate. A battalion would usually regard The Army as another organization. So it was with the Brigade of Guards in 1939 and this did not exclude Carrington's battalion.

We laughed at our deficiencies of equipment, we mocked 'The Army', which we thought of as a vague, remote, enormously incompetent authority quite outside ourselves. We reckoned we were very good. We knew our Regiment's history and traditions. Many of us had fathers who were Grenadiers. We were supremely confident. If war came – and it was obvious throughout 1939 that sooner or later it would come, I don't think anybody doubted we would do as well as our parents had in the war which had culminated in total victory only 21 years before.[4]

This was yet another illusion held by even the inspirational battalion commanding officer, Boy Browning, who had neither the resources nor the training time between the far more important ceremonial duties in London to bring his Grenadiers up to a state in which they would be ready for war. One of the difficulties was that hardly anyone was sure what state that was.

Many of the officers – and this went in too many cases right up the line to general officers commanding – still lived in a military dream so successfully lampooned many years later by Joan Littlewood's *Oh What a Lovely War!* Carrington's regiment, like much of the rest of the army, continued to parade their colours behind which many of them would fall within a short time. A concentration on *esprit de corps* was considered of the utmost importance by an army that believed still that the twelve battalions within the First World War Guards Division constituted one of the finest fighting forces in military history. As Carrington was to find out, no army, and none of its battalions, can march far on its image.

When on 1 September 1939 the German army entered Poland, Carrington's battalion put away its bearskins, donned its berets and

4 Lord Carrington, *Reflect on Things Past*, p. 31.

shifted to Sherborne in Dorset as part of the 7th Guards Brigade. This in turn was part of 3 Division, which was to be sent to France as a spearhead of the British Expeditionary Force.

The first casualty in that move to Sherborne was Browning, who was clearly thought far too good to command even the second battalion of the Grenadiers. Browning was despatched to do grander things and eventually become a general. An indicator of how the army was still trying to sort itself into some sort of battle shape and fitness was the fact that the new commanding officer, who was a nice enough man, appeared to be more at home with thoughts about hunting, toppers and early marriage than the essentials of bringing a frontline battalion up to speed.

It was at this point in Carrington's life that Bernard Law Montgomery entered the scene, albeit at arm's length. Neither knew then, of course, that they would become firm friends and sometime later political colleagues in the House of Lords.[5] Montgomery, then a major general, arrived as Carrington's divisional commander. It was he who, immediately seeing the flabby and unprofessional state of his soldiers, set them on a training programme that should have been started five years earlier. Even Wellington's observation more than a century before, that his own men terrified him, would have been discarded.

The battalion was set to wait for the first fair wind to France. Carrington would have to wait for his war. He was not old enough to go into battle. No soldier in the battalion under the age of twenty-one would be sent overseas. So, Carrington was now sent to the training battalion at Windsor and then, in April 1940, to his first command, a demonstration platoon at the Small Arms School at Shorncliffe on the Kentish coast near Hythe. During the daytime Carrington's team demonstrated personal weapons. In the evening he deployed his forty-eight-strong unit as part of the south coast defence system. The military jargon should not hide the pathetic

5 When Field Marshal Lord Montgomery entered the Upper House he did so as a Conservative peer. Most military peers tended to demonstrate their impartiality by sitting as cross-benchers.

state of that deployment. For example, Carrington was armed with a pistol, forty-five of his men had rifles and bayonets and three, light machine guns. No one realistically expected that they would hold off a seaborne invasion. Indeed, their role had more to do with the need to make some disposition of forces while expecting they would give way to bigger and better units once the invasion threat – then thought to be real – materialized.

These were eventful and frustrating times for a young soldier who wanted to get into the war. In 1940 Neville Chamberlain had been forced to make way as wartime Prime Minister for Winston Churchill. It was also the year of the Battle of Britain and Carrington had a grandstand view. It was, he thought, all very remote and unreal, as if he were attending an exercise as an umpire.

The summer of 1940 was especially beautiful, and there was a curious unreality in watching, without danger or involvement, the ships steaming slowly along the Channel with German bomb-bursts bringing up the columns of water around them while, overhead, Spitfires fought it out with Messerschmitts and occasionally a pilot drifted down by parachute towards the cliffs of Kent or the Hythe marshes.[6]

There was that same year, 1940, an altogether less unreal spectacle: the vision from that same Channel vantage point of scores of small vessels steaming backwards and forwards with their miserable, vanquished survivors from the British Expeditionary Force's retreat to Dunkirk. Far away from Carrington's sight the army began its long-awaited North African offensive. Between Dunkirk and the victories in the desert there were, for Carrington, moments of more sombre reflection. The Royal Navy lost the *Prince of Wales*, the *Repulse* and then HMS *Hood*. Carrington's view was that the public mood changed. Their invincible Royal Navy had lost major vessels and hundreds of men during the spring of 1941. To a young army officer, the impact was enormous. An army unit was part of a great campaign and somehow the news of casualties was tempered

6 Lord Carrington, *Reflect on Things Past*, p. 36.

by the breadth of that campaign; there was a conditioning in people's minds that soldiers died one by one – almost anonymously to all but family and battalion. But when a ship went down, the name of that vessel would be on every lip and that loss had a greater impact on national morale than almost anything else in the war. Carrington later reflected that he had understood this and had to cope with the potential effect on his soldiers who, after all, were as vulnerable to mood swings, and therefore inefficiencies, as any civilian.

Little wonder that by its instincts and nature, the army would not as a system hold his affection and attention once the war was over. Carrington had the highest regard for the men he commanded and many of those who commanded him. However, his short temper with incompetence and inefficiency had already developed. When the war was over the army, even the Grenadiers, for all their promises of a great future, would not be able to hold him. On 6 June 1940 Carrington celebrated his birthday commanding his lightly armed men on the beaches of Hythe. He was now old enough, should he have been a commoner, to vote and he was of an age to go overseas to fight for his country. For the moment he had to remain along with much of the British army in Britain. The war in Africa would come but he would take no part in it. The British Expeditionary Force had retreated to Dunkirk and had escaped across the Channel to the uninvaded Britain, a military evacuation that even then he thought of as some sort of victory when it was patently a defeat.

Carrington felt disappointed at not having gone to France. But he had been back to Sandhurst, this time for the Guards officer's tactics, wireless, gunnery and driving courses. The army records show that tactically he was considered 'quick and intelligent' and that he should 'be good with more practice'. He was to get that on D-Day.

The major running the wireless course wrote that he was a 'good worker, keen, competent, intelligent. Did well.' Forty years later his Private Office at the FCO (Foreign and Commonwealth Office) also gave him straight 'A's as a communicator.

The gunnery officer thought Carrington had 'done very well

and seems to be interested in gunnery'. Considering there was a war on that was somehow reassuring. He got top marks for driving and practical maintenance, motorcycle riding, truck driving, Bren carrier driving and light tank driving: 'His vehicle handling is good, he is a fully competent motorcyclist over all types of country.' This was all the more remarkable because Carrington was perhaps the most short-sighted officer in the Grenadier Guards. When he drove perfectly in a straight line there was no tactical judgement, it simply seemed the safest thing to do, especially without glasses.

Carrington then went back to Windsor and even though the scarlet was mothballed to London Duties, Guards were still mounted. In spite of the Blitz, Carrington and his brother officers found London a jolly place. The so-called wartime spirit was bolstered by dances and a smart social life. Young officers certainly danced all night to the music of the time. It was on one of these occasions that Carrington reached another changing point in his life far earlier than he and his regiment had imagined possible.

In the summer of 1941, almost to prove that reasonable life went on, Carrington went to a cricket match at Eton. One of his brother officers, Dick Westmacott, also an Old Etonian, introduced Carrington to his sister-in-law, Iona McClean, the daughter of one of Britain's most celebrated pioneer aviators, Sir Francis McClean. After the match they went to a restaurant in Curzon Street. Carrington was smitten. It was, he thought in later life, perhaps the best cricket match he had been to. However, what was he to do about the regiment's age rule? He was only twenty-two and after all, as they said in the variety theatres, 'there was a war on'. On the day, it was all rather simple:

I marched into the Commanding Officer's office, known as the Orderly Room, immediately after he had dispensed justice for the day at a midday ceremony we called 'Memoranda'. A large genial man, his name was Mike Dillwyn-Venables-Llewellyn. We were stationed in billets at Warminster in Wiltshire and the Orderly Room was in St Boniface's School. I stood rigidly to attention[;] it was the hour when officer applications were received or rebukes administered. I was a (temporary) Captain.

'I thank you, Sir, for leave to get married.'

A few friendly enquiries and I received it, with congratulations. The injunction given to me on joining the Regiment three years before had been disregarded.

They were married the following April. Paraphrasing his famous Uncle Charlie, the third Baron Carrington, on his own marriage, Carrington always said that marrying Iona McClean was by 'far the most sensible thing' he had ever done. Given the way in which she stood with him and often advised him during the following sixty years, there were many of their contemporaries and friends who regarded this as something of an understatement.

Iona Ellen McClean was not simply some society young lady passing time and waiting for marriage. Strikingly beautiful, she was also frighteningly intelligent. It was this intelligence that was put to good use during the war. Apart from English, she spoke German, French, Italian and Dutch. She was interviewed in a small office in Brooke Street, Holborn, to join the wartime Postal Telegraph and Censorship Department. Her examination had her graded A-Exceptional in all four languages. She was appointed in December 1939 as an Examiner Grade I. She stayed there until a few days before her wedding.

It was hardly surprising that she was good at languages. The young Iona McClean had a Swiss governess who, apart from teaching her some English literature and history, made sure that she had fluent French, German and Italian. When the war began she had not immediately thought of censorship and had tried to become a driver. She was not suited. She scraped through her driving test and also managed to scrape a bus. The censor gave her a job and billeted her with a baker and his wife. During the day-time she translated letters from German refugees in the south of France and occasionally Spain who had managed to get out of the wartime Reich.

Iona and Peter were married on 25 April 1942, appropriately at the Guards Chapel in London with a detachment of Grenadiers forming the guard of honour. The Carringtons were lucky to get that. The battalion had been sent off on what was to be the most important training exercise, apart from the D–Day landings, of their war. It was only because Carrington had put in his request to get married before the orders to move were posted that he too was not on exercise with the rest of the battalion.

They were even allowed to get away for a honeymoon, a week in the finest suite at the Lygon Arms Hotel at Broadway in the Cotswolds. Carrington had inherited his father's title in 1938, but the £19.10s honeymoon bill made quite a dent in his bank account. Although the family estates and investments were large, stretching as they did from Millaton through to the Home Counties and the Wash, it was not easy for Carrington to lay his hands on any ready money. His wealth was tied up in bundles of trusts and estates, in freeholds and leaseholds. Moreover, his father had been the third holder of the Carrington title to die in ten years[7] and consequently the Carrington finances had been considerably weakened by three-fold death duties.

The Carringtons began their married life together in the back of a butcher's shop, along Boreham Road at Warminster. It was on the road from the military camp by Salisbury Plain to Heytesbury, the home of a more famous observer of war, Siegfried Sassoon. Carrington always claimed that to get to their rooms they had to dodge and duck beneath sides of beef, which certainly indicated that the battalion was reasonably fed – the only reason that drove a large number of them to join up was hunger.

On 25 April 1942, while the Carringtons were exchanging vows in the Guards Chapel, the second battalion began a divisional exercise on Salisbury Plain with their new weapon – the tank.

To many of the soldiers it was an absolute puzzle why this undoubtedly important fighting vehicle should be given to the Guards. It most certainly could be argued that with the tank becoming more important in ground formations, it was essential to turn the very mobile infantry into at least a mix of foot soldiers

---

7 The third Lord Carrington died in 1928, the fourth in 1929 and the fifth in 1938.

and armoured crews. Thus the Guards Armoured Division was formed.

A large number of officers in the Brigade, holding the general view that armour rather than infantry was becoming the predominant arm, were keen to embark on the venture, the Regimental Lieutenant-Colonels all welcomed the idea, and the Major-General commanding the Brigade of Guards ... after consultation with his Majesty the King, expressed himself as being strongly in favour of the proposal.[8]

This decision was taken in 1941. It came at a time when, as we have seen, there was an air of desperation among those who believed they understood how to modernize the army in the short time before the planned D-Day invasion of Europe. The British determination to modernize its ground troop formations contained a certain element that based the restructuring plans on the German armies. There was nothing new in this; after all, when the British army was reorganized before the Great War, it took the German example as its model. However, in 1941 and 1942 Carrington – perhaps reflecting the tactical grasp that he had demonstrated at Sandhurst – believed his superiors to be wrong. He accepted the need for an increased armoured capability. He was of the firm opinion, however, that when the European offensive came, a key requirement for its success would be airforces that could suppress enemy supply and resupply from factory to frontline unit, and the harrying of those frontlines together with the Allied army's ability to move rapidly to take advantage of its air superiority.

To Carrington's mind, even in 1941, it was clear that there would be a continuing shortage of rapid reaction and mobile infantry for the rest of the land campaign. Perhaps twenty-two-year-old acting captains were not asked for strategic opinions. But while Carrington continued to believe it was wrong to have turned

8 Earl of Rosse and E. R. Hill, *The Story of the Guards Armoured Division*, 1956, p. 114.

so much of the infantry into armoured troops, he was realistic in one insight that was not necessarily to do with the tactical and theatre assessment of the war's prosecution: the infantryman is the most vulnerable soldier. Fewer of his Grenadiers died than might have been the case if they had not become part of the Armoured Division.

Inevitably, the transition from footslogging to one-ton charger had its lighter moments. Grenadiers have a long tradition of fighting their wars in formation with the absolute obedience that only comes to foot soldiers. Their instincts are those demonstrated and practised by the Carringtons of this world on the drill square and parade ground, where every discipline and command remains unquestioned until the inevitable barrack-room inquest. Thus the infantry soldier will rarely give ground until ordered. The routine and respect for hierarchy, certainly in the early 1940s, relied very much on that unquestioning discipline first learned together as young recruits and always in full view and respect of authority, which the guardsmen understood to mean anyone of a higher rank. Montgomery called the Brigade of Guards 'the best troops in the army, without question . . . because you can trust them: they do what they're told'. By that, Montgomery meant they did not have to exercise any imagination but just got on with it. Whatever the intellect and imaginations of the Foot Guards, their whole training and culture were not designed for them to take individual initiatives at speed, something that would be necessary in the quick manoeuvres of tank warfare. Putting a guardsman into a tank hid the foot soldier from leadership. The senior non-commissioned officers (NCOs), used to keeping their guardsmen in sight and, therefore, under almost touchable command, found it far more difficult to continue the old ways of inflexibility in command. Add to this the concept of a six-foot-plus guardsman, perhaps three of them, squeezing into the claustrophobic bin that was a Second World War tank and we have an almost inevitable comic strip of curious errors.

Shortly after Carrington returned from his wedding leave, he found himself on manoeuvres with his tank squadron. His tanks were bouncing and pounding across Salisbury Plain. He was puzzled why his sergeant major, huge and commanding in the Grenadier tradition, but now wedged into another tank, was taking so long to respond to radio orders. As he remembered in 1998:

There was always a pause before he acknowledged a transmission, and one day, when his tank happened to be close to mine, I discovered why. When an officer's voice come through his earphones he stood to attention and saluted before tackling the microphone.

Whatever the rights and wrongs of the restructuring of the Brigade of Guards, Captain Lord Carrington's duty, in the same tradition as the sergeant major's, was to carry on training, be ready to do as he was told and if necessary, as many of his friends did, die while doing so. In July 1944 his battalion in their tracked steel boxes crossed the Channel and took part in the first of many painful fiascos that would lead to the Allied victory over the German army. Carrington crossed too, on his way to the sometimes bizarre personal adventure of the next twelve months that would result in his own Military Cross for gallantry and the decision that would change yet again the course of his life – the first of his official resignations.

Carrington found himself in Operation Goodwood, in which three armoured divisions drove their way south beyond the eastern part of Caen. This was Carrington's baptism of military fire. It was not encouraging. The unremitting bombing of Caen was part of the great plan that was supposed to result in German submission, with column upon column of the surrendering enemy. Like many great plans it did not happen that way. Instead, their antitank guns and dug-in tanks killed too many of Carrington's comrades. Carrington's first battle showed very little of the enemy, who

in spite of having been shaken to pieces by our air bombardment, had recovered enough to start picking off British tanks with enthusiasm and in large numbers. What we did see was our own blazing hulls – our battalion lost over twenty tanks from one cause or another in the first hours – and very soon we found ourselves halted while a more deliberate attack was put in on the village of Cagny. The cavalry charge – for the initial advance had resembled exactly that, and a fine sight it was – had ended.[9]

At the end of his first day (18 July 1944) in a war that had neither manoeuvre umpires nor observers to tick boxes and award fictitious results, it became clear that the master plan, not surprisingly, had run into difficulties if not the sand. Carrington and his brother officers had been told, and had in turn told their men, that the German forces they faced had been irrevocably weakened by their actions on the Russian front. They had been bombed to the verge of submission. They were hugely outnumbered. Carrington's impression was that he may have been told this and he may have told his men, but no one had told the Germans. To his mind they remained effective. It was a very thoughtful Carrington who ordered his men to dig a five-man trench that night, and then drove his tank over it as a protective lid to give some defence from the inevitable shellfire from an army which had failed to realize that it was weakened and defeated.

The Carringtons were not very good at being parted. They had been married for two years, were devoted to each other and would remain so for the rest of their lives. Much later, in 1998, when Iona was in an intensive care unit, Carrington was devastated to the extent that someone close to him realized for the first time that if 'anything happened to Lady Carrington' then he would not survive without her.

They wrote to each other every day, yet in 1944, with their separation just three months old, Iona became quite low. Daily letters did not always get through very quickly and the physical distance between the two agitated Carrington, as a letter from him in November of that year shows.

9 Lord Carrington, *Reflect on Things Past*, p. 49.

2nd Armoured Battalion, Grenadier Guards. BLA [British Land Army]
2.11.44.

My Darling,

Two letters from you this evening, both very depressed. Your stay at West Coker[10] doesn't seem to have cheered you up very much. I know it will be very lonely for you at Woolacombe[11] without anybody there I only wish I could do something about it. I am very angry to hear that you think you are useless. You are a silly old fool. In the first place what could Algy [the family dog] do without you and secondly and most important, you have simply no idea how useful you are to me. If you ... were not there waiting for me to come back, then this whole business out here would be quite pointless ... you are the only person in the whole world that I care two hoots about & don't you forget it ever. I should loathe to have a wife who was mad about breeding dogs or something & who never had time to think about me & didn't really care whether I was there or not. I do realize how horrible it all is for you, but it won't go on forever & two days after I get back you will have forgotten it all. You will realize from all this that not only am I rather fond of you, but the thought that you are my wife & like me makes such a difference that you obviously have no idea how completely positive you are – not in the very least negative.

I have seen people out here who never have a letter or anything from someone they really care about. Nor have they anything to come back to after the war. I know I have & am very lucky. So be a good old trout & cheer up & remember that I love you so much I am pink in the face at the thought of you & can also remember every bit of you so much that I am aching all over.
Peter

10 West Coker in Somerset, where Iona Carrington's friend lived.
11 Rockenore, Woolacombe, Lord Carrington's mother's rented house. She refused to live in London and certainly not in Buckinghamshire, which she found closed in. Carrington disliked the place, referring to it as a horrid little bungalow.

Carrington's letters were not always so moving. Often he would be writing for Iona to send his brand of Turkish cigarettes, not, as he called them, 'this Virginia muck'. By contrast, he then wrote home about a scene that was to remain with him for ever: his first sight of a concentration camp.

5.11.44

Jock Gilmour arrived early & this morning offered to take the Baron [Richard Trotter][12] & myself round a concentration camp. The camp was extremely interesting. Exactly as I imagined it would be. Most depressing. It was very large in fact I believe there were about 20–30,000 Political Prisoners there. It was partly run by the Germans & partly by the Dutch S. S. who were I believe just as bad. We were shown the gallows, the crematorium, including a portable one. The lime pit where they throw the ashes & also a gas chamber. They didn't show us [inside] a chamber as it was forbidden to go in but I gather it was pretty unpleasant . . .

Carrington's war in 1944 lived with him for the rest of his life. More than half a century later, that experience made him question the tactical doctrine that believed it possible to simply bomb a Bosnian army into submission without putting in a large, effective ground force to confront a tired but still effective enemy. War does not always conform to the strategic plan. This lesson in 1944 was part of the reason that Carrington was most certainly not surprised when column after column of undamaged tanks and self-propelled guns withdrew from Kosovo in spite of the NATO claim that they had been destroyed or damaged beyond repair by the bombing might of the American-led airforces.

Whatever his thoughts at the end of that first battle concerning its planning and the training and efficiency of his own battalion, that phase of the attempt to drive the Germans out of France

12 Trotter was called Baron by the Carringtons because he was big and a caricature of a baron.

was, in spite of the doubtful start, successful. He now witnessed something else that was to be invaluable in later years as Defence Secretary and Secretary-General of NATO, when decisions and propositions were necessarily judged by the application as well as the intention.

The image of warfare was the broadside of six-inch naval guns, the dogfights of squadrons and the cavalry illusion of tank warfare and slogging infantry. Carrington did not question the bravery of those in the frontline. However, from his lowly position, he wondered at the enormity of the logistical battle. Set in that war zone of northern France was not the confusion of mangled armies but the bewildering sight of square mile after square mile of the logistical tail that kept the frontlines on the move. Miles of transporters, trucks, fuel bowsers, field hospitals at various operational levels, recovery lorries, communications units and convoys supplying basic needs such as food and water. All of this had to be moved, parked, moved again, dispersed, redesignated and above all defended. It was another lesson for Carrington for the future.

In spite of the display of military superiority, Carrington's impression was that the whole of Operation Goodwood was ill-conceived. He believed that the inability to manoeuvre the vast frontline and logistical army owed more to desktop and sandpit planning than to any understanding of the complex terrain over which they were expected to fight, and defeat, an enemy which could, with little effort, position itself to hold up the advance of a superior force. This was a long-lived view and one which influenced his judgement of the military realities in the Balkans fifty years on.

Carrington's battalion then became part of the famous story of the confrontation between Generals Montgomery and Patton with Eisenhower on how best the war might be prosecuted, the great military debate between fast-moving attack, which Montgomery favoured, or the broad sweep eastwards.[13]

13 See, among others, John Keegan, *The Second World War*, London: Century Hutchinson, 1989.

Montgomery was about to hand over land command to Eisen-hower and be promoted to Field Marshal. Captain Carrington was about to play an important part in Montgomery's final effort as land commander: a two-fold operation called Market Garden. This was in September 1944, three months after the Normandy Land-ings had begun. The beachheads, having been secured after many false starts, remained the clearing house for follow-on forces and, most importantly of all, supplies. Part of the original Overlord campaign, that is, the Allied assault on Continental Europe, had involved heavy bombing of German supply lines, including the French railway and its bridges. This had been claimed as an enor-mous success. Carrington remembers thinking it obvious that the success in destroying much of the rail-lines and fords also meant they could not be used, without considerable repair, by the Allies. Consequently when the Allies were at last able to advance from the Normandy bridgehead they had created (which was not until August of that year), virtually all the supplies had to come by road. This meant congestion. Because of the very nature of logistical organization, the fuel, food, spares, ammunition and support ser-vices could not keep up with the fast-advancing armour and infantry.

The Allied commanders supposed that the logistical nightmare could be overcome because the frontline forces would capture the Channel ports, thus making it easier to get supplies through and, at the same time, cutting the length of the logistical tail. The Germans would not play this game. The four main ports, Dunkirk, Calais, Boulogne and Le Havre, together with the Scheldt estuary (the important port of Antwerp is the most easterly navigable part of the Scheldt), were so heavily defended that it took until the end of September to secure Le Havre, Calais and Boulogne. The Germans could not be dislodged from the Scheldt until the end of Novem-ber. Dunkirk was not captured until the end of the war.

The inability of the Allies to secure the Channel ports and the Scheldt meant that the Canadian, British and American armies could not be resupplied. Why this logistical priority was not executed remained a mystery long after the war was over. On

10 September, which was the day that Eisenhower formally took over the command of north-western Europe from Montgomery, the English commander made ready his last operational initiative. Market Garden started on 17 September.

The term Market and the term Garden referred to two operations. Garden was the assault of the British airborne division on the Rhine bridges at Arnhem. This horrendous failure, in which 1,000 men were killed and 6,000 taken prisoner by the Germans, was due to bad planning and the inability of the armoured units to reach the 1st Airborne Division to enable it to successfully overcome the 9th and 10th German Panzers. Carrington was in the other operation, Market. It is often thought that the securing of the bridges at Eindhoven and Nijmegen was all due to the American airborne divisions. Carrington, in a minor masterpiece of understatement, could be persuaded to point out that this American 'victory' was 'mistaken' – it simply had not happened that way. After all, on the matter of the bridge at Nijmegen, Carrington was an authority. It was there that he won his Military Cross.

Carrington's colour sergeant major, Peter Robinson, had a vivid impression of what happened, as he described to me:

The battle started at about five or six in the evening. I was LOB [Left Out of Battle]. Lord Carrington came and sat with us most of that night and we had a few sips out of the whisky bottle. Next morning I was the first over. My tank was hit so I had to change tanks. Then my troop Sgt overtook me but I caught up with him. Then two tanks got hit. One caught fire, the other was OK, so I was left with just two. Lord C was on the south side. He then came over to the north side and couldn't find me so he came up to see where I was.

This further understatement of a situation where Carrington's troop of tanks, on a bridge they believed to be mined, were being blasted from German positions, and were being hit; where soldiers were changing tanks as one was knocked out; and where Carrington and Robinson drove across, then back, and held enemy fire while the whole troop got across – this understatement, then, explains why

Carrington told everyone that Robinson was the hero of the occasion. Nevertheless, it was Carrington who had the letter from the War Office on 9 October 1945, to make himself available for an Investiture in which King George would pin to his chest his Military Cross.

A year after the landings in Normandy the war was more or less at an end. The Guards Armoured Division was disbanded and Carrington's charger, the faithful Sherman tank, withdrawn with the rest of the herd. It was a strange event. Carrington had never been convinced that the Grenadiers were tank men and yet, at the enormous parade at the Rothenburg airfield on 9 July 1945, there was a certain poignancy as, for the last time, tanks rumbled past Montgomery. Many of those tanks had landed at Normandy with the Division and had truly been the shield between life and death for Carrington and so many of his friends. After the tanks came the Foot Guards, back to what they did best, fighting men stomping in perfect time. It was, for Carrington, almost full circle from the days he had first joined the Grenadiers in January 1939. Perfect drill to show off immense pride.

Carrington's part in the fighting war was done. He now witnessed some of the consequences of that war. The desolation caused by the fighting, the destruction of homes and infrastructure, the consequence of the Final Solution, a whole society haggard-eyed from war, each left images he never forgot. In every job that followed, from junior minister to Secretary-General of NATO to Bosnia, Carrington never underestimated the terrible possibilities of any conflict.

Edward Heath told me in 1989 of his belief that he shared with Carrington a concept of a politically unified Europe partly because of what they had both gone through and had witnessed during the Second World War.

It was in 1945 that Carrington made the third most important decision of his life – the first being to go to Sandhurst, the second to marry Iona McClean. As the war came to an end, he decided to leave the army. Carrington was a regular soldier. He had not simply signed on for the duration of the war. His senior officers believed him cut out for an exceptional career and certainly higher command. One of his contemporaries, David Fraser (later, General Sir David Fraser, Vice Chief of the General Staff), observed to the author in 1998 that Carrington's sense of political diplomacy as well as his military faculties made him a natural long-term candidate in the chiefs-of-staff corridor. So, why did Carrington decide to give up the prospect of an enviable career in a world in which he had excelled? There is no single answer. It certainly was not postwar stress.

Carrington first thought about leaving in 1943. This was the year in which he and Iona decided that they must have a family home. Their first child, Alexandra, was born in April that year. Carrington had decided that they would not stay on at Millaton, no matter how fond he was of the house and the countryside in that part of Devon. Their new life together was centred in London and at Windsor. Their friends were in London, and even in abnormal times the Grenadiers remained committed to London Duties. Millaton was simply too far from the capital. At the same time, Carrington was hardly pushed to find somewhere to live. When, in November 1938, he had inherited the barony, the sometimes mixed blessings of the estates had come with that inheritance. Moreover, unlike his father, Carrington felt confident in his inheritance. He was not the colonial boy who had taken the title as a result of the tragedy in Charlie Lincolnshire's family.

So in 1943 the Carringtons looked through the inventory of his inheritance and went to Buckinghamshire and the village of Bledlow. One of the houses he had inherited was the Manor House there. It had come into the Carrington family when the first Lord Carrington bought it in about 1800 from the brewer Samuel Whitbread. It was a mellow, mostly Georgian pile, with the earliest part dating from 1648. When Peter and Iona Carrington went to see it, they were confronted with a spartan and much neglected building partly occupied by a tenant farmer. They looked it over, thought it would more than do and began to plan that this would be the seat of the sixth baron. A family seat demands commitment. Yet Carrington was not simply looking to be a country gentleman.

Somewhere deep in his young mind was the notion that although he was clearly good at soldiering, it was not the profession that he should follow. Carrington believed that he had proved himself with a distinguished career at Sandhurst, followed by a 'good' war. He had seen action, been decorated for gallantry and was still only twenty-six years old. Yet in spite of his success Carrington was never really interested in the army because it had not caught his imagination.

David Fraser later discussed with the author this apparent contradiction in Carrington's military abilities and his developing philosophy of social justice. As a subaltern, Carrington was always quick to detect and resent injustice and often found himself disturbed that many of his men had had a raw deal in life. He did not wear these feelings on his sleeve, but they knew that he minded about people who had a hard time. Equally he was not in the least sentimental, even at that age. There was no affectation in his feelings, although there was an increasing degree of awareness that his privileged life could only be publicly justified if he used it for the good of others.

He had also started to think about the rights and wrongs of the social and political system in Britain. He talked for long hours with his soldiers and listened for even longer as they told him their views of Britain. Many of his guardsmen told him they had joined the regiment well before the war to escape the poverty in which they lived as civilians. He began to believe that the war had changed nothing. The anxieties and the disaffection of many of these men had nothing to do with victory over Nazism. A soldier who had joined the second battalion of the Grenadier Guards in the 1930s because he was hungry may have been thankful for surviving the gruesome years of the Second World War, but saw nothing in his home town that led him to believe life had much changed in British society.

Carrington was also struck by the way in which many of his soldiers and local villagers saw the political future in these islands.

Consequently, he was not at all surprised that the nation voted Labour in the 1945 election. He did not accept the thoughts of some of his peers who believed that the people were ungrateful and had turned their backs on Churchill, who, in that curious historical assessment, had delivered the victory. Carrington's view was that the majority of people would vote Labour because the promises they held out for social reform and the nationalization of the great industries would be sufficient to distinguish them from the Conservatives, who offered nothing new. Carrington also believed that in the voters' mind there was a further oddity in their perception of postwar politics. A vast number of the electorate in 1945 had never voted for anything but National Government. The older voters had memories of the constitutional handover of power in 1924 to the first Labour administration. Although it was short-lived it did nothing to frighten the electorate. In 1929 nothing was done that suggested the Labour Party was an extension of the Communism some had feared and wondered about. The National Governments that followed suggested that same electorate felt safer with coalition politics, but with the decline of Ramsay MacDonald's powers and the domination of the Conservatives, National Government was in effect Tory government.

Carrington was beginning to believe that without any sophisticated analysis, the voters were likely to blame Conservatives for the bad times and for preventing Labour ideas from coming through. Churchill's vain attempts to continue the National Government in 1945 by, for example, promising to implement Beveridge's social reforms smacked of the desperate tactics of a man who was trying to cling to power because it was the only office in which he felt comfortable. Even with a limited knowledge of political history, Carrington was minded of the similarities between Churchill and Lloyd George twenty or so years earlier. Given some of the comments on his essays at Eton, perhaps we should not be surprised at the depth nor the tendency of Carrington's political analysis in 1945.

There were two added considerations in his mind when he decided to resign his commission. First, Carrington sensed that he had had his war, that he had 'done his bit', and that nothing that would follow would live up to those formative years of his adult life. Second, he had inherited his title in 1938 but because of the war he had not been able to 'assume his responsibilities'. He believed he had a duty to act as steward for the Carrington estates. The second responsibility was political. He had not taken his seat in the House of Lords. Carrington was not a 'fashionable' peer. He understood that if he were to take his seat then he would not be a backwoodsman. He wanted to become politically active. At twenty-six he regarded himself as privileged. He did not feel uncomfortable with this special status. Carrington was coming to admire the idea that someone in his position had the opportunity to attend to that most high-minded (and therefore dangerously bogus) form of charity work – public service. The new generation of politicians who believed deeply in public service as opposed to simply political dogma included the young R. A. Butler, whose wartime Education Act was to be such an influence for the next thirty years and who sincerely believed that public service was a duty. In 1945 Butler and Carrington met and became friends.

From that time, Carrington forever understood that the major weakness of anyone in his position going into politics was that he would always lack the coalface experience of the House of Commons. Although it was a quite different place in 1945 than it was in 1982, he sometimes wondered if that lack of Commons experience contributed to his undoing as Foreign Secretary during the Falklands crisis.

Carrington had exhibited bravery under enemy fire. He had now to exhibit a quite different courage under friendly fire. He planned to resign at a time when he was desperately needed. Some thought his action unforgivable. His regiment was simply appalled by his behaviour. In 1945, with the war at an end, came the huge conundrum of quasi peace. A large part of the conscripted army had to be demobilized. Tens of thousands of those who had 'escaped' the war in uniform and a new generation in their late teens were now being conscripted into the army to take the place of those who had served their time and were now due for release, particularly the tradesmen and artisans desperately needed to rebuild blitzed Britain. At the same time, the military responsibilities were expanding and the government was committed to being part of the four-power occupation of Germany.

There were still military commitments in Palestine, India, South-east Asia and Hong Kong. The army was needed to safeguard those dangerous transitions to independence in Palestine and the Subcontinent and to fight the new enemy, Communism. There would soon be confrontation in Malaya, Borneo and the first United Nations war: Korea. The army needed, therefore, a highly trained, experienced and bright officer cadre to manage and lead the new system and organization immediately necessary to implement these postwar commitments. While the army understood perfectly that officers who had signed up or had been drafted in just for the war had a right to go and were in many cases needed outside, the system relied heavily on the professionalism and, above all, the loyalty of their regular officers. The army was not about fighting a war, it was about guaranteeing a peace. Carrington's decision to resign was seen by some as an act of disloyalty, an abandoning of the military lodge in which he had been received and encouraged.

Carrington was aware of and felt the strength of this criticism towards him but he had decided on a political life and a new direction. In crude terms he had paid his dues and, as the army records of October 1945 put it, 'relinquished rank of temporary major and [was] placed on unemployed list at own request'. He was now single-mindedly bent on going his own way.

Carrington's life was changing in so many ways during the twelve months that followed the end of the war. His first daughter, Alexandra, had arrived in 1943 and Iona was now carrying their second child. This was the bright light of the young family. But there was a dark shadow hanging over it too. His mother was dying. She had been ill for some time and he knew that she would not recover from her cancer. Sybil, Lady Carrington, was taken into hospital for what even fifty years later would be considered major surgery. Get-well letters winged their way to The Clinic in

London and so did a very special bunch of grapes. In wartime Britain grapes were not imported. Any that appeared in fruit bowls were some of the few cultivated in Britain. The grapes were sent by Princess Mary, the Princess Royal. As a letter to Sybil Carrington's sister Madge showed, close attention was paid to the way they would arrive.

Harewood House, Leeds
August 10th 1945

Dear Madge
I just cannot tell you how distressed I am to hear of your great anxiety. Please tell Peter and Elizabeth [Lord Carrington's sister] how I feel for them at this time. This morning I sent Sybil some grapes by passenger train which our servant is meeting and have let him know he is to take the grapes round to the Clinic for Sybil – I should be grateful for any news of her and do *please* let me know if there is anything she would like, possibly more grapes if I can manage them. Am sending this letter care of Miss Jacob, the Matron, who I know. I do think of you all in your anxiety over dearest Sybil – yours sincerely,
Mary

Sybil died in September the following year, 1946.

The centre of the Carringtons' life for the rest of the century would not be Westminster and Whitehall, but Bledlow, the estate in Buckinghamshire. Scattered throughout the Home Counties, the Carringtons had 10,000 acres, a third of which were in-hand as farmland.

Carrington's mother may have thought the county, and Bledlow within it, claustrophobic, but for the Carringtons, the good farming land of the Chilterns and the Manor House were exactly what they wanted in spite of its condition. So it was only now that the Carringtons decamped from Devon, not from Millaton, but from the small house at Woolacombe in the north of the county which had been rented for the duration of the war. During that time, the

Bledlow house had been occupied by Tom Wooster, tenant farmer, and by evacuees from London. This had not been a great luxury for the Londoners as the Manor House was virtually in its original Georgian state, with primitive plumbing and almost no electricity. In April 1946 the Carringtons swapped their London rented accommodation in Campden Hill Square for Bledlow.

The Manor House is a square building of small mellow brick with large-paned sash windows on two floors. In the roof are the attic rooms for servants and later the children. It was then, and has remained, a proper working house, whether for the seemingly endless stream of political and diplomatic guests as well as friends, or discussions about harvests and what always seemed to be Carrington's joy, the gathering of 'the fruits of the earth'. In 1946 it was hardly the comfortable home of later years. The immediate conditions in Britain as the war came to a close and during the years that followed were against the restoration of great houses. Resources were few and demands on them considerable. Regulations were seemingly impenetrable. Even a peer of the realm had to apply to the local authority for planning permission to do the simplest work on a house. One way of controlling who could build what was to limit the amount that could be spent on a house. The Carringtons managed to get £400. That, in 1946, was a lot of money. On paper, they looked wealthy. In fact, they had little money, certainly when compared with other aristocratic families with stately houses. Also, as mentioned earlier, three lots of death duties in a decade had taken quite a few resources. Moreover, they were very well aware that anything they did have was tied up in the estate.

During the war when the Carringtons had first seen Bledlow they thought that they would have to spend some £10,000 putting it in order. That transposes as not much short of £400,000 at 2008 prices. Bledlow was not in stately home condition. Carrington later reflected that once the rose-tinted view of newlyweds faded, the best description of Bledlow was 'fairly derelict'. No Carington had lived in it for a hundred years. Originally it was kept as the home of the eldest son of the Carington family, while the family

seat was about eight miles away at Wycombe Abbey; but Uncle
Charlie got rid of the family home. He sold it off to a girls' school
and then built in the grounds one of the more hideously styled
bungalows in Buckinghamshire. The bungalow had the rather
grand name of Daws Hill. It became something of a fortress for
Uncle Charlie, who, perhaps, came to resent the fact that the family
home was no longer his. There was never an easy relationship with
the school. It was Peter Carrington's father who eventually sold the
bungalow to the school. He was rather thankful to get rid of what
he regarded as the ugliest house he had ever seen.

All this meant that Peter and Iona Carrington were reopening
the estate and they moved into the Manor House at Bledlow in
April 1946. Two months later their second daughter, Virginia, was
born. With his military life more or less behind him, Carrington
set about rebuilding Bledlow.

This was very much a task for both of them. It was also carried
on in addition to their more public lives. Neither had idle moments.
Peter was getting on with the business of learning the political
ropes at the local and county levels as well as in the Lords. Iona was
not left out. She became an active chairman of the Buckingham
Land Army. In this period there were few titular heads of any
organization. Britain was broke and there was a social as well as a
political urgency to rebuild the country, its fortunes and lifestyle.
Therefore as chairman – Iona Carrington never, even years later,
saw herself as 'chairwoman', certainly never 'chairperson' – she
spent three years between 1946 and 1949 taking a deep interest in
the way that land army girls were treated and particularly how they
were housed. Just as it never entered her head that the war would
not be won, so she never believed that it was impossible to make
life better for everyone – rich or poor. Her attitude was very simple: one just got on with married life, including learning to cook
on a solid-fuel range, and then tried to make what was often a very
gloomy time for others more comfortable and full of hope rather
than anger and disillusionment.

At home, the immediate task was to put in essentials, such as
plumbing and electricity. Everything needed official permission,

not because the house was of extraordinary architectural interest but because that was the way of postwar Britain. Nationally, the term 'War Damage' had become a ubiquitous catchphrase. Building materials were in exceedingly short supply and there were much greater priorities than the refurbishment of a Georgian mansion for a young peer, whatever his war record. Consequently the Carringtons made Bledlow habitable but not much more. Carrington regarded politics as a harder building job than Bledlow. His view was that it was always possible to sleep soundly at home, whatever its state. That could never, he thought, be said of politics.

Carringtons, from the first baron in the late eighteenth century, had been in politics, mostly at national level. Uncle Charlie had been a successful Agriculture Minister.[14] Peter Carrington's father had been active in West Country politics – not Westminster perhaps, but he took it as seriously. As we have seen, Carrington had been deeply aware through the opinions of his soldiers of the deep distress of many communities unable to cope with the economic frailties of the 1930s. His was a patrician view of the world, yet it seems to have been deeply felt. Time and again, images from his wartime experiences and a closer interest in the way that British society, with all its vulnerabilities, was moving, made Carrington believe that what he saw sometimes self-mockingly as the dying instincts of the British Whig should really have been translated into a sense of duty.

Yet it was still a time when many on Carrington's side of the House entered Parliament with no burning ambition. Parliament was a less strenuous institution in the 1940s than, say, forty years on. It was quite common for an MP to spend his day in the City or at the Bar and then turn up at Westminster in time for tea. This certainly made it easy for Carrington, who when he first went into the House was, not uncommonly, still wearing his army uniform. He long insisted that he had taken his seat to go about the business of politics and not as some charity worker. In later life

14 See pp. 39–40.

he was absolutely certain that had it been possible in those days, he would have given up his title in order to fight a seat in the Commons. He claimed in conversations with me that his political instincts would have been better satisfied if he could have become an MP. Wistful hindsight? Quite possibly. Peter Carrington thoroughly enjoyed being a peer and this was as true in the 1940s as it was sixty years later, even though he was an active and sometimes vociferous champion of House of Lords reform. Indeed, his proposals in 1968 were more draconian and seemingly democratic than those put forward by the Labour government in 1999.[15]

Carrington's baptism was a gentle immersion in the British political font rather than the total and exciting ducking he might have expected if he had gone into the Commons in that post-war period. The 1945 election had been, on occasions, a bitter affair. Churchill, in apparent desperation and disbelief that he (probably even more than his party) might be discarded by the electorate, resorted to the terrible accusation that an Attlee government would need to adopt the characteristics of the Gestapo to remain in power.[16] The new Labour government was bright and abrasive and determined to travel at a brisk political pace to implement the reforms that the electorate had voted for. The Conservatives were led in the new Commons by the same old guard that had lost the election and that had, certainly in Baldwin's time, so dominated the coalition government. There was a creeping sense of fear among some of the Conservatives of the new dominating theme in British political thought: the Welfare State. But Carrington's belief then was that the need for social reform through National Insurance and the Welfare State was obvious, and should be accepted by anyone with half a political brain and an epsilon of social conscience.

When he took his seat in the Lords, Carrington freely admitted his political ignorance and his enormous lack of understanding of

15 See p. 235.
16 See Martin Gilbert, *Churchill: A Life*, London: Heinemann, 1991, p. 846.

what society wanted and what it could afford. Yet in later years, he maintained that he then understood that there was no going back to the attitudes and ways of the 1920s and 1930s. For him, there was a desperate need to understand how government could implement changes without damaging the sound areas of the British social fabric and without alienating large parts of society which by and large had no immediate need for change.

Carrington was no radical social reformer. He was never an aristocrat who felt embarrassed by his accident of birth. Indeed, he enjoyed each and every trapping of privilege. Certainly in the peacetime 1940s, Carrington would not have numbered himself among those who condemned privilege. The management of the welfare of society would also take place alongside the radical legislation which Carrington's own party so opposed, especially nationalization of the railways and other great industries including coal. Labour would deliver on its promises but, as in the case of coal, most of them would not solve the inherent problems of those industries. In fact, within months of the miners getting exactly what they wanted in 1947, the pits nationalized, they were out on strike. Between 1945 and 1950 Britain witnessed the fastest changing half-decade of the century, changes which had been forecast in November 1944 when King George VI gave his address from the throne in which he announced that his government (still a coalition) was thinking towards a comprehensive health service and a universal system of National Insurance.

In May 1945, with the war in its last days, the Labour Party withdrew from the coalition government, and in July won a landslide majority. Labour had got nearly 48 per cent of the vote, the Conservatives less than 40 per cent.

The clear difference between the 1945 government of Clement Attlee and that of Ramsay MacDonald a decade and a half earlier was that Attlee's was the first Labour government with an absolute majority over all other parties, and by 1946 it was hard at work. The Bank of England was nationalized, the legislation to nationalize the coal industry was passed, as was the National Health Service Act, although it would not take effect until the middle of 1948. In

1947 the school-leaving age was raised to fifteen, electricity was nationalized and the Act to take the railways into public ownership passed.

It was also in 1947 that the government was panicked into bringing forward the date to give independence to India, thus bringing about the bloody partition of the Subcontinent. The frailties of that transition from colonial dependence to independence, and the inability of previous governments to devise a system with all parties in India for peaceful changeover, were to leave a wretched mess in India and Pakistan for the rest of the century. The ignoble retreat from the Subcontinent under cover of constitutional and diplomatic agreement was mirrored during 1947 and 1948 in the way that Britain had to get out of its Palestinian mandate responsibilities when in May 1948 the Jews proclaimed the state of Israel. These were therefore Carrington's formative political years and influenced his attitudes and decisions for the whole of his time in political and international office. The years from 1947 to the death of Stalin in 1953 were a tumultuous period in British political history, and clearly loomed large in Carrington's life.

The place of the House of Lords in British politics during the 1940s should not be underestimated. When at the end of 1945 Carrington took his seat, it was a very small legislative community; there were no life peers. (The life peerage system was introduced in 1958.) The position of this elite club in British political life was emphasized in 1945 by the fact that it did not sit in the Lords but in the King's Robing Room. The Palace of Westminster had been badly damaged during the Blitz and was still not repaired. MPs had therefore taken over the one place the Luftwaffe had failed to destroy, the Lords' Chamber. The irony of this was not lost on Carrington.

Given the natural composition of the hereditary peers, the day's business resembled a Conservative debating society. In fact, the Tory majority was so overwhelming that they had to sit on both sides of the chamber. Carrington always dated his interest in the future of the Lords from this period. He saw not only the need for eventual reform, but also the importance of a balanced and reforming second chamber.

We might imagine the instincts of the Conservative majority in the Lords to be exercised enough to attempt to put down the pile of legislation intended to take into public ownership core industries and institutions. Carrington's belief that it was in 'the traditions of the House' not to habitually make the life of government ministers intolerable by the sheer weight of numbers and noise in the Lords is ill founded. Previous administrations (Liberal mainly; only latterly Labour) had always been bedevilled by the strength of Tory majorities in the Upper House. The pre-1914 Liberal governments found it almost impossible to get anything through that the Lords did not want and this had led to the only satisfactory reform of that place in the whole century.[17]

There were, however, two moderating influences in 1945 when Carrington entered Parliament. One was the Leader of the House, Lord Addison, and the other was the Leader of the Opposition, Lord Cranborne, whose descendant was to be such a leading personality in the Lords reform debate during the Blair government of the late 1990s. Addison had been in that pre-First World War Liberal government. Like many in the first half of the century, Addison had shifted on to other benches, although he had not abandoned his beliefs. Now in his late seventies, he was the ideal Leader of the House, even though many of his instincts were not with his own government. He was particularly opposed to the brutal determination to implement the famous Clause IV of the Labour Party manifesto. This was the creed recited by every party activist in favour of – as it seemed to Carrington at least – wholesale

---

17 The 1911 Parliament Act was the result of a conflict between Asquith's Liberal government and dyed-in-the-wool Tory peers who were determined to block the Budget of Lloyd George. The 1911 Act limited the power of the Lords to delay legislation of so-called money bills sent from the Commons and for no more than two years any other legislation. Although this is the main reason the 1911 Act is remembered, it was also this legislation that reduced the period between General Elections from seven years to five. This Act lasted until its major amendment in 1949.

nationalization. To the Conservative peers this was not simply political change, but the fulfilment of a nightmare first experienced in
1917 when news came of the Bolshevik Revolution. Many Tory
peers saw no further than a socialist conspiracy, a way of completely changing the United Kingdom's way of life. Against this
debate, Carrington balanced neatly on his two seats: one in the
Lords and one at Bledlow.

In Buckinghamshire he had started the long haul of improving
the estate. He had become, not quite overnight, a gentleman farmer
so was not taken too seriously by some. Tenants and hands were
well aware of his background and he made no secret of his shortcomings. Moreover, there was very little sophisticated agriculture
in these islands in the late 1940s and no indication of the commercial and scientific influences that would be visited on British
farmland during the coming couple of decades. Although there
was a certain amount of mechanization, many farms still used old
methods including horse ploughing; indeed the horse, even in sub-
urban areas, quite commonly pulled the milk and bread carts.

The Second World War had enormously influenced the way
agriculture was managed during the 1940s and beyond. An estate
such as Bledlow had usually run at a loss or was able to, at the very
most, break even. Consequently, even if they had been inclined to,
most landowners never made large investments in their farms.
Many of them, of course, did not regard themselves as farmers.
Their estates, however small or large, were very simply viewed as
what they owned; their bit of England. Tenants did the farming but
rarely had any money for themselves. It was common in the first
half of the twentieth century for farm labourers and their families
to live in the most primitive conditions.

Britain had not really been self-sufficient in food since the late
nineteenth century. During the Second World War, the whole
nation had been told to dig for victory. When peace came, the
shortages were still there. For example, meat was rationed in Britain
and so was bread, which had not been the case between 1939 and
1945. Because the system of agriculture and landowning was badly
structured, it was actually cheaper for Britain to import a lot of its

food than try to grow even the most basic crops on a large enough scale for the nation to be self-sufficient. The cereal prairies of the eastern counties were yet to be ploughed. There were few places where corn was grown on any grand scale. When Carrington took over the Bledlow estate, which at that time was just 350 acres, most of the land in the county was for grazing and hardly ploughed.

Little wonder then that the war changed so much in the way Britain was to be farmed. Agriculture was now seen as an essential industry. Price structures, productivity targets, cross-fertilization of ideas and a corridor of advisory bodies throughout Britain amounted to a national effort that had not been seen before. The immediate postwar years in agricultural planning laid the ground for Britain to become the most cost-effective farming nation in Europe.

Apart from the economic need to do all this, there was the drive of the postwar Labour government to implement change, for which it had a mandate. It had a large majority. It had the sense of social revolution and it had the brains on its front benches. Just as Ellen Wilkinson was making education work (largely thanks to the template provided by R. A. Butler's Education Act), so Tom Williams matched her inspiration and cleverness in agriculture. Carrington, as a farmer and later as an Agriculture Minister (in Churchill's government), called Williams the best Agriculture Minister of any government of the second half of the twentieth century. (Presumably he thought the third Lord Carrington the best of the first half.) Certainly at no other time in the century did the industry have such a revolutionary air about it as it did after the Second World War. So the opportunity to make agriculture work, and for a minister to leave his mark, was great. Williams had the added advantage that he was thoroughly likeable. He was popular with everyone in farming and even on the opposition benches at Westminster, which is more than can be said for his junior minister, George Brown, whose farming connection was that he had been an official in the Transport & General Workers Union Agricultural Section. For the time being, these matters were of little consequence to the young master of Bledlow Manor.

Carrington's farming qualifications were being improved. During the war, Agricultural Executive Committees were set up throughout Britain to get as many acres under profitable production as possible. Like any other industry during wartime, there was enormous room for improvement. Ideas that had perhaps been around for some time but through a lack of opportunity had not been put into practice were now exploited. During the Great War, the government had been able to coordinate industry, systems and efficiency targets, and production had been impressively high. After 1918, the government had found it difficult to understand why many industries were no longer efficient. One reason was that there was no longer a government-led – and in some cases enforced – effort. After the Second World War, the coincidence of the Agricultural Executive Committees and the politically and socially revolutionary programmes coming from Tom Williams's Agricultural Ministry meant the continuation of the national farming and horticulture policies that had benefited the country during the war.

As a landowner, Carrington had been invited to join the Buckinghamshire Agriculture Committee. He had been fortunate enough not to be thrown in at the deep end of agriculture immediately after the war. Although he had taken over the estate at Bledlow, at that time he did not have the farm, which was run by the tenant, Tom Wooster. When Wooster died in 1949, Carrington at last had his own farm. He also had a son and heir, Rupert, who was born in December 1948.

Fortunately, membership of these agricultural committees was not confined to gentlemen farmers. A typical committee would include the local vet, a tenant farmer, a farm owner, a manager and an agent as well as the large landowners. Consequently, the fund of knowledge was considerable. So too were the powers of these groups. For example, a committee might look at a badly run and maintained farm and 'advise' the farmer how he should improve his lot. This could be anything from range and breeds of livestock to machinery and accommodation. If the committee did not think much of the farmer's response then they had the power to kick him out. So much for freedom and democracy in postwar Britain.

Carrington was a very quick learner. Although he was no expert, the sheer level of expertise and advice gathered by his committee was enough for him to begin to become a knowledgeable agriculture debater in the House of Lords. He was also considered an increasingly influential figure on the basis that not only did he know people in high places, they knew him. Not surprisingly, he was asked to become chairman of the executive committee of the Country Landowners' Association.

The committee system wasted no time in recruiting Carrington. Nothing was left to chance, even train times.

Ministry of Agriculture and Fisheries
55 Whitehall
London SW1
3rd January 1946

Dear Lord Carrington

We are anxious to get a representative landowner on the War Agricultural Executive Committee for Bucks., and I should very much like to put your name forward to the Minister if you would be willing to serve.

In view of the fact that these Committees are ultimately to become a permanent feature of agricultural organisation I think you will agree that their constitution becomes a matter of very great importance and that those who serve on them will be performing a most useful and important task in furthering the future prosperity of the countryside.

I am wondering if you would be willing at any rate to have a talk about the matter? If so, would it be possible for you to call here on Thursday, the 10th, at about 3 PM. This is the only day I shall be in London until the succeeding Thursday, the 17th, which would be a suitable alternative if the 10th is impossible for you.

Hoping very much that I may have the pleasure of seeing you.
Believe me,
Yours sincerely
[Sir William Gavin]
Chief Agricultural Adviser

The Lord Carrington
Millaton
Bridestowe
Devon[18]

Ministry of Agriculture and Fisheries
55 Whitehall
London SW1
14th January 1946

Dear Carrington

I am delighted to think that you are willing to serve on the Bucks.
War Agricultural Executive Committee, and I am putting forward
your name to the Minister tomorrow. You may, therefore, I hope,
expect to hear from him within the next day or two (unless he
knows of any just cause or impediment etc!) and the object of this
note is to let you know that the next meeting of the Executive is at
County Hall, Aylesbury, on Friday next, at 10.30, and the Chairman,
Mr Raffety, says he would be delighted to see you then if the
appointment comes through in time. While you are living in London it would not be essential for you to be there at the beginning of
the meeting if you find this inconvenient. I see there are trains from
Baker Street as follows:

Baker Street	Aylesbury
8.36	10.04
9.16	10.42

18 The Carringtons still had the house near Okehampton. However, it might
be thought the Ministry of Agriculture would have known he was living at
Campden Hill Square in Kensington.

(I am afraid I have taken these from a July timetable, so perhaps they should be confirmed.)

Another point I should like to suggest if I might is that you should join the Country Landowners' Association, and I have written to the Chairman as per enclosed copy warning him that he may be hearing from you.

Yours sincerely

William Gavin

Carrington also became a member of Buckinghamshire County Council. He was always rather proud to have held at least one elected office, and he stayed on the County Council until 1951 when he went into Churchill's government. His departure from the County Council was not treated with undue graciousness. As Carrington remembers it, the local Tory leader, V. W. Gurney, made it clear that he was not much impressed with his decision.

Woodlands
Burkes Road
Beaconsfield
17th March 1951

Dear Lord Carrington

Thank you for yours of the 14th inst. from which I note that you are not seeking re-election to the County Council.

I am very sorry that you find it necessary as I had formed the impression that you would be a very useful member.

You have youth on your side and of course we require young members. Unfortunately young men now have to earn a living owing to high taxation and in consequence cannot spare the time to attend meetings. It may be that the Conservatives will in due course have to go into opposition, then perhaps you will find time to return to Aylesbury.

Yours sincerely

V. W. Gurney

Carrington's instincts for leadership had been nursed and developed at Sandhurst and in his regiment under particularly trying circumstances. Even in the apparently parochial environment of local government at county level, during those three years he was to learn the power of officials over elected representatives. He quickly saw that leadership and the authority of the voters was not nearly enough to overcome the Machiavellian and often downright self-serving pettiness of unelected officials who, after all, had to carry on the functions of local and regional administration for election after election and political persuasion after political persuasion.

Once more Carrington's military background was put to good use. He understood perfectly the need for planning and mastering a brief and applying it to an objective. It was a simple military rule which he applied at regional government level to overcome those sometimes unhelpful officials and departments. Even as a peer in the 1940s, he was aware that elected government at whatever level had to ensure that it remained a servant of the electorate and not the bureaucracy. Many years later in Margaret Thatcher's and Ted Heath's Cabinets, Carrington had an enviable reputation for understanding the essentials of any brief. At the same time he had critics who suggested that later in life he often chose not to do his paper homework before even essential meetings. Sir Roy Strong, for example, claimed that, for this very reason, Carrington was a disaster as chairman of the Trustees of the Victoria and Albert Museum.[19]

Carrington's further easement into his political career was blessed by his being able to sit on the opposition benches during those turbulent years of the second half of the 1940s. He was not to be overwhelmed by the political helter-skelter of pushing through a mass of new legislation, much of it the subject of complex parliamentary draughtsmanship. For example, the 1947 Agriculture Act needed all the skills of the minister, the former miner Tom Williams. Farmers would be guaranteed prices – almost a licence

19 See p. 458.

to grow money. The political sensitivities of the period were such that although this was a Labour government giving the farmers perhaps the biggest boost since the early nineteenth-century Corn Laws, the rural vote never wavered from the Conservatives.[20] With his growing expertise in agriculture, Carrington found himself best able to follow the Upper House practice of speaking only on those subjects of which he had direct experience.

The determination of the Labour government to put through legislation that would provide sensible regulation for the country-side as well as the urban sprawl was, again, good practice ground for Carrington. The Town and Country Planning Act went through both Houses by 1947 and was on the statute book by the following year. This legislation would force the county councils to, for the first time, plan the development in the shires. Those same councils would also have compulsory purchase powers, which, apart from in times of emergency such as war, was a new and controversial move. It was this 1947 Act that introduced the need to seek planning permission for big alterations to buildings and the way that land was used. It was therefore the introduction of the whole rural and urban planning system as a basis for procedures and legislation for the next half century. This was not party dogma. Just as James Wheatley had by his 1924 Housing Act recognized the need to plan for the building industry, so the 1945 Labour government understood that some order had to be brought to the way in which the whole country went about construction, reconstruction and the use of precious land resources. The draft legislation and the ensuing debate were necessarily complicated. Equally there was an opportunity and a temptation for voices to

20 In 1815 Lord Liverpool's government banned the importation of corn once it had reached a certain level. This meant that there were bread shortages and riots but it took seven years before the Corn Laws were amended in 1822 and heavy customs duties imposed. The political differences over the Corn Laws led to hugely damaging splits in the political parties. It was not until 1846 that the Corn Laws were repealed, but not before there had been an irreparable schism within the Tory Party from which some believed it never recovered; the trust broken and the mistrust established were set for the rest of the century.

be raised against the Town and Country Planning Bill because personal interests were threatened and sensitivities raised. Could this not after all be nothing more than an increasingly dictatorial government telling landowners and landlords what they could not do with their own property?

The make-up of the Tory opposition in the Lords in the postwar period was largely, although not entirely, traditional backwoodsmen and landowning classes. Carrington, although a landowner, was very much part of the younger generation which included people like Onslow and Townshend (whose ancestors had helped govern Britain since the eighteenth century). It was Lord Chesham who became their tutor in parliamentary procedure and encouraged the younger peers to study draft legislation, to question its structure and to speak politely, usefully and often, as it was debated during its passage through the Lords. The Town and Country Planning Act was a pretty good practice ground for any budding politician. The procedures and sense of change, albeit Labour inspired, confirmed in Carrington his belief that he should have a political career rather than simply seeing the Lords as a delightful club and a place to exercise the Whiggish tendency. With Buck De La Warr[21] as the Shadow Agriculture Minister in the Lords, Carrington was again encouraged and seen as future ministerial material. In 1947 he was given his first job – junior Opposition Whip.

The twenty-eight-year-old Carrington decided that his knowledge of what went on in the Palace of Westminster should not be confined to the House of Lords. He spent much time in the gallery of the House of Commons learning and watching. Below him was his own party front bench of names that were already well known and many who would be known for generations to come. The young Major Lord Carrington (at this stage it was still common practice for people like him to continue to wear their uniforms even in the House) could not have been anything but impressed at the sight of Churchill, black morning jacket, pinstriped trousers, waistcoat, spotted bow-tie and surprisingly pink face. There too

21 The ninth Earl De La Warr.

was the languid Anthony Eden and the slightly pasty R. A. Butler. But Carrington had met many famous men and was indirectly related to many of them. This was a man for whose mother the Princess Royal had sent a servant bearing grapes.

The men who impressed him from the peers' gallery were on the government benches. The quiet, seemingly ordinary, cricket-loving Prime Minister, Clement Attlee. There also was the man whose room Carrington would one day inherit, the brilliant and persuasive Foreign Secretary, Ernest Bevin:'Large, burly, rather ugly with heavy horn-rimmed spectacles and a continually moving mouth, he conveyed power and authority.'[22] Carrington remembers that he continued to be impressed with Bevin and his determination to bring about a transatlantic alliance of the United States and the main nations of Western Europe. A future Secretary-General of NATO, he never forgot the origins of the alliance or the persuasiveness of Bevin's argument for it.

Carrington was going through the reasonable transition from one career to another at an almost leisurely pace. True, he was intensely busy, but, in the manner of the day and his place in society, he was charmingly moving from one platform to another. It is an impression that he gave throughout the whole of his adult life – the gifted and agreeable aristocrat whom others assumed would always be the right person for anything they put his way. For example, when much later in life he was invited to join a bank at a very senior level, he offered the mild objection that he did not know anything about banking. That did not seem to worry his fellow directors. Now in the 1940s he knew little about politics, but the instincts of the ruling classes are simply defined and so very soon he did. The drift from 1946 in the Lords to 1951 in government could not have been better planned. It suited him politically to quietly learn the routine and a few of the vagaries of politics without the rough and tumble of the Commons, even though they were far less boisterous during that time than in the early 1980s when he was to suffer for his ignorance.

22 Lord Carrington, *Reflect on Things Past*, pp. 82–3.

It was too a very comfortable and pleasant period of transition in the Carrington family life. Peter and Iona Carrington were gradually pulling the Bledlow estate together. The children had arrived at an undisturbingly regular rate.[23] Scattered about the family's holdings were fine bits of furniture and splendid and sometimes huge portraits. The house at Bledlow continued to be what it was, a manor house rather than a stately home. It became a jolly place to live in for a growing family and lots of friends. Iona Carrington was in her element. She was thought 'sensible' by the county. She was, and remained, extremely strong-minded, tempered with a sense of humour. At this time she began to make a mark with trowel and hoe. Apart from the round of committees and societies which she was expected to join and even chair, Iona Carrington's great ambition was in the design and laying out of the gardens of Bledlow. Indeed, it would have been rather comfortable for Carrington to have become 'something in the City' and Iona a busy hostess when she was not creating the Manor House garden. However, a political path rarely allows a quiet herbaceous border in any family.

When in February 1950 Attlee's government went to the country (their fixed term was up), both major parties knew the election was to be a close-run thing. Of the 625 seats, Labour won 315, a majority of 17 over the Conservatives, but there were 9 Liberals and 3 others. Labour was back, but only just, and Attlee could hold power only until the autumn of 1951. The election was called for that October.

Considering the social changes that had taken place, most of which were favourable to the general population, it may seem curious that Labour should lose to the Conservatives. However, the phenomenon of a majority Labour administration had meant such a scurrying of legislative draughtsmen that to some extent Attlee's government had nothing else to offer. Between 1945 and 1951 Britain had seen the end of the war, the foundation of the National Health Service, the nationalization of the Bank of England, the

23 Alexandra born 1943, Virginia born 1946, Rupert born 1948.

coal industry, the electricity and gas industries, transport, the steel industry, the famous 1947 Town and Country Planning Act and the Representation of the People Act. With this political and social revolution now given statutory legitimacy, there was no excitement in government. It was as if Attlee had run out of big ideas. At the same time the teething troubles of nationalization were there for all to see. None of this had made people better off. Britain was still broke from the war effort and war damage and bomb sites were still an everyday feature of the British urban landscape. The economy was messy. Moreover, the longed-for peace dividend was never paid. Britain and her allies may have defeated the Germans but the cost in financial and social terms had been enormous. Perhaps to simplify it, the British did not feel victors. And so in spite of Herbert Wilcox's *Spring in Park Lane* and the romantic images floated by Anna Neagle and Michael Wilding, together with the New Look from Paris and even a fairytale wedding in 1947 of a princess and her handsome naval officer, Britain was still a desperately austere place in which to live.

Even the threat of war had not retreated. In 1948 the Berlin airlift began. In April 1949, with government warnings to the people that the Soviet Union was now a direct and very real threat, NATO was formed and teenagers were told that for the foreseeable future there was no way National Service would be abandoned. In September 1950 British troops were fighting in Korea. In January 1951, far from turning swords into ploughshares, the government did much for the shares of the defence industry by announcing an unprecedented £4.7 million peacetime rearmament programme. Moreover, the jewel in Attlee's crown, the National Health Service, was going through the first of its many public difficulties. The government had never really worked out how much it would cost and, in April 1951, the Cabinet was forced to bring in prescription charges, something which it had promised not to do and indeed was against the whole principle of cradle-to-grave healthcare. Aneurin Bevan, the father figure (although not the parent) of the NHS, resigned in protest.

This then was the atmosphere in Britain when in October 1951

Labour went once again to the electorate. The Conservatives were returned with a majority of 26 seats – Churchill as Prime Minister, his heir apparent Anthony Eden as Foreign Secretary. With Churchill back in Downing Street, Carrington took the next step in his political career.

5. Churchill's Shoot

One morning, very much in the image of the landowner, Carrington was shooting partridges at Bledlow while Churchill was in Downing Street aiming off for his junior ministerial list. Carrington knew this, but it certainly was not his style to sit nervously by his telephone. He shot for most of the morning, during which time there was a call from Downing Street. The butler explained that his lordship was after partridge, but he did promise to mention Downing Street's call when Carrington came in. After lunch, Carrington returned to the Manor House and the telephone. Churchill said to him, 'Have you had a good shoot?' Carrington, who really had not got much of a bag that day, said yes, he had; then, said Churchill, 'Would you like to join my shoot?'

At the age of thirty-two, Peter Carrington was to be a junior Agriculture Minister. It was the start of a government career during which he would serve every Conservative Prime Minister from Churchill to Thatcher. In spite of memorable moments and much success, it was a political career that would end in tears.

His appointment as one of the two parliamentary secretaries at the Ministry of Agriculture and Fisheries was a straightforward decision. The other junior minister was Dick Nugent. He was in the Commons. Churchill needed a spokesman in the Lords. In opposition Lord De La Warr had been the Conservative spokesman, but he was too senior and, anyway, Churchill wanted him as Postmaster General. Carrington's apprenticeship to Buck De La Warr and his practical experience during the past five or six years as farmer, landowner and member of the Agricultural Board in Buckinghamshire, as well as chairman of the executive committee of the Country Landowners' Association, made him an easy choice. Just as an earlier Carrington, Charlie Lincolnshire, had been involved in legislation that had affected agriculture, landowners and especially tenants half a century on, so Carrington was involved in the debate that for decades and more would anger landowners and ramblers alike.

In the 1990s Carrington recalled that it was in the early 1950s that he had understood the need to prepare for what in the final decade of the century became the controversial subject under the headline, the Right to Roam. In the 1950s Carrington was saying that a balance had to be struck between what was then an intensive effort to farm Britain to something close to self-sufficiency and the desire for the whole country to get into the countryside, especially the national parks. He said as much in a letter to *The Times* on 21 May 1951.

Sir,

Country dwellers welcome visitors to the countryside, but at the same time they hope they will observe the very reasonable and simple rules put over in this code, which explains the reasons for making them. Most of the damage to farming and amenity that now happens is the result not so much of wilful perversity as of thoughtlessness and ignorance owing to a lack of understanding of the processes of agriculture and forestry. Given a reasonable stand- ard of behaviour on the part of visitors to the country, there should be no clash of interests on that score between townsmen and coun- try folk. But the ideas of the Country Code should be spread widely by all available means of publicity, including the films, broadcasting and posters. The maxims of good behaviour cannot be instilled in a day.

For that reason the Country Landowners' Association attaches the greatest importance to putting the ideas of the Country Code into the head of every schoolchild in the land, just as he or she is taught the rudiments of 'safety first'. This proposal need not in any way encroach upon an already overloaded curriculum. School teachers can give invaluable help to the campaign in their method of approach, e.g. to nature study, and their contacts with the children out of lesson time. My Association, therefore, sincerely

hopes that the school authorities will do all they can to encourage
the observance of the Country Code.
I am, Sir, your obedient servant,
CARRINGTON,
Chairman, Executive Committee,
Country Landowners' Association.

In November 1951 Carrington reported for his first job in government. He spent the previous weekend reflecting on the reputation of his famous ancestor, the third baron, who had been President of the Board of Agriculture in Asquith's government. Charlie Lincolnshire had become famous as the author of the legislation known as the Farmers' Charter and the pre-First World War Smallholdings Bill. Forty years on, the sixth baron would also make a name for himself in the same ministry. However, it is most unlikely that Uncle Charlie would have thought highly of the circumstances.

Just as at the end of the twentieth century a ministerial workload was considerably more than that of fifty years before, so Carrington's was considerably more than that of his predecessor, who, by one account, used to arrive at the Board of Agriculture at about 11 a.m. and was gone for lunch and for the day by a quarter to one. Carrington had to work harder than that.

Agriculture had never been seen as much of a controversial subject since the Corn Laws debates of the nineteenth century. Yet Carrington was, in his very short time in the job, embroiled in two controversial issues. The first was myxomatosis – the fatal disease designed to curb the rabbit population but which incensed the human population. The second issue was the Crichel Down Affair, in which Carrington was so discredited that he was forced to offer his resignation to Churchill. More immediately, even as a junior minister, Carrington found himself grappling with the huge problem that Britain could not feed itself in spite of the imaginative leadership of Tom Williams, Attlee's Agriculture Minister. Whatever Tory policy and aspirations, Carrington's albeit brief experience on his own estate, his six years in opposition studying the practical politics of agriculture plus his time on advisory boards and committees, suggested that British farming needed to operate on a bigger scale.

Williams had done a great deal to push through reforms and subsidies for the agricultural industry. But there were other priorities. For example, war damage throughout the urban areas of Britain was so great that it already had been estimated that the nation needed about 300,000 new houses a year. This was seen by many as an impossible figure to achieve. The then Minister of Housing and Local Government was Harold Macmillan. He was to exceed this target. With the issue of housing a priority, the task of feeding the nation did not attract the public scrutiny and political momentum it deserved. Now he was in government, Carrington could see the broader picture which had been obscure in opposition. Britain was expected to be 'short of food indefinitely'; moreover, half Britain's food consumption was having to be bought in 'a hungry, competitive world'.[1] And although Britain was becoming more widely mechanized throughout her industries, farmers were very often inept managers. Farmers who could bargain to their satisfaction at a sheep fair did not necessarily have the commercial wit to take advantage of mechanization on their farms. Shortages would continue into the foreseeable future but the concern went much deeper than where to find food. It began to bite into the very dangerous area of the health of the nation. Six years after the end of the war, Carrington found himself grappling with the very real problem that Britain would be pushed to feed the nation above subsistence level. He had never forgotten some of his own soldiers telling him that they had joined up simply to escape hunger. He saw hunger as an injustice in British society of the 1920s and '30s. Now, in the 1950s, Britain was not starving, but she was hungry. Within three weeks of becoming a minister, Carrington was telling the Lords that calculations had been made purporting to show that it would be physically possible to produce

1 Dick Nugent, the junior Agriculture Minister in the Commons, November 1951.

sufficient calories for the bare subsistence of the British population. He announced that the diet would hardly be exotic and
would be made up very largely of 'bread, oatmeal, and barley meal,
or their products, potato, sugar, and such vegetables as carrots and
cabbages together with a very small quantity of milk and meat,
largely cow beef. There would be little or no bacon, eggs or beer.'
There was a further conundrum for him: to actually produce that
diet, Britain would have to import huge quantities of fertilizers and
feed stuffs. To pay for them, Britain would need equally large exports.
Yet, as Carrington told the Lords, those exports would not be available because so large a proportion of the population would be
working on food production. It did seem rather a hopeless position,
especially when Britain was expecting to import from Commonwealth sterling countries and the colonies 4.5 million tons of food
and feed stuffs and, for example, about 30,000 tons of meat from
New Zealand alone. The British government had already had to go
to the New Zealand Dairy Products Marketing Commission asking
for butter and cheese exports to be increased. Fortunately, New
Zealand was willing to reduce its dairy exports to other markets in
order to supply its often malnourished 'homeland', Great Britain.

There was a second question for the landowning Carrington:
what to do about building on green belt sites. He was not so much
concerned with factory and light industrial development, which
accounted for little more than 10 per cent of encroachment on
agricultural land. Macmillan's drive to produce 300,000 houses was
the main 'culprit'. For about a decade some 50,000 acres a year had
been lost to development. In 1953 Carrington estimated that, by
the end of the century, land developers would have grabbed about
2 million acres of Britain's countryside. Perhaps anticipating the
public debate that would follow (although hardly imagining its
form in the late 1990s), Carrington's estimate suggested that the
biggest demand would come from housing, accounting for some
70 per cent of the development of agricultural land.

It was in 1953 that an apparently local and, at first, hardly noticed
argument about who owned a small piece of land nearly finished
Carrington's political career before it had got any further than the

most junior ministerial job. The future of land use, and who should
have a say in how that land was used efficiently, prompted a letter to
The Times that was to result in a ministerial sacking, and also to
fundamentally question the nature of authority in postwar Britain.

Sir,

There have been a number of references in the Press recently to
what may be called the veiled nationalisation of agricultural land.
An outstanding example of this procedure is taking place in this
locality, which will, I believe, become a matter for much wider
interest.

In 1939 the Air Ministry acquired by compulsory purchase
700 acres of down land, belonging to several owners, for an R. A. F.
bombing range. In 1950 this land was handed over to the Land
Commission, and has since been farmed by the local Agricultural
Executive Committee. As the area was no longer required for
defence purposes I, as one of the previous owners, applied to the
Ministry of Agriculture in 1950 to buy back the 330 acres which
formed an important portion of one of my tenant's farms. After a
delay of nearly 18 months my application was refused, though
neither then nor at a subsequent meeting with the Parliamentary
Secretary were we told what was to be done with the area. At this
meeting I offered to buy or rent the entire 700 acres and laid out
my plans for doing so. I was told that they would be given sympathetic consideration.

Shortly after my application was again refused, and as a result
three MPs for this neighbourhood sought an interview with the
Minister to protest at this treatment. He informed them that some
months previously, before my application had been turned down,
the Ministry had committed themselves to sell the land to the
Commissioner of Crown Lands, and though he regretted that it
was too late to reconsider this decision there was no obstacle so far
as the Ministry was concerned to my acquiring the land from the
Commission. Once again I applied and after a serious delay was
informed by the Commissioner that as a condition of the transfer
he was committed to the Ministry to erect a farmhouse, cottages,

and buildings, which were, of course, quite superfluous to my needs as I already had them. He also said that though he had not bought the land he was already committed to a prospective tenant.

To my own distress was then added that of a large number of local farmers who had applied or hoped to rent the land. One of them has a written assurance from the Land Commissioner personally that before the land was let it would be advertised in the public press and that his application would be carefully considered. No such advertisement ever appeared. A committee of protest has been formed and a public meeting is to be held this week to ask for an inquiry into the matter, as it appears that the rights of farmers and landowners and extravagance with public money may be involved. Yours faithfully,
MARY ANNA MARTEN
Crichel, Wimborne, Sept. 21

Mary Anna Marten was the daughter of Lord Alington, who was the original owner of the land. She had inherited it and had married Commander Toby Marten. On the face of it, the Agriculture Ministry was faced with a very simple situation: war had been expected and so the Air Ministry had not unreasonably taken over land as part of its preparations for the war effort. None grumbled that it had gone from private ownership to public ownership. But after the war, should it not have been offered back to the original owners or their descendants? Reasonably, the answer would be yes. Yet these were unreasonable times. As we have seen, Britain could not feed itself. This was one reason that the Air Ministry transferred the land to the Ministry of Agriculture, an act some might have seen as a roundabout method of nationalization. The Agricultural Land Commission in 1950 (still under a Labour government) took the decision to seek a tenant for the whole 700 or so acres. Why? Largely because this unit could operate efficiently rather than letting it, or selling it in smaller lots. When the Martens tried to buy 328 acres, which by inheritance would be Mrs Marten's, the ministry said no.

This was more than a confrontation between the Ministry of

Agriculture and an aggrieved landowner. Even in the opening years of the twenty-first century that ministry is seen as one of the most secretive, and sometimes one of the most arrogant, in Whitehall. Fifty years earlier this seemingly unreasonable attitude produced a deserved reputation and might be understood more easily when we remember the importance of agriculture in Britain. Williams had set in motion the legislation that would subsidize and devise agricultural systems for the foreseeable future. The British obsession – as an island nation this was perfectly understandable – to protect and promote its ability to provide basic feeding overrode any uneasiness that the Ministry of Agriculture might be the most feudal of government ministries.[2] Agriculture, which even in the year 2000 produced little more than 1 per cent of the nation's Gross National Product, could easily command 70 per cent of political and national debating time in Parliament and newspaper columns.

That autumn there seemed no great urgency in the department. The 725 acres at Crichel Down in Dorset had been bought by the Air Ministry in 1937 for £12,106. Mrs Marten's father, Lord Aling-ton, had owned 328 of those acres, so he got £5,603. As far as the ministry was concerned, that was perfectly reasonable. Moreover, the ministry believed it was within its rights to do what it wished with the land, whatever the public thought. The Land Commission also thought it right that it should, without any questioning, select its own tenant for Crichel Down – which the Commission did. He was Mr Christopher Tozer.

Carrington was told that he had better make a local visit, talk to a few officials and decide what to do. It could be that Carrington was not best placed to discover the rights and wrongs of the Crichel Down Affair. He appears to have been less than capable of separating the original government need from what, certainly a

2 The concern among the English that the country could not feed itself dated back at least to the sixteenth century. Champions of colonizing America, for example, claimed that it would be one way of getting rid of England's surplus population.

few years later, would be a reasonable gesture of restoring the land to those who had some legitimate interest – in this case the daughter of Lord Alington. It was true that, in theory, the land would be more efficiently farmed over 700 acres.

Carrington's reaction to this request for the land to be returned to its previous owners appears to have been, by today's standards, high-handed. The evidence seemed uncomplicated: the land had been taken during a national emergency; the emergency was ended; the land should be given back. Carrington's celebrated sense of justice failed. The ministry did not accept any criticism. These were the 1950s and the arrogance of bureaucracy was legendary and unreformed. Crichel Down was now part of bigger thinking, whereby big farms were better than small farms.

The ministry was unbending in its view that it was right and should not be examined on the matter. Carrington was a junior minister and supported this view. His judgement was wanting in the findings of the Clark Inquiry (chaired by Sir Andrew Clark QC), which found that the decision of the Land Commission in August 1950 to let Crichel Down as a single unit (i.e. Big Farming) was financially unsound. One of Clark's conclusions was that the Lands Service and the Land Commission had become 'so infatuated with the idea of creating a new model farm that they were determined not to abandon the scheme for financial reasons'.

A junior official, D. S. Brown, who was comparatively inexperienced in these matters, was told to produce an assessment of the rights and wrongs of Crichel Down. Brown was also instructed by his superiors that as the job was extremely confidential, he was not to approach previous owners (including Mrs Marten) and was to base his assessment entirely on information supplied by the ministry's bureaucracies and its agents. Consequently, it was impossible for Brown to do anything but make a misleading report. According to Clark, this arose solely from the 'passionate love of secrecy inherent in so many minor officials'.

Carrington grasped none of this. Nor did he understand properly that the previous owners wanted to buy back their property at current market prices, which were considerably higher than the

Air Ministry had originally paid. Nor did he seem to be impressed with the simple fact that the people that wanted to buy had reputations as first-class farmers and publicly demonstrated that this was so. Carrington was supposed to bring to the Agriculture Ministry his experience as a reasonable farmer and all the advantages of his committee work on the Agricultural Advisory Board. His failure was his inability to challenge his officials.

Sir Andrew Clark's report went so far as to publish the names of the officials he criticized. He said that he regarded the actions of C. H. M. Wilcox, an Under-Secretary at the ministry, C. G. Easterwood, the Permanent Commissioner of Crown Lands, and H. A. R. Thomson, a Crown Receiver, as demonstrating 'a most regrettable attitude of hostility' and that this attitude was 'engendered solely by a feeling of irritation that any member of the public should have the temerity to oppose or even question the acts or decisions of officials of a Government or State Department'.[3] The decision of the Agriculture Ministers, led by Tom Dugdale, endorsed the concept that land that had been forcibly purchased from its original owners for one use (in this case a bombing range) could be kept by the state for an entirely different use.

The fact that Carrington was sent to Dorset to see for himself the state of the land and its prospects and to reflect on the justice and common sense of the Martens' claim only enforces the Clark Report's scathing conclusion about his department's attitude. The public interest and disquiet at the time and Clark's damning judgement meant that the Martens would get their land back.

The Agriculture Minister, Tom Dugdale, was forced to resign. Dugdale's junior ministers, Nugent and Carrington, survived.

Carrington claimed that he and Dugdale had not understood the way in which the paths of centrally controlled economic recovery and public perception of personal rights were in danger of crossing rather than running in parallel. However, Carrington further claimed that his fellow junior minister, Dick Nugent, was not so ignorant of this convergence and that 'he was always per-

3 The Clark Inquiry report, published as a White Paper, Command 1976.

fectly clear in his mind that the Martens should be offered back the land which had been theirs before Government took it from them'.

If Nugent was so minded, why did Dugdale and Carrington fail to understand his argument, if indeed it were ever put to them? Forty years on, Carrington, in conversation with the author, insisted it was too long ago to remember. Dugdale took the brunt of the criticism because he was the senior minister. Nugent felt that because of his beliefs, he was equally guilty. He too decided to offer his resignation. Many MPs believed that Carrington had been let off by the Clark Report and that his judgement was unsound.

Yet Carrington did not think to resign until Nugent said he was going to. Prompted by a bitter debate in the Commons on 20 July 1954 (during which Carrington in the Lords was protected from the harshness of the criticism), they wrote their letters of resignation, compared them and then sent them over to Downing Street.

House Of Commons, July 21

Dear Prime Minister,
After yesterday's debate it is clear that the general feeling in the House is that the Crichel Down affair is the result of a Ministerial failure. As I am associated with this I feel that I have no alternative but to ask you to accept my resignation. In doing so I would like to express my gratitude to you for the honour of taking part in your Administration.
Yours sincerely,
Dick Nugent

Ministry Of Agriculture, July 21

Dear Prime Minister,
I have been considering the position which has arisen out of the debate on Crichel Down in the House of Commons yesterday. There has been much criticism of the way in which this matter

was handled and as I have been associated with it I am now writing
to ask you to accept my resignation. It has been a great privilege to
have had the opportunity of serving in your Government and I am
very grateful to you for it.
Yours sincerely,
Carrington

But there was no way in which Churchill could afford to lose all
three ministers. It was enough for Dugdale to have apparently done
the honourable thing. It is too simple to accept the popular idea
that he was going because it was his position to accept responsibility for what Clark had identified as maladministration in his
department. It seems far more likely that Dugdale went because he
believed that the original decision (to hang on to Crichel Down as
one big farm as part of the government policy of agrarian development) was correct. Furthermore, that July debate in the
Commons made it clear that a ministerial scalp was demanded.

It is very likely that the honourable course of ministerial responsibility, which either leads to a seat in the Lords or resignation, was
forced upon Dugdale and Churchill by the vehement criticism in
that Commons debate from his own colleagues and not simply
from the Labour opposition. This was certainly the view of Tom
Williams, who believed that Dugdale went because of 'the hounding from his back-benchers . . . not his clinging to that pillar of the
constitution, the doctrine of ministerial responsibility'.[4]

What of Carrington's decision? There are still people, including
some in the Conservative Party, who believed that Carrington had
not behaved honourably and that he should have gone. If he had
done so, it is very possible that he would have ended his ministerial
career in the summer of 1954, for there was no way in which
Churchill would have forgiven him. The Prime Minister believed
very strongly that Clark was right and that Dugdale, Nugent and
Carrington were wrong. Churchill's public response to the letters
from Nugent and Carrington was just as expected.

4 Peter Hennessy, *Whitehall*, London: Secker & Warburg, 1989.

I have carefully considered the reasons for which you offer your resignation. I regard the reflections that have been made on the part you have played in the Crichel Down case as wholly unjustified. Moreover, your chief has full responsibility in the matter and it is his earnest desire that you should retain your office. I therefore ask you to withdraw your resignation.

Yours very sincerely,

Winston S. Churchill

So, Carrington was saved for the nation. However, his credibility at the ministry and in Parliament was not so good. Within three months of the debate,[5] Churchill moved him sideways. In October, Carrington became a junior Defence Minister. This was a ministry which he more easily understood and with which he would be connected for the rest of his public life, in and out of government. It was also a department from which he would be forced once more to write a letter of resignation.

Carrington went to the Defence Ministry at the same time as Harold Macmillan became its senior minister. (There was no secretary of state at that time.) Macmillan was not there long; Carrington was. He much admired Macmillan, but not simply because they came from the same 'family' – Macmillan had also been a Grenadier. He had joined up at the start of the First World War in the King's Royal Rifle Corps and had soon transferred to the Grenadier Guards, thanks to a few strings being pulled on his behalf rather than any military judgements. Macmillan had wondered about the

5 The Home Secretary, Sir David Maxwell Fyfe, made the closing speech in the 20 July 1954 debate, during which he defined ministerial conduct and how and in what circumstances a minister should protect a civil servant. In broad terms the minister was always responsible for his bureaucracy unless an official did something which the minister disapproved of and did not know about. In every other case ministerial responsibility would extend to defending the official to the point of resignation. Therefore the Crichel Down Affair and the actions of officials and Messrs Dugdale, Nugent and Carrington became a constitutional reference point for the rest of the century.

privilege of this manipulation of the system, especially into a smart regiment, but he was later to reflect that really the only privilege that he and many others looked for was that of getting themselves killed or wounded as soon as possible. Macmillan was wounded (more than once) and suffered the effects for the rest of his life. He, like Carrington, was decorated with the Military Cross. He, again like Carrington and most certainly unlike Churchill, did not seek medals. There is an aside to the brief army careers of the two men. It is the coincidence that each had a Sergeant Robinson. When Macmillan was severely wounded on the Somme it was to his Sergeant Robinson that he shouted to take command and press on with the attack. In the Second World War, Carrington won his MC for his part in the attack on, and the taking of, the bridge at Nijmegen. In that action, Carrington too turned to his Sergeant Robinson to press the attack. Today this is a point of almost no significance, but in times past it was a strand of understanding in the bond that was to grow between the two men of very different generations, but not so different temperaments. Carrington could always relate to lower rather than middle orders.

When he took up his next post, Macmillan was already a political hero for having delivered what many had seen to be an overambitious target of 300,000 new homes. Now he was given an even harder task: to be Minister of Defence under Churchill. His dilemma was obvious. Churchill knew more about defence than anyone in government and certainly more than any Prime Minister of the century. Although he recognized Macmillan's capabilities, Churchill sent a steady stream of notes telling his minister what he should be doing and what he should not be doing. Macmillan was not even allowed to prepare and introduce a White Paper. Macmillan had gone to the ministry because, frankly, there was nowhere else he could go. He might have become Leader of the House, yet that did not much interest him. He would have liked to have been Foreign Secretary; however, Anthony Eden was firmly in that office and would remain there while he waited for Churchill to leave Downing Street. So Macmillan became a political eunuch: he looked the part, he sounded the part, but where it mattered, he was quite ineffectual.

The matter was made worse by the structure of the ministry to which he and Carrington now moved. These were the days when each service had its own ministry: the War Office, the Admiralty and the Air Ministry. Many thoughtful political and military planners, including the by then retired Field Marshal Montgomery, had campaigned for what would eventually become a single ministry with a secretary of state in overall charge. It was not until the 1960s that this came about, when Macmillan himself was PM. Carrington was not in the least surprised that Macmillan then went along with the reconstruction. The five months Macmillan had spent supposedly in charge of the ministry had quickly convinced him of the need for change. Carrington immediately recognized that as a junior minister he had absolutely no power whatsoever, and his boss not much more, other than the right to chair interministerial meetings. Carrington quickly understood that this was a hopeless position for any minister. Even an important process such as the discussion of funding for the individual services would not be decided by the central ministry run by Macmillan but could, if the individual service minister wished, be referred to Cabinet, with that minister having the right to attend to put his service's case. It effectively meant that a minister junior to Macmillan always knew there was a system which could overrule him.

When Carrington went to the ministry in the autumn of 1954, the Second World War had been over for only nine years, and the Korean War had only just finished. The Malayan emergency had been going on since 1948, and a large part of the British army was committed to that conflict. There was still a military presence around Suez. The negotiations to withdraw from Egypt now signalled a potential confrontation as a result of the determination of Colonel Gamal Abdel Nasser to drive the British from the region. Preparations were being made to reposition Britain's Mediterranean headquarters on Cyprus. The start of the Cyprus emergency was already in view.

To keep the military going, the received wisdom was that there had to be a huge intake of civilians. In 1954 there were 800,000 people in uniform, more than a third of whom were National Servicemen. There was also a standby reserve of 600,000 men. But with garrisons in Hong Kong, Singapore, Malaya, Aden, Suez, Cyprus, Gibraltar, Belize and the Falkland Islands, and postwar commitments in the Rhine army, there was seemingly no way in which this global defence policy – there is a case to be argued that it was not a policy but simply a consequence of empire – could be maintained without keeping a conscript army going. Equally, as Carrington soon recognized, a National Service system was mightily expensive and not particularly efficient. The resources available to the services and the systems of training would never bring the conventional military up to the standard needed to support the United Kingdom's postwar colonial and international commitments.

Carrington was known as the under-lord in the modest ministerial building at Storey's Gate. It was really little more than a complex of committees and minor bureaucracy living in reduced circumstances. Yet, as we have seen, the questions faced by the United Kingdom were intricate.

Carrington later recalled in conversation with the author that although the Defence job might have been seen by some as a sideways move, its complexities and international as well as national ramifications made the local difficulties suffered in Agriculture appear somewhat tame.

Carrington arrived at Defence during the closing weeks of 1954 and discovered what he had long suspected (as a soldier): that the overambitious plans of the postwar Western allies had to be accepted for the nonsense that they were. Carrington saw that within a four- to five-year period spanning the late forties and early fifties, the whole strategic outlook of world military and political thinking had been changed by the development of nuclear weaponry.

When he had left the army, Carrington was aware of the received wisdom, often cynically presented by Montgomery, that it would take almost one hundred divisions to preserve the so-called balance of power in Europe. Carrington's assumption was that postwar Western Europe – which, of course, included the uncertain constitutional future of what was to become West Germany – could most certainly not find the money to build and maintain this goal. Later he would muse that it was more than money that prevented between ninety and one hundred divisions (each with approximately eight to ten thousand men) from being established. No European government (including Britain's) had the political and economic resources to promote such a rearmament programme. Apart from all that, where would Western Europe park such a huge army with all its equipment and logistical train?

Attlee's government had started a rearmament programme. Not unexpectedly, the Conservatives, when they came to power in 1951 under Churchill, continued that policy. The new junior Minister of Defence was now being told that these well-laid plans were quite incapable of defeating a Soviet army should it choose to head in a westerly direction towards the Channel ports. Carrington was learning to talk about 'trip-wire policy'. The function of the British army was to be an integral part of an allied force in Europe that did nothing more than hold the line until the political decision was taken (either with great care or in panic) to press the nuclear button.

By the following February (1955) Carrington had been involved with the presentation (largely sponsored by Churchill even though he was shortly going) that the West's and therefore Britain's deterrence policy must rest primarily on strategic air power with its nuclear weapons. Here, then, were the origins of MAD, the doctrine of Mutually Assured Destruction that the Americans, principally led by Secretary of Defense Robert McNamara, would adopt as their policy for dealing with what they saw as an increasing Soviet threat. Carrington's assessment was that this doctrine, although inevitable, was largely unsound because it could not anticipate technological development in a wholly secretive Soviet system that most certainly did not accept the situation as it was prior to the 1940s.[6]

6 US Department of Defense, *Effects of Nuclear Weapons*, DoD Publication, revised 1968.

In this he was correct. The technological development which he was not alone in looking for was in rocketry. Two and a half years after the February 1955 statement of British doctrine, strategic planners went into their darkened rooms to think again. When Britain had spoken about strategic forces with nuclear weapons, it had been referring to what became known as the V-bomber force. This was a manned aircraft squadron carrying nuclear weapons which, with skill and luck, might get through to Soviet targets, although they were unlikely, and therefore not expected, to return from such missions. What caused the rethink was the rapid development in space engineering. Carrington, as a junior minister, was not privy to American estimates of the Russian space programme. Yet in 1955 he knew that the Americans were working towards space flight. That was hardly secret. What he did not know, and what the Americans could not believe, was that the Russians were ahead of the Americans. When on 4 October 1957 Soviet engineers launched *Sputnik 1*, the first artificial satellite, into orbit around the earth, concern even in the relatively insignificant Storey's Gate office was not prompted by the loss of kudos to the Russians, but by the deeper and more startling military significance of the event. *Sputnik* was not important. The rocket that had put it into orbit was extremely important. The Soviet Union now had the capability of producing a rocket that could send a payload, and therefore a warhead, into orbit. The era of intercontinental warfare was born. This was the technological uncertainty that had concerned Carrington.

Carrington's thoughts at the time did not concentrate on strategic philosophy. He was awe-struck at the appalling capacity for destruction which man had now acquired. He then developed a personal belief which rested on the premise that nuclear weaponry made war less likely, largely because of the obvious horrors it would bring. This position was hardly surprising considering his military background, the briefings that he was continually getting and the fact that he was in a government which completely endorsed the concept of nuclear deterrence. It is true also that in the early 1950s very little was known about the destructive potential of the nuclear weapons now in the Western and Eastern armouries. It was certainly not enough to use the awesome destruction at Hiroshima and Nagasaki as benchmarks. Nuclear weaponry was moving from the era of kiloton to megaton. Even the American Department of Defense, which was compiling the official handbook of the effects of nuclear weapons, appeared to be working on the premise of survival rather than destruction.[7] Carrington believed, much later, that although doctrines were drawn with scant understanding, they would not have been altered by having more information. He remained a champion of nuclear deterrence for the rest of his life. However, an illustration of a sometimes naively expressed comparison with different forms of warfare was made by Carrington in the Lords when he said, 'Perhaps there are some who, faced with the unknown consequences of nuclear warfare, are apt to forget that conventional warfare as we have known it in the last two world wars is utterly degrading.'[8]

He never could accept an argument that focused on the scale of destruction and its longer-term consequences, and that very early speech was rephrased time and again during the coming thirty or so years.

Carrington's boss at Defence, Macmillan, did not last long. He had been in the job for not quite six months when Churchill resigned as Prime Minister. Eden went to Number 10 and Macmillan to the Foreign Office. Into the Defence Ministry went Selwyn Lloyd, an honourable but unremarkable minister. He too moved on quickly. Eden had found his feet at Number 10 but not his self-assurance. Eden had always seen himself as the classic Foreign Secretary, and just as Macmillan had found Churchill running the Defence Ministry, he now found Eden determined to decide foreign policy. Shortly before Christmas 1955 this unsatisfactory relationship descended to its nadir. Eden simply did not have the grandness to be Prime Minister; almost before Macmillan entered the Foreign Office, Eden wanted to get rid of him, as the

7 US Department of Defense, *Effects of Nuclear Weapons.*
8 Lord Carrington, *Reflect on Things Past,* London: Collins, 1988, p. 103.

number of directives (up to a dozen a day) he sent Macmillan suggested. Eden eventually moved Macmillan from the Foreign Office to the Treasury, and he searched for a lesser known and more compliant figure. Thus, Selwyn Lloyd left Defence for the FO. The new Defence Minister was one of the shrewder managers of Westminster and Whitehall during the 1950s, Walter Monckton.

Carrington watched all this with a little alarm. He thought the ministry needed the guidance and inspiration of Macmillan for a long, not a short, period. It disturbed him that Macmillan and Eden simply did not like each other. Although he regarded Selwyn Lloyd as a man of great principle, he considered him unsuited to the task. Very quickly he understood that Defence was what he would call 'arguably the most complex portfolio in the Cabinet'. No issue had a simple argument and each had a complicated answer. Decisions would have to survive for many years, sometimes decades, unlike, say, even the huge Health Ministry where a policy on prescriptions could be reversed or endorsed after twelve months. For example, once the planning staff had identified the need for a particular type of ship, the time from drawing board to launch and then putting that vessel into service might be fifteen to twenty years. It was difficult to understand the complex link between the sometimes conflicting forces of industry, the defence system, the Treasury and, most of all, foreign policy. Moreover, there were few if any votes in defence policy.

Carrington's first speech in the Lords as a junior minister was on the policy and technology needed to modernize the Royal Navy's cruisers. The still relatively young and undoubtedly junior minister had to make his debut speech on the Royal Navy knowing full well that listening closely to every word were three Admirals of the Fleet, Lords Chatfield, Cunningham and Fraser. He was aware also that the argument for modernization, especially if it were to convince the Treasury, had to be a little more sophisticated than the boldly stated fact that there were only six 6-inch guns left in a cruiser, damn it.

This was the only job for which Carrington could claim some formal training. Although towards the end of his life he was most remembered as Foreign and Commonwealth Secretary, it was in the Defence Ministry that he did best.

Carrington often said that he was just a dogsbody at the Defence Ministry. In March 1956 the dogsbody was sent to the Western Isles to tell the people of North and South Uist that even though the ministry, which did not need planning permission, was about to turn the land of their crofts into a rocket range, their views would not be ignored. The ministry was going through the motions. The plans for the rocket range were to be given to Inverness County Council. It was promised that if there were substantial objections, then the Secretary of State for Scotland might hold a public inquiry. Carrington, still with the public sense of injustice over the Crichel Down Affair, needed all his talents of persuasion to calm the uncertainties of the crofters. He appealed to their better nature and sense of patriotism – a risky tactic. For three days, Carrington and a small group of the ministry's guided-missile experts talked quietly to the crofters. Their leader was a priest, Father John Morrison. Carrington told him that no more than 200 acres on the north-western tip of Eochar would be used for the actual firing site. He then promised that, after all, no crofting homes would be demolished. He did mention that a further 1,000 acres would be taken over but that the crofters would be able to use them for grazing. And Carrington gave Father Morrison a personal assurance that the proposed carving of a 25-foot statue of the Madonna and Child on a hillside at Eochar would be allowed to go ahead.

The priest was impressed, especially as Carrington sold him this last point as a concession, hinting that the ministry had hoped to use the Madonna's site as a radar station. Father Morrison was won over and told the people, 'They have done their best to be decent with us ... I don't think a rocket range is a desirable thing to have in any area, but we realize it is a national necessity, no matter how evil, and the crofters of South Uist are a very patriotic set of people.'

Carrington's lasting impression of that visit was not so much the Madonna and Child, but the fact that Father Morrison had told him that this island was the fictional Isle of Toddy in Compton

Mackenzie's *Whisky Galore.* In fact, the key moments in Carrington's negotiations had taken place not in the formal surroundings of the island council, but in the local pub. There was still illicit whisky on the island and by the time Carrington and Morrison emerged from the pub, a solution had been found, although Carrington confessed much later to not remembering very much of the conversation that brought it about.

Carrington returned from the Hebrides a contented man. His minister thought it a job well done and that Carrington's diplomatic powers were well recognized. They were powers by which he would probably be remembered for the rest of his career. They were most certainly to be needed in his next posting, although whether the people of South Uist and the scattered nomads of Woomera had anything in common was doubtful.

6. A Green Rolls-Royce

In 1956 Carrington had been in politics for more than a decade. He had served his apprenticeship in opposition. For the past five years he had worked as a journeyman minister. By the way of modern politics, Carrington might be expected to be ready for a 'big job'. (John Major became Prime Minister just eleven years after entering the House.) In the 1950s British politics did not work that way. Furthermore, Carrington was now thirty-seven years old and safely established. What he had not anticipated was a sabbatical.

Britain needed a new High Commissioner to send to Australia. The then Commonwealth Relations Secretary was the Earl of Home. It was he who asked Carrington if he would like to go to Canberra. If an MP had been asked to go it might have been expected to signal the end of his political career. After all, it would have meant giving up an elected seat. If that MP had been a junior minister, even (or maybe especially) at the Defence Ministry, then the chances were he would not have expected to return to British political life unless he were to inherit a seat in the Lords. (In 1956 there were no life peers.)

However, Carrington was not an MP. His seat in the Lords would be there when he returned. He might even expect some preferment if the job was done well. Yet there was never a suggestion that a place in government would be kept open. Whatever the party's confidence in a minister, there were few certainties about the lifetime of a Parliament. It would only take what Macmillan was famously to call 'events', to overturn the government's stability. In fact, within a very few months of Carrington's going to Australia one of those 'events' occurred. The invasion of the Suez Canal Zone by British, French and Israeli troops was directly responsible for the end of Anthony Eden's political career; it is always a difficult moment for a governing party to misplace its Prime Minister.

Carrington's sense of curiosity, duty (he had no embarrassment using that word) and history encouraged him. Curiosity told him that the appointment to Australia was exciting, especially as he was only thirty-seven. As he reflected to me late in life: 'You imagine at that age being asked to become the High Commissioner of a very important post in a very politically sensitive country. It really was quite something.' At first he did not accept the post. He went home to ask his wife, Iona, whether she felt that the job was either (a) a good idea or (b) something which she was prepared to do. She simply said she thought it might be and that it would be a pity not to have a try.

History was on Carrington's side. His father was born in Australia and had not come to England until he was a young man, and then not to claim his title, but to fight in the Great War. Even more intriguing was the sense of following in the footsteps of the last Carrington to don a plumed hat in that most unceremonial of countries, Australia. For his great uncle Charlie, whom Carrington so often resembled in political instinct and sometimes character, had served as Governor of New South Wales.

As British forces gathered in the Mediterranean to join in the disastrous assault on Suez, the Carrington family plus entourage sailed on 10 October in the P&O liner *Oronsay*. The ship went via the Cape of Good Hope, the Suez Canal being shut. They sailed in the proper style of the day, accompanied by three children, their governess Sally Shaw, a butler, a cook who had been Iona's mother's cook, and two maids. The voyage was an introduction to what was sometimes the most tedious appointment of Carrington's career, with so many afternoon receptions that he never again drank tea.

The weeks slipped slowly by. The boredom was compounded by the fact that, as incoming High Commissioner, it was necessary for the Carringtons to be very sociable with the other passengers, many if not most of whom appeared to be Australians returning from holidays in Europe. As Carrington remembered it, 'The crew rather unkindly called them the Returned Empties. Every evening we had to turn up dressed as the title of a book, or we played Housey-Housey. It was not a very enjoyable experience.' The ship was to take them to Sydney, but via Perth, Adelaide and Melbourne. At each port, the Carringtons disembarked to pay their respects to local dignitaries. Carrington was effectively presenting his credentials to each state. Perth and Adelaide were politely formal. When the *Oronsay* docked at Melbourne, the Carringtons were soon introduced to the full-blast formalities of Australian life. The general image of Australia as an easygoing society occasionally flirting with republicanism was not one which greeted the Carringtons. They arrived in time for the Melbourne Cup – the most important day in the Melbourne social calendar – and the Carringtons had been told that Melbourne was much more formal than Perth and Adelaide put together.

We got the trunks out of the hold, dressed ourselves in morning coats and elegant hats and set off for Flemington Racecourse. In the Royal Box, a figure in grey morning coat greeted us. I naturally assumed he was the Governor and bowed my head. It turned out that he was the most unpopular man in Melbourne, the Governor's military secretary, Colonel Spragget. Not that the Governor, Sir Dallas Brooks was very popular either. He had the unpardonable habit of asking for presents if he opened anything. When he left, the Melbourne City Council asked what he would like as a farewell gift. 'A Rolls-Royce', he replied. I'm sorry to say, he got it.

Carrington had been appointed partly because the then Australian Prime Minister, Robert Menzies, wanted a safe pair of political hands in the British High Commission. Menzies, known as Pig-Iron Bob, never let his grasp slip on his Scottish ancestry. To him his Scottishness was as important as his Australian identity. So here was a Prime Minister who, although fiercely Australian, was determined that the destiny of his country should be surely linked to the Crown. While many in Australia followed Menzies' credo, at least enough to keep voting him in, a far less traditional view

came from Menzies' External Affairs Minister Dick Casey, who
had been at school with Carrington's father and whose wife Maie,
before she married Casey, had been his father's first girlfriend. This
did not mean that Carrington and Casey always had everything in
common.

Casey was very English in appearance and manner. However,
appearances did not hide the fact that he did not believe that
Australia's future was in her past. London and the monarchy were
the past and should no longer be Australia's focus of political,
strategic and economic attention. In 1956 Casey was probably
more right than wrong. He believed that the whole nation had to
recognize that they lived along one arc of the Pacific Rim. To
Casey, Australians lived in Asia. This, remember, was in the late
1950s. Australians had fought with enormous distinction – Casey,
who won a DSO at Gallipoli, among them – and sometimes with
terrible consequences in two World Wars. The battle in and for
Europe was easily understood, but it was not the major threat to
Australia; men like Casey took their strategic values from recent
history. The Australians had been physically threatened not by
Nazism, but by the Japanese. There had been a period when first
Hong Kong and then Singapore had fallen; at that time the British
were seen to have abandoned the war against Japan. It was the
Americans who had dominated that war, thus lessening and then
later removing the Japanese threat to the Australians. Little wonder
that Casey saw Australia's future in Asia, alongside eventually
powerful Japan and most of all America. Here was a contrast with
Menzies. Menzies recognized the importance of the Pacific in strategic, military, political and commercial terms. But he was not
willing to jeopardize the traditional ties with the United Kingdom.
Holding such clear views, Casey might be expected to be the caricature of the modern Australian while Menzies could be a late
nineteenth-century Anglo-Australian. Yet this was not the case.
Casey (much to Menzies' annoyance) was precise, correct in his
style and very much the Foreign Service officer and Crown servant,
whereas Menzies was a barn-stormer and carried all before him
with a sometimes brutal charisma. Most damning of all, according

to Casey, was that Menzies, who had once said that he was British to his boot-straps, was never critical enough of the constitutional and economic laces that tied London and Canberra.

Carrington was not Governor General, but High Commissioner. In theory, he was just another member of the diplomatic community. Yet because of the sensitivity of the Anglo-Australian relationship, the job required more than general diplomacy. He knew that much of the work was ceremonial and even in the late 1950s a posting of no obvious powers. He set himself a timetable to meet everybody he could who knew anything about Australia before his departure from England.

He talked to bankers, diplomats and to some of the few experts in the Pacific strategic tapestry. In 1956 Britain still had a considerable presence east of Suez and the region was not taken lightly by those who briefed Carrington. On 4 October 1956 Carrington went to see the Prime Minister – his final call before setting sail for Australia. He really did believe that Anthony Eden would give him his views of the main personalities he was about to deal with on behalf of the British government, and of the Prime Minister's hopes for the years that Carrington would be in Canberra. In the event Australia might not have existed. Eden was vague. It was as if neither Carrington nor Australia mattered to him. At that point in 1956, they did not.[1]

Anthony Eden was a sick man who was totally obsessed with Suez and particularly the Egyptian leader Abdel Gamal Nasser. Seemingly, every waking moment of the Prime Minister was spent thinking how to react against Nasser and how to cling to the Suez Canal. Eden's allies in this were the French and the Israelis – but few of his own military advisers. The French had a similar agenda to the British. The Israelis' sense of self-interest (the state of Israel was only nine years old) recognized the importance of maintaining British and French influence in the region. Here, then, was the last throw of Britain's colonial dice. To be defeated by Nasser

---

1 See Richard Thorpe, *Eden: The Life and Times of Anthony Eden, First Earl of Avon, 1897–1977*, London: Chatto & Windus, 2003.

would be the end of Britain's ability to militarily and imperially exert its foreign policy. That imperial authority was about to crumble with Eden's decision to invade the Suez Canal Zone. Little wonder he was distracted when Carrington went to see him in Downing Street. The High Commissioner designate did not fully engage the attention of his Prime Minister. At least he would be in a position to explain his government's views soon after arriving in Australia and he knew more than most because, as he observed later, 'Suez was about to erupt, not something that surprised me very much, since while I was at the Ministry of Defence, half the department was involved preparing for it.'

Nineteen fifty-six might not have been a watershed in postwar British history, but it was the year in which so many signposts were erected pointing to the social revolution that was about to occur and that would be known as The Sixties. This was the year when the phrase Angry Young Men appeared, from the play *Look Back in Anger* which had been staged at the Royal Court Theatre. Its author, John Osborne, and other writers like Colin Wilson were indeed the angry young men of British letters, suggesting that it was time to not simply forget but kick away the nostrums and fancies of what they saw as a complacent, unquestioning society. Certainly an old order had slipped away. The obituary list of 1956 included such figures of an earlier age as Sir Max Beerbohm, C. B. Fry, A. A. Milne and H. L. Mencken. Within a few months, in March 1957, Belgium, France, Italy, Luxembourg, the Netherlands and West Germany would sign the Treaty of Rome, to give birth to what was then known as the Common Market. Britain would not take part in that ceremony. This then was some of the social and political background as Carrington – at the age of thirty-seven the youngest High Commissioner ever to be appointed to Australia – his wife Iona and their children Alexandra, Virginia and Rupert plus a domestic entourage sailed for the southern hemisphere.

The land to which they went had a reputation for being quite unsophisticated. It was a place that, in spite of its irreverence, maintained many social traditions and values that would be soon lost from British homes. There was certainly some justification in the image of an outback dressed in wide-brimmed and cork-decorated hats; of floral frocks in Melbourne, especially on race day, and sherry kept in bottles in refrigerators rather than decanted in sitting rooms. It was a very good place to send an aristocrat. Carrington was sailing off to the sort of posting that people might expect towards the end of a long and usually modestly distinguished career. The Statute of Westminster defined the working relationship between the self-governing Dominions and the government at Westminster. This fundamentally meant that although Australia had the union flag in the corner of her own banner, she decided and determined all her own policies from local by-laws to international treaties. Carrington, as High Commissioner, was the Queen's representative, which reminded everyone that Australia still had some allegiance to the British Crown. But even in 1956, few defined the country in colonial terms. Australia was seen as a land of great opportunity in perhaps the same way as the Irish had seen America. The Carringtons immediately discovered this when two of the staff they had taken with them from England resigned within two weeks of arriving in Australia and went off to much better-paid jobs.

On the day the Carringtons arrived in Melbourne, 31 October, the RAF bombed the outskirts of Cairo and the Suez Canal Zone. Airborne troops from 16 Parachute Brigade landed around Port Said, the northern part of the canal, as marines went ashore from the Mediterranean squadron. In Moscow, Nikita Khrushchev, the Soviet leader, was at his belligerent best, and on 5 November he gave the order to send Soviet tanks into Budapest to put down the Hungarian uprising. The British and French were distracted and hardly in a moral position to criticize another invasion with any credibility. The United States, which had opposed Eden, was simply mad at everyone.

Carrington's background for the past twenty years had been soaked in the consequences of warfare and political differences, which meant that he was almost the ideal person to explain exactly what was going on and why in the Suez Canal Zone. He was also expected to give some up-to-date assessment of an increasingly belligerent Soviet Union. Khrushchev was yet to face the humili-ation of the Cuban missile crisis and was supremely confident – so much so that he had denounced the late Joseph Stalin in the spring of that year. As Carrington said in his memoirs, 'It didn't seem entirely impossible that my first task in Australia would be trying to negotiate Australia into the third world war.'[2]

In April 1957 Britain had carried out its own fission test in its development programme for a hydrogen bomb. The growth of the Campaign for Nuclear Disarmament (CND) was politically linked to the left wing of British politics. Indeed it was Labour that found itself caught between the moral dilemma of nuclear policy and the political and public debate that affected the future of its own party. Some leading members of the Labour Party believed that a cam-paign against the so-called H–Bomb could be manipulated into a vote winner. There were many in the Conservative government who feared that this view might be correct. It was not quite a par-allel with the political choices facing government and opposition in the 1990s during the complex debate over European member-ship and commitment, yet the membership of the nuclear weapons club and the commitment it involved once joined would be equally long-lived.

This debate had started long before Carrington had gone to Australia and, during his three years in Canberra, he of course saw the briefing papers from Whitehall. At the same time he did not have to go through the Whitehall and Westminster wringer that was grinding his former government colleagues during one of the most bitter of post-Second World War defence reforms.

When Carrington had left for Australia there had been an equally devastating fire-fight taking place in Whitehall and in his old ministry. In November 1956 Harold Macmillan, the former Defence Minister and now Chancellor of the Exchequer, tied in Britain's future defence policy with his own economic strategy. Antony Head was then the Defence Minister, the man whose thoughts Macmillan directed. Macmillan believed the economy

2 Lord Carrington, *Reflect on Things Past*, London: Collins, 1988, p. 116.

could not afford to maintain the then imperial and colonial commitments. Not quite three years after the death of Stalin, the British military task was beginning to centre on the containment of what was seen as the Soviet threat to Western Europe – the Warsaw Pact had been formed two years earlier. Moreover, the weakness of Britain's economy, which was threatened by oil shortages and declining gold reserves, meant there had to be belt tightening in all departments and therefore the usual round of defence cuts. With a cumbersome, mostly ineffectual and very expensive system of conscription (National Service) imposed on military thinking, Macmillan wanted reform of the military rather than straightforward reductions in spending. In this approach, Macmillan had an ally in Mountbatten, the First Sea Lord and later Chief of the Defence Staff, whom most found to be a curious mixture of sailor, grandee, politician and royal relative. This was the man who had at one point believed that the marriage of Prince Philip to Princess Elizabeth would mean that one day the throne would be occupied by the royal house of Mountbatten. Mountbatten was as keen on reform as Macmillan and made that clear in a memorandum left by Macmillan's bedside during a visit to Broadlands. That document outlined the case for the reform of the Defence Ministry, together with thoughts on future defence policy. Although it was not totally fulfilled until the 1980s, here was the basis of the next thirty years' defence policy.

Head was not to last very long. Macmillan had a very simple philosophy: Britain needed a nuclear deterrent which was big enough to show the Americans that it was a true ally and committed to the philosophy of using nuclear weapons to deter Soviet aggression. It followed on from this that the only way Britain could afford to provide this so-called independent deterrent was to get the Americans to pass on the military technology, or at least some of it. This, Macmillan believed, would go some way towards reducing the financial burden of the military budget. But, and this was the third aspect of his policy outlined to Head, the armed forces had to be cut and one of the ways that this could be done was to cash in a few of what he called 'insurance policies', for example making huge cuts in Britain's Middle East and Far East core structures. Carrington, in Australia, was beginning to view South-east Asia in particular from quite a different angle. He had seen the need for an Asian version of NATO – a collection of states with similar interests and the need to act together in order to deter the extension of Communism throughout the mainland and littoral states. Macmillan told Head to reform and to make the cuts. Head said he could not and resigned on a matter of principle. Macmillan was not impressed, and famously gave the job to Duncan Sandys. Sandys was not universally liked. He was often indifferent to people's feelings and single-minded unless distracted by an extremely convincing argument against his prejudice. The Chiefs of Staff intrigued and Mountbatten intrigued more than anyone.

And so the April 1957 Defence White Paper, the Sandys White Paper, was one of major cutbacks. National Service conscription was to go, which meant that within five years the size of the armed forces would be reduced by nearly 50 per cent. The Navy would lose its four battleships and transport command in the Royal Air Force was to be enhanced. The debate was protracted and there were threats and counter-threats of resignations from within the services for the rest of that year and into 1958. Here was the basis of Britain's defence policy for the foreseeable future. It might have been an easier one to get through Whitehall and Westminster if Duncan Sandys had been an agreeable character. He was not. Perhaps a Peter Carrington type of diplomacy would have made life easier for Macmillan. But Carrington was far away in Australia and too junior for such a task. Sandys in not even his most belligerent mood would have probably been quite contemptuous of Carrington's style, and whereas concessions by Sandys would have been regarded as tactical moves, any by Carrington would have been treated with derision by Sandys. Carrington, in a personal role, did not care for what Sandys was doing to the Defence departments. But who was Carrington in this debate? Now a far-off diplomat, yet one who had a wide network of influential friends who reflected his views at Westminster. Sandys was never fussed. Two decades later he poured some of his vitriol on Carrington when the latter negotiated the handover of white Rhodesia to its black leadership. Twenty-three years earlier, Carrington was arriving in Sydney certainly unaware that he would ever re-enter British politics in such a position as to be vulnerable to personal attacks.

The journey had been long and, even after the social faux pas at Melbourne races, mostly uneventful. There was seemingly more interest in the new High Commissioner's habit of bowing to the wrong people and in Lady Carrington's fashion sense, which was more Bond Street than Flinders Street. After Melbourne came Sydney, where they were greeted by the Governor of New South Wales, Sir John Northcott, at the Governor's mansion. It had once been the house of Carrington's Uncle Charlie, the third baron, when he was Governor of New South Wales between 1885 and 1890. On the veranda was carved the Carrington coat of arms. From Sydney they moved on to Canberra in the High Commission green Rolls-Royce, a vehicle that seemed as big as the ship that had brought them from England. Carrington detested the pomp that car suggested. The children most certainly disliked it and would hide on the floor in case their friends saw them in it. Carrington, with the help of his obliging chauffeur, Paddy Coyle, resolved the matter by driving the Rolls down from the Cape North Peninsula to Sydney along what were then some of the bumpiest roads in Australia. As Carrington remembers it, 'At Rockhampton the body became detached from the chassis and our mission was accomplished.' The Rolls and Canberra were, according to Carrington, both out of place in Australia.

In 1956 Canberra, a purpose-built capital, was home to about 35,000 people – by English standards a very small provincial town, which is what it was. Yet there were some elements of the enjoyable casualness of that sort of place no longer possible in Britain. For example, Carrington quite often rode on horseback to his office in the morning. Because Canberra was largely a community of bureaucrats and diplomats, it suffered from the constant round of lunches and dinners with the same people. It was quite likely that a diplomat would be sitting at lunch alongside someone with whom he would be sitting at dinner that same day. It could become an irksome existence. Virginia Carington was in the official car with her father going to one of the less formal lunches in the city when he reminded her of an important lesson in diplomatic party-ing. One could spill drink, drop a fork, even hiccup, but one must never, never allow conversation to lag. Silence at a formal luncheon or dinner table was unforgivable. It not only suggested an unsuc-cessful occasion, it also laid bare the fact that these luncheons and dinners were often a complete waste of time. With this lesson firmly in her mind, the then ten-year-old Virginia spotted the deliberate mistake at lunch that day – a lull in the conversation. So she piped up: 'Shall I tell you who Daddy hates most in Canberra?' Young Virginia at that point quickly learned another diplomatic lesson. If you get it wrong, someone is likely to kick you under the table.

There was a great distinction between the role of the Governor General and the position of the High Commissioner in the late 1950s. Each territory or state had its own governor. Therefore the Governor General was something of a commander-in-chief figure. He (it was, until Quentin Bryce's appointment in 2008, never a woman) was the monarch's representative. The High Commis-sioner had no powers whatsoever; he was nothing more than any other ambassador in the capital, hence the need for lots of bowing and curtsying to state governors and to the Governor General. The real power in the land was, of course, the Prime Minister.

In 1956 there was an interesting juxtaposition of political styles. The Governor General was an Australian, Field Marshal Sir William Slim, or Bill Slim as he was generally known. Slim had a conspicuous reputation as a celebrated soldier and an abrasive character. The two easily go together and, in Slim's case, reflected the fact that he was a very honest and fearless individual. Slim was appointed Governor General in 1953, partly because of his reputation during the Second World War, and for the way in which he had understood, during that conflict and the period after, the special position of the Australians in the region. When Carrington arrived in 1956 the Australians had got used to Slim and rather admired him, although Carrington's assessment was that the say-what-you-mean nature of many leading Australians who had dealings with Slim had been somewhat bruised during those three years. It was Carrington's belief that although Slim and Menzies quite liked each other as individuals, each found the other's political and diplomatic style exasperating.

The relationship between Carrington and Slim was warm. However, the protocol of the Governor General's position could not be compromised. Slim could not be seen to be favouring Carrington. Equally, there were particular interests, which started in London, that concerned them both. Consequently, Carrington found himself having to make a number of unofficial calls, usually via a side door, to discuss these matters. It was all a very sharp learning curve for the new High Commissioner.

Given his inexperience, his personal feelings, the strong views and advice of the Governor General and, most importantly, the contradictory views of Menzies and Casey, it might easily be imagined how difficult Carrington found his first official days in Australia, where the diplomatic and political topic had to be the British action in the Suez Canal Zone. Carrington had his instructions. The British government's position was very simple: Nasser had wrongly taken over the Suez Canal, thus usurping Britain's position in the region and compromising stability – or what there was of it – in an area which had increasingly obvious dangers. Britain could, and did, list the ways in which Nasser inspired unrest among the peoples of the region, and the cult of Nasserism was well established and growing. Apart from regional instability being bad for pan-Arabic relationships, there were two overriding interests for Britain and of course France: unfettered access through the Suez Canal, and oil. The two went together. Middle East oil was essential for European survival. Apart from being the conduit from Europe to the Far East and Australasia, the Canal was the essential waterway through which oil was transported. Whoever controlled the Canal could, if not control the flow of oil, then influence its price. The third aspect of the British government's case was that Nasser's influence and actions represented a direct threat to

Britain's concept of its position in the world. Eden certainly seemed to think that Nasser was effectively challenging Britain's political, economic and military status. Matters were hardly eased with the West's well-founded suspicion that Egypt was becoming, or had already become, a client state of the Soviet Union.

This position was so open to criticism that even though it had a strong ally in France, Britain's foreign policy on the Middle East was anything but well supported. Eden, with a reputation of having been a fine Foreign Secretary, insisted on policies towards Nasser that were hard to sustain outside the Cabinet he ruled. It was nevertheless Carrington's task to represent his government's views. As someone irreverently said, the task of an envoy is to lie abroad for the good of his country.

Carrington had a difficult hand to play. He accepted all the arguments, or at least their general thrust that Nasser was bad for the region. What he did not agree with was his own government's military action. Yet he had to 'sell' that Anglo-French adventure. Moreover, his Prime Minister, Eden, had compared Nasser with Hitler. Carrington could not do that. Nothing in Nasser's actions suggested that he was going to war to support his pan-Arabic vision, nor did he appear to have any intention of allowing his increasing reliance on the Soviet Union to influence his policies. Nasser understood the political as well as the economic souk. He struck no bargains that were not his alone. Here then was Carrington's dilemma: how to represent his government's view, for which he had but qualified sympathy, and worse still, his government's actions, for which he had no sympathy at all. If ever there was a case of a diplomat quickly learning his primary function to go out and lie for his country, this was it.

Carrington's conflict began with the politician with whom he was expected to have direct relations, the External Affairs Minister Dick Casey. Casey believed that the Anglo-French action was wrong morally and practically. He argued from the beginning that for it to succeed the British and French would need international support in general, and American backing in particular. They would get no general support and only anger from Washington.

What was the point in supporting Britain, since it was going to lose, and since South-east Asian leaders would not think much of Australia for having supported such an irresponsible cause.

While Casey could not agree with Britain's position as espoused by Carrington, he understood that Carrington's personal views did not necessarily accord with his government's. Also, Casey was in conflict with his own Prime Minister. Menzies was more pro-Eden than Carrington and was not simply being pro-British. He believed that the Canal had to be run as an international waterway to guarantee some sort of stability in the region and to keep open the commercial and strategic routes from Asia and Australasia to what Menzies regarded as the centre of the world – Northern Europe. Carrington recognized that as international opinion set more firmly against the Anglo-French position, Menzies' instinct was to be even more supportive of Britain. Carrington's note to himself was that Menzies' view of the whole Suez operation and Australia's response was determined not by strategic, economic or political thinking but by instinct. Carrington thus found himself reporting back to London a conflict between the Australian foreign ministry and the Prime Minister's office.

However, there was agreement that America's opposition to Eden's decision to attack Egypt had meant from the outset that the invasion, even if militarily successful, could not have a lasting political and diplomatic future. Carrington had little idea of his political future in 1956, but he had already formed the opinion that the United States did everything on its own terms. The so-called Special Relationship did not even translate into American English. Seventeen years later he would be reminded of this thought during a flaming row with the Americans, once again over Egypt. Against Carrington then, in 1973, would be, among others, Donald Rumsfeld, who even in those days had abrasive views of Old Europe.

Carrington's stance over Suez in 1956 was even further troubled because when asked what Britain's ambition was, however he represented it, he knew there was only one real thought in Eden's mind: to get rid of Nasser. To Eden that was all that mattered;

everything would fall into place once the evil Nasser was overthrown. In later years Carrington was to reflect that perhaps this
single-minded strategic thinking, based on an obsession with an
individual, was not confined to the 1950s and Eden. The United
States was to spend more than forty years obsessed with the idea
that Fidel Castro should be overthrown. Successive British governments were convinced that the evil of the Balkans and the Middle
East would be resolved if only Serbia's President Milosevic and
Saddam Hussein of Iraq were overthrown. That Britain and America could hurl billions of dollars' worth of their most sophisticated
weaponry in support of their obsessions reminded Carrington that
Eden had by no means exclusive rights to strategic paranoia.
Throughout this time nothing had changed Carrington's mind
that the United Kingdom needed the support and understanding
of its former colonies and possessions. As the *Sydney Morning Herald*'s London correspondent observed, 'the appointment of a man
of Lord Carrington's calibre shows the importance being attached
here [in London] to Australia'.

One of the ways in which Carrington brought about better
understanding was through quiet recommendations that wherever
possible British Cabinet ministers were to go to Australia to see
for themselves what was going on. Both the Queen Mother and
Princess Alexandra went south and, not unexpectedly, they both
presented a more relaxed, almost informal, picture of royalty,
which at the time was quite important from Britain's point of
view.

Carrington's sense, even in the 1950s, was that the public and
international perception of royalty and its constitutional function
was changing, or should be. Therefore, and especially in Australasia,
he recommended that both the government in London and Buckingham Palace needed to be encouraged to present royalty in a far
more informal way. He accepted that instinct and protocol could
not be abandoned, yet they might be tempered, and he firmly
believed that although perceptions often defy logic, Australians still
saw royalty as reflecting the general character and attitude of all the
British. His recommendation was that royal visits to Australia

should be more informal and 'more and more a matter of course'. During a television interview in Australia, Carrington was outspoken, defying the then formal and reserved approach of Whitehall. In his view, 'the more members of the royal family who visit Australia the better it is'. Equally he made it clear to the Foreign Office that the Australian High Commission in London was a backward-thinking legation. The High Commission was not properly doing all it could towards breaking down the average Englishman's ignorance of Australia. It was this sort of thought process that Carrington, still a relatively inexperienced High Commissioner, was determined to push to London and the Australian foreign ministry.

Carrington had a great opportunity to 'rebrand' Britain with a visit by Princess Alexandra, who, in the late 1950s, was one of the more popular members of the royal family. Making her first official visit to Australia, Alexandra was so well received that the far from obsequious Australian press corps gave her red roses at the end of her fourteen-day tour. The Australian press called her 'a smasher' and, at a farewell dance given for her by Governor General Slim, Alexandra apparently danced more than one young Australian off his feet well into the early hours of the morning.

The most important visitor for the long-term view of the Australian government – and probably Britain's too – was Harold Macmillan, who was on a Commonwealth tour. Macmillan had become Prime Minister when Eden could no longer carry on. He arrived at the start of 1958, election year in Australia. Both governments saw a need to build a different form of relationship. The Commonwealth was changing, colonies were getting independence, Australia was the senior partner in the Old Commonwealth. More immediately, Macmillan's old wartime friend Robert Menzies was determined to milk the British PM's trip for all it was politically worth. Macmillan arrived on 28 January 1958 and did not leave until 11 February. In those days tours tended not to be whistle-stop and, after all, apart from Canberra, the Macmillans (his wife Dorothy was with him) had to visit New South Wales, Queensland, Victoria and Tasmania. There were civic receptions, dinners with administrators, exhibitions of lifesaving displays to applaud, sugar-growing techniques in Nambour to look interested over, Dandenong industrial developments to view, hands to be shaken at the Nunawading migrant hostel and lunches with Victorian joint empire societies, wavings to be done at the Hobart Regatta and, for Dorothy Macmillan, the inevitable meetings with 'women's page' journalists. Quite an itinerary and quite an opportunity for Lord Carrington to show off his Prime Minister and for Menzies to pick up any advantages for his election that might be going. Neither had an easy task. Macmillan was not a natural star performer and, at first sight, not easily a man that could bring many votes to the Menzies campaign. Outwardly, and perhaps inwardly, Macmillan represented everything that most old Australians were impatient with and the atmosphere from which many new Australians had escaped Europe – including the United Kingdom. In short, he was not the sort of person to receive bouquets of any sort from the Australian media.

The trip did not get off to the best of starts. New Zealand was first on Macmillan's itinerary and his aircraft made a refuelling stop in Queensland on the way. It was only a staging, and Macmillan, who had taken a sleeping draught, slept through the stopover. The problem was that he was a Prime Minister and therefore an Australian minister was sent to attend him. There was not much attending to do, as Macmillan remained fast asleep. As far as the Australian press was concerned, the pommy PM had snubbed a good Australian. Carrington himself was not getting the best press at that time. His official Rolls-Royce had been smashed up, which he did not mind because he did not like it. The press loved the story, especially when news leaked out that two of his staff had walked out. Carrington's belief was that they had come with him as a way of getting to Australia without paying and never had any intention of remaining in his employ. He had been at a conference in Singapore with Macmillan, who was then on his way to New Zealand. He had no idea that there was a refuelling stop in the middle of the night in Australia.

Iona and I, who arrived back from the conference that evening, were greeted with banner headlines 'British Prime Minister Snubs Australian Minister' and the news that the chauffeur had smashed the Rolls which was being prepared for Macmillan's visit, and on top of that, a letter announcing that two of the servants had walked out.

The snub incident was rather bad management. It would have been perfectly easy, as well as truthful, for a member of his staff to say that he was ill and had taken a sleeping pill, but in spite of having warned them endlessly about the horrors of the Australian press they did not take the elementary precaution.[3]

Carrington had done his best, but Macmillan was not entirely in tune with the new Australia. For example, he had a disconcerting habit of greeting people with 'Hello there, I bring you greetings from the old country.' There was, Carrington thought, a sense that he was either under the impression that he had arrived on Mars, or his understanding of what Australians were about in the 1950s was somewhat wanting. Macmillan tried. In fact, he believed that if he were a young man he would have gone to Australia, even though the Australians were 'rather tiresome people'.[4] Macmillan, not unnaturally, appeared to feel uncomfortable in Australia and with the Australians. There were times when he had to perform for the press photographers in the standard way of all visiting dignitaries. This usually meant doing something very Australian. Photographs of him with a koala showed that he was not quite certain how he should behave, and he managed to give the impression that the animal had much in common with a leaking baby.[5]

Carrington did what he could to relax the Prime Minister. Macmillan was now sixty-four – he celebrated his birthday, 10 February, on the island of Tasmania. He travelled with the trappings of what he really was, an Edwardian aristocrat. Carrington, at thirty-eight and an hereditary peer, was not inhibited by his

3 Carrington notes, 24 February 1958, private papers, Bledlow.
4 Alistair Horne, *Macmillan, 1957–1986*, London: Macmillan, 1989, p. 86.
5 Ibid.

background, and in the year that he had been High Commissioner he had taken to the Australians and they to him. Carrington's enthusiasm began to work through to the Edwardian gentleman, yet another advantage of an enforced stay. Macmillan began to relax, particularly in a Melbourne club.

During the tour I was determined that the Prime Minister was going to meet not only the politicians and Lords Mayor et al. but also some of the more important business men and others who really made Australia go round. I therefore gave him dinner both in Sydney and in Melbourne in the leading clubs there. Macmillan was very fond of clubs. At the Melbourne Club, which is a mixture between the Turf and the Carlton – only very much more so – he was delighted with his dinner. Unfortunately we had to go to a Civic Reception of fifteen hundred people in the Town Hall and it was due to start at 9.30pm. At 9.15 I edged up to him and said 'I really think we ought to go now'. 'Nonsense!' he said, pouring himself out another glass of brandy. Five minutes later I tried again. 'Go and tell the Lord Mayor I'm drunk,' he said angrily. By then I was getting pretty desperate so I said to Bob Menzies, who was dining with me, 'We've got to do something'. Meaning he had to do something. He went and touched him on the shoulder and said, 'I'm going to the Town Hall now and expect you to be there in three minutes' and disappeared. Greatly fearing I left him three minutes and tried again. This time he got to his feet, wagging his head angrily, 'Very well, I'll go, but Churchill wouldn't.'[6]

By the end of his Australian visit, Macmillan had become so popular that his farewell reception was almost heroic. Again, Carrington would never have claimed credit for Macmillan's transformation but the general opinion was that the visit gave him a new kind of confidence. In many ways he was experiencing the fresh perspective that Carrington had himself gained in Australia. The British political scene was often stifling, and the world did look quite different when seen from the southern hemisphere; so

6 Carrington notes, 1958.

did the role of individual political leaders. Macmillan was going back to a cold, gloomy and disrupted Britain with confrontations between government and dock and transport unions plus the ignominy of seeing a Conservative candidate beaten into third place in the Rochdale by-election.

Carrington had the luxury of waving off his Prime Minister, tucking his white handkerchief back into his top pocket and pressing on with yet another visitor.

No sooner had he [Macmillan] disappeared than the Queen Mother arrived. This has caused the Australians to lose their heads completely. The Secretary of the Cabinet and the Head of the PM's Department has been struck off from all duties for six months in order to arrange her three weeks tour. Practically every road in Australia which she intends to drive down has already been shut and the precautions taken are such that the average citizen of UK extraction is infuriated. Nevertheless, she has received such a terrific welcome and her visit will do so much good one cannot complain. We had the alarming experience of having her to dinner in my house. Ostensibly this dinner was given by all the Commonwealth High Commissioners but food, the servants, the flowers and all the trouble were provided and taken by us. It passed off fairly well, except that Keith, the other half of Prowse [Keith and Prowse were Carrington's dogs], being a great Royalist, decided that he wanted to see her and escaping from the clutches of the children in their bedroom rushed into the dining room and sat underneath her skirts. The Queen Mother, I don't think, noticed but there was an ugly scene whilst the butler tried to remove him from this rather unusual position. Eventually he was got away but it was a nasty five minutes.

Carrington did not go to the Tower and had certainly learned that being High Commissioner was hardly a diplomatic sinecure. He saw it as an increasingly important job that had taught him a lot about foreign, particularly South-east Asian, politics and policy making. It was an experience that he would put to good use on his return to government and later in opposition.

This posting was very much a double-act. Iona Carrington was

as much a success as her husband. She had to go through all the
rounds of taking everything that was offered: coffee, lunch, tea,
cocktails, dinner and criticism. Back home in Buckinghamshire,
Iona Carrington had sat on the County Council's Children's Welfare Committee. That committee spent much of its time looking
after children who had been abandoned or were victims of family
poverty. In Australia she saw solutions to problems for children that
could never be applied in England. To her, Australia meant wide
open spaces. She saw that many Australian children could get to
beaches and did not have the same sense of being hemmed in by
the peculiar poverty suffered in England – in spite of the new welfare state and sometimes because of the simple fact of living in a
northern climate.

For both Carringtons, the Australian posting was to have long-
lasting effect. It was no sabbatical. On 10 October 1959, three years
to the day since they had sailed for Australia, the Carringtons
boarded the liner *Oranje* for home. It had been a successful posting
both from the Australian point of view and certainly from
London's. When he ended his tour, the *Melbourne Herald* described
the 'hon pom', as he became known, as the right man at the right
time.

He has proved there are times a layman can do a better job of top level
diplomacy, particularly in a robust field such as Australia, than a career
diplomat. He also proved that a young man can fill a key post of representation as well as an ageing senior. He captured from the outset the
free-wheeling, roving, inquisitive, sometimes blunt and occasionally
shrewdly indiscreet approach to Australia and Australians which has
always given the North American envoys a slight edge over most colleagues. For three years he has lived with vim the Australian way of life.
As one of the bright younger men of the Conservative Party knocking
on the door to high Cabinet Office he was seconded, rather than transferred, for a term in Australia. This has meant that his links with the
British Government and his channels into high places in Whitehall have
remained direct. Points of friction have been subtly oiled and centres of
misunderstanding have disappeared since he arrived.

Throughout his career, Carrington's admirers would say that he always appeared to know about the region and subjects and people that he had to deal with. It was said that he was quite a good Agriculture Minister, simply because well out of the public eye he had had to learn the business of agriculture though his own farming and the postwar County Committee system. He had gone as a very junior minister to the Ministry of Defence and although hardly exclusively so, as a professional soldier and because of his grasp of European history, he had quickly formed what turned out to be a far-seeing approach to the future of the North Atlantic Treaty Organization and Britain's role in it in economic, political and military terms. The facility to brief himself beyond headline issues stood Carrington well. Very quietly, Carrington got more than was obvious from his time in Australia. He had a very good tutor in Dick Casey and another in Bill Slim. Long before it was time for him to go, Carrington had understood the argument for developing relations with South-east Asia for the three corners of the international triangle of cooperation – economics, politics and defence. He agreed with Casey. The world did look quite different from Australia. It was possible to drive across Canberra without getting out of second gear, especially in the whispering High Commission Rolls-Royce. But in Canberra, in spite of the impression that someone had built a suburb but had never found a city to tack it on to, there was for Carrington the opportunity to understand that while Britain may have been shedding her colonial trappings, a quite different and more important future lay ahead for her in Asia. At the end of his time in Australia, Carrington could see the importance of the Pacific Rim, something that very many British politicians a generation or so later mistakenly believed was new thinking.

7. First Lord

The Carringtons sailed from Sydney at 4 p.m. on Saturday 10 October 1959. Four days earlier they had started on the final round of official goodbyes. Commonwealth Societies reception, calling on Lords Mayor, State Premiers, tea parties, even a Guinness and cheese party – quickly and apparently rightly followed by tea with the archbishop. There were more cocktail parties and dinners before the ship sailed. But High Commissioners in Australia do not get away that easily. On the Monday, the *Oranje* berthed at Melbourne and then on the Friday at Fremantle. More cocktails, more lunches and then at last, on 16 October, after morning tea with the Governor of Western Australia, they finally put to sea heading for Jakarta and Singapore. They had planned to relax and enjoy a quiet holiday together: sightseeing in Singapore, then off to Bangkok, across to Kuala Lumpur, back down to Singapore, and almost a month later boarding the P&O liner *Chusan* and back to England. It all sounded rather civilized and too good to be true. Sadly, it was too good to be true.

Carrington may well have found a refreshing view of the world in the southern hemisphere. He may have thought it reasonable to take a holiday in the sun before returning to a freezing English winter. But the thermometer was not dropping in Westminster as far as Macmillan was concerned. If Carrington had packed his plumes he could jolly well unpack his pinstripes. The ship had not even reached Jakarta when the captain told Carrington that he had a coded signal for him: 'Will you become First Lord of the Admiralty QUERY Come straight home'.

Carrington had no choice but to abandon Iona in Singapore (she did come home at leisure aboard the *Chusan*) and flew straight to London. He was met there by his new private secretary Patrick Nairne, one of the brighter civil servants in Whitehall. Two years younger than Carrington, Nairne was to form a fascinating partnership with the new First Lord and would in the early 1970s become Deputy Under-Secretary at Defence when Carrington was Secretary of State.[1]

The Carringtons were immediately faced with the prospect of living in the very grand Admiralty House with its four drawing rooms, three dining rooms and floors of bedrooms. It sounded all very well until they realized that they were expected to provide their own staff to run it without any help from government money to do so. It was all very different in the late 1950s and early '60s from today. Relief came in the form of a stern survey report on 10 Downing Street. It appeared ready to fall down. Macmillan preferred Admiralty House and so moved in while the Carringtons moved into a flat over Admiralty Arch, complete with view of the Palace and the sound of grating gears (not all cars then had synchromesh gear boxes) coming through the floorboards from the traffic entering and leaving Trafalgar Square. Mountbatten would take great delight in telling the Carringtons that their drawing room had been his night nursery when his late father – Prince Louis of Battenberg – was First Sea Lord.

Carrington was not perhaps a strange choice as First Lord, but it was all very new to him. He knew about soldiering but next to nothing about the Navy and its customs – even their language seemed foreign. It was a big job in those days. The Royal Navy still had the second biggest fleet in the world. He was also aware that he was entering a service of very odd traditions and treasures, among them broken furniture. The First Lord's room overlooked Horse Guards Parade. In one corner was a breakfront bookcase with a split panel. Carrington suggested that it might be repaired. The senior civil servant looked horrified. 'Mr Churchill kicked that in when he was in a temper.' He was then introduced to the Admiralty Board Room in which the table has a section cut out

1 Nairne eventually became Permanent Under-Secretary at the Department of Health and Social Security, Master of St Catherine's College, Oxford, and Chancellor of Essex University, where he gave Carrington an Honorary Degree.

to accommodate the considerable stomach of a previous Civil Lord. Carrington was also struck by the large chart of the English Channel on one wall with an arrow depicting the direction of the wind from a weathervane on the Admiralty roof; this was to alert their Lordships to the danger of a French invasion.

The new First Lord was somewhat alarmed when he met his Permanent Secretary, Sir John Laing. Laing, having been in the Admiralty for forty years, knew his way about like no one else and, as Carrington soon found out, was in a position to frustrate almost anything that happened – and did.

Carrington remarked to the author: 'He told me once that he had a loose floorboard in his room and when he got a particularly difficult file, to which he didn't know the answer, he buried it under the floor. "It made very little difference," he said, "and nobody seemed to notice. These things usually solve themselves."'

One issue that would not resolve itself was the future of the Royal Navy's carrier fleet. Carrington was thrown in at the deep end of this inter-service shark pool. There were only three vessels, but at stake was the very principle of operating carriers and there-fore the Fleet Air Arm, destroyer, frigate and submarine escorts and Britain's so-called power projection capability. Some lofty reputa-tions were also on the line, including that of one man who cared more about reputation than any other in Whitehall – Lord Mountbatten.

Carrington had mixed feelings about Mountbatten, as he wrote to me late in his life:

He was in many ways a most extraordinary man: brave, intelligent, per-sistent and, until he became First Sea Lord, the Navy had done very poorly compared with the other two Services. His predecessors, though splendid in war, were not very good Whitehall warriors. Dickie was. He was, however, impossibly vain, always referred to his royal connections, loved medals and dressing up and was cordially detested by a large number of his brother officers. Caspar John [the brother of the artist Augustus John and who succeeded Mountbatten as First Sea Lord in Carrington's time], for example, never referred to him as 'Dickie' or

'Mountbatten' but always as 'That bloody fellow Burma'. Many years later, when I was Secretary of Defence I was carrying the Cap of Maintenance at the Opening of Parliament. Alongside Dickie, who was carrying the Sword of State, he had a heart attack as he arrived in the Chamber of the House of Lords. He was really suffering, had to hand over the Sword and leant against the wall, recovering. At the end of the Ceremony, he picked up the Sword and walked back along the Royal Gallery and we stood opposite each other as the Queen went into the Robing Chamber. When the doors closed behind her, he came over to me, pea-green and sweating and said to me 'Now look here, Peter, we've really got to get these aircraft carriers tied up'. A brave man, but flawed.

Here was the most important defence issue of the day. The Royal Navy wanted to replace its three ageing aircraft carriers but the RAF was lobbying for the money to be spent on aircraft that would be based across the world on colonial islands. It was a daft Island Strategy because the islands would be independent within a decade or so. However, so strong was the debate and so devious and determined the lobbying (as Mountbatten had shown) that, as Carrington remarked to me, 'No admiral went to bed unless he had looked underneath to see if an air marshal was hiding under it. No air marshal went into any room without looking behind the door to see if an admiral were concealed.'

Carrington's opposite number at the Air Ministry was Hugh Fraser as Secretary for Air. Carrington believed Fraser daily became 'more anxious and worried and paranoid. It was all pretty disagreeable, since tempers ran high.' The irony of course was that although the Navy in theory won the day and the Cabinet agreed to build three big carriers, in the end they were never built because the Treasury, having let the debate rumble on, had never intended to give the Navy any money to build them. Such was the way of defence strategy even when blessed with such strong-willed advocates as Mountbatten and quiet diplomats as Carrington. Fraser could really have spared himself the trouble.

Important ships forever cause aggravation to ministers and chiefs of staff because they are enormously expensive to build, usually altered during design and construction processes and, unless there is a conflict, rarely appear to do anything much that justifies their size and cost. At least aircraft carriers look menacing because of their size and aircraft payload. Carrington did battle over the aged carriers in his fleet and with that other dubious investment, the Royal Yacht. He had not long been in the Admiralty when the bills started to arrive for *Britannia*'s refurbishment – the Navy call it refit. The cost was estimated as £2 million and rising – a considerable sum at a time when, for example, the average wage was £700 a year. The editor of the *Sunday Express*, John Gordon, whom Carrington regarded as a 'noisy Republican', attacked not the Admiralty, but the Queen over the extravagance of expecting the taxpayer to spend such a large sum on her yacht. Other papers followed his argument. Carrington had hoped it would all blow over, until a call from Sir Michael Adeane, the then Private Secretary to the Queen, informed him that the monarch would like to see him at Buckingham Palace at six-thirty that very evening. That meeting remained very clear to Carrington for the rest of his days, as a letter to the author revealed:

I realized that I was not going to get the Garter and set off full of foreboding. At the stroke of 6.30pm, the door opened and I was told to come in. I was not asked to sit down. The Queen said to me, 'I hear the Royal Yacht is being re-fitted for £2 million – why?'

I said, 'Oh your Majesty, the yacht was very badly built after the war and we really can't have the possibility of her breaking down with Your Majesty on board.'

The Queen was not amused and made it clear.

Meanwhile, in Australia there was much speculation that Carrington might return, to succeed Bill Slim, the retiring Governor General. The Macmillan visit had been a huge success and Carrington had done rather well from it. The reports of the royal tours had been equally favourable. To many in Australian politics and in the media, the Carringtons would have made a good First

Family. He admitted to having been flattered, but not persuaded. Carrington had always made it clear that his three-year tour in Australia was an honour but simply a secondment from British politics. Macmillan had decided that Carrington would not return to London simply to hang around the House of Lords waiting for a sinecure – political or otherwise.

In October 1959 Macmillan had called a General Election. The government had been in power since the spring of 1955 and could have stayed on until 1960, but that would have been imprudent, especially as the Labour Party was in some disarray, and anyway Macmillan's personal popularity was extraordinarily high. Supermac, as the cartoonists were calling him, could hardly fail to persuade the electorate that it was worth keeping him and his colleagues. Moreover, Macmillan raised a convincingly quizzical eyebrow to the much publicized but widely ignored 'tell the people' tour of the constituencies by the Labour leader Hugh Gaitskell. Macmillan had other advantages. Television would for the first time play a crucial role in the election and Macmillan appeared to have become something of a television personality. He also had a very good speechwriter in George Christ. The Tories increased their lead over Labour from the 1955 General Election to 107 seats. It was the first time that a British political party had won three elections in a row with an increased majority each time. That election was Macmillan's election. He needed now to get down to the harder task of building a new government. It was to this administration that Carrington was called, to take up what was then a post of Cabinet rank. As Macmillan said of Carrington, he was

The last of the Whigs, full of common sense, a sense of history, and very good nerves ... any Government of the nineteenth century would have been full of Carringtons – always able to bugger off home to his estate if Parliament no longer wanted him.[2]

2 Quoted by Alistair Horne, *Macmillan, 1957–1986*, London: Macmillan, 1989, p. 158.

There were times when Carrington's life appeared like a script for a television drama: the history of a family with all its ups and downs and passions – a saga of snubbed northern bankers to royal favourites in two generations; family feuds and tragedies; and then the sixth baron, Peter Carrington, even more publicly known than the famous Uncle Charlie. What is often forgotten is that Carrington went from ministry to ministry on the back of unfortunate events. Yet, in spite of the fact that those incidents involved him, he managed to come out for most people as a hero. As a quite knowledgeable and not overtly ambitious junior Agriculture Minister, he was brought close to ending his political career when it had barely begun. At the first possible moment afterwards he was shuffled into the relative safety of the Defence Ministry, at the time an establishment of considerable responsibility but little power. Now, in the late autumn of 1959, Carrington was about to become First Lord of the Admiralty, the civilian head of the Royal Navy[3] with a salary of £5,000 a year – about seven times the average wage at the time. He was to earn it, although some would eventually say he did not. He would wear the yachting livery designed by his hero and the most famous twentieth-century First Lord, Winston Churchill. Churchill carried the office with some certainty but not a little controversy. Carrington was to do the same and was to yet again find himself forced into writing his ministerial resignation. This time, as far as the public was concerned, the matter was somewhat more serious than Crichel Down.

Carrington went back to the Admiralty at a time of important rethinking in transatlantic and East–West relations. In October 1957, while Carrington was just a third of his way through his tenure in the High Commission in Australia, the Soviet Union had launched the first artificial satellite, *Sputnik 1*. This had generated much activity in departments of state in the major NATO capitals. The long-range rocketry made America vulnerable. Continental Europe had always been vulnerable. The United States now understood more clearly what was meant by having a constant frontline,

---

3 The Royal Navy's senior admiral is First Sea Lord and Chief of Naval Staff.

even in peacetime. Now, its own frontline was a trip-wire which zigzagged from the Kola inlet to the Black Sea and in the east just a few miles across the Bering Sea from North America. The United States therefore had a greater stake in military thinking, although this was not always understood in the American capital, especially in the US Congress. The timing therefore of the damaged relationship between the United Kingdom and the United States over Eden's Suez adventure was more important than many understood at the time.

The importance of the international dimension to Britain's defence policy was also undergoing change. From a global responsibility based on her colonial possessions, the United Kingdom was now going to spend far more time and effort redistributing a limited military budget on supporting the deterrence concept in East–West relations. Here was an important aspect of Carrington's position within the ministry. Although he was First Lord, he was also the government minister in the Lords, and therefore obliged to speak on a much wider aspect of defence than his Number One Dress uniform suggested.

When Carrington got up to speak for the first time as First Lord in November 1959, he addressed the Upper House not on the Royal Navy but on the increasingly vexed subject of the British nuclear deterrent. He was an excellent champion of the nuclear deterrent case. He had taken part in a war which had come to its conclusion with the use of atomic bombs. More important had been the effect on him of the news in 1952 that the United States had developed and tested the hydrogen bomb. Carrington had accepted the truism that from that moment in 1952, the genie could not be returned to its bottle. Indeed, one of his tasks as a junior Defence Minister in Churchill's government was to explain the White Paper on the defence estimates. Four years earlier in 1955, the Defence White Paper rehearsed the simple concept that nuclear weapons were the only feasible deterrent against increasing Soviet ambitions. Carrington's view then was that everything should be done to make the leaders in the Kremlin understand that Britain believed in as well as supported the doctrine of retaliation.

There was no half-way house in this belief. The nuclear deterrent hypothesis was either ludicrous or sophisticated. No one really knew which notion was true and few dared think what might happen if the so-called nuclear capability extended beyond the original and rather exclusive membership. By the time of Carrington's first defence debate speech in 1959, the major change was not so much in nuclear warhead development as in the means of delivering that warhead. Carrington had to convey this message to an interested but rightly suspicious House; it is easy to understand why there was an intellectual as well as a popular argument against the emerging British policy.

The British nuclear capability was first developed under the authority of the Labour government of Clement Attlee. Churchill, who followed Attlee, was determined that once the hydrogen bomb – an enormously more powerful system – had been created, Britain had to produce her own warheads. Because the United States did not trust any of its allies, the 1946 MacMahon Act (named after its sponsor, Senator Brian MacMahon of Connecticut) went through Congress in order to stop technology leaking from the United States into Europe. This was why Britain had to develop its own H-bomb. Carrington thought the American position on technology transfer reasonably understandable from the American point of view, but unhelpful when trying to argue for and strengthen the European nuclear deterrent. 'Deterrent' was a euphemism which the public by and large accepted. The Labour Party was famously split, which was hardly surprising considering its origins and social ambitions and, moreover, it was not yet a party likely to attract the middle classes of Britain. What people like Gaitskell (the Leader of the Opposition) and Macmillan did not yet know was what the British middle class thought about the nuclear debate.

Carrington returned from the Australian sunshine to a bitter wind blowing through the Admiralty. He believed that the department would give him great pleasure and the appointment made him immensely proud. This emotion was not simply an expression for his diary and speeches. To understand Carrington, it is necessary to accept that he was a man with a profound sense of what was right and wrong, someone who really did feel honour in the most junior task. If we understand his belief in honour, then we can better understand his emotion when he believed he had failed. A test of that honour would come in his new job. Once more he would be accused of incompetence and feel moved to offer his resignation.

Many of the issues Carrington faced had been explored when he was at the Ministry of Defence as a junior under Macmillan. Debate, both public and private, was demanding greater skills than simply being on top of a ministerial brief. As a later Defence Secretary, Labour's Fred Mulley, remarked to the author, shortly before the May 1979 General Election, 'Anyone who's not a fool can do that. To keep on top of the system, you need a bit extra.' Carrington did not follow too closely the reams of paper prepared by officials and compensated by having 'a bit extra'. He had started to show the sense of humour in negotiation and debate that was later to give him the reputation of being a person who could defuse an argument in that self-effacing way which Macmillan regarded as so typically Whiggish. For example, before Carrington went to Australia, during the 1955 debate on Britain's nuclear weapons capability within that year's White Paper on the defence estimates, many peers were concerned that Britain's so-called independence was far from guaranteed. Lord Jowitt, Labour leader in the Lords, had expressed most of the argument when he said that although the White Paper had set out that Britain had no option but to make a hydrogen bomb, as Carrington told peers, it was still almost impossible to go along with the concept that

we should use it only if the other side used it, for we should face the pressure of conventional weapons, visibly with the Russians advancing to channel ports . . . hydrogen bombs in Great Britain, whatever their source of manufacture, would never be used from this country without the consent of the Government of the day.[4]

4 Lord Carrington, notes for speech in the House of Lords, 17 March 1955, in Carrington papers, Bledlow.

This concept of 'no first use' was one which would hang over Britain's nuclear policy for the rest of the century, certainly during Carrington's political lifetime. Carrington successfully tempered the debate with the following observation to his fellow peers:

We have declared unequivocally where we stand and we must be prepared, whatever the consequences, to defend what we believe to be right. If David, in his fight with Goliath, had announced beforehand that he intended to stick to conventional weapons Goliath would have strolled over and annihilated him with one blow of his sword.[5]

The remark had the desired effect. The peers laughed. The tension in the debate was gone. The government won its motion and their Lordships were off to their dinners by 8.30 p.m. that evening. He did the same thing during the debate on National Service in July 1955.

Most people accepted that the conscription of young men needed to be abandoned. It soon would be, but in the meantime the debate was centring on those people who were avoiding the call-up. If a young man could have his conscription papers deferred until he was twenty-six, he did not have to go into the army. Another way of getting out of the call-up was to join the Merchant Navy. At that time, the British mercantile service employed some 148,000 men, almost a quarter of them in the catering departments – cooks, stewards and waiters. When Lord Glyn launched into a motion against the government for allowing people to avoid National Service by becoming sailors, it was Carrington who once more gave the light touch that demolished the opposition's argument and those who championed it in his own party.

I gathered from the terms of the motion that Lord Glyn was uneasy about the deferment of merchant seamen, in particular those who worked as waiters. The noble Lord has performed a satisfying and unfortunately

5 Ibid.

far too rare feat of putting down a motion and answering it himself. He has concluded that they also serve who stand and wait.[6]

Back in the government, in 1960, Carrington's sense of humour was not always so effective. Britain had to decide what to do about extending its nuclear weapons capability. The issue covered the so-called delivery system. The simplest way until the late 1950s was to put the warhead in a plane and if necessary carry it to Moscow, and drop it out. Rocketry development had made this simple system not exactly outdated, but certainly second-line. In 1958 the Americans had agreed that Britain should be exempted from the MacMahon legislation which blocked the transfer of certain military technologies to other countries. The Ministry of Defence then put money into a British project called Blue Steel. It was a sophisticated rocket that could carry a nuclear warhead. Blue Steel was an expensive project and was abandoned in favour of a long-range missile called Blue Streak. Blue Streak was even more expensive and the Chiefs of Staff persuaded the government, in early 1960, to abandon that too. This was the subject on which Carrington first addressed the House as First Lord in November 1959. He said at the time that the policy had not changed but it was very clear that Blue Streak would be scrapped. The opposition accepted that the project had been enormously expensive and in principle supported what the government intended. But it was the way the decision had been taken that caused such resentment. Here again was Carrington facing no serious charge but being part of a team that was not up to speed on such an important subject. As Lord Shackleton told the House on 3 May 1960,

There had been hesitation and vacillation beyond any reasonable degree ... the consequence of the ministerial collapse and the ultimate cancellation of Blue Streak was disastrous and it would be good to recognise that fact now.

6 House of Lords debate, 17 March 1955.

Six months earlier, Carrington had told the same House that government policy had not changed. This position was now attacked,
with the general charge being that the government was suffering
some form of neurosis and had, according to Shackleton, 'shrunk
from facing the consequence of the collapse of Blue Streak'. Carrington was sent into the House on the offensive.

The suggestion has been made that the Government has been following
a rake's progress, pressing on with Blue Streak at great cost in the face
of facts so obvious that we should have stopped the project much
earlier – and some have said it should never have been started. That attitude is wholly unjustified although perhaps in some quarters politically
convenient.

The Blue Streak story demonstrates most vividly some of the major
difficulties that confront any Government in the circumstances of today.

There have been uncertainties in the past and there will be in the
future but one certain thing has emerged from all of the discussion that
has taken place – it remains the policy of the Government to maintain an
independent contribution to the nuclear deterrent ... the Government
has nothing to be ashamed of, we have been open, straightforward and
consistent about our problems and policy.

Help was supposedly at hand when the Americans offered, in
March 1960, a long-range missile they were developing called Sky
Bolt. Carrington's Royal Navy did not think much of it but the
RAF loved it. Sky Bolt was designed to be carried by aircraft and
therefore the RAF's ageing V-Bomber Force could be justified.
Although none recognized it at the time, it would have been well
to beware Americans bearing gifts. No one could foresee then –
or at least they said so later – that the Americans would pull out
of the Sky Bolt deal. In fact the following year, in March 1961,
Carrington was back on his feet in the Lords explaining that Sky
Bolt was a good arrangement and that it was being sold to Britain
as our 'independent contribution to the nuclear deterrent'. Of
course it was not, nor would it have been even if the Americans
had kept their word. What no one would admit was that the Sky

1. *Top left* Rupert Carington, Carrington's grandfather, in Australia – a big and not always prudent spender. 2. *Top right* Edith Carrington, Peter Carrington's grandmother by marriage to Rupert Carington, in 1891. She was a considerable heiress as the eldest daughter of John Horsfall. 'My grandfather ran through his wife's fortune with the same ease as he had shown in England.' They had one child, Carrington's father. 3. *Bottom left* Peter Carrington's parents in 1912. 4. *Bottom right* Carrington on his mother's knee, 1919. Of his mother, Carrington said she was 'a gentle, sweet-natured person' whose character tended to soften the sternness of his father's outlook.

5. *Top left* Peter Carrington's father, the 5th Lord Carrington, in Grenadiers No. 1 dress uniform. The Grenadiers were the family regiment, but the 5th Lord Carrington was kept out until his father's illegitimate son was killed in action in 1915.

6. *Top right* Carrington's father in 1916.

7. *Bottom* Peter Carrington's father with his regiment, centre front with gloves and moustache.

8. *Top left* Peter Carrington at his first boarding school, Sandroyd, aged about eight.
9. *Top right* Sandhurst, 1938: digging trenches during the Munich crisis.
10. *Bottom left* Sandhurst, 1938: with other cadets. Carrington is third from left.
11. *Bottom right* Sandhurst, 1938: bicycling to PT, with Carrington, bottom right, 'commanding' from the flank.

12. *Top left* Newly commissioned Second Lieutenant the Lord Carrington, 1938. The only instructions from his colonel were: do not speak in the officers' mess for three months; do not marry before the age of twenty-five; and do hunt two days a week. Carrington disobeyed the first two. 13. *Top right* 'Much the most sensible thing I ever did was to marry Iona.' Wedding day, 1942, then off to a Worcestershire pub and the start of married life at the back of a pub. 14. *Bottom left* The baptism of Alexandra, the first Carrington daughter, in 1943. 15. *Bottom right* Lieutenant Colonel Sir Francis McClean, Iona Carrington's father. An Irish engineer and pioneer aviator, he provided the aircraft and facilities at Eastchurch that began what became the Fleet Air Arm. (Drawing by Edward Rawling.)

16. *Left* Princess Elizabeth with the Grenadiers in June 1944, just before D-Day, at Hove, Sussex. Carrington appears out of step with his brother officers but not with the future monarch.

17. *Middle* Princess Elizabeth inspecting the 1st and 2nd Battalions, Grenadier Guards at Hove before the invasion in 1944. Carrington is in the back row, directly above the princess.

18. *Bottom* Field Marshal Montgomery sitting, centre front, in December 1944 with Major General Alan Adair, GOC Guards Armoured Division, on his right and Lieutenant General Brian Horrocks, GOC XXX Corps, on his left. Montgomery was investing members of the new Guards Armoured Division with campaign medals six months after D-Day. Carrington is centre in the back row, and the only peer in the group.

19. The Manor House at Bledlow, Buckinghamshire, Carrington's family seat. When in 1946 Carrington and Iona decided to move in, one side was occupied by the tenant farmer and the house's facilities were very basic.

20. Carrington's first ministerial job was Junior Agriculture Minister in Churchill's 1951 government. His background in estate farming and the Buckinghamshire Agriculture Board could not properly prepare him for the often tedious European meetings. This is a Food and Agriculture meeting in Rome in December 1951.

21. Signing the Mayor of Grimsby's book in 1952. Grimsby meant fishing, meant jobs, meant ministerial visits.

22. *Above* Prime Minister Harold Macmillan with Carrington in 1957 at a news conference on his arrival in Australia. When he called out 'I bring you greetings from the old country,' young High Commissioner Carrington was surprised to see this piece of imperial theatre greeted with pleasure.

23. *Left* Carrington had an uncanny ability to smile through difficult occasions. Here he is with Archbishop Makarios of Cyprus, who was exiled by the British to the Seychelles in 1956.

24. *Top left* The popular image … 25. *Top middle* but should he hear a ring of untruth …
26. *Top right* and the less true it seemed … 27. *Bottom* then Carrington would drop the façade
of the easy-going aristocrat.

Bolt deal left Britain relying on the Americans for technology and supply.

It has been challenged at every level of consideration: on purely military grounds, that it is an unnecessary duplication of the American deterrent; on economic grounds, that we cannot afford it; on political grounds, that it is a barrier to disarmament and on moral grounds, that it is iniquitous.

As Navy Minister, Carrington was now directly involved in the setting up of what would be known as Britain's Polaris fleet. Macmillan had negotiated the Sky Bolt deal with the outgoing President of the United States, Dwight D. Eisenhower. There was more to it than simply taking delivery of missiles. One of the things the Americans wanted in return was a Scottish base for their own Polaris submarines armed with this early form of submarine-launched ballistic missile (SLBM). Macmillan had agreed, in the spring of 1960, that the Americans would have a Scottish base but needed to go through the rigmarole of how this might be publicly announced. The sensitivities of the anti-nuclear groupings were predictable enough and the political fallout in Scotland was easily anticipated. The nuclear argument was now established on the simple lines that its deterrent value was unquantifiable and, should it fail, then the first targets would be the bases from which nuclear systems operated as well as the major command and control centres. Little wonder that anyone living in Scotland close to one of the proposed sites was not entirely supportive of the Anglo-American concept for nuclear deterrence. The needs of a nuclear submarine site restricted the choices. The boats had to have quick access to deep-water exits into the Atlantic, thereby spending as little time as possible on the surface. The vessel was always most vulnerable when it was leaving port to go on patrol. If it could be picked up, an enemy could follow it more easily. Satellite reconnaissance did not exist in 1960, but no military strategist believed it was far away and exaggerated claims were already being made for its future capabilities. The base had to be reasonably remote in order that it could find deep-water sites and because the development that would go on in support of the operation would mean creating new infrastructures. The third reason, which really went hand in hand with the need for remote deep-water bases, was the fact that it was much better to keep any such major target as far away from centres of population as possible.

Macmillan agreed that the US Polaris fleet should be based in Holy Loch off the Firth of Clyde. The Americans had wanted to be quite close to Glasgow, the third largest city in the United Kingdom. Between March and September 1960, most of the details were sorted although some of the assurances the Americans were asked for were inconclusively given. Carrington, for one, never believed that the American deployment could be seen as a joint operation. Moreover, he could hardly believe that, in time of war, the Americans would definitely honour any guarantee and that they would never fire their missiles from their Polaris submarines in UK territorial waters without first consulting the British government. The best the Americans would go along with was a rather vague statement that in time of tension and transition to war, Washington would 'take every possible step' to let Britain know what she planned to do. This worked very neatly with the American notion of consultation, which was telling her allies what had just taken place.

Carrington was proved absolutely correct in this judgement when America went on high alert at UK-owned bases without telling Number 10. This was in 1973. (See p. 318.) In December 1960, when the whole matter came to the House of Lords, it was presented as an American concept for a so-called multilateral medium-range ballistic missile base for NATO. This was not a decision that had been taken; it was simply something for consideration and in fact would never see the light of day. The Americans had, however, said that they were committed to deploying five Polaris submarines to NATO before the end of 1963. The Foreign Secretary, Lord Home, apparently thought he was reassuring Parliament by saying that the submarines would 'operate in accordance with existing procedures. Thus no change in the control arrangements for nuclear forces is involved.' In other words, if it happened at all, there was no way in which the Americans would let their allies get even a little finger on the operational detail, procedure and command of these nuclear forces. It is some evidence of their Lordships' grasp of what Home was telling them that they seemed more concerned that day in the House, Tuesday 20 December, with the state of the Royal Navy's coastal defences. Carrington, forced to his feet, found himself not deep in the detail of strategic nuclear thinking, but discussing whether there might be something in his budget for a couple of gunboats that might operate out of Littlehampton.

The value of coastal forces is not in dispute, but it is virtually confined to one set of circumstances – global warfare. They make no contribution to winning the Cold War. It has been decided that resources would be better spent on ships with greater all round capability. That doesn't mean that the Navy has abandoned coastal forces altogether.

The Royal Navy might have been a bit puzzled by their First Lord's assurances.

When the House resumed the following month it had started to take on board the depth of the nuclear debate. There was open scepticism about NATO control. No one believed that it was simply a matter of having one nation's finger on the nuclear trigger (America's) but the other fourteen members' fingers on the safety catch. Not that the more conventional scenarios brought any comfort. Certainly by that time, 1961, Britain's army in Germany was thought quite incapable through its existing organization and equipment of reacting effectively against any advance by what were then called the Group of Soviet Forces Germany (GSFG). So, many in Parliament were waking up to the fact that policy had shifted to nuclear retaliation at the first signs of aggression rather than the last resource. Carrington tried to calm the debate in the Lords without much success:

Tactical and strategic weapons had been spoken of as though there were a readily discernible difference between them. Between the hydrogen bomb and the bazooka with a nuclear warhead there is a whole range of weapons whose use could be strategic or tactical depending on the targets at which they were aimed . . .

He argued that while the Supreme Allied Commander in Europe (SACEUR; always an American) would have a more flexible weapon in the Polaris warhead, he would not have a greater flexibility in when he might use it. Carrington's point that a new weapon did not mean loss of NATO control to the Americans was not received with much conviction. He was on much safer ground when discussing the non-nuclear weapons capability of his Navy.

The Royal Navy was now in the business of having nuclear-powered, though not nuclear-armed, submarines. But the more the government advanced its plans for the Navy, the more three aspects stood out in Carrington's mind. First, the Navy had two great advantages when demanding increased spending: it was a force that could deploy in something akin to the old gunboat diplomacy and then withdraw without the difficulties that a land-based operation would present. Second, it was still the only military system anywhere in the world which could properly defend the lines of communication that Britain relied upon, the so-called sea lanes that brought everything from fuel to food necessary for Britain's short-term, never mind long-term survival. Third, there was no easy way in spite of these telling arguments to find the money to maintain the increasingly expensive fleet.

The serious risk, if risks there were, of going short in any particular respect could not be ignored but we cannot be blind to the consequences to the economy when too much money and too many resources are devoted to defence. In all big issues of policy there must be a balance between what would be liked, what can be afforded and what we must provide . . . the most striking change in the navy is the tremendous increase in capability. In 1940, the crippling attack on Tarranto was delivered by forty aircraft on the carrier *Illustrious* one hundred and seventy miles away. A similar result could be achieved today by a single Scimitar with one nuclear weapon flying from a carrier more than twice as far away.

It was a sign of the times that the boast of the power of that Scimitar aircraft with its nuclear weapon was seen as a matter of achievement rather than its fiercer and more gruesome possibilities.

On Trafalgar Day, 21 October 1960, the Queen launched the *Dreadnought*, Britain's first nuclear-powered submarine. Here was a very public example of defence policy development based on the need for devastatingly powerful forces for all time, rather than an illusion that swords into ploughshares was a credible option. In general, Carrington's message was that although there was some measure of agreement among NATO allies about the possibilities of disarmament, it was better to produce a government review of defence thinking ahead for the next ten years on the basis that no disarmament would happen, than be ill prepared when hopes were proved vain. So, in March 1960 Carrington was back to Westminster with a defence review, telling the Upper House that it was wrong to shut its eyes to what the Russians had achieved in their rocket programmes. He would not accept the widespread criticism that the government was having difficulty making up its mind on where to go next with its own rocket programme, which everyone knew was reliant upon the Americans. As First Lord he seemed rather pleased that Britain now had V-Bombers with improved engines and bombs.

The RAF has developed techniques which could get four bombers into the air from one airfield in under four minutes and that time is being improved. No one can count on destroying at one go our V-Bomber force and armed with the Blue Steel stand-off flying bombs our bombers will be capable of hitting enemy targets for a number of years yet.

In this same March 1960 speech Carrington told the Lords that the first American Polaris missile submarine was in commission.

The possibility of having submarines of that kind which are about twice as large and twice as expensive as the nuclear [powered] submarines which we are developing presents difficult technical and financial problems ... the United States is giving us the fullest information about the weapon and the submarine.

They were not, but at that stage it did not matter. Carrington had thought for almost a decade about what he believed nuclear weapons strategy should entail. He saw beyond the narrow debate of the Cold War which necessarily meant that Britain's defence policy, especially its nuclear weapons policy, was largely determined by three factors: perceptions of Soviet capabilities, the limitations of technological transfer from the United States, and, inevitably, the Treasury. Whatever the limitations, Carrington believed that the European trip-wire should not be the focal point of a threat to stability.

The concept of stability could not be credible unless Britain's existing weapons, and those on order, were the best available. They were of little value unless they were internationally recognized as deterrents. There was no point in being able to mount a splendid guard at Buckingham Palace if the same soldiers were either badly trained, useless or had poor weapon systems in time of crisis. Certainly by the end of the 1950s, defence policymakers were having to accept that Britain's worldwide military commitments – NATO membership, deployment of the Rhine army, nuclear weapons held on the basis that the Soviet Union, or at least the Warsaw Pact, was a recognizable enemy – now sat uneasily under the heading National Requirement. In a debate on the defence White Paper in 1961 Carrington's speech reflected this reality.

The changes in weapons and their method of delivery in the last twenty years or so mean that defence is no longer a narrow question of national politics. What happens in the most backward and far off country might affect the peace of the world. The increasing complexity, technicality, and cost of modern defence has made it impossible for Britain on her own to build up forces on the same scale as those of the two giants of today, Russia and the United States, with their huge industrial capacity.

The purpose of policy must be to maintain stability and peace throughout the world and Britain can only make her proper contribution if the economy remains strong. The Government has carefully considered all considerations before coming to the conclusion that Britain should and must retain her independent nuclear power.[7]

The anti-nuclear lobby dismissed this thinking as the work of dull scholarship. The campaigners had been on the march for more than a decade since Britain first tested its own nuclear weapons in 1952, in Australia. Carrington thought then, in March 1961, that any idea of unilateral disarmament was quite pointless and that anyone who believed that such an action would change the world was a very sanguine man.

To his mind the five-year defence policy to which he was contributing had an untouchable element – nuclear weaponry. A bigger headache for defence planners was one that would persist into the twenty-first century: Britain's conventional (that is, non-nuclear) forces were overstretched and often underequipped. In theory they could be brought within days to operational readiness in their main theatre, Germany. It was a fragile theory. The minimum manpower requirement was for 165,000 soldiers. Yet, as one of Carrington's close allies, Viscount Montgomery of Alamein, said in the 1962 defence debate in the House of Lords, looking at figures tended to divert too many from the real question of operational efficiency.

If a man spends twenty-one years in the army he spends seven years in bed ... two years cleaning his boots and equipment, at least two years waiting about outside the orderly room, probably two years cleaning the barracks and on fatigues, and two years on leave. That makes eighteen years, and so far he has done no training. In the end he spends three years training, and that is enough.

Montgomery's bit of fun had a grain of truth which Carrington, as a soldier, picked up. As early as 1961, Carrington was pointing

7 Command 1288, HMSO.

out that one of the weaknesses of the system in Whitehall was that the Air Ministry, the War Office and the Admiralty operated as separate bazaars and therefore made what he thought to be the main task of defence policy-makers – a more flexible, if necessary smaller and faster-reacting group – that much more difficult to implement. None of this would change until Lord Mountbatten, as Chief of the Defence Staff, fully had his way and the three separate ministries were brought under the wing of the Secretary of State two years later. Even then it took another twenty years before the concept of a joint service ministry that Carrington wanted to develop began to be set in place, largely due to the political energies of Michael Heseltine when he was Defence Secretary.

Carrington sought reform, but in truth he had few if any real powers. He also wanted small rapid-reaction forces, a theme echoed forty years on. In 1961 he was able to demonstrate the practical need for such a force during an emergency in Kuwait. The developing maritime strategy was far removed from the cumbersome land forces of the Rhine army. Kuwait, to which Britain had defence commitments, was threatened during late June of that year, a threat that gave Carrington the unexpected opportunity to demonstrate the usefulness of quick-reaction forces in what was called Operation Vantage.

On 25 June President Kassem of Iraq claimed Kuwait as Iraqi territory. Two days later the Amir of Kuwait asked Britain for help when it became clear that an armoured Iraqi brigade was about to invade. 42 Commando Royal Marines were in Karachi embarked in HMS *Bulwark* and by 1 July were standing off Kuwait and had men on the ground before lunch that day. 45 RM Commando were sent from Aden and a detachment of Coldstream Guards was flown in from Bahrain. By the evening of 1 July, Britain had half a brigade group and air support in position within five miles of the Iraq border. Britain sent more than a gunboat. Carrington seized upon this to tell the House of Lords, 'this quick and decisive action undoubtedly helped to discourage and deter any move to overrun the Sheikhdom'. He was delighted with what he called the 'clear demonstration' of naval amphibious operations.[8]

Carrington was to have far more to worry about than the success of 42 Commando in Kuwait, the rights and wrongs of nuclear weapons and the need to restructure Britain's conventional defence forces. He was yet again about to be forced to tender his resignation to the Prime Minister. For this was the year both of the Portland spy ring and of one of the more tawdry espionage stories of the postwar Admiralty, the Vassall Affair.

The year 1961 should have been an agreeable time for the whole of Harold Macmillan's government. The Conservatives had been in power for a decade and Macmillan had been Prime Minister for almost half that time. He had weathered political difficulties, particularly a little local one three years earlier when the Chancellor, Peter Thorneycroft, and two of his juniors, Enoch Powell and Nigel Birch, had resigned over the direction of British economic policy. The internal pressures of government, which resulted in the mass sacking of many of his Cabinet – forever known as Macmillan's Night of the Long Knives – would not take place until the following year. Yet many of the enemies of government and Britain were hidden. This second half of the twentieth century was marked by constant and highly motivated espionage and counter-espionage. It is easy to understand why. First and foremost, the alliance with the Soviet Union that had been so important in determining the outcome of the Second World War had collapsed by 1945. Any hope of cooperation in managing the peace was totally fanciful.

The second feature that led to such high-powered espionage was the deployment and capability of nuclear warheads on both sides. The North Atlantic Treaty Organization was a collection of states whose single purpose, according to a remark attributed to NATO's first Secretary-General, Lord Ismay, was to keep the Americans in, the Russians out and the Germans down. By the

8 One of the first ashore in 42 Commando was a young officer who later became leader of the Liberal Democrats, Paddy Ashdown – an officer at that time unknown to Lord Carrington.

middle of the 1950s, West Germany was a member of NATO and as far as many in the Russian leadership were concerned, the Soviet Union's single greatest threat. The Soviet Union, rightly or wrongly, saw itself threatened by an alliance which was led by the United States and contained its historic enemy, Germany. From the Soviet perspective, its homelands and what it called the Near Abroad – the other Warsaw Pact States – were surrounded by an aggressive force, NATO. Moreover, the alliance's senior member, the United States, certainly with the support of the United Kingdom, had demonstrated publicly that it was willing to use the most awesome weapon of the modern age, the nuclear warhead. By 1961 the American programme to produce intercontinental delivery systems had more or less wiped out the Soviet lead in this area demonstrated in October 1957 with the launch of *Sputnik 1*. The Soviet Union understood perfectly from public pronouncements that in spite of restrictions imposed by Congress, strategic technologies were being passed to the United Kingdom, a nation which was determined to operate its own so-called independent nuclear capability, especially in submarine-based systems. For their part, in this period of mutual suspicion, the Soviet Union had demonstrated between 1945 and 1948 a ruthlessness in bringing neighbouring states to heel. It had also produced its own successful nuclear weapons programme plus the development of two major navies, the Northern and Pacific fleets, and two lesser fleets, the Baltic and Black Sea. Finally, the Soviet Union had developed more than thirty divisions in the Group of Soviet Forces Germany (GSFG) and the covering airforces which included intercontinental bombers. All this mutual suspicion resulted in intelligence gathering by both NATO and Warsaw Pact states on an international and uncompromising scale. In London alone there were some sixty KGB officers and nearly as many from the GRU (*Glavnoye Razvedyvatelnoye Upravleniye*) – the Soviet military intelligence.

This then was the atmosphere of 1961 when the intelligence services uncovered two Soviet espionage incidents, both in Carrington's department, the Royal Navy. The CIA had been debriefing one of their Polish agents, Michael Goleniewski. It was he who told the Americans that a Soviet spy ring was operating at the Underwater Weapons Establishment at Portland in Dorset. The Americans informed British Intelligence, in this case the Security Service, MI5. The Metropolitan Police Special Branch then arrested Gordon Lonsdale, who, in spite of his adopted name, was a Russian, two Americans called Helen and Peter Kroger, and Harry Houghton and his mistress Ethel Gee, Britons being run by Lonsdale. Lonsdale was a thirty-nine-year-old Muscovite who was not on the KGB list of London operators but was one of the so-called 'illegals' – spies who could pose as local people with a totally verifiable background that was beyond suspicion. His real name was Konon Trofimovich Molody. In 1954 Molody had assumed the identity of Gordon Arnold Lonsdale, a dead Canadian whose birth certificate he had stolen. Houghton was a clerk in the Underwater Weapons Establishment and Gee, his mistress, was a filing clerk. They were the ideal intelligence gatherers for Molody because no one ever questioned why they should be looking in the files because that is what they did for a living. Both Houghton and Gee had access to nuclear-powered submarine files and a whole range of operational details of Britain's anti-submarine warfare programme. The Krogers, whose real names were Morris and Lona Cohen, were supposedly secondhand booksellers but at one time had been members of the infamous Rosenberg espionage system in the United States. In 1961 they were living in a small, undistinguished house in Ruislip along with their radio transmitters and receivers tuned to Moscow and all the bits and pieces of their trade, including cipher pads and false passports.

When the captured agents went to trial, Molody was jailed for twenty-five years but was out three years later, when he was exchanged for British agent Greville Wynne. The Cohens were given twenty years. Houghton and Gee each went to prison for fifteen years. (Molody died in 1970, it is said after an enormous drinking session.) And that should have been that.

Prime Minister Harold Macmillan appeared sometimes to give the impression that he did not want spies caught. He much preferred them either tipped off and told to get out or turned. His logic was understandable and generally ran along the lines that capturing spies only causes political trouble. He was certainly right in 1961. The Americans most certainly did not think much of the British for allowing the Portland ring to operate undetected, especially as this was not long after the fiasco over Kim Philby. Equally, the Americans were hardly in a position to give Britain a lecture on security. William H. Martin and Bernon F. Mitchell were analysts for the US National Security Agency. They did not give the KGB information, but when they escaped to Moscow in 1960, they gave a news conference denouncing the American social system and told the world that the American intelligence community spied on its allies as well as its enemies. (Forty years later, a similar claim was made by a British GCHQ worker over the Iraq War of 2003.) Furthermore, an American staff-sergeant, Jack Dunlop, was also spying for the Russians. Dunlop was the chief of staff's driver at the NSA and managed access to highly classified documents, which he handed over to the GRU. There were others, including an army sergeant, Robert Lee Johnson, and an Arabic-speaking security employee who was suspected of working for the Soviet Union's intelligence services, but was kept on by his department because the Americans were short of fluent Arabists. So, Macmillan's difficulty may have been local but was certainly not little on this occasion. When there is a failure on such a scale, people – driven on by the media – want to know why. More urgently and politically damaging, they want to know who is to blame in order that they can do just that. Portland was Navy, therefore its political head, the First Lord of the Admiralty, Lord Carrington, was the culprit.

Here was a perfect illustration of how ministerial responsibility is impossible to exercise fully. Does a new First Lord of the Admiralty simply study a list of everything that he 'owns' and then begin a national and, in the late 1950s and early 1960s, an international tour of his property, to reassure himself that every single aspect is being run as it should be? Carrington, not yet ready, as Macmillan would have put it, to bugger off to his estate, certainly understood this role in his private life. He did exactly that on his own estate.

The principle was the same, but the Admiralty estate was huge and bewilderingly complex. Equally, should not the First Lord, understanding the enormous changes in military doctrines and policy during the fifteen years since he had left the army, have been more aware of the vulnerabilities of his Admiralty? Even allowing for input from his officials, extracts from his parliamentary speeches and interventions reveal that Carrington was more than aware of the Soviet determination to match and, in many instances, exceed British and allied nuclear and conventional capabilities.

Today the security leaks may seem astonishing. Could there be a connection between Carrington's personality and the lapses in keeping a check on the Navy's secrets? The spying started long before Carrington arrived in the department, yet is that excuse enough? In discussing Carrington's personality and how he worked in all the offices of state he held, including the Admiralty, his admirers, and there were many – certainly more than detractors – talk about his sense of humour, intelligence, friendliness and his effort to see the best in everyone. He liked to run a relaxed ship. Too relaxed? Indeed, was it not the job of the First Lord of the Admiralty, with his military background and a good understanding of Soviet Intelligence, to insist that everyone should be reminded that penetration was likely and should be at all times guarded against? Maybe Macmillan was, after all, correct in believing that it was best not to publicly expose spies but to simply control and, if that were not possible, to stop their activities. Whatever the reasonable and unreasonable arguments, Carrington once again found himself telling a Prime Minister that he was willing to resign.

The Portland Affair surfaced in January 1961. Harry Houghton's activities had not gone entirely undetected before then. Five years earlier, Houghton had been identified as a possible disloyal member of the Portland staff. Nothing much was done about it – certainly, as it proved, nothing worthwhile. A telling point in Carrington's favour was the fact that the Portland establishment had apparently seen no grave risk to security. Therefore why, or, more properly, how, could the First Lord of the Admiralty?

Once the trial had produced guilty verdicts, Macmillan announced that a committee under a High Court judge, Sir Charles Romer, would inquire into the circumstances of the security lapse. Macmillan had to set up an inquiry for two reasons: it was the reasonable thing to do and, to some extent, it took pressure off Carrington, who was being publicly castigated through the media. He was the man in charge. Should not the man in charge resign? Carrington went through the motions of telling Macmillan that he would of course go if asked. No prime minister was less likely to accept a ministerial resignation, until it was inevitable, than Macmillan. He did not like fuss. Carrington had announced that the security agencies should be congratulated on catching Houghton, Gee, the Cohens and above all Molody. Carrington thought that a positive move; the Prime Minister might have positively preferred that there had been no need to congratulate the security services.

The Portland ring had hardly surfaced when in April 1961, George Blake, a Secret Intelligence Service (MI6) officer, was arrested. He had been recruited by the Soviet Union, probably as early as 1951, and his treachery resulted in the deaths of a number of agents. He was jailed for forty-two years, but escaped with the help of an IRA terrorist and two members of the Campaign for Nuclear Disarmament. For the moment, Carrington could breathe more easily. Blake had nothing to do with him and it was likely that the inquiry into Portland would clear him of responsibility, even if the department's weaknesses – many of which he had started to repair – were revealed.

The Romer Committee did clear Carrington of any responsibility. Yet the circumstances of Houghton's treachery made very miserable reading for those charged with implementing a security system. The trail from Houghton was long and not very winding. In fact, it remains a puzzle that he was allowed to get as far as he did in his career as a traitor.

In 1951 Houghton had been appointed clerk to the British naval attaché in Warsaw. He was recalled to London when his heavy drinking became professionally unacceptable in the Polish capital.

That was in 1952. He was then appointed to the Underwater Weapons Establishment in Portland, across the causeway from the seaside town of Weymouth. In an efficient world of security at this stage of the Cold War, Portland should have been told that Houghton had been recalled from Warsaw because he drank. Portland was not told. In 1954 another clerk in the department reported that Houghton was taking home classified documents. Houghton's immediate superior was informed and did nothing. It was not until 1960 that an investigation began into the activities of Houghton and his mistress Ethel Gee. Even then, it was because of the CIA tip-off and not as a result of the British security services. As the summary of the Romer Inquiry showed, there were no grounds for back-patting.

In 1956 Houghton was twice brought to the notice of the authorities in the Underwater Weapons Establishment as a probable security risk. Insufficient investigations were made and a report which was both incomplete and misleading was submitted to the Admiralty. The security officer at the establishment is gravely to blame for the casual way in which he dealt with this matter. Even so the captain of the establishment should personally have ensured that proper inquiries were conducted and that the matter was fully reported to the Admiralty.

The main responsibility for the failure to make a proper investigation of Houghton in 1956 rests therefore with the authorities in the Underwater Weapons Establishment at that time. The evidence discloses that there was a general want of 'security mindedness' in the establishment; and responsibility for this must rest with the captain of the establishment. But the Admiralty and the security service, although they received only an incomplete and misleading report from Portland, cannot escape criticism for failing to press the matter to a positive conclusion.

With one minor exception the committee found no inconsistency between Government security policy and the security rules issued by the Admiralty.

The committee consider, however, that apart altogether from the incidents in 1956, the Admiralty are to blame for the manner in which they discharged their responsibilities for security, particularly in regard to supervising security arrangements at Portland. In particular the method of keeping the personal records of Admiralty civilian staff gave no certain means of ensuring that all the available information about the conduct and capabilities of individuals was to hand when they were considered for particular posts or when security doubts about them arose . . .[9]

Carrington later suggested that the demand for his head was nothing much more than a media trial. This is not quite true. In Parliament there was considerable debate and a not unreasonable demand from the Labour opposition that someone should be accountable. A brief and polite exchange between Hugh Gaitskell, then the leader of the Labour Party, and Harold Macmillan on 23 June 1961 in the Commons reflects what many were saying in more robust terms.

> MR GAITSKELL: It is immensely important to preserve the political responsibility in matters of this kind. Would the Prime Minister not agree that here is a case where a service department is severely criticised by an impartial committee for want of security? Is it not clear that it is the responsibility of the political head of the department, the First Lord, to prevent that kind of situation arising? In those circumstances how can he defend his decision not to accept the resignation of the First Lord?

> MR MACMILLAN: In the circumstances it is the right decision, and I hold by it. I recognise that we cannot avoid our responsibilities. They are there. But in modern conditions it would not be reasonable to apply it quite in the same way. This is a general criticism of organisational methods. I do not think it would be right

9 Romer Inquiry report, summary paragraphs 5, 6, 7 & 8. June 1961.

to visit that on the First Lord. Many Boards of Admiralty have been involved. It is more efficient to try to put it right, as I am sure we can.

In the Lords, Carrington was on his own turf and the going was easier, as his response to their Lordships' discussion on 6 July 1961 in that place shows.

I wish to say something about the Portland security case and the steps I have taken about Admiralty security since the arrest of Houghton and Miss Gee.

I am grateful to your noble Lordships for what you have said about me personally.

Your Lordships will realise that it was impossible to take any overt action before the arrests were made because it was important not to alert the spies. Indeed it was only after the arrests were made that the extent of the weaknesses which have since been disclosed became apparent.

As soon as I was free to do so, I instructed all departments and establishments to review their security arrangements and at the same time all senior officers were reminded of the special features of personnel security in the report of the Committee of Privy Councillors in 1956. I then set up an internal committee to review the organisation for security within the Admiralty and at the same time ordered an examination of the working of the security system, both at headquarters and elsewhere. All this was before the Romer Committee was appointed.

This second examination is not yet complete. But as a result of the internal committee report I have now decided to set up a new security department within the Admiralty in which all the threads of personnel and material security, as they affect both the civilian establishment and the Fleet, will be brought together. The detailed organisation and staffing of the new department is now being worked out and I intend to appoint a Director of Security as soon as possible. This step will remedy what I think was the most serious weakness criticised by the Romer Committee.

As the new department will deal with both naval and civilian security, which of course does not happen at the moment, it will have to be staffed by naval officers and civilians, since there are a number of differences in the conditions of service of uniformed and civilian personnel. The head of the department will be the best man I can find, whether he is naval officer or civilian.

The new department will be responsible for ensuring that the security arrangements at headquarters and naval establishments are working properly and for seeing that the regulations are fully understood and applied, and it will have the staff to enable it to test this by inspection in the field.

Another duty of the Director of Security will be to look into the whole question of the appointment, training, status, and duties of security officers.

There is one thing I would like to make clear. If on security grounds it becomes necessary to take any disciplinary action or to make any decisions likely to affect the employment or career of any individual, these decisions will be taken by the Board of Admiralty, as they have always been in the past, and not by the Director of Security. This new appointment should not be looked upon in any way as interfering with the accepted conditions of service of naval and civilian staffs. Finally, I am examining the Admiralty system of maintaining personal records which was another weakness to which the Romer Committee drew attention, to see whether it can be made more effective. I shall of course wait and see what further recommendations may emerge from the broader review now being carried out by the Radcliffe Committee.

In the middle 1950s there was uncertainty in Parliament, the country, and the Navy about its future in a nuclear age and, as a result, there was a certain amount of malaise and lack of purpose in the Fleet. I believe today this has entirely disappeared and the events of the last few days have proved most strikingly the need for the sort of Navy that we are building.

There was still the question of Carrington's own position. On 22 June 1961 the Labour politician George Brown – whom Carrington came to dislike intensely – had confronted Macmillan in the Commons. Referring to the report of the Romer Committee, Brown attacked Carrington's competence.

GEORGE BROWN: The Committee considered … that the Admiralty are to blame for the manner in which they discharged their responsibilities for security.

In the light of that very flat and frank criticism does it not make nonsense of ministerial responsibility if no minister accepts the corollary of that and resigns? Should not the First Lord of the Admiralty have done that? Is it not indecent to keep telling us what happened to a couple of junior officers when a minister who was flatly criticised stays in office?

HAROLD MACMILLAN: No. The doctrine of ministerial responsibility is well known – it is the ultimate responsibility. But in modern conditions it must be recognised that the minister's duty is to carry out his task as efficiently as it is possible. The First Lord comes into this fairly recently, but since the matter has been raised, I think all of us who know him well will not be surprised to learn that he did offer his resignation to me. I came to the conclusion, after going carefully into it, that I did not think this was a case where I would be right to submit his resignation to the Queen.

Brown was not easily put off and he voiced in the Commons that day what many others believed, that there was a parallel with the ministerial responsibility involved in the Crichel Down Affair, in which Carrington once more had been criticized, had offered his resignation but had remained in office.

BROWN: To return to ministerial responsibility. Does not the Prime Minister consider that what has happened by his refusing the First Lord's offer to resign marks a considerable deterioration from the time of the case of Lord Crathorne, when the Minister of Agriculture resigned over the Crichel Down breakdown – which was much less serious than this? Does the Prime Minister not really understand that to the public outside, whatever the sophistication in here, this covering up at the top will seem an alibi for doing nothing about it?

Macmillan appeared to give careful consideration to Brown's words and perhaps sensed that the Labour Member for Belper had struck a reasonable note in his last sentence. Public opinion was important. It was equally important not to lose Carrington. Furthermore, Macmillan really did not believe that Carrington's resignation would have been much more than a token political execution. The whole matter of the Portland spy ring and Houghton's reliability had been in doubt since 1956, during which time Carrington had been High Commissioner in Australia. Macmillan therefore concluded that as many Boards of Admiralty were concerned over many periods it would not have been wise for Carrington to take responsibility for the whole wrong-doing. Carrington himself returned to the subject in the new session of the Lords in November 1962.

No blame can be attached to anybody for the existence in my department of an individual who was willing to become a spy. Nor is it blameworthy to have caught a spy. The real issue of blame, if there is to be blame, is whether he should have been caught sooner. That is to say, were there or were there not faults in the application of the Government security system in the Admiralty?

These are precisely the matters which the committee appointed by the Prime Minister are investigating. In the first instance their task will consist of gathering all the relevant facts, many of which, of course, are not confined to the Admiralty. The report of this committee will not be published but as has already been announced, a statement on their findings will be made in due course.

It has been said that a committee of officials will not have the necessary authority when it comes to dealing with a matter of ministerial responsibility for the actions of a department.

The argument seems to me fallacious. I do not imagine that anyone could question the competence of these senior officials to sift the facts thoroughly and to form a completely objective judgement on the part played by the Admiralty in this case. What is more, the committee are expressly charged to have regard to the recommendations of the Radcliffe report, which dealt very fully with the question of how we ought to run our security.

If the committee should find that there was culpable negligence in the application of the Government's security system within my department during my period of office as First Lord, and particularly since the Romer and Radcliffe committees reported, then I shall naturally accept full ministerial responsibility . . .

This last point was not unreasonable. It was all about fault having occurred during Carrington's time in office. The length of time spent on the inquiry and the discussion which followed suggested not only disquiet, but frustration that somehow the blame was not to be settled on any public head. That might have been that. The crisis was averted and the second Carrington resignation in less than a decade torn up. Macmillan had followed Romer with an inquiry, chaired by Lord Radcliffe, into all aspects of security. Radcliffe was swift and his finding went to Cabinet in January 1962 with a few recommendations and not very startling observations. Generally, Radcliffe seemed to think all was in order. It was not. Now came what Carrington later described in his memoirs as one of the 'unpleasant episodes of my political life'. Once more, his resignation letter was prepared.

The First Lord was now faced with the Vassall Affair. William John Christopher Vassall was a homosexual. He was, in 1955, working as a clerk to the British naval attaché in Moscow when he was photographed at a party actually organized for homosexuals by the Second Chief Directorate of the KGB.[10] The photographs depicted Vassall taking part in a complicated array of sexual activities with a number of different men. Blackmail was easy. In 1957 Vassall finished his tour in Moscow and returned to the Admiralty in London. He worked in Naval Intelligence and as private secretary to the Civil Lord, Thomas Galbraith. He started to hand over Admiralty and NATO documents to his KGB handler Nikolai Rodin, who escaped before he was compromised when George Blake was arrested. Vassall carried on spying until September 1962,

10 See Christopher Andrew and Oleg Gordievsky, *The KGB*, London: Hodder & Stoughton, 1990, pp. 363–4.

when he was arrested. Here was an occasion when Macmillan made it clear that he preferred spies to be detected but turned rather than arrested. Carrington went to see the Prime Minister and told him of Vassall's treachery and, or so Carrington supposed, the triumph of his arrest. Carrington said Macmillan sighed, 'Oh, that's terrible. That's very bad news . . . It's when we find a spy that there's trouble, more trouble than if we don't. When one catches them it can be most troublesome!'[11]

Certainly deep trouble and misery followed. Vassall was sent to prison for eighteen years on 22 October. Meanwhile, Carrington and the rest of the ministry had another matter on their minds: the Cuban Missile Crisis. They may have been looking in the other direction, but the media were not. Galbraith was no longer at the Admiralty. He'd been shifted to a junior Scottish Office job. His move did not protect him, nor the Admiralty, even when Radcliffe made a further report and cleared all ministers of any responsibility. The press, perhaps not unreasonably, sensed a cover-up. Galbraith was thought to have been too close to Vassall, although there was nothing sinister ever proved in their relationship. Nevertheless the press kept on. Carrington claimed that the press hounded Galbraith out of office: an apparently honourable resignation. Some at Westminster believed that it was not so honourable and that Galbraith had to be told to resign. Whatever the case, he went. One down and one to go. Carrington was once more vulnerable to public accusations of ministerial inefficiency. Carrington felt he might have to go, but the Radcliffe report saved him.

Twenty years later, after Carrington had fallen because of the Foreign Office's failure to understand Argentine intentions over the Falkland Islands, the Defence Minister John (later Sir John) Nott, who stayed in his department, observed that Carrington was totally unable to judge the mood of MPs. He believed that Carrington had been unreasonably swayed by the rough and tumble of the real and often bruising world of the Commons. Carrington was ever vulnerable to the accusation that his self-

11 Ibid, p. 367.

assurance slipped when he stepped beyond his own rarefied atmosphere. In 1962, with the media at his every move, he was certainly rattled. Carrington may have come through a very mucky and bloody war with a reputation of being a first-class leader. He may have been popular as he reorganized the family estate and learned to talk sense with his farmhands. But now, as the Vassall debate intensified, so did the pressure on Carrington and his family. Fleet Street (as it then was) loved nothing better than to get a celebrity on the run. Door-stepping a politician who might look haggard enough for the front page, whose wife might look worried enough for a good inside spread and who might whisper just one phrase to kick off the lead story, was great sport for photographers and reporters. A by-line or picture credit on a story like this could change careers. Carrington simply regarded it as hounding.

Macmillan saw the stress on Carrington. He needed to shore up his junior minister and did so by telling him how Mountbatten had spoken in his favour.

Dear Peter,
I hope you are not worrying too much about the Vassall case. You must not feel alone in your responsibility since I share it as well. I have an idea that will be helpful to your position. If you had been a fly on the wall at Broadlands [the Hampshire home of Mountbatten] this last weekend you would have heard much to give you pleasure, satisfaction and confidence.
Yours ever
Harold Macmillan[12]

Carrington was reassured but not out of the range of Fleet Street. He was photographed in white tie and tails at the Royal Naval Cinematograph Association dinner. The picture was good, the headline, to Carrington's mind, devastating: 'Doesn't Lord Carrington Care?'

The intense atmosphere might be imagined when the *Daily*

12 Undated letter from Macmillan to Carrington in Carington archive, Bledlow.

Express claimed that Carrington was not only incompetent, but had known about Vassall and had tried to cover up the matter and kept it from the Prime Minister. Carrington regarded this as an accusation of treason. He was morally offended and regarded the matter as libel and went to see Macmillan. Carrington decided that he must take the *Daily Express* to court. He had already been cleared and the *Express* knew they would lose. Carrington had been told by his libel lawyer, Helenus Milmo, that the action might fetch £150,000, a considerable amount in 1963. He wanted to go for the *Express* and then give the money to the King George's Fund for Sailors, an appropriate gesture by a First Lord of the Admiralty. Carrington's political judgement here was not very sound.

Harold Macmillan stopped him taking the *Daily Express* to court. Macmillan had no regard for the paper, nor any of them for that matter. However, he had no intention of letting Carrington triumph over a mass circulation daily newspaper when the General Election was not much more than a year away. It would, Macmillan told him, not be sensible to get the *Daily Express* against them. The best he would allow was Carrington to settle out of court for his costs. Milmo had expensive tastes.

Apart from the Vassall Affair and the Night of the Long Knives,[13] there was to be a further major event to shake the government before the end of Macmillan's premiership: the Profumo affair. More sex, more spite and more lies.

The way in which Galbraith and Carrington had been hounded by the press influenced the way in which Macmillan handled the Profumo scandal, in the summer of 1963. When Macmillan had asked Carrington if Profumo were guilty of anything, Carrington, to Macmillan's mind, could be trusted when he said, no, he was not. Macmillan made the mistake of believing John Profumo. Profumo was the War Minister, but the matter had nothing to do with the Admiralty.

13 This action on 13 July 1962 prompted the remark from Liberal politician Jeremy Thorpe that, 'Greater love hath no man than this, that he should lay down his friends for his life.'

Carrington was not directly involved in the Profumo scandal. Nevertheless, he was naturally sensitive to the wholly distressing political and personal circumstances. Profumo was generally recognized as being efficient and talented. He became involved with Christine Keeler. She was briefly his mistress. Miss Keeler had also been close to a military attaché at the Soviet Embassy who was a member of the GRU. An outline of the facts are these: the Minister of War was having an affair with a woman who had been variously described as a model and a society prostitute and who was a friend of a Soviet military intelligence officer and, most importantly, the minister denied all this to the Prime Minister and the House of Commons. He was therefore also a liar. The fact that he apologized to the House and to the Prime Minister for lying was to his credit, but nevertheless did not detract from the seriousness of what he had done. Here we see a reflection of what George Brown was talking about in the Commons. Brown made the distinction between what the public apparently thinks and expects, and what some find acceptable in more supposedly sophisticated circles. Carrington's reaction to it all clearly aligned him with the broader view of what happened. He saw much of the outcry against Profumo as sheer hypocrisy, as he described in his memoirs:

It is, of course, true that he lied about it to the House of Commons. I accept the seriousness of this and its difference from lies in private life. Nevertheless people tend to lie at first about such matters, where others are concerned. Let those who have never tried to conceal some episode in their private lives throw the first stones at Profumo; I don't think he would be much bruised.

In the bruising world of public life and politics in particular, Carrington's was indeed a sophisticated if not universal view. It reflects also a quite different view to that held by most voters. But then Carrington never had to rely on voters. There is a footnote to this story which might begin, 'There but for the grace of God ...'

One of the scenarios of the Profumo affair which was much

covered by the media was the involvement of the so-called Cliveden parties. Cliveden was the Buckinghamshire home of the Astors. The media described how Christine Keeler and her friend Mandy Rice-Davies cavorted naked in Lord Astor's swimming pool at Cliveden. During the summer of 1963, Astor gave a lunch party. Afterwards Astor suggested those who wished to should go down to the pool, already famous for its frolicking. The guests at that party included Christine Keeler and Lord and Lady Carrington. Wisely, the Carringtons left while the others went off to the pool. Considering the efforts of the media and many politicians, it is interesting to ponder whether or not Carrington would have survived had they gone to the poolside instead of sensibly and fortuitously going home.

Thirty years on, as Profumo approached his eightieth birthday, Carrington was one of those who tried to persuade the PM John Major that Profumo should be resworn a member of the Privy Council. He saw good reason for that when he wrote to Major on 18 May 1994:

Frankly, nobody could have worked harder in the intervening years to have restored his image and to do public service. I wonder whether it would be possible to do this. It would give all his friends such immense pleasure and I think it would be a proper award for a really rather good man.

As Major put it a few days later to Carrington, 'I will certainly see that this suggestion is carefully considered.' How carefully is unclear.

During the autumn of 1963 Harold Macmillan, who had been ill for some time, was forced to resign. He had suspected for very many months that he had prostate cancer. The symptoms were uncomfortable. Yet he was too embarrassed to tell his doctor. This 'old man's disease' was, as far as Macmillan was concerned, a private affair. Maybe he simply did not wish to believe how ill he was. Macmillan suffered a painful attack which he could not conceal and went into King Edward VII Hospital for Officers in London for surgery. Even then the political callousness of some of his party managers was evident. They wanted him to carry on because Macmillan was indestructible and the best electoral asset they had. They knew also that there would have to be a General Election the following year, and that there was no natural line of succession as there had been from Churchill to Eden to Macmillan.

There was no established electoral procedure within the Conservative Party. Usually the successor was a natural choice. There was another aspect to consider. Whoever was chosen would be Prime Minister – a point of considerable constitutional importance. In theory the job should have gone to R. A. Butler, who had the title First Secretary of State and Deputy Prime Minister. Macmillan resigned as the great, and presumably some of the good, were gathering for the Conservative Party Conference. Carrington was not there; he was in the Far East as First Lord of the Admiralty inspecting the deployed Royal Navy. It is unlikely that he would have been there anyway. Carrington disliked party conferences intensely, and did his best to avoid them. If he had been in a position to directly influence the selection of the new leader he would not have voted for the man his party chose, Earl Home, later Sir Alec Douglas-Home. Carrington wanted Rab Butler. He believed that it was Butler who had been responsible more than any other person for the rebuilding of the Conservative Party following the 1945 General Election defeat. He thought him wise and the right man to lead the party, a view not shared by his colleagues. Even with Butler out of the running, he still would not have voted for Douglas-Home. Carrington's vote went to Lord Hailsham, an altogether livelier figure than Butler. Carrington's view was that Butler was unlikely to be elected, whereas Hailsham might be but would not make as good a Prime Minister. (Viscount Hailsham disclaimed his hereditary title and fought and won a by-election as Quintin Hogg, in the hope of winning the party leadership.) To Carrington, Hailsham was one of the few people who could pull together the patently disheartened Conservative Party in 1963 with his exuberance, political instincts, sense of mischief and fun and above all his ability to wring votes from a largely disenchanted electorate. Why then would Carrington prefer Butler? Rab Butler appealed to Carrington's personality. Both loved gossip, both could be very good sources of supposed secrets. He found Butler enormously amusing and wonderfully indiscreet; he delighted in many of his famous and sometimes embarrassing asides, particularly the occasion when Butler described Alec Douglas-Home as 'the best Prime Minister we have'. For all that, he wondered if Butler really had what Carrington called the 'touch of steel' and 'ruthlessness' to be an effective PM. Neither Hailsham nor Butler got to Number Ten and Carrington believed that the man who did become PM, Alec Douglas-Home, had neither the public appeal of Hailsham nor the depth of Butler and certainly not the steel that would be needed to run through opponents. On balance, he still thought Butler, once in Downing Street, would have turned out to be the best choice as Prime Minister.

Carrington's view of Douglas-Home was that he was selfless, sensible, sound and honourable. He presented sometimes difficult arguments with a simplicity that made all clear and he was forever trusting in the sincerity of others even when he felt he could not agree with them. Carrington believed this was all very well but once Douglas-Home had translated from the Lords to the Commons, it was unlikely that he would get the better of the Leader of the Opposition, Harold Wilson.

Douglas-Home had supported Harold Macmillan's candidacy for the premiership and had been a very effective Leader of the House of Lords and Lord President of the Council. He had been deeply involved in the House of Lords reform and had been very influential in Macmillan's reaction to the Cuban Missile Crisis the previous year, 1962. He it was who had announced at the party conference Macmillan's intention to resign; he had even had to undergo the indignity of a medical examination himself in order to satisfy the grey suits of the party that he was not about to keel over and to anticipate the public speculation that he was too old for the job. He was only sixty. The formal proposal for the leader-

ship was made by Carrington and seconded by R. A. Butler –
Carrington, in a seemingly odd move, was proposing someone
whom he thought ineffectual. Such was the party machine.
Douglas-Home got the job, and was grateful for Carrington's support. He believed, as he had in 1956, that Carrington would one day
be on the high table of British politics.

Foreign Office,
July 30 [1963]

My Dear Peter,
This is just to thank you for all that you have done to help me in
the last few years both in Australia and then in the House of Lords
and as First Lord.

Nothing has given me so much pleasure as to see your progress
and it will be complete when I see you one day in the place where
I have just been.
Yours ever Alec

Carrington had got the job as First Lord of the Admiralty when
he was in the Far East. He now lost it when he was in the Far
East. Douglas-Home decided that Carrington had been at the
Admiralty for long enough. The need for a new Cabinet meant
Douglas-Home had one particular difficulty. What to do about
Butler? One thing was obvious – Butler had to be given a very big
job. Douglas-Home made him Foreign Secretary. He understood
also that Butler would need a good spokesman in the Lords on
foreign affairs and someone with a broad understanding of the
subject to support Butler, who might not always be relied upon,
especially if he got bored and switched off, as he occasionally did.
Carrington was the obvious choice. His time as a junior Minister
of Defence following the Crichel Down affair was a period when
Carrington matched his practical military experience with an
excellent grasp of international tapestries, including the increasingly difficult nature of East–West relations, and the responsibilities
of colonial defence. It was Douglas-Home whose recommendation

had sent Carrington off to Australia for three years as High Commissioner with the full knowledge that Carrington would not simply learn about koalas and gum trees but would come to see the world from a different geophysical and political point of view and would, on top of this, learn the importance of Asia in British political and colonial policy. More recently, as First Lord of the Admiralty and government Defence spokesman in the Lords, Carrington had needed a credible knowledge of the wider concepts of maritime operations throughout the globe. The Lords at the time was sprinkled with peers who really did know the subject and had strong views. The general impression was that Carrington had spoken with authority on the international implications of Britain's overseas defence and foreign policy. Douglas-Home had been one of those red bench experts because he had had a certain influence on the formation of British policy. As his 30 July note revealed, Douglas-Home also believed that Carrington would one day become Foreign Secretary. Therefore it was no slot-filling exercise when Douglas-Home appointed Carrington to be Butler's deputy at the Foreign Office and, perhaps more importantly, to come into the Cabinet as Leader of the House of Lords.

This was not going to be a long term in office because Douglas-Home was going to have to call a General Election and it was likely that he would lose it. Nevertheless, within a few months, perhaps weeks, of Douglas-Home's Cabinet gathering, it became clear that it contained a major weakness: Rab Butler was not a good Foreign Secretary. He was bitter and, as Carrington observed, he did not have the depth of character to conceal his bitterness at having been rejected by the party. He was a man of contradictions. Perhaps he would have made a great and memorable bureaucrat, perhaps a celebrated Whitehall mandarin rather than a rejected politician.

Sir Nicholas Henderson, who was then Butler's private secretary, described him as something of a paper addict. Referring to the famous red boxes of official papers ministers have to go through every day of their ministerial lives, Rab's wife Mollie was of the opinion that he would rather go through what she called 'the beastly boxes' than enjoy himself at a dinner party or the theatre. Carrington's view was that Butler had the sort of mind and experience of more than a quarter of a century in Whitehall and Westminster that enabled him to skip through those papers with apparent enjoyment. Yet this did not make him a good Foreign Secretary. Henderson wrote that the Private Office soon became aware of 'the characteristics for which he had become famous in Whitehall; inability to make up his mind or confront an issue or person'.[14] Perhaps it is not so remarkable when one remembers that Butler much admired *War and Peace*, which contained his favourite literary character, Pierre Bezukhov, whose tactic during the French invasion was one of delay and retreat. Butler preferred withdrawal to retreat but the object and the outcome remained the same. Butler himself said that it was often better to do nothing. His detractors put this down to indecisiveness, yet on big issues, Butler regarded doing nothing as a sound tactic. Carrington, certainly later in life, thought Butler had often been right about this. Carrington also saw dangers in taking decisions that might check or change the course of events without first being perfectly certain that the newly created political or diplomatic tributary was simply and easily contained. The first test of the Butler–Carrington relationship came that very year. It was Cyprus.

Cyprus had been British since 1878. During the nineteenth century one of the most important issues in European diplomacy was the gradual disintegration of the Ottoman Empire, exacerbated by the rivalries of France, Britain and Russia in that region. A prime consideration for all three was access between the Black Sea and the Mediterranean. During the nineteenth-century wars between Russia and Turkey, Britain had always supported the latter, believing that while Turkey and its empire stood, then so would the important trading routes between India and the Mediterranean. A patch in the diplomatic and strategic quilt of the region was Cyprus and had been so since the eighteenth century.

14 Sir Nicholas Henderson, *The Private Office*, London: Weidenfeld & Nicolson, 1984, p. 71.

This was a period when Britain believed that control of the eastern Mediterranean was essential to maintain overland military and commercial routes. Cyprus was well placed to reinforce that control (especially against – or for – Napoleonic ambitions) and Pitt the Younger had said as much in 1791 in a denunciation of Russian intentions towards the Ottomans. During the 1800s the rise of nationalism and Christian opposition to Muslim Turkey increased and Orthodox Russia supported Christian Balkans with the stronger motive of keeping open a route from the Black Sea to the Mediterranean. The result was three Russo-Turkish wars. Britain did everything it could to stop Russia taking the Bosphorus straits as it intended to do. Here was the cause of the Crimean War (1854–6), after which the Bosphorus was closed to all foreign warships. But in 1877 Russia and Turkey once more fought each other. The following year a ceasefire was agreed and an international congress called that summer in Berlin. Britain, represented by Disraeli, attended the congress because Turkey had seized control of Cyprus. Disraeli, coincidentally a friend of the third Lord Carrington, who saw Cyprus as our asset, somehow arranged for the Turks to allow Britain to administer the island. During the 1914–18 war, Turkey joined the side of Germany and Cyprus was then formally annexed by Great Britain. In 1925 the island became a Crown Colony. Five years later the Greek Cypriots on the island were stirred by *enosis*, which was a movement for the island's unity not with Turkey, but with Greece.

In the 1950s and early 1960s, Cyprus, with its complex loyalties of Turkish and Greek islanders, once more occupied the What-Shall-We-Do? trays in the Foreign Office and departments of Defence. Carrington's involvement was hardly a surprise to him in that he had what he saw as a genetic interest in almost every British policy subject. This sense of ancestral connection should not be underestimated. Although an exaggerated view, he felt there was rarely an issue facing him that an earlier Carrington had not seen. Carrington knew his family history and often approached an issue as another episode in the family history. So it was now with Cyprus.

Archbishop Makarios became the leader of the Greek Cypriots in 1950. His tactics were to resolve the question of possible union with Greece in the most peaceable way. He failed but remained the single most important figure in the Greek community. The terrorist war which followed in 1955, and which resulted in Britain declaring a state of emergency, meant the British could no longer tolerate Makarios on the island. In 1956 they exiled him to the Seychelles for a year but even then refused to let him back into Cyprus. Instead, Makarios went to live in Athens. This charismatic, bearded figure became an international hero partly by the publicity of his exile. The inevitable happened: Makarios was at last seen by the British as the only person who could lead the Greek Cypriots. Thus in 1959 he was invited to London for independence talks and then installed as President. But independence was complicated by the fact that nearly a quarter of the population of Cyprus was Turkish, and they actively resisted union with Greece. In 1961 Cyprus became a member of the Commonwealth and therefore was the responsibility not of the Foreign Office, but the Commonwealth Office and its Secretary of State Duncan Sandys, an acerbic politician who was later to be one of Carrington's most vitriolic critics over the latter's handling of Rhodesian independence. Butler did not like dealing with Sandys. It is worth remembering Henderson's assertion that Butler simply did not like dealing with people if there was any likelihood of a collision of views.

The Cyprus situation when Carrington went to the Foreign Office was more than a problem within the Commonwealth. Centuries of bitterness between Turks and Greeks would not be simply resolved. Carrington's view was that Cyprus would continue to exist for a very long time as a divided island, although he did not anticipate that the formal division that followed the 1974 Turkish invasion of northern Cyprus would last. A complication in the efforts to look for a solution was the strategic importance of Cyprus. It had a key role in British and NATO's strategic thinking because of its threefold military function: an air base for military operations in the Middle East; a support base for continuing naval and army deployments in the region; and a base for electronic intelligence gathering. For the rest of the century and beyond, its antennae would continue to monitor Soviet activities during the Cold War, and Russian air and naval movements and electronic communications after the Berlin Wall came down; today, electronic intelligence (ELINT) gathering continues against Russia in the Caucasus, as well as Iran, Syria and Iraq.

Tension existed more than peace during this period. The Second World War had been over for less than twenty years. Almost all military and strategic decision-makers in the 1960s had vivid memories of not only that war (and therefore the realities of conflict), but also the immediate origins of the Cold War in the late 1940s. They had witnessed the retreat from Palestine, the disturbances during the Kuwaiti invasion and, just seven years previously, the debacle of Suez. Many in British government circles felt that the lesson to be learned was a need to maintain a solid transatlantic relationship between Washington and the major West European capitals. Certainly the Americans had taken the Cyprus situation seriously and George Ball, Under-Secretary of State in the State Department, was sent to London to talk to Butler, Carrington and Sandys about a common position.

Towards the end of 1963, Greek and Turkish Cypriots were fighting throughout the island, and Britain had to reinforce its garrison in an attempt to maintain order. At that stage in Cyprus there was no UN peace-keeping force. The government in Ankara made increasingly aggressive sounds suggesting it would not long tolerate what it saw as the oppression of the Turkish minority. The relationship between Butler and Sandys, respectively heading the Foreign and Commonwealth interests, was not in the best temper to put on a united British front. The personal relationship was not one of expressed animosities, more simply that Butler did not want to involve Sandys. He remarked to Henderson in his Private Office that 'when you see the bull lying quietly in its pen it seems a pity to kick it and stir it up. Duncan's been quite easy lately, quite reasonable really, hasn't he? and it seems a pity to wake him up.'[15]

15 Ibid., pp. 71–2.

Butler left the negotiations largely to Carrington, who, instinct-ively the diplomat, spent a great deal of time nipping through a small archway between the Foreign Office and the Commonwealth Office. Sandys, as the senior minister and also the department head responsible for the island, chaired meeting after meeting. At those meetings, Carrington thought Sandys not very bright. Car-rington's style was to have short meetings, except on the rare occasion when confrontation might be resolved by stamina rather than intellectual argument. According to Carrington, *all* Sandys' meetings relied on stamina and the tactic of wearing down the opposition.

Carrington was not a newcomer to the Cyprus problem. When at the Ministry of Defence in 1955, he had attended that year's Cyprus conference. Greek terrorism under the banner of EOKA had been hitting at British troops on the island with enormous success. Macmillan, who by then was Foreign Secretary, had chaired the London conference in August 1955. Then, Carrington was generally sympathetic to the Turks. It may be interesting to note at this point that the British government felt that the Americans were interfering in what both Eden and Macmillan saw as British territorial interests. The Foreign Office was instructed to warn off the State Department. It may have done so but the Americans did not even blink. Carrington, very much the junior, also kept his inquisitive eye on Cyprus. It was a perfect example of a seem-ingly unimportant ailment that could so easily fester into an incurable sore.

This was the year before Suez, and the then Colonial Secretary Alan Lennox-Boyd made the policy statement that Cyprus was not simply a domestic problem but an island that was extremely important in Britain's strategic thinking. Given the planning that went into the Suez operation it was easy to see why Lennox-Boyd and his then Prime Minister Eden saw Cyprus as one of the key points that had to be protected diplomatically and militarily. The conference that Carrington had attended in 1955 had got nowhere and its failure had resulted in increased terrorism. Cyprus was such a sensitive matter that in 1956 Lord Salisbury, Carrington's mentor in his early days in the Lords, resigned in protest at government policy towards the island. But it should be noted that Salisbury was always in a mood to resign over something or another, and his going probably had more to do with his relations with Macmillan (a kinsman) than the detail of the Cyprus issue.

By 1963 there was still no reasonable solution in sight. Perhaps little wonder that Butler, having no obvious enthusiasms and not a little introspection, threw the whole matter to Carrington. Carrington had no magic formula that would resolve the dispute. He was mindful of Macmillan's view in 1957 that it was best to 'get clear' of Cyprus. In 1963 Makarios proposed that all power sharing between Greeks and Turks should come to an end. There followed the inevitable violence and the Turks unilaterally withdrew from the power-sharing arrangement. This was the moment that the UN set up its peace-keeping operation on the island, an operation Carrington had wanted for some time. He little believed that more than four decades later it would still be there and that the island would remain divided. No one in Whitehall had a way to bring about peace on an island that in Carrington's view would have corrupted even a perfect solution. So Cyprus was left to fester and Carrington turned to spending much of his short time as Deputy Foreign Secretary getting on and off aeroplanes and rushing back to London for what he saw as his main post, in the Lords.

Carrington's role as deputy to Butler was really a part-time affair. His Cabinet post was Leader of the House of Lords. Yet he always thought that he was Leader by default, since men more senior to him, including Hailsham and Home, had disclaimed their peerages in order to be considered for the party leadership and Number 10. The constitutional issue of disclaiming titles was something that did not attract Carrington. He was by then certainly eligible and an attractive enough figure among the party faithful to have had a reasonable chance of getting to be leader of the party and so perhaps Prime Minister. If it had been possible to disclaim in 1945, he might well have done so and tried for a seat in the Commons. Or at least that is always what he claimed in conversation with the author, but Carrington was never entirely convincing on this point.

It may have been that he could never muster the patience and certainly not the grass-roots support to run for the Commons. More than that, for all his social conscience developed among his soldiers, Carrington very much liked being a baron. He would have felt vulnerable without a peerage. There was not even a baronetcy to fall back on. As for the idea of joining the fashion for becoming a commoner and therefore a candidate in the 1960s, this simply did not arise. Carrington was not senior enough to be considered as a credible candidate for party leadership. Altogether, nothing in his life convinced him that there might be any advantages in being a commoner.

As Leader of the Lords he did not have much time to think about all this. The party was going through a miserable time and even in that rarefied place dissatisfaction with the government had not gone unremarked.

In October 1964 Alec Douglas-Home went to the country. The Conservatives had been in power for more than a decade, and there was a feeling throughout the land that the time had come for change. Douglas-Home had put off the election for as long as possible, hoping that extra weeks would repair the damage caused by the leadership change in which he became Prime Minister. Perhaps he hoped for an economic miracle that would show that economic recovery was on the way.

Carrington later told me that he too privately took the view that it was time for a change. In 1964 he felt that the Conservatives did not deserve to be in government.

Carrington's Whiggish philosophy was that if all is well with domestic policies of health, education, law and order and, most importantly, the economy, and if the nation's foreign policies protect her interests, then not much needs to be done but maintain course and speed in order for a nation to be quietly governed until 'an event' changes the tempo. However, Carrington had the uneasy feeling that in 1964 his party did not properly and quietly govern. He believed that the Conservatives did not have a single new idea that would give them a legitimate hold on Downing Street.

As it turned out Douglas-Home lost, but to the surprise of many of the pundits the margin was not very wide. There were only 200,000 or so votes' difference between Labour and Conservative.[16] However, not very much is enough in a democracy.

Carrington gave up his red boxes and left the office he loved best. He walked across the dead-end that is Downing Street and joined his colleagues in the Cabinet Room for a noon-day glass of something; such is the nature of a political wake, no one stayed to lunch. Outside, the Pickfords van loitered. So began the Wilson government. A few days later, Carrington had a note from Douglas-Home. It was typically generous and the final line gives an insight into both characters greater than all the speeches they made.

HoC 21st October 1964

My dear Peter
I have seen you since you wrote but thank you for your letter all the same and for all the loyal and splendid support you have always given. It is that which makes politics bearable.
Yours ever Alec

Politics in opposition is rarely so interesting and, even in the Lords, less bearable. This was Carrington's second life on the other benches.

---

16 Conservatives 303, Labour 317, Liberals 9. Labour got 44.1 per cent of the total vote and the Conservatives 43.4.

8. Lords Reformer

In that late autumn of 1964, when the Tories pinched themselves and woke up in opposition, Carrington was seemingly luckier than most of his former government colleagues. Twenty-four hours after the polls had closed, many Tories were probably thinking about what might have been. Like Carrington, most probably felt empty and rather flat. Even a junior minister had an official car, red boxes, a private office, a routine and someone to call him minister. For Carrington, unlike a commoner, there had been no risk of losing his parliamentary seat. Carrington became the Leader of the Conservatives in the Lords. But it was not much of a job. Most of the time he was bored and thought the whole thing ineffectual. He attended Shadow Cabinet meetings but was able to take little effective part mostly because politics is largely about being in the Commons. So Tory Members of Parliament were not much interested in what their Lordships might think, and Carrington was not inclined to remind them that in his House at least the Conservatives still had a clear majority.

By 1965 Carrington was regarding his leadership in the Lords as a part-time job. In the 1940s he had used the time to learn more about his new life as a civilian and, Crichel Down apart, put it to good use in government. Now, very respected and soundly connected, Lord Carrington began to enjoy the thought that there was life after government. In the Lords the network is interesting and well connected.

One day in the Lords, an old friend from Eton days, Viscount Bridgeman, asked him quite casually if he would like to become deputy chairman and, eventually, chairman of the Australia and New Zealand Bank. The fact that Carrington knew nothing about banking did not disturb Bridgeman, so presumably the bank's stockholders would be equally relaxed about the appointment.

Moreover, Carrington did understand Australia and New Zealand –
it was only six years since he had been High Commissioner in
Canberra. He had, however, the grace to feel something of a fraud as
the organization's deputy chairman without any idea how a bank
worked. But the chairman, Geoffrey Gibbs, who was about to move
over for Carrington, did not seem to think this particularly remarkable. The general feeling was that Carrington would eventually 'pick
up' the idea and that he was not to worry. He did worry. Part of him
was delighted with the idea of being chairman of a bank since he
was only ever interested in what he called big jobs. Part of him
simply wanted to understand what he was supposed to be doing.

So it was arranged that he should go along to see one of the
partners, John Glyn, of the then private bank Glyn Mills. The firm
had been bankers to the army since the eighteenth century and the
notched sticks of pay rates were still kept there. The earlier partners
had known the earlier Carringtons when they were still Smiths
and so it seemed quite natural for a Carrington to go to Glyn Mills
twice a week for lessons on how to be a banker. For much of the
rest of his life, when not in government, Carrington continued to
sit on the boards of different banks, and although he never described
himself as a professional banker, something of the Smith genes
must have survived.

The Australia and New Zealand Bank was not one of the
larger counting houses but it was one of only two London-based
Australian banks. The other was the English, Scottish & Australian
Bank, which ANZ was to take over. In 1967, when Carrington
became chairman of ANZ, perhaps his main use was threefold. His
experience of thirteen years in government had given him a
thorough working knowledge of Westminster and Whitehall as
well as an interest in many overseas governments and non-
governmental organizations. Second, Carrington's connections,
including those with courtiers and royalty, were seen as impressive
credentials in themselves. And finally, he had an extensive list of
friendships in Australia, together with experience and knowledge
of the southern continent and an understanding of the politics and
commercial possibilities within South-east Asia. Consequently his

role in ANZ was not simply a job for one of the boys, but one to which he could bring political and commercial understanding as well as personal contacts. He was closely acquainted with almost every person and system that affected the daily operations and strategic ambitions of the bank.

One of the first tasks was to take out the only opposition, the English, Scottish & Australian Bank, in a hostile take-over bid, which meant that Carrington was to be introduced to the harsher side of commerce, which included the sacking of employees and, closer to home, of many of the unsuccessful board. ANZ was successful and therefore Carrington survived the take-over. In fact he did rather well out of it all in the long term. One of the smaller shareholders in ANZ was the British bank, Barclays. After the take-over Carrington was given a seat on the Barclays board. When not in government it was a seat he kept for the rest of his business life, just as he did with another directorship that he took on about this time, at Schweppes, which later became Cadbury-Schweppes, where his former political boss at the Ministry of Defence, Harold Watkinson, was now chairman.

So courtesy of the employment exchange operated by the inner circle of Westminster and White's Club, Carrington was now into one of his other successful careers. The connection between politics and commercial life with Carrington, as with some other ministers, was more than simple patronage. Carrington never did know much about fizzy drinks, although he always prided himself on being able to mix a stiff gin-and-tonic for his guests, and for much of the final two decades of his life, his health meant that tonic water replaced wine. Carrington never regarded himself as an expert in banking, although his influence and observations were extremely useful in the boardrooms at ANZ, Barclays and, later, Chase Manhattan. It might be imagined that Carrington was hired not so much for what he knew, but whom he knew – or, again, who knew him. He did more than renew friendships in Australia. He began the commercially important task of understanding the interlinking of business and political interests across continents, and he began to learn more about a continent that would be so important in his future political career and that would cause him so much personal distress. Carrington 'discovered' Africa.

But in December 1969 Carrington set out wearing not his commercial but his political hat to Nigeria, where a furious civil war was being fought. His purpose was very simple: as a foreign affairs specialist he was probably the best person to send to find out for the Conservatives what was going on in that country.

The Wilson government did not really like the idea of Carrington, or any other Conservative politician, going to upset a very delicate relationship with General Gowon. The difficulty for anyone trying to get both sides of an argument in wartime is that instinctively the inquirer is viewed with suspicion by both sides, especially if there might be a suggestion of traditional bias. This was the difficulty faced by Carrington. Going to Nigeria and then to the south-east of the country, where the Ibos wanted to establish independence for Biafra, was not simply a question of arranging transport. There was certainly a large element of politicking in this trip. Alec Douglas-Home had been replaced in 1965 by Ted Heath as party leader. Heath was no more invulnerable to the sense of helplessness in opposition than any other political leader. He wanted to use Carrington's Africa trip as a publicity tool: it would show the Conservatives continuing to think about big issues as well as domestic programmes.

On the eve of his departure, Carrington received a message from Downing Street. Although the High Commission in Lagos had drawn up his itinerary – which they would not have done without government approval – the Wilson administration was making a last effort to stop him going. It appears that the authority for this decision had come, not from Downing Street nor from the Foreign Office, but from General Gowon himself. He was furious when he found Carrington intended to go to Biafra. Carrington was not about to turn back and, in spite of the fact that their accommodation at the stop-over in Gabon had mysteriously disappeared, they continued via Paris, where Carrington picked up his powerful minder for the trip, the Paris correspondent of the *Daily Express*, John Ellison.

Ellison, one of the most respected correspondents in Beaver-brook's empire, was a good insurance policy in case Carrington ran into flak. Also, in Carrington's mind there was no point in going through all the dangers and hardships of a so-called fact-finding mission unless it was worthwhile in publicity terms. Yet as Carrington took off in an ancient DC4 cargo plane flown by two Frenchmen, he wondered at the wisdom of the trip, especially as his first stop at sometime after midnight was to be Uli in Biafra and then into Owerri. This was something of a coup for Carrington because Owerri had been in Nigerian hands. But now it was the headquarters of the breakaway Biafran government, led by the formidable Colonel Ojukwu. Here was a puzzle for Carrington.

Biafran leaders – but not on this occasion Ojukwu himself – had to go through the motions of haranguing British imperial policy as the former colonial power. In his memoirs Carrington recalled how he had to go through the motions of carefully considering what they had to say. 'I sat through it,' he wrote, 'merely saying stiffly that I accepted none of the premises or conclusions put forward. It was not possible to walk out. Not in Biafra.'

Carrington found Ojukwu arrogant and conceited, yet this did not overshadow his intelligence. Having gone through the motions of opening speeches to each other, Carrington surprised Ojukwu by asking him what he thought General Gowon would tell him. Ojukwu's answer was obvious but accurate. Biafra was in Nigeria. Gowon would point to it as being a small part of what was supposed to be one nation but for tribal reasons it could hardly ever be that. As far as Ojukwu was concerned, his people would never accept Nigerian sovereignty and Carrington concluded that would make an agreement between the two sides impossible. Equally, he did not support Ojukwu's idea that the Nigerian Federation, led by Gowon, would eventually get bored with the war and at that point the Federation would split. Carrington then toured villages where the Biafrans were trying to maintain everyday life by keeping schools open and even dispensing civil as opposed to military justice. Stories of starvation were clearly true, although Carrington was puzzled by the way the British press represented some aspects of the war. He was told, for example, that the Nigerian Federation airforce had killed 500 Biafrans in one raid. Still they fought on. Was it true? Whom should he believe? On balance, neither side could be trusted with the truth. To Carrington, truth was supposed to be an expression of reality. He recalled his own practical experience of battle, where every witness to events and especially those in higher command could invent truth. Why should Ibo or Nigerian be any different from other nations at war? However, he concluded that the Ibo people who wanted to break away from the Federation were among the most intelligent of Nigerians; like their leader Ojukwu they tended to regard other Nigerians as inferior. By the time he was due to fly to Lagos to see and hear the other side of the Nigerian story, Carrington was finding himself sympathetic towards the Biafran people.

If this seems of little consequence, we must consider that the impressions were lasting and that, one day, Carrington would be Defence and later Foreign Secretary when his views on Nigeria and its recent history would indeed be important – in international as well as national contexts.

In Lagos Carrington almost immediately formed an impression of General Gowon as a total contrast to the often theatrical and conceited Ojukwu. Gowon and Carrington had one thing in common: both had been at Sandhurst. In what Carrington thought to be a bizarre expression of the old boy network, Gowon declared that he was sure the Englishman would understand that the whole conflict had to be judged by one huge difference: Ojukwu had not been to Sandhurst. Instead, he had gone to the National Service Officer Cadet School, Eaton Hall in Cheshire. Carrington told me that before him was a thoroughly 'likeable, honest and devout' man. To him these were characteristics expected of a brother officer whose instincts were uncompromisingly pro-British. At such meetings, British foreign policy might be influenced if not made.

By the time Carrington had returned to London he was depressed about what he thought would be the future of the war.

While on the Biafran front, with the Nigerian Federation forces not much more than a bayonet charge away, Carrington had sympathized with the Ibos. Yet the quiet and transparently sincere Gowon had convinced Carrington not so much of the Nigerian cause, but of the fact that Gowon's relatively moderate prosecution of the war would lead to his downfall before it did to Ojukwu's.

Carrington's political and commercial interests did not clash but they certainly ran on parallel lines. He believed Britain had responsibilities in her former colonies. He was doubly interested in Nigeria because there were huge UK investments in the Federation, not least in oil. But Nigeria failed to arouse many public sympathies in the UK, perhaps because the geography was remote, the colonial history only vaguely understood and the main characters little known. A much greater dilemma in the African continent for any British government – Labour or Conservative – was one which had caused public as well as political anguish for four years by the time Carrington returned to London: the unresolved question of what to do about Rhodesia.

In the autumn of 1965 the white-led Rhodesian government of Ian Smith had declared unilateral independence from Britain. Carrington realized immediately that the Rhodesia question could divide his own party. Ever since 1961, the Rhodesian Constitution had accepted 'unimpeded progress to majority rule'. Wilson had attempted to get a resolution by having an amended constitutional agreement and by using the influence of other Commonwealth leaders. Smith probably knew after talks with Wilson in January 1965 (in the 'margins' of Winston Churchill's funeral) that progress as he saw it was unlikely. He certainly saw no value in being pressured by senior Commonwealth members, for example, Sir Robert Menzies. He had telegraphed Wilson:

... I am willing at all times to receive suggestions from you and to listen to what the British government has to say on Rhodesia, but, frankly, I am not interested in what other members of the Commonwealth say about our affairs, and what they do say will not turn us from what we consider to be the right thing to do in the interests of our country ...[1]

Carrington's wide circle of colonial, political and business friends had by 1965 convinced him that unless there were to be a remarkable unbending from Smith's position, then a unilateral declaration of independence (UDI) was inevitable. One of his friends, the Tory intellectual Iain Macleod, had announced during a television interview that the law on UDI was 'by no means clear'. Conservative pressure to abandon its policy of standing firm with Wilson against Smith was growing. By the party conference in mid-October 1965, there was a deep gloom. Heath and Douglas-Home were being pulled into line by the Tory old guard.

Many Conservatives were what might have been called in the mid-1960s typical *Daily Express* readers. Indeed, in those days, it was quite common for a Conservative household to take two newspapers, the *Daily Telegraph* (for him) and the *Daily Express* (for her). The Beaverbrook Press, owners of the *Daily Express*, by then run by the late Lord Beaverbrook's son, Sir Max Aitken, supported Ian Smith. Aitken had flown in the Royal Air Force during the Second World War, as had his two chums Douglas Bader and Ian Smith. Bader with his heroic personality and Aitken with his newspapers (both the *Sunday* and *Daily Express* were still high-circulation broadsheets during this period) made formidable champions of Ian Smith's cause. He was portrayed as a gallant airman who had fought and risked his life for Britain against Nazism. Smith was shown as someone who had seen what had happened to other parts of Africa as it was 'handed back' to black Africans. He believed that Rhodesia, as it then was, could easily collapse into a corrupt society that would be forever torn between the tribal differences of the Shona and the Matabele (or Ndebele). He also made much of the fact that the majority of white Rhodesians had been there for generations and that the country was as much

1 Harold Wilson, *The Labour Government 1964–1970: A Personal Record*, London: Weidenfeld & Nicolson/Michael Joseph, 1971, p. 144.

theirs as anyone else's. Many in the United Kingdom did not need convincing by Aitken's editors and leader writers.

As Leader of the Conservatives in the House of Lords, Carrington was acutely aware that many grassroots Tories as well as those in both Houses of Parliament were pro-Smith. Harold Wilson's Labour government also had an internal difference to resolve: Smith was a rebel and there were those in Wilson's Cabinet who insisted that the government should not negotiate and therefore be seen giving into rebellion. Wilson had no option and neither would Heath had he been Prime Minister. The possible alternative to negotiation – other than ignoring the matter – would not work.

The Cabinet had to consider the possibility of military intervention in Rhodesia, but the force needed to attack Rhodesia would have been bigger than the UK could mount. The logistical task would have been impossible to maintain. Worse than all this, public opinion would never have supported an attack on loyal Rhodesians, the sort of people who had stood by Britain against the Nazis and whose sin was to desire to remain loyal to the Crown. Or at least, that was how it looked. It was an impossible challenge, quickly recognized as such and therefore abandoned. The obvious retaliation was instituted: sanctions.

The Royal Navy sailed on what became known as the Beira Patrol, hoping to stop illegal shipments entering the port of Beira and on to Rhodesia. It was a futile exercise in that the Navy could not intercept all vessels and there were other ways through to Beira. Nevertheless, while Smith retained his general support, the white farmers could see little ahead but conflict; many decided to leave what was known as the garden of Africa, making what became the notorious 'chicken run' to South Africa and, they thought, a more certain future.

What of the black Rhodesians? Some black leaders, such as Joshua Nkomo, Ndabaningi Sithole and the cleric Abel Muzorewa, remained in the towns. But others beneath the revolutionary banner of ZANU (the popular acronym for the Zimbabwe African National Union) took to the gun and to the bush. Their leader was Robert Mugabe. Mugabe had been in political detention during 1962 and when released in 1963 started ZANU and became its secretary-general. He was back in detention in 1964, where he was to remain until 1974 when he escaped to Mozambique and led the rebels from their bush camps. In 1965 few recognized the importance of Mugabe.[2]

Carrington's military judgement was that if the bush opposition grew (and in 1965 there was every possibility that it would) then the conflict would go on for some time because guerrilla-based opposition could survive setbacks that conventional armies could never do. His political nous suggested that it was increasingly unlikely that the diplomatic tactics then adopted by Harold Wilson would bring down Smith. Therefore, it was quite possible that Rhodesia, like Cyprus, would be yet another unresolved question when Conservatives returned to power. Maybe, at the time, this seemed unduly pessimistic, but as it turned out he was correct. Moreover, it was not unreasonable for him to believe that he might return to the Foreign Office and therefore the Rhodesia file would land in his red box. As it turned out he was both right and wrong. He was right that Wilson would not resolve the problem. He was wrong that he would be in the Foreign Office when the Tories returned to government under Ted Heath. His long-term forecast had not foreseen, though, that ten years later, having been out of government again, the Tories would return and that he would be Foreign Secretary and that his then Prime Minister Margaret Thatcher would make it his first task to find a Rhodesian settlement.

In the meantime, Carrington had the problem of deciding how best to handle the differing Tory opinions expressed in Parliament over the question of sanctions. Wilson's government, although not forced to, had gone along with the UN proposal that Rhodesia should be subject to sanctions. Carrington believed sanctions to be a nonsense. Every piece of military and geographical advice suggested they would be broken. As a result, sanctions would do nothing to bring about a settlement, indeed they would serve to

2 President of ZANU-PF (Patriotic Front) and of Zimbabwe from 1988 to 2017.

strengthen the resolve of the Smith regime since it would see that it was beating the international system. Under British law, sanctions could not simply be imposed and then left in place; they had to be renewed by both Houses of Parliament every year. Carrington found himself in a difficult parliamentary and party position. The Lords were tacitly bound by what was known as the Salisbury convention, an understanding devised after the Second World War by the then Tory Leader in the Lords, Lord Salisbury, that while peers would make their opposition known to any legislation sent from the Commons, they would not ultimately stand in its way if it was clear government policy expressed in its General Election manifesto. The Salisbury Rules/Convention did not quite cover Sanction Renewal Orders. Furthermore, it had always been much harder for a Conservative Leader in the Lords to control his peers in opposition than in government. There was a huge and hereditary Tory majority over Labour, Liberal and cross-benchers. In government they would naturally support their own legislative programme. But in opposition Tory peers were quite likely to take it upon themselves to maintain a running battle with Labour Bills sent from the Commons. They either had a genuine objection to those Bills, or they simply saw the debates as an opportunity to express their frustration at being in opposition by challenging government legislation.

When the Sanction Renewal Order came to the Lords, Carrington's task was to show the party's disapproval of sanctions without engineering a constitutional crisis by voting against what was clearly the express wish of the House of Commons and, equally germane, therefore his own leaders in that place. The parliamentary trick was not to vote against, but to abstain. The difficulty was that the sanctions had post-dated election issues and were not therefore part of the Labour manifesto, and hence did not come strictly within the Salisbury Rules. Many Tory peers told Carrington exactly this, in strong terms. The animosity that some of his own people felt towards him for insisting upon abstention rather than provoking a constitutional fight over this issue would not, in some cases, disappear for the rest of his life. Many members of the Lords, the Commons and not a few in the grassroots membership of the Conservative Party continued to believe that Carrington's policies on Rhodesia were wrong. They accused him of selling out and of not being a proper Tory. When President Robert Mugabe set his ZANU-PF supporters on white farmers and their workers – long after Carrington had retired from public life – the hate mail in his post bag was considerable. It was, said the writers, all Carrington's fault.

The irony was that Carrington always believed that sanctions were morally wrong; their effectiveness against UDI was of secondary importance in his mind. Equally, he understood the constitutional position of the Lords and that this was the wrong issue on which to challenge a government and thereby question the role of the House of Lords.

It was not until Carrington took on the leadership of the party in opposition in the House of Lords after the defeat of Douglas-Home that he began to properly question the role of the Upper House. During his time in opposition during the 1940s he had learned the ways of the House and, as a very junior member, been hard pressed to keep up in this new environment. Moreover, the House of Lords in the 1940s was quite a different place from what it was in the late 1960s. In the immediate postwar years Carrington sensed the hangover from the patrician community prior to the war. It was, too, a period of social and political revolution. For the first time there was a powerful Labour government which had an overwhelming mandate from the 1945 electorate to implement the social and industrial changes that even Churchill had acknowledged, albeit in his political desperation, during the election campaign. Here then was the basis of the Salisbury Rules, which Carrington was not alone in accepting as reasonable and politically easy to follow. After all, only the Tories needed them because of their huge in-built hereditary majority.

When Carrington took on the Tory leadership in the Lords, the issues, such as Rhodesian sanctions, were demanding enough for him to put his mind to the future of that place. He quickly came to believe that if the Lords were to survive as an effective second

chamber, then there needed to be a revision of its role and composition. Since going into politics, he had more or less accepted the
received wisdom on the role of the Lords. The two basic functions,
as he saw it, were to revise and thus improve legislation sent from
the Commons. Revising and hopefully improving a Bill were not
procedures necessarily considered to be opposition to the legislation contained in the Bill. It was, and is, very common to improve
a Bill with amendments to the draft. Often this could be with the
government's encouragement. Parliamentary draughtsmanship was
vulnerable to scrutiny and although a Bill might have received a
reading in the Commons, perhaps with a large majority, there was
no hardship when further scrutiny revealed a flaw, even though a
government might go through the political antics of disapproval of
Lords interference. The Lords could, in Carrington's view (and
here again this was the accepted idea), delay legislation with
amendments. He believed that peers could sometimes see public
concerns and urgencies which governments either ignored or were
unable to provide debating time for in the Commons. Therefore,
the Lords could initiate a debate and hope to bring to government's attention sometimes divisive issues.

These crucial roles of the Lords were to be exercised rarely, if at
all, in Carrington's mind. His greatest fear was that either by incompetence or, worse still, political pique, government would push
through legislation that would usurp the accepted institutions of a
nation and therefore its basic liberties. He was, in effect, thinking
about the fundamental idea of kingship: the protection of the
people from their enemies, including bad law-makers, in return for
allegiance. Carrington held that if an unelected House believed it
could be in a position to effect all its self-ordained roles, then it
needed the consensus of the people.

Therefore, Carrington was convinced that the Lords needed to
examine themselves and be encouraged to put forward such
reforms as would make their place a more credible forum for
British democracy. This, in the late 1960s, might have sounded
rather pompous. There was a practical notion to be considered.
That decade was not one of political revolution but it was one of

extraordinary social change. Throughout the British Isles, people were questioning the old order. In the winter of 1960 Macmillan had famously observed the wind of change. That wind blew throughout the decade. Carrington was never certain of the consequences in Britain, yet he understood that it was not possible to keep explaining to the people why an empire was being dismantled; why a government was laying out its plans to withdraw from almost all its commitments East of Suez;[3] why many of the basic institutions, particularly education, were being reviewed; even why Britain was moving closer to the concept of European Union, without at least putting forward the idea that one of its most unrepresentative institutions might be reformed.

In his soundings on all sides of the House, Carrington came to two conclusions. The majority of the peers and many of those to whom he spoke in the Commons felt that the Lords, although out of date, remained a useful institution, mainly for the reasons that he had considered. His second observation was less satisfying. Many, probably the majority, of the Lords believed that the House could no longer be defended in its present form in those times, yet none, it seemed, had any sound idea of what might replace it or how it might be amended.

Carrington felt quite strongly that a large number of hereditary peers really did have a contribution to make to political debate. Moreover, when life peers had appeared in the Lords in 1958, it was hoped that they would be there for their ability rather than their pedigree. There was also the Bench of Bishops who, by definition, were supposed to be extremely wise if not in every way. On paper, and especially in the tearooms, the authority of the Lords was established; yet Carrington had no doubts that the people of these islands read little paper and rarely heard conversations in the tearooms.

Although he supposed it was time for change, Carrington appreciated that the problem of reform was that if the peers were to be seen to be more constitutionally efficient and carry greater

3 See Denis Healey, *The Time of My Life*, London: Michael Joseph, 1989.

weight, then their political standing would be strengthened and thus would threaten the very place that was most critical of them: the House of Commons. Make the Lords more efficient, weaken the authority of the Commons, was a sound assumption.

Yet when the Lords found its will reasonably opposed by the Commons it invariably backed down, having made its protest. An example of this occurred in May 1967 when the House of Lords tried to amend the London Government Bill. When it left the Commons, the Bill declared that the London Borough elections, which were to have taken place in May 1967, should be postponed for twelve months. The peers did not like this and so changed the wording back to May 1967. The Commons rejected the amendments from the Upper House. The Labour front bench in the Commons was angry with what they saw as the in-built majority of the Tory peers interfering in government. Carrington said in the Lords that this notion was entirely wrong.

It is often remarked that the Conservative majority in the Lords is a great handicap to any Labour Government and grossly unfair. The truth is the exact opposite. If anything goes wrong, the Labour Government could use the House of Lords as a whipping boy.

We have conducted ourselves with restraint and moderation and allowed a lot of legislation to go through to which we were utterly opposed and about whose effect on this country we had the gravest misgivings.

We have done it for this reason. We believe that this House, the unelected Chamber, should not, except in the last resort and in quite exceptional circumstances, overrule the opinion of the House of Commons which has been elected by the people of this country. If we did not adopt such a course, it would be impossible for any Labour Government to govern.

This Bill has no mandate from the electorate. Indeed it deprives the electorate of their right to vote. It is a nasty piece of political jiggery-pokery. There are those who feel that this is such an important issue that the Opposition must face the consequences of a firm stand. But there are powerful arguments to the contrary. They have always maintained that they should delay a Bill in order to enable the Commons to think again and to allow the electorate a period for reflection ... It has always been my view that we [the Lords] would use our powers only once. Labour MPs will make sure that the House of Lords is abolished or its delaying powers removed if there is a direct confrontation. One should be completely and utterly convinced of the importance of an issue before staking the future of the House on it.

After much thought I have come to the conclusion that this is not such an issue, not because it is not important but because it is not of such national significance and constitutional gravity as to fit the criteria which I have outlined.

Carrington then followed up his position with a letter to *The Times* which clearly stated what he felt was the role of the House of Lords.

First, it has a revisionary function. The usefulness of this has been proved over and over again, most recently in the work the House has done on the Land Commission Act and the Companies Bill. I do not think that these two Bills would have been amended to such an important degree had it not been for the work of the House of Lords, and I believe this to be a most vital role.

Secondly, the House of Lords, owing to the experience of its members and its less rigid timetable, can debate the important issues of the day with great authority. I believe that the influence of the House of Lords in forming public opinion is growing and the House in recent years has gained in public esteem.

Thirdly ... there could arise a matter of great constitutional and national importance on which there was known to be a deep division of opinion in the country or perhaps on which the people's opinion was not known. In a case of this kind ... the House of Lords has a right, and perhaps a duty, to use its powers, not to make a decision but to afford the people of this country and members of the House of Commons a period for reflection and time for views to be expressed ... we have always maintained that the House of Lords should not in the end make the final decision, but its delaying powers should be used for a period of reflection.

... In the course of arguing that this was not the right occasion to use these powers I said I thought it would be possible to use them only once. This is because the Government in their manifesto published before the last General Election stated that they intend further to curtail the powers of the House of Lords.

Should there be a clash between the two Houses no doubt legislation would be introduced for this purpose. This makes it all the more important to choose the right issue. *That is not to say that I do not absolutely disagree with any proposal to reduce our powers* [author's emphasis]. The 1949 Parliament Act passed under the Labour Government gave these delaying powers to the second chamber. They can and should be used in the sort of situation I have outlined above.

If such an issue arises I shall have no hesitation in advising my Conservative colleagues to stand firm regardless of the consequences. It would be their constitutional right and duty to do so. Yours faithfully,
Carrington – House of Lords, Feb 23.

This was not new thinking from Carrington. He had believed as much since the day he had taken his seat in the House under the guidance of Lord Salisbury. Both his speech during the London Bill debate and his letter to *The Times* reflected Salisbury's teachings. An earlier Lord Salisbury, the last one to be Prime Minister, had, in 1888, suggested the introduction of life peers. This had not been a popular idea until yet another Conservative PM (Harold Macmillan) had recommended the first of the non-hereditary peerages to the Queen in 1958. Until that point, it was simply assumed that a man went to the Lords as Carrington did – because the right came with a coronet – or as Lord Northcliffe supposedly said, 'When I want a peerage, I shall buy one like an honest man.' Five years after the introduction of what became known as working peers, reasonably serious ideas had been put forward to reform the way the Upper House itself worked. In 1965 a House of Commons

Select Committee had reported on procedure in that place. This amounted to an attempt, albeit a tentative one, at modernizing the workings of the Commons. Not unexpectedly, therefore, there was some pressure for the Lords to put their own House in order and to appoint another Select Committee. Equally, peers on both sides accepted that the Lords should not simply mirror the Commons because, as Carrington insisted on 29 April 1965, their House 'had always been at its best when it had been least like the Commons in the conduct of its functions and procedure. It would be a mistake if the Lords regarded itself simply as the Commons writ small.'

Carrington sensed that whatever reforms the Lords might bring about themselves would satisfy (for the moment) the Commons because the Upper House was not yet an election issue – certainly not as it had been prior to the 1911 Parliament Act – and that, with a certain amount of management, the Conservative majority would not force the issue. Although in that debate of 29 April Carrington laid out his belief in the function of that House, there remained a sort of Whiggish temperament to his ideas when he noted that one of the functions of the Lords was to 'act as a Council of State in the sense that owing to the rather slower tempo of affairs there we have time to discuss at our leisure important issues of the day ...'

Politicians on both sides of both Houses believed there should be changes. However, and inevitably, not everyone agreed what those changes should be. Finally, in 1968, the Wilson government introduced a Bill to reform the House of Lords, following an all-party conference on reform. Everything should have been in place. But everything was not.

The Leaders of both Houses (Lord Shackleton and Richard Crossman) led the consultations with Carrington and his deputy Lord Jellicoe, and with the Shadow Leader Iain Macleod in the Commons. The one thing both sides agreed on was that the Lords should have a proper function rather than some Ruritanian role that every so often annoyed government, particularly a Labour one. The conclusion of this group would probably be the only one that would be considered for any length of time by Parliament. It therefore had to be workable and acceptable to the vast majority of MPs and peers.

Carrington thought that if the five of them failed to come up with a workable programme for reform, then there was every chance that the Lords would face some not too distant threat of abolition. At the same time, he was more or less convinced that abolition would fail because no one would agree on what should replace the Lords. He assumed also that there would never be serious discussion of the more intriguing question: should the Lords be replaced at all? It would seem that Carrington became the architect of the group's proposal. He devised a method of Lords reform that within reason could be sold to all but the extremists on both sides of both Houses.

Consequently the Labour government's Lords Reform White Paper, published in 1968, bore Carrington's imprint. He believed that the House of Lords should sit at two levels: Level One would be voting peers, Level Two non-voting peers.

At Level One, there would be up to 250 peers created – some of whom might already be ennobled – and they would be called Lords of Parliament. They would be paid just as MPs were. They would, unlike MPs, have a retirement age. The importance of cross-benchers would be recognized since they held the balance of power between the two main parties. There would be no room for backwoodsmen because a Lord of Parliament would have to attend at least one-third of sittings otherwise he or she would lose the right to vote. The main power of these Lords of Parliament would be to delay Commons legislation for up to half a year.

Level Two would be peers without the right to vote but, as prominent people in their fields, they would be encouraged to speak and therefore add to the debate.

Carrington did not believe this plan to be ideal. In fact, he was rather afraid that it was nothing more than the best one they had – sadly, the best in the best of all possible worlds. He accepted also there was a weakness in his idea, reflected in the views of his old mentor Salisbury. While it sounded very reasonable to have the great and the good speaking in the House either as Lords of Parliament or as non-voters, those same people, because they were well established in their fields, would necessarily be old. Salisbury argued that having, say, fifty hereditary peers in the reformed Upper House would give an opportunity to bring in young blood if not blades.

Anomalies in the plans were obvious. Yet Carrington's view was that a committee of the Privy Council could keep an eye on the reform and recommend amendments as everyone thought necessary. He accepted and helped promote the concept of Lords reform during that year's debate but he never really believed that what might be put in its place would be better for the country than what was already there. It was a case of putting in a reasonable alternative when an unreasonable alternative could easily be made to take its place.

In November 1968 the Lords began to debate its future. Always in Carrington's mind was that the basic function of the House of Lords depended on the extent to which the public recognized it as a defender of the constitution and all that went with it, and the extent to which that same public believed their Lordships' intentions were honourable and should be supported.

When the Lords voted, they supported the idea of their reform by 251 votes for, and 56 against – or Content and Not Content, as the Lords signify a voting result. Yet the Commons, where the whole debate had begun, proved incapable of carrying through the legislation. This was the moment of the unlikely partnership of Michael Foot and Enoch Powell, who stood not shoulder to shoulder but on opposite sides of the House.

Powell was regarded by Carrington – who rather liked him – as a romantic. Powell made it clear that he regarded the Lords as very much part of the parliamentary tradition of democracy. To Powell, what he called the 'parliamentary peerage' was essential to that form of democracy. Therefore, when the government, having won the approval of the Lords, took their Parliament Bill into the Commons three months later, Carrington was convinced that Powell would demand more than the peers had asked for. He was sure that the peerage, without a parliamentary duty, would be defunct. Therefore Powell demanded that the hereditary peers had to be numbered among the Lords of Parliament. His sense of logic would not tolerate the idea of a nominated second chamber. Powell would vote against the legislation because of his fundamental and, according to Carrington, romantic belief in parliamentary tradition.

On the other side of the House, Michael Foot said he too honoured the tradition of the British Parliament although his concept of it was different from Powell's. The fundamental difference between Foot and Powell was that the former was a republican. He had no time for the hereditary peerage nor could he accept the concept of patronage that would put so many placemen in the Upper House.

Where Foot and Carrington agreed was on the ill-conceived idea of a reform which would constitutionally overcome the anomaly of the inherent Conservative majority in the Lords. It would not be possible for the Lords to carry out its function of checking and balancing legislation from the Commons if it were expected that the Upper House would always have a built-in majority of opposition views. Carrington accepted Foot's premise that there was simply no constitutional arrangement that could make sure that when a Labour government was in power there would be a Conservative majority in the Lords, and when a Conservative government was in power there would be a Labour majority of peers. Carrington's memory of that occasion was that it was 'enjoyable stuff, no doubt, but it was purely destructive and intended so to be'. Like Powell, Foot objected to the basic premise of the Parliament Bill and intended to kill it. Here then was the joint aim of the two opposing MPs. Powell did not want the Bill because he wanted to leave the Lords as they were. Foot did not want the Bill because he believed it would give the peers a seemingly more legitimate role.

In 1968 the debate was no more sophisticated than it would be thirty years on. A Labour government and a considerable number of peers – including Carrington on both occasions – wanted change

in the structure and work of the House of Lords; but however long
the debate continued, no one could come up with an alternative –
either in 1968 or in 1999 – that did not look downright wishy-
washy and uninspiring. It was as if the Wilson government had
simply put dull and unimaginative words to a political hymn and
the more verses sung the more obviously wretched and dull the
scholarship that had drafted the lines.

In the autumn of 1968 everyone in both Commons and Lords
understood that the opportunity for reform had been missed yet
again. Only the Cabinet could not bring itself to accept this. It was
not until the following April that Wilson used the excuse of pressing time on the parliamentary programme to announce that the
shabby Parliamentary (Number II) Bill was to be abandoned. There
is an irony that Wilson used Barbara Castle's famous White Paper
on industrial reform, *In Place of Strife*, as one of the supposed priorities. Mrs (later Baroness) Castle was to have her White Paper
dumped because of Cabinet and trade union squabbling and Wilson's indecision. The government had a majority of seventy, but
still could not get through its parliamentary reform. Wilson was
leaving himself open to accusations of incompetence, particularly
by the Conservative Leader in the Commons, Edward Heath.
Heath accused Wilson of personally breaking off party consultations in what he called 'a fit of pique and petulance'.

At this time, Carrington believed that the proposals that he, with
others, had put forward would have led to worthwhile reform
of the Lords. However, though he supported it, he was uncertain
as to how long the new system would have survived. He was, by
then, an experienced parliamentarian and had given almost a quarter of a century of service to government in one form or another;
he had had plenty of time to question not only the constitutional
position of the Lords, but the broader views and examples of
people beyond Westminster, many of whom had no particular
self-interest in the place. For example, his three-year 'sabbatical'
from day-to-day politics while in Australia had allowed him to
absorb the influence and opinions of some who had very particular
views on the working of Parliament in London and of the peerage.

Powell's belief that without Parliament the peerage had no constitutional function, only a social structure, had occurred to Carrington before he had heard it from Powell. Yet he appeared blind to the fact that tinkering with the structure of the Lords (which is what the 1968 debate was all about) would satisfy no intellectual or constitutional demand.

Carrington's proposals had been based on arguments presented before the Great War, even when his famous Uncle Charlie Lincolnshire was in government. What Carrington could not grasp in 1968 was that if there were to be change in the Lords then it had to be radically imposed. This left two possibilities: either abolish the Lords altogether or make it an elected House. At the time Carrington could not stomach either suggestion. Thirty years later, in 1999, he believed that the House of Lords in its existing form should be abolished and replaced with an elected chamber. Nevertheless, in 1999 he accepted a seat as a nominated peer in the system that the Blair government had instituted. As well as his hereditary title, Carrington became a life peer, Baron Carrington of Upton.

When, in April 1969, the government at last admitted that it could not get any further with the Bill, Carrington and the Tory benchers were not overjoyed. Yet, as he told the House, it was hardly a surprise.

This Bill has been as good as dead for some time, and although the Government talk about not proceeding with the measure further at this time, I do not think we will expect to see this Bill in its present form again.

I am disappointed. I am sad because I see an opportunity to reform this House with a considerable measure of agreement between the parties wasted. The White Paper proposals were approved by this House by an overwhelming majority. In future it will not be easy or even possible to get such agreement again. I, and probably Lord Shackleton [Lord Privy Seal and Labour Leader in the Lords], believe that the White Paper proposals would have been workable, acceptable, and authoritative.

Seven years later, Carrington had refined his ideas. In April 1976 he anticipated devolved government in Northern Ireland, Scotland and Wales, together with the increased influence of the European Union.

Unless members of the European Parliament are directly associated with Westminster, there will be real danger of the two parliaments drifting apart. Jealousies, misunderstandings, rivalries will grow. It has proved nearly impossible for a member of the House of Commons to combine membership of both assemblies [Westminster and Strasbourg]. Would it not be worthwhile considering the automatic election to the second chamber of those who have been directly elected to the European Parliament? Coupled with this there could be elections from what eventually emerges as a result of the devolution debates now taking place. This second chamber could then consist of one third directly elected members of the European Parliament, one third directly elected from whatever assemblies emerge from devolution and one third from the existing house – partly to ensure continuity and partly to provide a forum for those eminent in public life who are peers, or have been made life peers.

The *Guardian*'s political correspondent Simon Hoggart reported the speech (made in Scotland) and observed quite correctly that, 'His suggestions virtually amounted to the scrapping of the Lords as it is now.' Tory Central Office immediately claimed this had nothing to do with party policy and was purely Carrington's personal opinion. As the ever perceptive Hoggart noted, 'On this subject at least, his views must carry more weight than any other Conservative.' They did then, but not some twenty years later when during a storming row among senior Tories Carrington tried to mediate only to be literally told to 'Shut up!' by the Conservative Leader William Hague. That was to come and would be a reflection of the way the party had turned to a new and very different generation of leadership and values.

9. The Road to Bloody Sunday

In the summer of 1969 the government was trying to push through changes to the parliamentary boundaries. Here was a confrontation that Harold Wilson, with a false sense of history, imagined would provide him with the sound reason to create bench upon bench of life peers in order to get command of the Upper House. From the 'kitchen cabinet' in Downing Street emerged rumour that if Carrington and his peers opposed what they regarded as gerrymandering by the government, then Wilson would introduce a short Bill in the Commons that would remove the delaying powers of the House of Lords, might even expel hereditary peers and could quickly introduce new life members.

Carrington could see the reason for the opposition to the Boundaries Bill, but he was determined to be in total command of the way in which his ennobled troops fought it. He called a meeting of peers, who all had different ideas of how the matter should be treated; he told them that the Bill should be allowed through without a division on its second reading and then, during the committee stage, they should bring forward an amendment, or even a series of amendments, to stop the gerrymandering. Carrington's task was to obstruct the government without damaging the Lords constitutionally or, equally, its public esteem. Could Wilson have carried out his threat to flood the House with his placemen? Carrington at the time judged that Wilson would fail for one simple reason: he did not know a couple of hundred people whom he might ennoble and who would turn up regularly to outvote the Tories.

Wilson's own people did not like the confrontation because if boundaries were not agreed then a series of pending by-elections would be delayed even further. The longer the elections were put off, the greater the chance of the government's increasing unpopularity setting the electorate against the Labour candidates. The political management of the whole affair may have seemed right at the time but, twelve months later, it did not matter. Wilson was gone (for the moment) and the Tories were once more in power (for the moment).

In 1966 Wilson had returned to power with 363 seats. All had appeared well. Three years later his government was in a mess and, by 1969, parliamentary reform and, perhaps more importantly for Labour, Trade Union Law Reform as it appeared in Barbara Castle's White Paper *In Place of Strife* had been abandoned. On 18 May 1970 Wilson announced that a General Election would be held on 18 June. By the end of the month, Wilson was telling his Cabinet that they were being too complacent. One curious aspect of that election was that the opinion polls seemed to think that Wilson would win – which was one of the main reasons he dissolved Parliament. Certainly the difference between the two party leaders was marked, as Carrington remembered:

On the one hand, Ted Heath, stiffened and uncharismatic, had had an unsympathetic press while Harold Wilson was sailing through the campaign radiating presidential bonhomie backed by favourable polls. On the other hand I sensed an undercurrent of detachment among our own activists and party audiences.[1]

Carrington believed the opinion polls. He did not believe that Heath had the personality to impress the electorate. He imagined the depressing prospect of many more years in opposition, and he said as much to his close friend William Whitelaw. He was convinced that Heath's belief that he would win was misguided and that the Tories would lose that June election. On election day, Carrington went down to Heath's constituency at Bexley in Kent. He had not arranged to do so and Heath was surprised and suspicious. The story at this stage is one of contradictory views: Carrington suggested in his autobiography that he had gone to Bexley to support Heath,

1 Conversation with author.

whereas Heath believed that Carrington had gone as grim political reaper.

At lunchtime there was an unexpected visit from Peter Carrington. After congratulating me on the fight, he told me that, should we lose, I would be expected immediately to stand down. This advice was well meant, but quite unnecessary. This election campaign had been a fair contest and I would have stood aside without any prompting if the result had gone against us. It did not. From the declaration of the first result, David Howell's victory at Guildford, I knew that my instincts had been a better guide to the result than the supposed science of the opinion pollsters.[2]

Ironically, when many years later Carrington advised Thatcher to go, she assumed he was still a Heathite, never realizing that the party had once given him the unenviable task of telling Heath that he may have to stand down. Whatever the differences in confidence, Heath had and continued to have high regard for Carrington. His experience in the old Defence Ministry, the Admiralty (in spite of the difficulties over Vassall and the Portland spy ring) and, after that, as deputy to Rab Butler at the Foreign Office, made Carrington a natural choice for a Cabinet job. Heath also took into account the fact that because Carrington had been in the Lords he had as First Lord of the Admiralty had to speak for the government on a much wider defence brief than the Royal Navy. He gave him the defence portfolio.

Defence is one of the biggest spenders of public money, yet, apart from the Foreign Office, the least accountable. At that time it had the third biggest budget in Whitehall and the department was the largest employer of civil servants. It remained the bedrock of enforcing British foreign policy and, in spite of Denis Healey's restructuring of defence commitments in the previous administration, the British military retained a global role with a sensitivity that went beyond the uneasy confrontation in Cold War politics.

2 Edward Heath, *The Course of My Life*, London: Hodder & Stoughton, 1998, p. 307.

The Royal Navy was still deployed worldwide along most lines of latitude: the enforcement of policy in the Falkland Islands, Belize in Central America, a full garrison in Hong Kong, a South-east Asia commitment, an active deployment including seconded troops in the Gulf States and in support of Sultan Qaboos of Oman in his war against the People's Democratic Republic of Yemen, the protection of sovereign bases in Cyprus, commitments in Malta and Gibraltar – all of these, on top of the enormous deployment of Royal Navy, Army and RAF in the NATO commands and the British Army on the Rhine.

There was also the continuing and sometimes vexed question of Britain's nuclear capability. The spearhead of the nation's nuclear weapons power was contained in four Polaris submarines, each of which carried missiles with multiple nuclear warheads. It was Carrington's task to take the decision to update Polaris and although the modernization programme, known as Chevaline, provided a controversial subject some years later, it was Carrington who started it.

The sixth floor of the Defence Ministry, where the Secretary of State then reigned, turned out to be an outpost of the Guards' Club. Carrington and his deputies Robin Balniel and Ian Gilmour had all been officers in the Grenadiers. There were those along that corridor who had not been Grenadiers and quite frankly made it clear that they did not entirely support this club spirit. Carrington felt at home in the ministry, which was hardly surprising considering his background. However, it was not a job without burdens.

As well as the Polaris issue, it was left to Carrington to implement the draconian restructuring that Healey had designed. This was the famous, or to some of the military infamous, plan to withdraw Britain's military presence east of Suez. In opposition Carrington had been instrumental in preparing the Conservative case against the Healey cuts. This was a more complex task than might be imagined because Carrington saw the sense of and privately supported some of Healey's reorganization. Carrington's experience told him that admirals, generals and air marshals always wanted more of anything but this military kleptomania did not necessarily provide for efficient armed forces. Manpower was an obvious example of services that were more efficient without National Service but nevertheless they had to accept that few young men wanted to join up. Carrington had defined one of the advantages of doing away with conscription as an opportunity to have highly motivated and professional forces. But when he arrived as Secretary of State for Defence ten years after conscription ended he did not find the recruiting offices crowded. There was a huge manpower shortage in the services. He quickly concluded that manpower, both in recruiting and retention, was the biggest problem that he faced as Secretary of State. In October 1970 he went to speak at the Royal United Services Institute for Defence Studies in Whitehall with a message that many of the audience had anticipated. The Healey cuts had – partly thanks to the Conservatives – been portrayed not as a rational assessment of what Britain needed to do and what it could afford to do but as an indication that Labour did not care about defence. This was not true. In reality, many of the Chiefs of Staff believed that they did rather better under Labour. The opinion was that Labour was always reluctant to cut back too much on equipment spending because it risked the knock-on effect of cutting jobs in the defence industries. Carrington argued at the RUSI that one of the main problems of recruiting was that would-be soldiers, sailors and airmen were certainly not going to sign up if they did not believe the government gave any importance to the whole matter of Britain's military system. Yet this was hardly the whole truth. There remained other employment opportunities and the services retained much of their National Service image. And, unlike his soldiers when he joined his battalion, young people in Britain in 1970 were not hungry.

To add to the manpower problems, there was now a new responsibility. The previous year, 1969, the then Home Secretary, James Callaghan, had approved a direct request from Gerry Fitt (later Lord Fitt) to send extra troops on to the streets of Northern Ireland. Callaghan had wisely noted that it was easy to send troops but that it would be difficult to get them back again. Carrington

would be the Secretary of State for the next four years. It was a
time of enormous bloodshed and controversy in military deployment in the Province, including the January 1972 event known as
Bloody Sunday, the inquiry into which would still be going on
thirty years later, long after Carrington had retired.[3]

The immediate task, however, was to continue the withdrawal of
British troops from far-off commitments, some of which were
hangovers from Empire. The two major areas from which to fall
back were the Far East and the Middle East.

Carrington did not have a unique insight into the strategic
importance of the Far East nor how it might be developed without
the physical presence of all three services. It was now exactly ten
years since he had returned from Australia. Thanks to his time in
Australasian banking and with an increasingly wide circle of international friends, he had kept in touch with developments in
South-east Asia. In Australia he had learned the importance of balancing emerging political and economic ambitions with the need
to provide reassurance that old obligations would not be abandoned. An example of this was the regional understanding that
some defence pact that included the United Kingdom would be
an enormous advantage. Defence agreements usually come when
there is a common enemy or threat. In South-east Asia and the Far
East, that threat was thought to be Communism. Britain had been
a major part of the United Nations force that had gone to war in
Korea in 1950, and British troops had countered Communist insur-
gency in Malaya. Furthermore, the possibilities outlined by strategic
think tanks of the spread of the conflict between North and South
Vietnam was certainly taken seriously by the incoming Heath
government.

In 1970 Carrington's view was that he did not believe that Britain
should be involved militarily in the war in Indo-China. His position
was that Healey's Far East withdrawal programme should be imple-

3 Work on the second Bloody Sunday Inquiry, under Lord Saville, started in
2000, finished hearing evidence in 2004 and was published on 15 June 2010.

mented, but some marker had to be left that showed that Britain recognized her traditional obligation within the region. This recognition was not simply to support Singapore and Malaysia, but reflected the traditions and obligations that Britain felt towards Australia and New Zealand.

One option was to reverse the Healey withdrawal programme. This was never seriously considered. Healey's East of Suez assessment was not some dogmatic socialist ploy to strip Britain of its defence capability. It was a carefully constructed plan by a man considered by many – including those in the military – to be the best defence minister in the postwar era. Dr Henry Kissinger regarded Healey as a man with a brilliant mind which had been put to careful use when judging what Britain's defence policy needed to be in the decades following the 1960s. Healey saw no point in having a military posture that had been cut out of an old imperial picture book. Money was limited. Manpower, after conscription had been abandoned, was in very short supply and existing levels could not be guaranteed. Equipment costs for all three services spiralled. Looking at Britain's worldwide defence obligations in the second half of the 1960s, Healey said that they could no longer be afforded and the longer they were maintained, the less likely they could be honoured. Carrington agreed.

One of his first tasks was to negotiate the Five Power Pact with Australia, Malaysia, New Zealand and Singapore. The Pact provided for Britain to send forces if any of the other nations were threatened. This was no startling international treaty and none of the member states believed it to be so. But in July and August 1970, as Carrington went from country to country, it was clear to him that this was about the only way that Britain could give some token that it had not entirely abandoned its friends east and south of Suez. It was only a token. It was never clear at what levels UK troops could return to the region, still less what logistical resupply could keep them there. Nor was there a proper guideline that would speed the political process in London which had to be exercised in spite of the obligations in the Five Power Pact.

The one place Britain could not leave, not for another quarter of a century, was Hong Kong. Yet even here, force levels had been reduced. There remained an army garrison. HMS *Tamar* was still a naval base under a senior captain and there was a Gurkha camp up in the New Territories. Nevertheless, even by 1970 or so there was a feeling that the British were withdrawing and that the harbour belonged to the American fleet and the bars increasingly to US soldiers taking a rest from Vietnam.

At that stage in the development of British defence policy under Carrington, the more complex debate hinged on a simple argument: the rights and wrongs of British nuclear weapons policy. Here again was an example of the Secretary of State who came to the forefront of an argument which he had debated as a junior minister for more than a decade. Because he had led Conservative defence policy debates in the Lords, Carrington was possibly more aware of the general argument than most promoted to the senior job in the Ministry of Defence. The main thrust of the nuclear debate had not changed since Carrington last worked in the MOD.

Carrington had long supported the United Kingdom's nuclear weapons policy. To have the technology meant the opportunity to have the system. This in turn made the diplomatic argument for possessing nuclear weapons – the so-called voice at the top table – hard to dismiss. The United Kingdom was one of the five permanent members of the United Nations Security Council. The link between all five – China, France, the United Kingdom, the United States of America and the Union of Soviet Socialist Republics – was that each was a nuclear weapons state. The two most remembered clichés of nuclear weapons proponents would remain 'You cannot uninvent the technology' and 'You cannot put the genie back in the bottle'. Carrington had never doubted the effectiveness of this sentiment nor the power it gave the United Kingdom at a time when its international commitments were being reduced and with them its international authority.

As a junior minister Carrington had made the case for a transatlantic nuclear weapons policy, faced as the West was with a perceived threat from an increasingly sophisticated Soviet nuclear capability. This threat was at sea, in the air both from bombers and rocketry and on land from short-range tactical and theatre nuclear weapons within the Soviet army. On top of all that, during the 1960s the Soviet Union produced a development plan for Fractional Orbital Bombardment Systems. In the simplest terms, nuclear warheads would be carried in orbiting satellites which in a time of war could be directed back into the earth's atmosphere and then target areas in the United States. As Soviet scientists had demonstrated that they had the technology to bring back a re-entry vehicle with a cosmonaut on board, returning a random constellation of nuclear armed satellites was relatively simple.

In the early 1970s, once the practicalities of implementing the last government's retrenchment policy had been arranged and the shortage of manpower allowed for, then Carrington's reasoning for the Conservative defence argument was straightforward: the enemy was there for all to see. Twenty years on, defence expenditure would be harder to justify until Britain realized that it was reverting to something akin to a colonial policing roll. In 1970 there were no ambiguities.

The Soviet Union was in the East, Britain was in the West, the Soviet Union had the Warsaw Treaty Organization, Britain belonged to the North Atlantic Treaty Organization and the line between war and peace was visible. The Chiefs of Staff of all three services could easily look to the Soviet Union, the Group of Soviet Forces Germany, its strategic rocket forces, airforces, surface ships and submarines in all four fleets (the Northern, the Pacific, the Baltic and the Black Sea), the almost daily deployment of bombers and reconnaissance aircraft to the very edge of British air space and then on to Moscow's client state, Cuba, the accelerated submarine-launched ballistic missile programme, the training and deployment innovations inspired by Admiral Sergei Gorshkov,[4] together with a formidable list of public statements from Soviet military and public leaders on capabilities (but not intentions) of all four Soviet services, as well as an active military intelligence gathering

4 Sergei Georgievich Gorshkov (1910–88).

apparatus. All this provided reasonable enough excuse, if excuse were needed, for the pressure Carrington was expected to apply in Cabinet and in the all important discussions with the Treasury.

In February 1971, during the Defence Estimates debate in the Lords, Carrington laid out what amounted to his own estimation of the Soviet threat and his belief in the way Britain should respond. He said that the Russians were threatening enough. They were determined to have forces that were on a par with American strategic weapons.

The Russians are aiming at parity ... and are well on the road towards it. The Strategic Arms Limitation Talks (SALT) offer hope of a check, but the European members of NATO can no longer take comfort in their superiority in strategic nuclear weapons of the United States.

The nuclear guarantee is still there, but its credibility will depend increasingly on the maintenance of NATO and of its capacity to deploy well equipped conventional forces in adequate numbers.

He then came to what was increasingly the theme of the Royal Navy lobby, which maintained that the growing superiority of the Soviet surface, sub-surface and merchant fleets threatened the traditional supply lines, the so-called sea lanes, to the United Kingdom. The UK was totally reliant on free sea lanes for its imports of raw materials, most foodstuffs and oil.

We as a nation depend so heavily for our livelihood upon the shipping lanes across the Indian Ocean as well as having substantial interests around its shores, that we can only watch this expansion with growing concern ... the Russians have not achieved this massive build up of their fleet and their military strength generally without a vast expenditure of money and resources. Bearing in mind all the other heavy burdens the Soviet economy has they can hardly have gone in for such expenditure without the most careful reasoning.

We are entitled to wonder what that reasoning is. They have certainly not been doing it for fun ... I am not seeking to rattle any sabres, even less am I trying to justify an imperial role for Britain in the 1970s ... In practical terms Britain must be ready, in association with their allies, to deploy their forces outside as well as inside Europe as part of the deterrent to aggression and our contribution to stability.

By 1972 the debate over Britain's nuclear weaponry was reaching a difficult state within Cabinet. There was pressure for what was called a comprehensive test ban treaty. This would, in theory, stop all testing of nuclear systems. The concept that computer testing would replace explosions of actual weapons, especially trigger mechanisms, had not yet gathered credibility. There were therefore four reasons to test: new weapons needed proving; old weapons needed checking; trigger mechanisms needed constant updates; weapons effects had to be monitored. Yet apart from testing modernizations, none of these reasons held much water.

What was particularly important for Britain, and not on the list of four, was the need to maintain Britain's right to test weapons in America. The UK had no nuclear test facilities after the weapon sites had been closed in Australia. Consequently, there appeared no way in which Britain would ever support a test ban, because their nuclear testing host, the United States, would never in the foreseeable future agree to banning tests at their Nevada sites. (An international test ban treaty is unlikely to be ratified by Congress.) Moreover, the principles of arms control were defined, not by global movements, but the two superpowers.

Any arms control agreement began as a bilateral treaty between the USA and USSR. Everyone else signed up to it if they wished, or could be persuaded to. Arms control treaties had one function, to indicate the state of East–West relations on the day the document was signed. Nothing more. No agreement in the history of arms control was ever signed unless either side no longer wanted the weapon system that was to be banned, or did not want the other side to have it, or could never work out the technology to make it themselves. Thus, arms control was nothing more than a reflection of how the Soviet Union and the United States felt about each other on the day. Britain, as Carrington would point out to Prime Minister Ted Heath, had no need to get involved. It had two simple concerns: nothing should be done to stop or high-light its own nuclear weapons deployments – especially new systems – and nothing should jeopardize Britain's top table seat as a nuclear power. Without nuclear weapons, Britain had no clout anywhere. That was the wisdom of the day.

Carrington raised a third concern: who had absolute command of Britain's nuclear weapons? This was the early 1970s and the government still had people who had served in the Second World War, including Heath, Whitelaw and Carrington. They had witnessed what happened after that war when Stalin created a cordon between Eastern and Western Europe. The Iron Curtain was not hearsay to them; they had seen the determination of Soviet forces towards the end of the war. All three had made lasting judgements about what was meant by the military-enforced partition of Europe. And each had been briefed daily on the expansion of Soviet forces. In particular, they had watched the growth of the thirty-one divisions (many Category A) of the Soviet Group of Forces Germany, and the huge development of Admiral Gorshkov's Northern Fleet, in which seemingly every day appeared new ships and nuclear-powered and in some cases nuclear-missiled submarines. Most importantly, considering this was a nuclear debate, each was impressed with the development of the Soviet strategic rocket forces – the weapons that carried the most sophisticated of the USSR's long-range nuclear weaponry.

In light of all this, it is hardly surprising that Carrington had definite views on maintaining Britain's independent nuclear weapons system – independent, that is, from everyone, including the United States. First and foremost in Carrington's mind was the tricky political conundrum of where Britain kept its nuclear weapons. In this period, the early 1970s, there was much speculation that British nuclear weapons were deployed in Germany. This was always denied, or at the very least 'neither confirmed nor denied', partly because of a natural sense of secrecy. Why make it easy for the Warsaw Pact commanders to know for sure what nuclear weapons were where? It was assumed that they thought they knew – which mostly they did – but why confirm it for them? Uncertainty is a valuable weapon. Second, great care had to be taken when considering the political sensitivities of the German people and their governments. Just as there was always opposition to American nuclear weapons on British soil, so the German protest was also a potential No Vote at any election. In 1971 all this was particularly important to Carrington, because he was about to authorize the deployment of new nuclear systems to Germany. In spite of speculation that Britain had long kept nuclear weapons in what was then West Germany, this was in fact the first time they had been deployed there. With this in mind, Carrington wrote to Heath on 10 March 1971 that:

I fully accept the need for us to hold as long as possible our public position of neither confirming nor denying the presence of nuclear weapons at any particular place, especially as it will be a year or so before these weapons are deployed in Germany. There is always the risk, however, of a leak which cannot be contained; and, if this should occur, we must be ready to present this deployment decision to the greatest political advantage. It seems to me that – notwithstanding the tactical nuclear weapons which we already have under our own control in Britain and at sea – we must regard the stationing of nuclear weapons on the Continent under British control for the first time as a matter of considerable political significance from the European point of view. I have in mind our present thinking on the development of closer European defence cooperation in general and Anglo-French nuclear collaboration in particular. I believe that this is a positive point that officials should follow up in preparing for the discussions with the Germans and subsequently the French.

Within that letter was the hint of a conundrum to be faced by Heath and Carrington. Carrington wrote that the weapons would be in Germany under British control. But what did that mean? As far as most in the MOD and the FCO understood, it meant exactly what it said. The weapons were British, so commanders would turn to the British Prime Minister for 'nuclear release' – permission to use them. That seemed straightforward. Not to

Carrington. His view was that the Americans would most likely
have an entirely different version of what it might mean. Carrington
argued that in the event of war, British forces and their weapon
systems would be under the command of the Supreme Allied
Commander Europe (SACEUR), always an American four-star
general. If a British commander wanted to use nuclear systems,
did he ask the PM or the American SACEUR? If that commander judged that nuclear release was unwise, did he take
instructions from Downing Street or SACEUR – in other words,
the Prime Minister or the President? This conundrum was addressed in a further letter from Carrington to Heath, this time
on 18 January 1972.

[SECRET]

CONTROL OF BRITISH NUCLEAR WEAPONS BASED IN GERMANY

1. As you know, the RAF Canberras in Germany which are
assigned to SACEUR in the nuclear role have been partly replaced
by Phantoms, and the remainder are now being replaced by Buccaneers. Since the Buccaneers will be equipped with British weapons,
I have been considering the control arrangements which should
apply to these aircraft.

2. The very long-standing arrangement governing the Canberras,
for which American nuclear weapons are provided, is that at the
appropriate NATO Alert stage – and subject to your authority –
the aircraft are transferred to SACEUR's direct command exercised
through 2nd Allied Tactical Air Force and not through RAF Germany. After that stage we cease to exercise control over them
through British command channels. Political control is maintained
by SACEUR's obligation to get the authority of the US President
for the use of nuclear weapons and, *time permitting* [author's italics],
to refer to the North Atlantic council. The President in turn has an
obligation to consult you, though this again is qualified by 'time
permitting'.

3. This arrangement has long been accepted as a special departure
from the general principle that you should exercise positive control

over all our nuclear forces through a British command channel. The reason for it is to avoid the complications and potential delays which would otherwise be introduced into SACEUR's arrangements for the control of his nuclear strike force on the Continent (of which the Canberras form only one – and a relatively small – element).

4. I have carefully considered whether the introduction of the Buccaneers with their British weapons requires any change in these arrangements. (No new point arises on the Phantoms which, as you will recall, will be equipped, like the Canberras, with American nuclear weapons.)

5. With the Buccaneers there is the vital difference that since they will have British bombs Britain will be the 'owning power' and therefore SACEUR will require your explicit authority (not that of the US President) before he may order them to make a nuclear strike. With this important difference I have concluded that we can safely maintain the procedure which we have long accepted for the Canberra aircraft (and which would in any case continue to apply to the Phantoms). In military terms it would make no sense to distinguish between the weapons and the aircraft, and identical arguments apply for passing the control of both to SACEUR at the appropriate stage (subject to your specific authority at that time).

6. We propose to remind SACEUR of his obligation to seek your specific authority before employing the aircraft on nuclear strikes (and of our own commitment to consult the Germans) when the Buccaneers are formally assigned to him, and to ensure that his standard operating procedures require reference to HMG before the British weapons are employed. This will give us direct and unqualified political control as compared with the Canberra arrangements, under which (para 2 above) our control is exercised only by virtue of our membership of the North Atlantic Council and/or our bilateral understanding with the US President, both being qualified by 'time permitting'.

7. The first squadron of Buccaneer aircraft is due to be declared operational in the nuclear role on 1st February next and it would be most helpful to know as soon as possible that you approve our proceeding on this basis.

Number 10 was uncertain of its position. On 20 January the PM's private secretary Robert Armstrong (later Lord Armstrong) sought to guide Heath.

Prime Minister
. . . It is, however, for question whether you should offer to consult the President, time permitting, before you authorise the release of British weapons; or whether this would in practice be covered by SACEUR's obligation to get the President's authority for the use of nuclear weapons. It is not clear that SACEUR's obligation to consult the President covers all nuclear weapons, ours as well as theirs.
Robert Armstrong[5]

Carrington's private secretary Robert Andrew attempted to reassure Armstrong and therefore Heath – which was perhaps the whole purpose of the exchanges.

Dear Robert,
In your letter of 20th January 1972 you asked whether the pro-posals put forward by the Defence Secretary for the control of British nuclear weapons based in Germany were likely to lead to a request from the United States Government that the Prime Minis-ter should consult the President, time permitting, before giving his authority for employing aircraft on nuclear strikes.
    The Understandings with the United States Government on the release of nuclear weapons, which are re-affirmed on each change of Administration, include a general undertaking that the United States Government will consult us, *if possible* [author's italics], before

5 Carrington papers, Bledlow.

using nuclear weapons anywhere. *There is no formal reciprocal undertaking on our part* [author's italics].

Although we cannot exclude the possibility that at some stage the US will ask for such a reciprocal undertaking it does not seem particularly likely that they will do so on this occasion. In the first place, the British-armed Buccaneers in Germany will be on the same footing as other British nuclear forces assigned to NATO (eg Polaris and the V force) for whose release the NATO guidelines already require HMG's specific agreement. Secondly, although under the NATO procedures SACEUR is formally obliged to get the agreement of the President only for the use of American nuclear weapons, we think it likely that he will in fact seek such agreement (and may indeed be required to do so by American rules) before using British nuclear weapons.[6]

That letter was written just four days before Bloody Sunday, and the nuclear weapons became operational the day after Bloody Sunday. Little wonder then that Carrington might have been distracted at about that time. For the rest of that year, he had to put the deployment and release schedules to one side, since much of his time was taken up with the consequences of Bloody Sunday.

Yet no Secretary of State for Defence can expect to escape the seemingly arcane world of nuclear debate. Positions, once in government, are different from those in opposition, when, apart from political opportunism, to have or not to have can be seen directly as party ideology. In practice and in government, the argument is more complex. A Labour Party against nuclear weapons is not the same as one in government. Thus, it was a later Labour government (Callaghan's) that modernized British submarine-launched nuclear warheads. It was also a Labour Cabinet which, in early 1979, agreed to introduce American so-called cruise missiles into Britain, even though one of the most public supporters of the Campaign for Nuclear Disarmament, Michael Foot, was a member of that Cabinet.

6 The National Archives, PREM 15/1363.

Conservatives have always voted for nuclear weapons in the UK military armoury. However, Carrington's view in early 1970 went way beyond the terms of the party manifesto. In government, he suggested, there were further legitimate considerations. These matters may be simple policy, but when a government found it necessary to deal with the day-to-day consequences of being a nuclear power, then extra minds and opinions had to be brought into the debate. The legality of weaponry meant the interest of the law officers. The deployment involved the Foreign and Commonwealth Office assessing territorial sensitivities. The danger of components or allied materials getting into the wrong hands involved the Departments of Trade and Industry, Customs and Excise and the Home Office. Operational ownership was in the hands of the Ministry of Defence. The further debate in which Carrington became involved, especially in 1973, was about the future of all weapons. The test ban treaty argument had once more surfaced. In the summer of that year, Carrington was concerned enough about British policy to write a personal, but still classified *secret*, letter to Heath:

27th July, 1973

Dear Ted

... Though we have supported the principle of a comprehensive test ban agreement in the discussions of the Disarmament Conference at Geneva, our own testing programme is such that we have no wish to see such an agreement come into force for at least the next five years or so. During that time, we shall need to test British devices underground and to take part in US tests of underground effects at their test site in Nevada. Our policy has accordingly been to maintain a low profile on this issue, leaving initiatives to other countries and keeping in step with US policy.

A great deal of seismic work is being done to help define a detection and verification system which could be incorporated into a comprehensive test ban treaty and which would give reasonable assurance that underground explosions in the low kiloton range could be detected and identified. But the difficulties are formidable and have not yet been overcome. Indeed it may be that no practical system could be devised which could not be evaded by shots on the low kiloton range. In Geneva we have concentrated much of our effort on these technical aspects of verification, and we have made and continue to make a useful contribution to this work.

The Foreign and Commonwealth Secretary will, I understand, confirm that neither of the two major nuclear powers appears to be pressing for a comprehensive test ban at the moment. We have been told that the National Security Council has recently decided that the US have no interest in a comprehensive test ban treaty at present [or ever, as successive US administrations demonstrated, whatever the personal ambitions of the President]; and the rate at which the US find it necessary to conduct underground tests makes it most unlikely that they would look with favour on a British initiative. The latest indication of the Russian attitude is that if a Western proposal for CTB negotiations looked like getting off the ground, they would insist that all nuclear powers, and especially the Chinese, would have to participate. This would effectively kill any initiative. In addition any step towards a comprehensive test ban treaty would be likely to deter the French from abandoning atmospheric tests in favour of underground ones. This would be regrettable not least because, if the French continued tests in the atmosphere, potential nuclear powers might feel freer to follow their example rather than adopt the more difficult and costly course of testing underground.

My view is, therefore, that an initiative by us at present would run counter to our defence interests. It is unlikely to be successful; it would antagonise the United States; and would complicate the problem of maintaining an effective British nuclear force.

I am copying this letter to the Foreign and Commonwealth Secretary.

Yours ever

Peter

SECRET AND PERSONAL[7]

7 The National Archives, PREM 15/1378.

It was this letter, in the summer of 1973, with the Geneva disarmament process living in hope of a lead from one of the great powers, which convinced Heath that British policy should be simple: no comprehensive nuclear test ban agreement in our time, and nothing should be done to fall out of step with the Americans.

In the context of the ongoing nuclear debate and the continuing horrors of Northern Ireland, it was almost a relief to be forced into another confrontation – this time in Malta.

Carrington believed the leader of Malta, Dom Mintoff, to be unbalanced. He thought him a man of mood swings who came from the same school as another erratic adversary, Colonel Qaddafi of Libya. To be bracketed with Qaddafi was no mean achievement. In fact, Mintoff's relationship with Qaddafi was reasonably close. The Libyan had been in power for only a couple of years, having led the coup against King Idris, and was now the Chairman of the Revolutionary Command Council. Dom Mintoff, in Malta, had his own idea about revolution which was, very simply, based on kicking the British military off the island.

Britain's position had hinged on the hope that when the Maltese went to the polls in June 1971 they would re-elect the relatively pro-British Dr Borg Olivier as Prime Minister. Olivier was no lapdog. He had gone to Harold Wilson's government for an increase in the payments that Britain gave the island under the 1964 Defence Agreement. In light of the Labour government's run-down of British overseas defence commitments, the idea of paying Malta any more money was not seriously considered. Four years on, in 1971, the Conservative government was at least talking to the Maltese about some improvement in the financial arrangement. The Foreign Office and the Defence Ministry, under Carrington, believed that they could fix the election by letting Olivier appear, just before polling day, to have wrung out of the United Kingdom government a package, mostly grants in aid, worth about £50 million. But this blatant pork-barrelling did not work. Olivier lost the election by one vote. Mintoff, the new

Prime Minister, immediately told the British that they were going to have to come up with a lot more money if they wanted to remain in Malta.

Mintoff has sometimes been seen as some kind of Mediterranean devil. That view is a very colonial one. Whatever Whitehall believed, Mintoff maintained (and continued to maintain) that he was not fighting the British for the fun of it. He was, in his terms, fighting for a new way of life for the island, which in the long run would mean getting rid of foreign military bases and becoming – so far as was possible – properly independent. Equally, Mintoff understood that in the short term the island economy relied on British funding, which in turn was based entirely upon rent in various forms for military bases. Mintoff therefore knew that the islanders could not be independent of the British military unless they could find the money from elsewhere. They hoped this could be done by building up their limited industrial base and exploiting the island's greatest assets: its climate, scenery and people. To develop those resources, Mintoff had to negotiate some way for the British to continue to have a presence on the island so that he could get the money that he wanted for his long-term plans.[8]

Carrington understood this. What he seems not to have understood was the determination of Mintoff to achieve exactly what he needed in his political and economic plan. From the first day of Mintoff's premiership he laid out a five-point demand. First, he wanted an increase in rent. Second, this increase would be payable in cash without any conditions as to the way it was spent. Third, it was to be a short-term agreement. Fourth, the British were to agree to run down their forces on the island so that they would all be gone by the end of the agreement, but that run-down would be implemented in such a way that the Maltese economy would not be embarrassed. Fifth, locally employed Maltese were to be given reasonable pay-offs and help in finding other jobs.

8 See Edgar Mizzi, *Malta in the Making*, privately published, 1995.

Carrington intended to go to Malta on 14 July 1971 to talk to
Mintoff about these demands. He was on his way to the airport
when he got a message from Mintoff saying that there was no
point in coming unless Carrington agreed to a big lump sum for
the rent. Carrington was not used to being treated like this and
cancelled the flight.

In Whitehall it was generally thought that Carrington could not
simply sit in his sixth-floor office and pretend Mintoff was of no
importance. If Britain had abandoned its imperial past, then it
could no longer treat small-islander PMs as house-boys. Five days
later he went to Malta. The talks were not successful. Carrington
more or less went along with most of Mintoff's demands except
for the first one, the rent. Mintoff said that he wanted £30 million
from Britain. What do we get for that? asked Carrington. An exclusive tenancy, came Mintoff's reply. So this was the difficulty for
Britain and the cause of so much argument for the rest of the year.
Mintoff told Carrington that unless the British government came
up with £30 million, he would go elsewhere for the money. He
went so far as to offer Carrington a deal: if he did not want exclusive rights, he could pay just £20 million, but then Mintoff would
look elsewhere for another tenant to make up the extra £10 million. At this point Carrington had to consider Britain's position as
a member of NATO. Britain and NATO did not want the Russians using the island as a refuelling stop for ships and planes; and
there were dark mutterings about revolutionary tendencies inspired
by Qaddafi. Moreover, two of NATO's southern states, France and
Italy, were close enough to the island to be concerned about who
might be the second tenant.

As ever, Carrington kept no record of that meeting other than
in his memory. But Lady Carrington did.

19th July 1971

Peter went off finally to Malta where Mintoff, fearful that his previous
discourtesy had been a mistake, put himself out to entertain him and
Robin Balniel [Lord Balniel, Carrington's deputy]. After explaining that
there had been nothing personal in his refusal to meet him, he announced

that he was going to give them a real Maltese meal. This banquet, cooked by Miss Mintoff, a student at Exeter University, consisted of: Black widow soup – very thick (the temperature outside in the 90s); Goat cheese tart – quite solid and cardboard pastry; Beef from Australia – it must have walked from Kimberley to Alice Springs; Maltese fruit. All washed down by home-made wine, the most palatable part of the dinner. This feast ended about 11.30pm and they were then invited to walk on the ramparts. They drove off accompanied by Mintoff's Communist secretary and tramped the ramparts until 1.15am. At one point a donkey stood across the steps. The secretary was too scared to brush past it so remained behind – perhaps he just disliked walking.[9]

Carrington in the meantime was having to face the fact that there was no way Britain could afford to meet Mintoff's terms. He was willing to pay about £5 million, and hand out the balance in overseas aid. This was normal procedure. This did not satisfy Mintoff, who wanted cash in hand so that his government could decide how to spend it, not some official from the Department of Overseas Aid. Moreover, Carrington had come to the conclusion that the reason to maintain Malta as a military base was not to directly protect any British interest but to enforce the strategic plan for NATO's southern flank. As far as he was concerned, NATO should come up with the rest of the money.

It was the view in Malta that Carrington miscalculated and did not understand Mintoff's determination to find alternative funding. Mintoff did not mind certain press reports suggesting that he might turn to the Soviet Union, but there was no way in which he either could or would. He knew too well that he would lose any hope of future independence once he went in that direction. The prospect of an arrangement with Libya was far less threatening and the Libyans were already praising Mintoff and publicly suggesting Malta as a potential example of a nation which had discarded its colonial and military masters and now represented one of the more peaceful states in the Mediterranean. At this point

9 Lady Carrington, private diaries, Bledlow archive.

British Intelligence confirmed that on 4 and 17 July 1971 Mintoff
had made secret night-time visits to Qaddafi to discuss Arab support. Carrington was told, but it made little difference to the British
position. Carrington was not going to give Mintoff the money he
asked for. Confrontation was inevitable.

Britain was quite determined that it was not going to back
down. At the same time, Malta was gaining confidence and quite
a lot of attention. The House of Commons was lobbied and what
to do about Malta became a regular subject for parliamentary
questions. Ralf Dahrendorf, the EEC Commissioner, flew to
Malta to discuss the matter with Mintoff. This visit bolstered the
latter's belief that diplomatic might was on his side, particularly
when Paul van Campen, the political adviser to the NATO secretariat, turned up in Valletta. Another significant occasion, not fully
understood by the British, was the opening of the Maltese Parliament on 16 August 1971. For the first time, the opening was
performed by a Maltese, the Governor General, Sir Anthony
Maymo. His speech from the throne, as Westminster would have
seen it, made it clear that the question of increased payments from
Britain was the main plank of Mintoff's government programme.
At the same time, Colonel Qaddafi gave $3 million in financial aid.
Mintoff never believed that the Libyans could take over the financing of a defence agreement but the British were less certain. They
were losing their imperial nerve. Three days after the policy speech
in the Maltese Parliament and the delivery of the Libyan loan,
Carrington made a quick visit to Malta. By this time he was telling
Mintoff that Britain and NATO were clubbing together to
provide £9.5 million. This did not really impress the Maltese government, which might, at that stage, have settled for a £20 million
package.

There was an aside to this financial bartering. The global economic system was stumbling over interest rates and devaluations.
The Maltese were forced to float their pound and sterling itself
was devalued by 3.5 per cent. Both Treasuries were having to
re-do their sums to see how much the British offer was now worth
in practical terms. Carrington returned to London on 21 August

with no agreement whatsoever and a good deal of frustration. A couple of weeks later, on 7 September, the Maltese tried a ploy that had worked in the past: they stopped the British forces getting duty-free fuel.

Britain was increasingly angry with Mintoff and was gradually turning off the financial aid tap. Relations between London and Valletta were dismal. Carrington should have been able to resolve this matter if he had had the support of other NATO states and his own Treasury plus a secretariat of his own that better understood Dom Mintoff. But not even Carrington's diplomatic and personal charm could make an impression. In fact, Mintoff was not impressed by the celebrated Whig. He thought his patrician values and attitude unwise, and, inasmuch that he believed Carrington was treating him as a recalcitrant colonial servant, insulting.

There was no sign of this deadlock being broken until Ted Heath decided that Carrington was getting nowhere. Heath invited Mintoff to London. Again, what Carrington's private office did not appear to understand and therefore failed to advise their master was that Mintoff's personality allowed him to agree with what he might previously have disagreed with if the other side was simply nicer about it.

Mintoff warmed to Heath, who he thought was wiser, less belligerent and certainly a better listener than Carrington. Heath did not give an inch on Carrington's position but his attitude was different and, although he would not agree to finding more money, he made it clear that at least he understood Mintoff and respected why he was arguing in the way he was.

On 18 September, thanks to Heath, both sides agreed to move things forward, including the negotiations for a new defence pact. Mintoff agreed that all the facilities that he had had previously withdrawn would be reinstated. In return, Britain agreed that during the next six months, that is until the end of March 1972, rather than starve Mintoff's government of all money, they would pay Malta half of what they were offering. There would be 'something on account'. On his way back from Britain in an RAF aircraft put at his disposal in recognition of his importance, Mintoff stopped off at Bonn to meet Chancellor Willy Brandt, who said that he had talked to Heath and that he was quite willing to go along with helping out the Maltese.

If anyone in Whitehall thought the matter was resolved and that Mintoff was a pushover then they were mistaken. It was clear that Carrington was not going to increase the rental offer beyond £9.5 million. The Americans tried to get Britain to move, but failed. Mintoff began insisting that if there was no agreement by the end of the year, then Britain would indeed have to get out. In the middle of November 1971, Carrington believed the affair had gone on long enough and that he would have to go to Malta and give Mintoff a good talking-to. Mintoff refused to see him and said there was no point in coming unless he was bringing a better offer. This was not the first time that Carrington had had to abandon a visit to Malta and he was not inclined to kow-tow to Mintoff. This was a proper stand-off. It was certainly true that not all Malta was behind Mintoff. There were many islanders who had not voted for him and thought it ridiculous to kick out the British, who, after all, may have been there for their own military purposes, but also con-tributed to the economy and provided a security presence which was not to be overlooked. Mintoff was left in no doubt as to the strength of feelings running against him when, on 29 December 1971, many in the Maltese House of Representatives argued against the Prime Minister.

By this time, Mintoff and some of his aides were receiving hate mail and threatening letters and were under police guard in excess of the normal protection. Carrington knew this and decided to go on the offensive. On the day that the Maltese House of Repre-sentatives debated the future of the defence agreement, Carrington had his officials draw up a statement of Britain's position and he immediately authorized that it should be made available to the public at home and abroad.

In accordance with the Chequers understanding of September 18th, £4.75 million was paid to the Maltese Government on September 30th and a team of British officers made three visits to Malta to discuss details of a possible defence agreement. Progress was made but the talks revealed a substantial difference between the two sides. In addition a number of NATO allies entered into bilateral discussions with the Maltese Government and made offers of economic assistance totalling £7 million spread over a period.

The Maltese Government rejected the offers as inadequate. No more progress could be made. On November 19th, Lord Carrington offered to pay a further visit to Malta and on December 4th repeated his offer proposing the date of December 16th/17th for talks without pre-conditions [i.e. without an increased offer on the £9.5 million and the offer to talk without pre-conditions was not taken up].

After a series of further exchanges Mr Mintoff sent a message on December 24th, received here early on Christmas morning, rejecting Lord Carrington's offer to go to Malta on 30th/31st or January 3rd/4th and stating that he was not willing to allow British forces to remain in Malta beyond December 31st unless an immediate further £4.75 million was paid to the Maltese Government.

The terms of the Chequers understanding made it clear that the agreed payment of £4.75 million related to a six-month period from September 30th, and that pending a new agreement there would be no restrictions placed on the British forces in Malta. The British Government are not prepared to make a further payment as demanded.

The British Government repeated Lord Carrington's offer to go to Malta on December 30th/31st or January 3rd/4th provided Mr Mintoff withdrew his latest demand and was willing to seek a basis for a new defence agreement. They also restated that they would not seek to keep their forces on the Island against the wishes of the Maltese Government.

In a message this morning Mr Mintoff reiterated the demand made in the message of December 24th. In the circumstances the British Government are setting in hand preparations for the withdrawal of British forces in Malta.[10]

10 Carrington papers, Bledlow.

Ted Heath thought the whole Mintoff affair less than important.

It was clear from the outset that Mintoff did not know what he really wanted, to get the British out and assert Malta's independence, or to extract more money from us. The hand he had to play was, in fact, woefully weak.[11]

During that September visit, Mintoff had delayed confirming that he would accept the invitation to London. Carrington did not know whether he would come until the day before he was due to arrive. He agreed a plan with Heath that he would give Mintoff a pretty stiff talking-to and then that Heath would continue the tactic of treating him robustly.

Heath did not have enormous regard for Mintoff and decided that he was bumptious and that one good tactic would be to flatter him. Heath the sailor and Heath the politician possessed great stamina on these occasions. At Chequers, on the evening that Mintoff arrived, Heath poured large drinks, started the conversation and then set Mintoff off talking about himself and what he wanted for his island. When Mintoff started to stumble and flag, Heath pressed him to go on until Mintoff appeared truly exhausted. At that point, Heath took a final sip of his brandy and suggested it was time for bed and that they would resume at 10.30 a.m. the following morning.

There may have been a certain one-upmanship about the tactic, yet Mintoff thought Heath was properly interested whereas he believed Carrington's celebrated jovial, kindly and humorous style one-sided. To Mintoff, Carrington had a harsh superior streak not far beneath his agreeable surface. For his part, as a result of that late-night session, Heath may have not changed his mind about Mintoff's personality but as a politician, who relied on votes to stay in power and even hold his seat in the Parliament (unlike Carrington), Heath sympathized with the depth of Mintoff's political conundrum.

11 Heath, *The Course of My Life*, p. 498.

He was concerned about the state of the Maltese economy ... and believed that British accession to the European Community would greatly reduce our interest in his island; he therefore needed to secure Malta's economic future on a new, sound footing, which is why he wanted so much money from us.[12]

Carrington later claimed that he quite liked Mintoff as a person. Mintoff never sensed this, especially during the final round of talks, which also involved the Secretary-General of NATO, Joseph Luns. Luns was a genial Dutchman who believed that one of the simplest ways to resolve any dispute was softly-softly rather than in what he then regarded as Carrington's old colonial style. When the three met in Rome, Carrington was not a little gratified when Mintoff showed his true colours. The discussions were really between Carrington and Mintoff, and Luns would now and then drop in a remark to the conversation. Suddenly, Mintoff, apparently now regarding Luns as being as bad as Carrington, leapt to his feet and screamed at the top of his voice, 'Shut up, Luns! Who the hell do you think you are? I'm not going to be treated like some Indonesian nigger.' (A disparaging reference to Dutch colonial history in South-east Asia.) From that moment, Carrington sensed he had Luns more on his side.

However, the politicking ended in smiles and handshakes by the spring of 1972. Mintoff did not really get much further than he might have done originally with the British government – although he did immediately touch the Chinese for £17 million. But this was the beginning of the end of the British military presence in Malta.

In May 1972 there was a footnote to the Malta affair, which also gave some insight into Mintoff's sense that he should keep in with the British. Curiously, it came in a letter from Prince Charles to Carrington.

12 Ibid., p. 499.

HMS Norfolk,
Mediterranean.
May 16th 1972

In two weeks' time we sail from Toulon and spend a few days in Malta before slowly making our way back home. While in Malta it looks as though I shall be going to several receptions & dinner parties & one suggestion I have seen is that I go on a barge picnic with Mr Mintoff.

When I heard of this I can only say I was astonished. Each time I have been to Malta over the past few years he has studiously avoided coming anywhere near me, but perhaps after all the recent events he is feeling more self confident & can afford to be less 'anti-British'.

If this tentative suggestion becomes fact I feel I ought to be forearmed and forewarned, and have no desire 'to put my foot' into anything I shouldn't! Is there any specific subject I should avoid and is there anything you would like me to mention if I had the chance? What exactly is our attitude towards him at the moment?

I am sorry to take up your valuable time like this, but there is nothing better than consulting the acknowledged expert on the subject!
Yours sincerely,
Charles[13]

This would be the last visit of British royalty to British-'owned' Malta but not the last time that the Prince of Wales sought Carrington's advice. The two became firm friends.

Carrington had a more disturbing task before him that year than the negotiations with the Maltese Prime Minister. The people of Northern Ireland were going through yet another wretched time in their history. Three years earlier, in 1969, the Wilson government had sent extra troops to the province to reinforce the numbers in the permanent garrison and to put patrols on the streets. The

13 Carrington papers, Bledlow.

terminology of Internal Security insists that the military is an aid to the civil power. The military constraints were, and continue to be, considerable in these circumstances. Moreover, the modern British army had no recent experience of a policing role within the British Isles. The disastrous military action in the island of Ireland during the earlier part of the century could not be compared with the task given to the British army in the 1970s. Moreover, the experiences of soldiers in the internal security operations in, for example, Cyprus and Aden, were not at all good grounding for what was expected in Northern Ireland. The anti-terrorist operations in, say, Cyprus were less sensitive than what the soldier was being asked to do in Belfast, Londonderry and Armagh. These were soldiers policing, in theory, their own people. The training establishments that were set up for the Northern Ireland deployment, for example near Lydd in Kent, and the intelligence-gathering operation based at Ashford, also in Kent, were designed and run without that essential experience of operating within the United Kingdom. Intelligence Corps, special forces and the Security Service and Special Branch practices of the 1940s, 1950s and 1960s did not truly prepare the army in 1969 for its day-to-day role in Northern Ireland.

As Defence Secretary, Carrington never took command of the Northern Ireland military role although as senior minister it was his ultimate responsibility. He was, in theatrical terms, a quick study. He decided that it was not a task that he could entirely leave to his juniors, and so he put in hand a series of visits every two months to Northern Ireland to find out for himself what was going on. He was hopeful that he still had the eyes of a soldier to understand the military predicament. He experienced in his words 'a series of traumatic events'. Traumatic events in political terms tend to be those the government has little power to prevent. Thus was the case in Northern Ireland during Carrington's term as Defence Secretary. Moreover, it was Carrington who took the lead in introducing clearly worded terms of reference for soldiers who he felt were vulnerable to uncertain operational conditions. According to Carrington, he understood from his own experience as a company commander in the Grenadiers that soldiers had to have explicit instructions about what they could and could not do in normal conditions of warfare. These were abnormal conditions because those same soldiers had to make their powers very clear to civilians who might at any time confront them. Those delicate terms of reference were written on the so-called Yellow Card each soldier carried.

The troops were deployed in Ulster within the Common Law of Great Britain and Northern Ireland. However, to put troops on the streets had, as Carrington observed, been a terrible failure of the normal way of the policing of these islands. And so in addition to Common Law, those troops were there within the Civil Authorities Special Powers Acts (Northern Ireland) 1922 and 1943. Moreover, additional regulations as amendments to those Acts allowed troops powers of arrest and search which normally would only be given to the local constabulary. Still less clear – yet passed over by Carrington as being less than important – was whether or not troops were on active service. The 1955 Army Act defined active service. However, to describe the insertion of troops in 1969 in this manner would have publicly suggested that they were on a war footing in the UK itself; clearly this was politically unacceptable and hence was glossed over.

What could not be ignored was the uncertainty in the minds of young soldiers and their officers (often equally young) who day after day were confronted on the streets and in the countryside of the province. This then was the origin of the need for a written instruction for each soldier (the Yellow Card). The immediate difficulty was that it was an almost impossible task for a soldier to be sure that he was going through all the procedures noted on that card during the heat of a contact with not simply a terrorist or suspected terrorist, but an ill-defined threat.

The task to produce the right wording for what were effectively rules of engagement for often very young soldiers was made harder by the numbers of departments involved. Far from giving the job to a literate officer and telling her or him to get on with it, the Defence Ministry had to seek the views of the Treasury Solicitor, the Home Office, the Foreign Office, the Lord President's Office and the Lord Chancellor. Carrington was ever reminded that soldiers were in no way different in the eyes of the law from civilians. They were in Northern Ireland as an aid to the civil power, as the jargon had it. But they had to follow the fundamental rules of Common Law. Moreover, under the Criminal Law Act (Northern Ireland) 1967, a soldier might use such force as was thought reasonable in the circumstances. Yet as Carrington argued, there was always the chance that what seemed reasonable in the circumstances at the time might be easily seen as unreasonable at a later date. To the end of his life he believed his troops, many of them untried, were operating with one arm tied behind their backs. As an experienced soldier he recognized that this was an unenviable pressure. As a Secretary of State he saw this pressure as an essential safeguard for the community. It was a discipline that would in many instances stop military action 'going over the top'.

The first Yellow Card appeared on 25 September 1969. The card was altered in July 1970 and, more importantly, in January 1971 when the third amendment emphasized the need for minimum force but, crucially, 'authorised the soldier to fire at a person carrying a firearm, thought to be about to use it and refusing to halt, at a person throwing a petrol bomb and in other circumstances ... but it was specified that a warning must be given before fire was opened ...'[14]

In November 1971 Carrington was personally involved in updating the card once more. His main decision allowed commanding officers to order soldiers to cock their weapons with a round in the breech but to keep the safety catch on. Also, he covered the impossibility of restricting soldiers to 'like for like' shooting. He decided that automatic gunfire could be used in the same circumstances as aimed single shots, although a soldier would not be allowed to use automatic weapons when persons not using firearms were in, or close to, the line of fire. Moreover – and this

14 'Employment of Troops in Northern Ireland from 1969 onwards – legal background'. Ministry of Defence briefing paper, undated.

was to have legal consequences at a later date – he decided that a soldier could shoot back against someone firing in a vehicle even if warning of returning fire would be impracticable in such cases. This was clearly more than just a Secretary of State squiggling his initial on a document the contents of which had been decided elsewhere. The Yellow Card was a definition of what was right and not right, and possible and impossible militarily. That there were no Yellow Cards in the politics of the Province became clear in 1971 when James Chichester-Clark resigned as Prime Minister of Northern Ireland.

The relationship between London and Chichester-Clark had always been tense. This Unionist Prime Minister in Northern Ireland in many ways represented the continuing apprehension of the Protestant community. They expected to be betrayed by the British government. Chichester-Clark had replaced another traditional Unionist, Terence O'Neill, who, in spite of his apparently moderate approach to the crisis, wanted a much harsher military regime in Northern Ireland. Although Prime Minister in the Province, he did not have control over defence. He wanted Carrington, in the summer of 1970, to send more troops and to go so far as to impose a curfew in traditional Catholic areas: the Bogside in Londonderry and the Lower Falls Road in Belfast. Carrington was one part of the troika to advise Heath on Northern Ireland, the others being Home Secretary Reginald Maudling and Foreign Secretary Sir Alec Douglas-Home. During 1970 Carrington believed that controlling or even banning sectarian parades might make policing easier to establish. But matters came to a crisis in February 1971 when the first British soldier was killed in Ulster.

Chichester-Clark tried to get Carrington to convince Heath that the 7,000 or so troops in Northern Ireland should come under the command of the Northern Ireland Prime Minister's office. Heath refused. Chichester-Clark, in March 1971, then told Carrington that unless Unionists could see that he, Chichester-Clark, had a firm grip on the security apparatus, he could not guarantee that there would not be civil war.

Carrington's response was based not only on the best advice of his military commanders but also on the experience of his formative years. What disturbed him most was that the Royal Ulster Constabulary did not have, in spite of its local – largely Protestant-based – knowledge, an intelligence apparatus that could counter terrorism. Scotland Yard's Special Branch was working in Northern Ireland. Carrington did not doubt their expertise, but he did not see it making an effective input into the security situation. He did not believe that reinforcements now being demanded by Chichester-Clark would make that much difference. Yet he understood the political importance of the request, and offered to send two further battalions to Northern Ireland.

Chichester-Clark was not impressed. He really wanted absolute control over the military and he threatened to resign. That was in the third week of March 1971. Heath told Carrington to get over to Northern Ireland and tell Chichester-Clark in no uncertain manner that he would gain nothing by threatening to bring down the Northern Ireland government. This he did, but an unimpressed Chichester-Clark resigned the day after Carrington got back. His successor was Brian Faulkner whom Carrington understood to be the last hope of Northern Ireland government. If he failed, then Carrington and Heath could see no other way but direct rule from London.

That summer of 1971 was probably, Carrington believed, a turning point for the Northern Ireland Parliament. Faulkner had tried to broaden the Cabinet to include more Catholic groups. It did not work. Gerry Fitt (who, incidentally, had telephoned Home Secretary Callaghan from a betting shop in 1969 to tell him that he had to get British troops into the province) led the opposition walk-out of the Stormont Parliament on 9 July. It was a signal for the IRA to increase its campaign. For the Heath government at that point, there was another pressure that should not be underestimated; it came from the military on the spot and it contradicted Carrington's assessment of the situation. Carrington had agreed that Brian Faulkner's request for internment made some political sense. It was his understanding that Faulkner was arguing more or less along the same lines as had the troika of himself, Maudling and

Douglas-Home, and therefore the Heath government. The General Officer Commanding Northern Ireland, General Sir Harry Tuzo, however, told Carrington that he did not believe internment would work in the long term.

Carrington went to a meeting with Heath and Faulkner on 4 August. With Carrington was the Chief of the General Staff (CGS), Sir Michael Carver, and General Tuzo. The Chief Constable of the RUC, Graham Shillington, the man who (as Assistant Chief Constable) had liaised with the Home Office to bring in extra troops in 1969, voiced the opinion that internment was one of the few resources available to the government. He said that about 400 IRA members and sympathizers were on his list of those who could be interned, but that no one should underestimate the Republican reaction in the immediate as well as the long term. Shillington warned that the process would create martyrs as well as relieve the security situation, but nevertheless believed – as he told me in 1979 – there was no option.

Carrington observed that if that London meeting took the decision to go ahead with an internment order, then, to reduce the possibilities of the reaction that the Chief Constable predicted, Faulkner would have to immediately publish a six-month ban on marches.

The Northern Ireland marching season represented more than a tradition: it was the most public demonstration of sectarian independence. There were very large 'Northern Ireland' marches in other parts of the British Isles, particularly Scotland, but only in the Province did the marches assume such political and social importance and therefore volatility. Faulkner agreed that such a ban would begin a week later on 10 August. Carrington had not anticipated (although Shillington and Tuzo had) the depth of IRA penetration in official circles in Northern Ireland. Within forty-eight hours of that London meeting having taken what was supposed to be the most secure decision, MI5 was reporting that the IRA knew all the details. Instead of the 10 August start date, the operation to imprison began on the previous day when 337 IRA members and sympathizers were arrested.

It was at this point that Carrington's involvement in seeking some sort of settlement in Northern Ireland began to touch upon his whole family. The intelligence services picked up a list of targets. Carrington and his wife were on it. Iona Carrington noted,

August 10th 1971
We have to be guarded against the IRA, the Angry Brigade and all other nuts. Clara, Pamela Onslow's [wife of the Earl of Onslow] elderly maid who is helping Franca [Iona Carrington's maid] – is not daunted by policeman and police dogs. Last night she said to Franca after turning down the beds, 'If we're all blown up tonight you will find the bedcover in the bottom drawer in the spare room.'[15]

During that initial round-up Carrington was mainly concerned with the role of the army on the ground under the GOC, Sir Harry Tuzo, including the role and actions of military intelligence and special forces, though he had a further responsibility as a member of the Inner Cabinet with Maudling and Douglas-Home.[16] The security forces, given the sensitivity of their role, performed professionally. What appalled Carrington was the basis of the arrest operation itself, which had relied totally on the information supplied by Shillington that had in turn come from his own RUC Special Branch and intelligence units. Much of the information supplied by these RUC special departments was about as much use as a pre-Second World War Christmas card list. Although the forces had arrested many IRA leaders, the majority of them had been warned by intelligence leaks and were now far away across the border into the Republic. Moreover, some of those arrested were old enough for pensions, having been active members of the IRA in the late 1920s and early 1930s.

By the end of 1971, 174 people had been killed in the new Troubles. The year closed with Carrington still having doubts

15 Lady Carrington, private diaries, Bledlow archive.
16 Heath was yacht racing and only returned to London to take charge when the operation had started.

about the wisdom of internment, but admitting that he had seen and offered no alternative. Most of all, he believed that internment might have had a more effective role if the RUC intelligence had been accurate, although he had no doubt that the reaction on the streets would have been equally violent. Worse was to come.

On 30 January 1972 Carrington was on his estate at Bledlow in Buckinghamshire when he was called to the telephone. It was his private secretary Robert Andrew at the Defence Ministry. There had been 'an awful incident in Londonderry'. It was a march; they had known about it but had not guessed at the consequences. In Londonderry's Bogside district, marches had been banned for six months as a condition for agreeing Brian Faulkner's request for internment. Security forces had attempted to contain the march. Shots had been fired. Men were dead. This would become known as Bloody Sunday. The march had been organized by the Northern Ireland Civil Rights Association (NICRA). The intended route was from the Creggan through the Bogside to the centre of Derry. The marchers turned right towards 'Free Derry Corner' and at this point some of them broke away from the main body to stone the British troops, members of the Parachute Regiment. The Paras fired 108 shots. Thirteen died that day and a fourteenth died from his wounds six months later. Support for the Republican movement including the IRA increased overnight. The Protestant population felt, with some justification, even more vulnerable.

To get a vivid view of the atmosphere of that time and the relationship between the armed forces and the Irish public it is worth reading the words of one of the more thoughtful generals-turned-academics. Major General Julian Thompson was a distinguished Royal Marine Commando who led the 3rd Commando Brigade during the 1982 Falklands War. He commanded in Northern Ireland and witnessed many demonstrations and led many security operations. More recently Thompson became a visiting professor at the Centre for Defence Studies at King's College London. In his history of the Parachute Regiment written in the 1980s, Thompson's description of what happened on Bloody

Sunday may appear less than circumspect but, when I asked him if he would have written it any differently ten or fifteen years on, he said that he would not, and that it would be wrong in the name of hindsight to tone down the bluntness of what he and many others felt. In the section where he deals with Bloody Sunday, Thompson had just described the death of Sergeant Willetts of 3 Para on 25 May 1971. Willetts, who was awarded a posthumous George Cross, was killed by a bomb. As his body was carried to an ambulance the crowd outside the police station 'jeered and spat on the stretcher'. Thompson continues:

On Sunday 30th January 1972, a protest march in the Bogside and Creggan areas of Londonderry included about 150 yobbos whose aim was clearly to provoke a confrontation with the troops keeping order in the streets through which the march was to pass. As the march reached a security forces barrier the yobbos steadily escalated the violence, throwing bricks and eventually using tear-gas (C. S.) grenades against the soldiers. The brigade commander ordered 1 Para to arrest some of the yobbo element. At 5.55 pm a shot was fired at a group of Paras: a moment later 2 Paras shot dead a man in the act of lighting a nail bomb. Almost immediately after this incident the Battalion entered the vicinity of Rossville flats, attempting to cut off the yobbos ... When predictably, the situation got out of hand the Provos deliberately, cold-bloodedly but without any thought for their own people, women and children, opened fire on 1 Para, using the crowd as cover, a tactic they had used many times before ...[17]

Carrington suspected that in spite of the inquiry into the incident by Lord Widgery, it was inevitable that the soldiers would be blamed for unreasonable action. To him, that blame was wrongly attributed. He felt that at the time, and clearly expressed this sixteen years after the event in his own memoir: 'the troops made what in any other country would be regarded as a pretty restrained effort

17 Major General Julian Thompson, *Ready For Anything*, London: Weidenfeld & Nicolson, 1989, pp. 310–11.

in defending themselves'.[18] In fact, this sentiment loses sight of at least one contrary reference in Lord Widgery's April 1972 report, when the firing of some soldiers was said to have 'bordered on the reckless'. But Carrington's recollection had not changed by the time of the second inquiry when that opened in 2000.

Carrington's statement to the Bloody Sunday Inquiry chaired by Mark Saville, the English Law Lord, which concluded in 2004, tells us far more than the Widgery Inquiry, which was speedy and served a political purpose. Indeed, Carrington remembers that Prime Minister Edward Heath told Widgery that his inquiry had political implications and that he should remember so. Carrington said Heath's remark was well meant, but utterly ill advised. The Saville Inquiry thirty years after the event was more aggressive. Carrington believed that it was entirely a political gesture to the IRA as part of the stumbling peace process of 1998 and onwards. He thought that the Republican lions needed more feeding and that any of the politicians, officials and generals of the time might be tasty enough chunks, especially as their actions – or inactions – thirty years on were even more vulnerable to criticism.

That criticism extended to the idea that somehow the Defence Secretary was responsible for the appointment of general officers in the province, almost as if a government would select certain soldiers to carry out its will. Carrington thought this nonsense. Yet it was rightly raised by the inquiry. A perfect example of this suspicion came when General Tuzo took over from Anthony Farrar-Hockley, who was – Carrington told the inquiry – more gung-ho than his successor. Carrington felt forced to explain that as Secretary of State he had nothing to do, nor would he presume to have anything to do, with the appointment of the General Officer Commanding Northern Ireland and most certainly not Tuzo's deputy, his commander on the ground, the Commander of Land Forces (CLF), Major General Robert Ford. As it turned out, Ford became a target for Saville Inquiry lawyers appearing on behalf of the families of those who had died on Bloody Sunday.

18 Lord Carrington, *Reflect on Things Past*, London: Collins, 1988, p. 248.

The sensitivity of the role of the CLF was that he was responsible for the day-to-day deployment and actions of soldiers.

Carrington had not been Shadow Defence Minister and so, at first sight, he came to the Northern Ireland debate only when he joined the government in 1970 – about a year and a half before Bloody Sunday. However, as Leader of the Opposition in the Lords, he had been part of the Shadow Cabinet Northern Ireland discussions, although his view was that the Shadow team, by and large, was not much interested in what the peers thought about anything. Of one thing Carrington was certain: the Heath Cabinet wished to avoid direct rule at almost any price. Apart from the injustice of directly ruling a province which had its own constitutionally devolved government, the consequences would be unrest of the worst kind and not simply from the terrorist organizations.

No one wanted direct rule as Northern Ireland had its own constitution and was responsible for its own affairs. We knew that to take those privileges away would cause trouble, not just with Sinn Fein and the IRA but also with ordinary Catholics and Protestants. Who were we to tell them how to run their country? I do not remember any financial considerations influencing our decision, we were much more concerned about the political aspects of the situation.[19]

The discussions in Cabinet had become increasingly detailed between the autumn of 1971 and January 1972, largely because of the apparent thoroughness in the way the IRA had established no-go areas in Londonderry. Yet Carrington's evidence suggested that the incident of Bloody Sunday was totally unexpected 'despite the fact that we knew that there was a big march planned. Nothing like this had ever happened before and we had no reason to expect it.'[20] There were no discussions in Cabinet about the dangers of the march nor a strategy for dealing with it. Yet, Ford had warned his GOC in writing that a confrontation could result in fatalities.

19 Saville Bloody Sunday Inquiry, written evidence.
20 Ibid.

I am also informed that there is in existence a memorandum prepared by General Ford which suggests that he thought it inevitable that a few Londonderry hooligans would have to be shot in order to settle the situation. All I can say is that we were 'Yellow Carding' for all we were worth. I was involved in drafting the amendments to the Yellow Card and we would never have agreed to any course of action which involved the deliberate loss of civilian life. I cannot believe General Ford meant this by his memorandum. He probably simply meant to indicate that given the situation, fatalities were inevitable. There can be no suggestion that he was actually seeking them. I am sure that no such plan was in existence and even if it had been, the MOD, the Government and Michael Carver [the CGS] would have had no part in it.[21]

The day following Bloody Sunday, it was Carrington, as Defence Secretary, who went to the Lords to make a public statement. Once more here was the difficult circumstance of having a Secretary of State in the Upper House at arm's length from the elected Parliament. Heath's Home Secretary, Reginald Maudling, told the Commons that Lord Widgery would take on the inquiry, and Carrington announced this in the Lords.

In view of the statements which have been made which publicly dispute this account the Government have decided that it is right to set up an independent enquiry into the circumstances of the march and the incidents leading up to the casualties which resulted.[22]

Their Lordships could be just as scathing as members of the Commons. Neither Carrington nor Maudling had made any personal references to the people killed or injured, nor to their relatives. Lord Beaumont of Whitley made the point that such sympathy for the injured and the relatives of those killed might have been included in the statement. The normally affable Carrington was not much impressed, as he made clear in his response to Beaumont.

21 Ibid.
22 *Hansard*, 31 January 1972, Cols 515, 516.

My Lords, may I answer one thing the noble Lord said? He took the Government and the Home Secretary to task for not having said something about those wounded and killed. I must say that it is my information that some of those who were killed were some of the IRA men who were shooting at the army. It is very tragic that that should have happened and I am sorry indeed that they should have been so misguided as to do so, and I am very sorry indeed for their relatives.

Carrington continued to spend little emotion on what he regarded as dead terrorists.

I would ask your Lordships to remember that this march was illegal and was known by those who organised it to be illegal. Indeed, they were warned on Saturday morning of this by Army Headquarters, Northern Ireland, who emphasised the illegality of the march and the responsibility which rested on the organisers for any violence which resulted as a result of that march. I think it a very great pity that this march took place.[23]

Carrington may have regretted that the march took place, but he was not surprised. Nor was he entirely surprised at the consequences. At 10.45 a.m. on Tuesday 11 January 1972 – more than two weeks before Bloody Sunday – the senior members of the Cabinet had been briefed by the CGS, General Sir Michael Carver.

The Home Secretary (then the minister responsible for Northern Ireland), the Chancellor Anthony Barber, the Foreign Secretary Alec Douglas-Home, the Lord President William Whitelaw and Carrington were all present. Carver told them that the Provisional IRA had failed to disrupt life in the Province as they had so threatened before Christmas. The security operation had been successful: eight leading Provisional IRA men had been arrested in Belfast and the organization was now 'virtually leaderless in the Ardoyne area'. It was at this meeting that the Cabinet was urged to come up with a political initiative before the Republican and

23 Ibid.

Unionist organizations were able to harden the minds and hearts of their respective communities.

The ban on marching was due to expire on 8 February 1972 and the Cabinet was told that Faulkner wanted to extend that ban until at least the end of the year so as to reduce the chances of violence and confrontation during the marching season some five months away. In this context, Carrington and Carver had discussed what to do about the no-go areas of Londonderry and told the Cabinet that a military operation to reimpose law and order would require seven battalions and probably involve the long-term commitment of four battalions to the city. It would be a major operation, necessarily involving numerous civilian casualties, and thereby hardening even further the attitude of the Roman Catholic population. Heath's Cabinet does not appear to have absorbed the implications of Carver's concise briefing and Carrington's understanding and endorsement of what the general was saying. Hence, the events of Bloody Sunday took the Cabinet by surprise. How these senior ministers failed to anticipate such an event remains a mystery, unless of course they never read or grasped what was being presented to them. The tendency to let other departments get on with their briefs was not an unknown feature of Cabinet government and did not contradict collective Cabinet responsibility.

Carrington had of course absorbed everything Carver told him, which is why even on reflection he was neither surprised nor moved by what had happened. He understood also that this was only the prelude to stronger action, including Operation Motorman.

Carver's report to Carrington and then to Cabinet, the day after the shooting, could not have been expected to be without its weaknesses. It was based on first reports and inevitably contradictions or uncertainties existed. Yet the language was precise and blunt.

About 200–300 hooligans ... began stoning the military barriers, and soon intensified their bombardment with some use of CS riot control agent. They were held at bay by the Army with water cannon, rubber bullets, and CS. When the hooligans began advancing behind shields towards the Army barriers, the local brigade commander ordered elements of 1st Battalion the Parachute Regiment (1 Para) to take the hooligans in the flank and rear and arrest as many as possible at the corner of Little James Street and William Street (locally known as 'Aggro Corner') ... soldiers of 1 Para came under fire with some 50–80 rounds from the third floor of Rossville Flats. An exchange of fire developed, and lasted for about 15 minutes, between 1 Para and the gunmen in the flats. After firing ceased, 1 Para claimed to have hit a number of gunmen firing from around the flats; and a number of persons in the flats had evidently been hit and were removed by ambulance.[24]

Carrington's recollection was that although Cabinet accepted that Carver's report was essentially correct, the conclusion was that 'there were numerous direct conflicts of evidence, and a quite different version had been given currency in the publicity media'.

He agreed with Heath that certain trusted defence correspondents in Fleet Street should be privately briefed on the content of Carver's report to Cabinet, which was classified *secret* and was supposed to remain so for at least the next thirty years. Here was a sign that the government was uncomfortable with the events of Bloody Sunday in spite of the tone of Carrington's report to the Lords and Maudling's to the Commons. They both knew that what had happened could not be entirely whitewashed by a sympathetic inquiry, even though many anticipated that was what would happen. There was a need to get the government's position on the streets to counter speculation and even selective leaking of the Carver report. Here too is a reminder that government spin did not start in 1997.

There was also a clear indication that although the level of violence on Bloody Sunday itself may have surprised some in government, few could have failed to understand that the Province would for some time be pock-marked by bullets and bombs. In his book *Memoirs of a Statesman*, Brian Faulkner claimed that at a meeting 'in London on 18 January 1971 [a full twelve months before Bloody Sunday] it was agreed by Maudling and Lord

24 Carver's report to Cabinet in Carrington papers, Bledlow.

Carrington, the Minister of Defence, that the Army must make arrests and not simply confine rioting to an area'. Carrington later claimed that he could not remember such a meeting nor, therefore, such an agreement.

And according to Faulkner, after three Scottish soldiers had been murdered in Belfast on 10 March 1971, Carrington and Carver went to Belfast and told Chichester-Clark that he could not have extra troops. This was the last straw for Chichester-Clark, who wrote his resignation letter at the end of the meeting.

On 7 October 1971 Faulkner met Heath and Carrington at Number 10 at 10.30 a.m. with Maudling, Whitelaw, Douglas-Home and Carver also present. Like his predecessor, Faulkner wanted more troops. Carrington said there were enormous difficulties in raising more troops. The best that could be managed was just three extra battalions 'with the prime objective of clearing the main trouble areas in Belfast, and secondly for the border task. Londonderry had lower priority, but the precise method of use of the forces should be left to the GOC.' (He thought also that making battalion areas smaller might deter terrorism and make arrests more likely. This was a tactic of the US army in Baghdad during 2007.)

Carver told Carrington in November, after the Faulkner meeting at Downing Street and the sending of the three extra battalions, that military action alone would not provide a solution. In his view it was up to the politicians to produce a political solution to coincide with the military providing a window of opportunity by having a tight grip on security. He told Carrington that if things went well by February 1972 then the IRA might be seen to be ineffective. There might then be a short period before the Protestants would begin to feel that the threat had been removed and that they need not therefore give anything away. 'A visit to Northern Ireland in mid-December [1971] led me to feel that the "window" was imminent. I therefore suggested to Carrington, that, unless the right moment for action appeared earlier, we should aim to take the political initiative in mid-February.'[25]

25 Michael Carver, *Out of Step*, London: Hutchinson, 1989.

Carver's proposals were put to Carrington in early January 1972. No action was taken. Why? Carver thought because the government was preoccupied with the miners' strike. Oddly, considering the urgency of the events of the time, Carrington always claimed to have no recollection of receiving these proposals from Carver. A former MOD civil servant suggested to me that Carrington did not always read everything set before him. (This was also a complaint of Sir Roy Strong when Carrington was chairman of the V&A Trustees when Strong was director of the museum.)

Within weeks Faulkner had resigned. There had been more deaths, including the IRA bombing in the Parachute Regiment's officers' mess at Aldershot. It was following this penetration of army security on the mainland that Carrington announced that Northern Ireland security powers had been taken away from the Province and transferred to London, and it was over this that Faulkner resigned. As Carrington suspected might happen once Chichester-Clark went, the Province could not govern itself and direct rule would have to be imposed. As he told the Cabinet, he did not believe Stormont would be re-established as a centre of government in the foreseeable future. Carrington had the support of his mentor, Foreign Secretary Sir Alec Douglas-Home, who made his and Carrington's views strongly known to Heath.

I really dislike Direct Rule for Northern Ireland because I do not believe that they [people living in Northern Ireland] are like the Scots or the Welsh and doubt if they ever will be. The real British interest would I think be served best by pushing them towards a United Ireland rather than tying them closer to the United Kingdom. Our own parliamentary history is one long story of trouble with the Irish.[26]

Carrington thought that Douglas-Home was right, but that there was no way in which the Unionists would be pushed or led to a united Ireland. The consequence of any such proposal would be political suicide for the government that made it and a bloodbath

26 The National Archives, PREM 15/1004, Prime Minister, PM/72/10.

in the Province. It was an occasion when Carrington could see no way in which the logical and, in the long term, inevitable solution could be implemented. Certainly 1972 was not the right time to float such a concept.

It would be unwise to underestimate the enormous pressures on Heath and his Cabinet from the very start of 1972. In January alone, Heath was attempting to cope with Northern Ireland, Rhodesia, Europe and sharply rising unemployment. Terrorism and the politics of Ireland simply took their place in the queue of immensely important and long-lasting issues for the Conservative administration.

In January Heath, with Sir Alec Douglas-Home and Geoffrey Rippon in support, went to Brussels to sign Britain's articles of accession to the European Community. Certainly this was a moment for Heath to celebrate, but all the time at the back of his mind was what was going on in Rhodesia. Home had agreed with the Rhodesian leader Ian Smith on a form of independence. Rioting had followed, and Smith had the former Rhodesian leader Garfield Todd arrested for leading demonstrations against the agreement. This was not a scene Douglas-Home and Heath wished to be broadcast around the world.

At the end of that first month of 1972 there was a flurry of bad news: unemployment figures rose above a million; there was a furious gun-battle between British forces and the IRA on the border; the Bloody Sunday killings on 30 January followed; there was every obvious sign of politically damaging industrial disruptions.

February opened with the burning down of the British Embassy in Dublin, a civil rights march in Newry and the miners' strike beginning to bite. Heath declared a state of emergency and by the middle of the month there were continuing power blackouts. On 21 February the official inquiry into Bloody Sunday began, and the following day the IRA bombed the Parachute Regimental Headquarters in Aldershot. Five cleaners, a gardener and a padre were killed.

The security difficulties in the province were not all arriving from one direction. Carrington noted the dangerous tendency to always think of the IRA as the sole danger, and to ignore the Unionists and the so-described Loyalist forces. In March some 200,000 Ulster Loyalists went on strike and the seemingly inevitable brick- and stone-throwing led to shooting.

The strikes had been prompted by the announcement on 24 March 1972 of direct rule from London, the principle of which was opposed by Carrington, Douglas-Home and Lord Hailsham. But the security system had collapsed. Direct rule was therefore inevitable. Even Carrington and Douglas-Home readily admitted that. Brian Faulkner, the Northern Ireland Prime Minister, was called to Downing Street to be told what he already knew, that security policy would for the foreseeable future come from London. Faulkner said that his Unionist-controlled Northern Ireland government would not accept this. Heath suspended Stormont. Faulkner announced that 'We feel we, in our endeavour to provide just government in Ulster, have been betrayed from London.'

Fifty years of Unionist rule were ended and, according to Carrington (in conversation with the author in 2004), the sense of betrayal was more widespread among Protestants than the British Cabinet ever anticipated. The IRA, of course, saw this as a victory for Republicanism (as Carrington said they would) because the 'armed struggle' was in their terms justified and because direct British rule could only add support to their cause.

This was not much of an introduction to Irish politics for the nation's first Secretary of State for Northern Ireland, Carrington's friend William Whitelaw.

In May this became even more apparent with Republican and Loyalist gunmen from the Ballymurphy and Springmartin estates fighting running gunbattles. When they were spent, eight people, one a teenager, were dead. In June a ceasefire of sorts was agreed between the British forces and the Provisional IRA. But it was meaningless. Nor did it give the Heath government any breathing space to tackle a new 'local difficulty', as Macmillan had once called political discomfiture. As much of Britain followed the

considerably hyped chess match between Bobby Fischer and
Boris Spassky in Reykjavik, Heath was reading secret reports that
meant he was about to lose one of his most trusted Cabinet colleagues. Because of his involvement with a discredited architect
called John Poulson, who had been implicated in a corruption
scandal, Home Secretary Reginald Maudling (a friend of Carrington's) was forced to resign. Heath and his Cabinet were having
a difficult year.

The Poulson affair knocked the Troubles off the front pages for
a while, but not for long. The government needed to take what at
other times would be inconceivable measures. There was an attempt
to bring the Provisional IRA into talks and the Republicans
announced a bilateral truce on 26 June. Carrington's view was that
it was a temporary move on the part of the IRA and that it could
not last because the leadership neither wanted it to nor had the
authority to enforce it. Carrington and Whitelaw were on a politically high-risk strategy because at the start of July they agreed
something that would have been unthinkable five or six months
earlier. At the Bloody Sunday incident, one of the outlawed Provisional IRA leaders was Martin McGuinness. Both Carrington
and Whitelaw would say publicly that men like McGuinness were
terrorists and killers with whom they would never negotiate. Yet
on the afternoon of Tuesday 20 June 1972, P. J. Woodfield, one of
Whitelaw's officials, and Frank Steele of MI6 met Gerry Adams
and David O'Connell from the Provisional IRA at a safe house in
Ballyarnet near the Donegal border. The report back to London
caused something of a stir in Whitehall. Carrington, while understanding the need to be hopeful, was sceptical when he saw the
summary of that meeting. (It does, however, explain why some
were always of the belief that Gerry Adams saw the possibility of
peace in the Province.)

The Top Secret document was short and very much to a hopeful
point:

There is no doubt whatever that these two at least [O'Connell and
Adams] genuinely want a cease fire and a permanent end to violence.

Whatever pressures in Northern Ireland have brought them to this frame of mind there is also little doubt that now that the prospect of peace is there they have a strong personal incentive to try and get it ... Their appearance and manner were respectable and respectful ... Their behaviour and attitude appeared to bear no relation to the indiscriminate campaigns of bombing and shooting in which they have both been prominent leaders.[27]

Because of this report, Gerry Adams and Martin McGuinness were taken with great secrecy to London to meet Whitelaw. Carrington provided the military briefing for the Northern Ireland Secretary. He offered the thought that there was always a chance that a longer truce could be achieved as long as Adams and McGuinness had absolute authority over the IRA. They did not, and Carrington further thought that even if they had they would not have wanted the truce to continue. He believed at the time that they had already planned the next stage of their campaign. It came two weeks after the talks.

On Friday 21 July, in little more than an hour, the Provisional IRA set off twenty-two car bombs and mines in Belfast city centre. Eleven died and 130 were seriously wounded. In the gruesome folklore of the recent Troubles, that July day became known as Bloody Friday. Indeed, 1972 became the bloodiest year of the Troubles. Some 470 people (mostly civilians) were killed that year, there were more than 10,600 shootings and almost 1,400 explosions. Thirty-six thousand houses and flats were searched and 1,200 firearms, 183,000 rounds of ammunition and 19,000kg of explosives were seized.

Of immediate concern to the army and to the Unionist-recruited RUC was that large areas of Londonderry were being run by the Provisional IRA. They organized everything including their own system of policing and punishments. These areas of the Bogside and Creggan were effectively principalities, no-go areas for the police, civilian authorities and the army. Inevitably there

27 The National Archives, PREM 15/1009.

was public demand for 'something to be done'. To the army, and to Carrington, this was a classic internal security operation to regain control of an urban area. British forces had been doing such things for the whole century.

Carrington had to assume that the Provisional IRA would attempt to turn the whole Operation Motorman exercise into a bloody confrontation. Moreover, he was perfectly aware from his own military background that taking an area was one thing; holding on to it peacefully demanded even greater organization and the ability to withstand long-term resistance. Was not the 800-year history of the British in Ireland about exactly this? The planning was revised a number of times until the weekend of Motorman; then nothing further could be done. All Carrington could do was wait.

That night, Sunday 30 July, Carrington stayed by the telephone at his London home in Ovington Square. Everything was put in hand. The RAF was on standby in Northern Ireland as well as on the UK mainland. A naval flotilla stood offshore. At six o'clock the next morning Whitelaw (who had spent the night with the GOC, Harry Tuzo, at the latter's headquarters at Lisburn) and Carrington were told that the army had achieved its aim of regaining control of the no-go areas. There were two civilian deaths – both shot by the army. The operation might have produced far higher casualties had it not been for the planning and, for once, good intelligence gathering and analysis.

Carrington's report to the Cabinet was clearly well received and with little surprise because it was always assumed that he had a safe pair of ministerial hands, although his political judgement sometimes usurped the faith others had in him. None doubted his sense of operational imperative learned as a professional soldier – and at the time there were three MCs in the Cabinet: Heath, Whitelaw and Carrington himself.

But his critics – and there were more than his lasting reputation suggests – believed his advice was never thoroughly sound because Carrington lacked a finely tuned political ear. His military and political judgement was now tested in one of the most controversial areas of Northern Ireland policy since 1969 – the interrogation of prisoners.

As Defence Secretary, Carrington had to have a view on interrogation. There had been an inquiry into interrogation techniques and it made controversial reading. This subject was not something to hand over to Number 10, William Whitelaw or the RUC. Disturbingly for some officials in Whitehall, particularly the Cabinet Office, Carrington seemed reluctant to make a judgement.

Carrington's soldiers (and in a few cases, people in the other services) were training day in and day out in the craft of interrogation; crucially, they were also training the RUC as interrogators at the Headquarters Intelligence Corps at Ashford in Kent.

The British army's interrogation techniques were based on two fundamental areas of expertise: what captured British troops might expect in a war with the Soviet bloc and, more importantly, about thirty years' experience of interrogating terrorists in Malaya, Aden and Cyprus. This was no hush-hush military operational process kept from the minister. Carrington knew what went on, what the techniques used were meant to do, and how they could be applied in Northern Ireland.

Interrogators were trained to isolate prisoners physically by keeping them apart and feeding them so-called white sound to block out other noises in an attempt to disorientate them. The actual interrogation techniques were based upon psychological and character assessments of each person. Thus, a prisoner who was a calm type would be subject to techniques different from those used on someone easily excited. The four basic character assessments formed the basis for all interrogations. So did the practice of disorientating prisoners and stripping them of any form of dignity that would encourage them to hold out.

The need for good intelligence in internal security operations was a key, perhaps *the* key requirement of any commander. Carrington perfectly understood its importance. Moreover, he understood the peculiar conditions of Northern Ireland. An interrogation team could work away for days and weeks gathering tactical and theatre intelligence in some former colonial outpost of British counter-terrorism operations, but using the same techniques in the United Kingdom was a much more sensitive adventure.

The internal debate between Heath, the RUC, the Northern Ireland Office, Carrington and their officials became intense during the summer of 1972. This was just seven months after Bloody Sunday and the Parker Report on Interrogation, so no one, particularly Carrington, was ignorant of the sensitivities involved. Equally, this was no exercise. This was the real thing.

There was, each minister and official agreed, an urgent need to gather intelligence on Republican terrorist groups and their supporters. The only way to beat the IRA, so Carrington believed, was to gather as much intelligence on their people as possible and get the analysis of that intelligence right, but in practice he was rarely impressed by the results. He told me in 2004 that, with the exception of Motorman, there was hardly an instance in his whole ministerial career when the intelligence community had been much help. It all sounded very good, he remarked, but in practice it left an enormous amount to be desired.

During that summer of 1972, the rest of Whitehall had made up its mind that two new centres could be opened to interrogate prisoners. They waited, some impatiently, for Carrington's view. But as far as he was concerned, there was much yet to be sorted. As a simple example, where was the interrogation process to take place and under what conditions? Shortly after Motorman, when Downing Street was pressing for some view, one of Carrington's Assistant Under-Secretaries, Derek Stephenson, threw the ball back into the Northern Ireland Office court, in a letter (classified *secret* and dated 3 August 1972) to his opposite number in that office, Neil Cairncross.

Dear Neil

It was, as you know, a part of the concept of Operation MOTORMAN that, once the Security Forces had occupied and dominated the 'no-go' areas, the intelligence obtained through interrogation would be a major factor in the neutralisation of the IRA. To be effective, the resources available to carry out interrogation need to be concentrated; and there needs to be adequate means of recording, evaluating and disseminating for tactical intelligence purposes statements made as a result of the questioning that is carried out.[28]

This alone meant providing a complex and twenty-four-hour Intelligence Support unit. This was an important step. More people were needed to be drafted in. Where were they to be put? Who would protect them? Who would make sure that what they worked on would not be leaked? As the army reported, and Carrington agreed, there was not the set-up in Northern Ireland to do the job that needed doing. Stephenson continued:

In the view of the GOC, interrogation following Operation MOTORMAN cannot be effectively carried out simply by using the existing facilities at RUC Police Stations. The subjects selected for interrogation would be those who come under suspicion, for one reason or another, but against whom no criminal charge can be brought. They would be held, initially, in Police Stations in various parts of the Province, where the resources of skilled interrogators cannot effectively be brought to bear on them and where no means at present exists for the evaluation and dissemination of the intelligence obtained. The GOC therefore advises, and the Ministry of Defence endorses this advice, that the RUC should be authorised to establish three Police Offices for the purposes of interrogation – one in Ballykelly (for Londonderry), one in RUC premises at Castlereagh (for Belfast) and one in Armagh for the country areas. The GOC proposes that likely subjects who have been selected at RUC Stations should be brought to one or other of these Police Offices for further questioning, for a period which might – subject to the authority of the Secretary of State – extend up to 5 days.

28 The National Archives, CJ 4/436.

With the exception of the holding time (still restricted to five days) this was a major step in the interrogation of UK nationals. It proposed to establish the sort of interrogation centres that the army had designed for the holding, questioning (the MOD was still nervous of using the word 'interrogate') and monitoring of Warsaw Pact prisoners of war. The one step that had yet to be taken was the use of army interrogators. The army did not trust the RUC, but under the law as it stood, they had no option but to leave interrogation to the police – officially, anyway.

> If the Secretary of State approves the setting up of these Police Offices, it would be for the RUC Special Branch to run them. But the Army would be ready to provide administrative backing, in the form of providing and maintaining such military accommodation as may be needed, and also providing extra guards for Police Offices where required, a detachment under the command of an Intelligence Corps officer to be responsible for the recording, collation and military evaluation of information obtained, photographic assistance and administrative support (for example, the supply of cooks). The Army would also be willing to provide medical support to meet the requirements for medical examination that are laid down in paragraph 8 of the JIC [Joint Intelligence Committee] Directive on Interrogation; and to arrange secure communications for each of the Police Offices. *There would, however, be no contact between Army personnel and the subjects for interrogation* [author's italics], apart from the medical assistance provided: the RUC would be solely responsible for the handling and questioning of subjects and the provision of escorts where necessary.
>
> I should add that, according to the advice we have received from HQNI [Headquarters Northern Ireland], both that HQ and the RUC Special Branch would, if the Secretary of State approves the proposal outlined in this letter, welcome a rather more detailed directive for the interrogation operation than that which the RUC Special Branch have already received. I attach, for your consideration, the draft of such a directive, which sets out the procedures

that are proposed and defines the responsibilities of the RUC and
Army respectively.
Yours sincerely,
Derek Stephenson
SECRET.[29]

Carrington remained concerned about the whole matter of
interrogation. He certainly wanted everyone to consider the sensitive nature of what was being proposed, particularly as he suspected it
would not stop with the army solely in a support role. At that stage,
the army was the only force with interrogation training apart from
a few individuals within police forces. Even the army's trained part-
time soldiers, the Territorial Army interrogators, outnumbered the
RUC officers with any experience and instruction in this field.
Moreover, there remained that deep army suspicion about RUC
loyalties. Carrington's misgivings were known but not officially
tabled. Why did he not put pen to paper there and then? Forty
years on, he said he could not remember why, other than that he
believed it was better to wait until everyone else had had their say,
a not unusual Carrington way of working. (He believed that was a
tactic he successfully deployed to get a settlement over Rhodesia
seven years later.) However, in March 2004 he expanded on this
reluctance. He told me that the condemnation and warning in the
Parker Report made the whole procedure repugnant to him. 'We
were horrified about what they had been doing. I didn't want to
go back to that sort of thing.' The correspondence continued to
flow, although not directly from Carrington.

Everyone was agreed that an interrogation phase was perfectly
necessary and lawful in the counter-terrorism campaign in the
Province. However, Heath, Whitelaw and Carrington remained
nervous of total commitment until all the terms of reference were
established. There were, in naval parlance, many cases of ministers
and officials clearing their yards. None was to have his name on any
directive that might be dredged up if the operation went wrong.

29 Ibid.

On a practical level, what happened to a suspect when there was no evidence to hold him? This interrogation procedure was against those who had been picked up, many of them targeted not on criminal suspicion but on suspicion of direct involvement in, or knowing something about, terrorist activities. An argument-cum-debate now followed about how such people should be treated. Would, for example, a detainee be kept in solitary confinement? Put him in a cell with other detainees and they would soon have a common story. They would also exchange information on their interrogations. Equally, there were supposed to be standard rules for the detention of prisoners. Should these apply? If not, that put the detainees on another level, akin to prisoners of war. Therefore, should not a representative of the International Committee of the Red Cross have access to detainees, as it would in wartime? Furthermore, at the end of the interrogation, what should happen to the suspects? Whitelaw did not want to get into the business of internment. Nor did he want to simply release people who had been through this new interrogation system for them to start rumours (or spread truth) on the treatment they had received. Who knew what these stories might lead to – internationally as well as domestically?

Finally, there was the very real possibility that the Northern Ireland Secretary did not, as yet, have the powers to direct the RUC Chief Constable to do anything that took the Constabulary beyond its normal field of operational practice. The best way to have achieved the desired outcome would have been to remind the RUC Chief Constable of the advice issued by the Joint Intelligence Committee, entitled 'Directive on interrogation by the armed forces in internal security operations'. No one in Whitehall thought to do so; most likely, they were reluctant to get involved in any way that would seem as if London planned to usurp the powers of the RUC leadership. All of which shows how the Northern Ireland Office, Downing Street and the Ministry of Defence were wary of anyone thinking they were interfering in the day-to-day running of the RUC, even though the terrorist threat was actively increasing and the RUC had so far failed to contain it. Linking the new emphasis on interrogation to the direct result of Operation Motorman may have seemed like an obvious operational requirement, but that was not how it was seen in the RUC, the Northern Ireland Office, Number 10 and even in some parts of the MOD itself. The army knew what needed to happen and Carrington was waiting to see how politically he could make it happen for them.

But he was in a spot with his own people as well as Number 10. The Chief of the General Staff, General Sir Michael Carver, had already told Whitelaw what was needed. Carrington still had misgivings and there was a feeling that he was deliberately waiting for William Whitelaw to ask him formally for his opinion. Consequently, some in the Northern Ireland Office, Downing Street and even in the MOD thought he was ducking the issue. The Butler rule – better to do nothing – was being applied. Or was it? Without getting directly involved, Carrington instructed his private secretary Robert Andrew to write to Ted Heath's principal private secretary Sir Robert Armstrong. On 7 August 1972, although some of Carrington's critics were never told, Andrew made clear to Armstrong that Carrington's concerns were not simply a cover for indecision.

Lord Carrington, while appreciating the military case for interrogation as a means of obtaining maximum information, is apprehensive about the political implications of reverting to a procedure which will involve the removal of persons to a special place for the purpose of lengthy interrogation, the nature of which is bound to be misrepresented. He has asked the CGS [Chief of the General Staff] who is going to Northern Ireland tomorrow, to discuss the matter further with the GOC [General Officer Commanding] and I believe that he will himself wish to have a word with Mr Whitelaw on the telephone before finally making up his mind.[30]

The view across Whitehall was that domestic and personal politics in London were holding up the process, which unless quickly

30 Carrington papers, Bledlow.

concluded would considerably weaken the whole operation. 'An opportunity lost' was how one army officer described the situation to me. Everyone wanted it to happen, but Carrington's support was needed and he knew that whatever he privately thought, the interrogation phase would go ahead anyway.

Everything to set up prisoner-handling units had been in place for some time. Everyone knew that interrogation centres would be established eventually, but no one really wanted to give it the nod. It was truly a political hot potato and it was something that had to be absolutely correct from the beginning. There was too much at stake in political terms and, as Carrington reminded me, there was a moral dimension that could not be ignored. Two police offices with interrogation rooms were finally set up, one at Ballykelly and one at Castlereagh in Belfast, by the Chief Constable in accordance with the terms of a memorandum dated 28 July 1972. Thus they were in service before Operation Motorman on 31 July. Carrington's MOD went ahead without telling the Northern Ireland Office and Carrington himself had not known the full details of what was going on. In spite of the sensitivities, the military and officials had got on with it knowing that once all was in train, then political endorsement would follow. That was what happened when a week later Carver and Whitelaw met on 7 August to agree the terms of interrogation techniques and the establishment of centres. The next day Carrington reluctantly agreed to whatever it was that had been agreed about interrogation procedure between Whitelaw and Carver. Interestingly – some might suggest conveniently – the person who should have recorded a minute of this agreement was ill on the very day. Moreover, no minute was kept of the crucial meeting between Carrington and Whitelaw the following day. That way there was no record of any differences.

Carrington's personal feelings over Northern Ireland reflected three areas of his thinking which did not much vary. First of all, as Defence Secretary he continued to feel deeply concerned that British soldiers with live ammunition were on active service in the United Kingdom. He had always believed that the purpose of the military was the defence of the realm. He continued to feel uneasy that the nation's enemies were not always overseas. Second, his understanding of twentieth-century history suggested to him that eventually the Irish Republic and Northern Ireland would be united. Third, in 1972 he sensed the mood of Great Britain was that the Irish should get on and resolve their own problems. In other words, he believed that most people on the mainland wanted nothing more to do with the divisive politics of Ulster.

In an emergency Cabinet meeting in August 1971, the subject of a unified Ireland had been raised. Ted Heath made a point of writing in his own memoir that Carrington and Hailsham had not gone so far as to support the idea for reunification. Carrington liked the idea but thought at that stage it was impracticable, and to promote it would be pointless and most likely to cause more rather than less bloodshed. Moreover, Carrington believed that the Conservative Party would support the Unionist view.

It was Carrington's talent to sense the party's mood that led Heath to appoint him its chairman in April 1972. As a party man, this was an important shift in his political career, more significant than that of 1979 when Margaret Thatcher appointed him Foreign Secretary. The appointment had everything to do with the state of the Conservative Party itself. It needed a good Establishment figure whom it could trust. The Tory grassroots has always gone for charm in the hope that behind it lies substance.

Carrington had now been in politics for a quarter of a century. The restructuring of the party after its defeat in the 1945 election was done by people like Rab Butler. This was not necessarily the back room of politics, but much of the bell ringing and morale boosting had to come from the then party chairman Lord Woolton. The role of Tory chairman had assumed a distinction in the Tory twentieth century, reinforced during the postwar years. The most popular managed to charm the grassroots activists and, equally important, their treasurers. As with other organizations, the most successful chairman was invariably a high-profile, likeable figure. The Tories wanted a chairman to be visibly all things the party thought it stood for, even when the parliamentary party knew it no longer did. In this respect Carrington was straight out of Tory

Central Casting. Moreover, he had Heath's approval, because the job was only partly to charm party workers; it also needed someone to prepare for electoral war. Between going into government in 1951 and 1972 Carrington had done nothing to disappoint the Conservative leadership, in spite of his brushes with resignation issues while at Agriculture and Defence.

Alec Douglas-Home had sensed from the earliest days that Carrington's ultimate resting place would be the Foreign Office, while others even thought he might one day be party leader – although he had never really shown any active interest in giving up his title. So by 1972 Carrington had had a good political career without having much of a political base. In the simplest terms, he was where he was because he was trusted by successive Prime Ministers and had yet to feel so unloved that he would 'bugger off back to his estate'. Equally, he was not close to the party in the way that MPs had to be. The last time he had had to face a selection committee of any form was on his entry to Sandhurst. Until Ted Heath's request came, Carrington's biggest collection of party points had come when the Conservatives were in opposition to the Wilson government. Carrington had chaired a fund-raising group which needed to find £2 million – a considerable sum in 1970. His success in this fund-raising was twofold: first, he got the money for the party, which earned him considerable gratitude, and second, it led him into making contact with a much wider section of his party. He learned more about those who were the real movers in grassroots support and he began to understand more of provincial politicking that had considerably changed since his time in postwar Buckinghamshire politics.

The party chairmanship was in many ways, then, the ideal job for Carrington. His personality appealed to the Tory lunch circuit and he really did know how to get the best from people. Most of all, chairmanship of the Conservative Party gave Carrington something approaching the political platform which he lacked. In the event it was to prove never enough: he went on to achieve high standing among the party membership, but never high enough among MPs.

In 1972 there was a distinct feeling that the distance between the grassroots of the Conservative Party and Westminster was greater than it had been for decades. It had probably widened since the going of Churchill. The Tory constituency membership lives on memories and comparisons, and Heath was no Churchill or Macmillan. Just as many Tories after 1997 spent years longing for a Thatcher (or even Thatcher herself), so Heath faced the reality of not being good enough for the political in-laws, the constituency membership.

Heath could see that the party was drifting and that the activists in the constituencies were becoming vocally more critical of their own government. Dissatisfied members protest by not signing cheques and putting pressure on local MPs, and in this way they spread the discontent on to the back-benches, which is too close for the leadership's comfort. Heath was also aware that the party did not have a credible communication system to encourage and reassure party workers.

Carrington's view was that there was considerable dissatisfaction which spread much further than the supposedly loyal Conservative members. He saw a greater danger that needed to be dealt with before Heath could call an election. Carrington was more concerned with the people that had voted for the party at the last General Election but who were not members of the Conservative Party. His belief was that the party could not rely upon floating voters for support at a General Election nor during the inevitable season of by-elections. Carrington assumed the General Election would come by 1974. He judged it insufficient time to turn round local party feeling, especially if the government did badly at local and by-elections. In this he was proved correct, which as he said later, 'was no comfort at all'.

During 1972 and 1973 the Liberals won five important by-elections – Berwick, Ely, Ripon, Rochdale and Sutton. Heath told Carrington that he needed his experience, his cheerful reputation among the party associations (Carrington, along with Margaret Thatcher and Michael Heseltine, became the most popular speaker at Tory grassroots functions during the last quarter of the twentieth century) and his seniority, which in Conservative terms remained an important badge of office. This was not mere flattery. Nor was it convincing to Carrington. He did not want the job and totally believed that he was the wrong person for it – not through any false modesty, but because he believed, rightly or wrongly, that by appointing him, Heath had demonstrated that he did not under-stand how much Britain had changed in just a decade. He believed that the irreverent mood of the 1960s had made it impossible for another peer to become chairman. While Ted Heath was the public image of the party, ideally the chairman had to complement this image by providing a sense of newness and renewal, balanced with the notion that the Conservatives remained the party to be trusted in government.

Carrington forecast in 1972 that the party would eventually be confronted by elements within the trade unions that believed they could do what the Labour opposition was incapable of doing: force Heath to call an election in such miserable circumstances that he would not be able to legitimately defend the right of government, of whatever persuasion, to govern on behalf of the people. Indus-trial anarchy would be the central enemy and not party manifesto against party manifesto. Carrington later told me that he believed that having demonstrated their power to defeat the Tories when Labour could not, then the unions would effectively run the incoming Labour government. For a man who was by all instincts a Tory, this was the very stuff of nightmares. With such a scenario, little wonder that Carrington believed that the Tories might not be best served by a party chairman who was an hereditary peer.

However, there was another reason why Carrington did not want to be party chairman. He already had one of the most demanding jobs in Cabinet, Secretary of State for Defence. This was not a matter of sitting in his sixth-floor office listening to the Chiefs of Staff, signing drafts of White Papers and then nipping along to St James's for lunch at White's. It was a job with enormous and complex international dimensions. Yet no matter how much Carrington protested, Heath could not grasp that he might not expect to be able to do both jobs as well as he should.

10. Musical Chairs

The domestic schedule in 1972 was time-consuming enough for any Defence Secretary considering what had been going on in Northern Ireland that year. The fall-out from Bloody Sunday was far from settled. Moreover, there was a new battle with the Treasury. This struggle extended beyond the usual struggle to get enough money to modernize forces. Carrington's predecessor, Denis Healey, had reduced defence commitments in his 1968 'East of Suez' review. To the Treasury, that suggested defence spending was not a priority. Carrington had to argue in Cabinet that given the surge in Soviet military spending – including armour, artillery, missile- and space-based systems – then Britain had a national and international obligation to modernize its own forces. It followed that defence spending was important to Britain's transatlantic relations, which both Carrington and Heath valued, and to its European aspect, which Heath valued even more.

Carrington's concerns over the future of NATO and the efficiency of combining allied forces was based very much on sound understanding of the defects in Britain's defence system and not least on the myth that went under the title of Joint NATO Doctrine. This doctrine too easily confused spending rates with military efficiency. Carrington argued in Cabinet and with his Chiefs of Staff that extra military spending did not necessarily mean extra military capability. Yet how much any NATO member spent as a percentage of its Gross National Product (GNP) was seen as a level of commitment to the alliance. This yardstick was typically used in Washington, where there was a general scepticism towards all European defence efforts. For example, the 1972 Defence Budget of £2.854 billion represented about 5 per cent of UK GNP. This was not an inconsiderable percentage in alliance terms, yet it did not offer what Carrington understood to be

necessary to provide combined forces that made a proper contribution to the non-nuclear deterrent factor in NATO. Carrington
argued (not always successfully in Cabinet) that if the UK appeared
less than committed to year-on-year defence increases then its
deterrent value was much reduced.

The Soviet Union's order of battle was laid out in clear terms of
numbers, readiness status and deployment, from the Group of
Soviet Forces Germany to the furthest boom defence vessel of the
Tikiflot, the Pacific Fleet base at Vladivostok. NATO therefore
had no doubts as to its task. What was in doubt was (and would
continue to be for the rest of the century) the contribution of
member states. Most were neither willing nor able to spend
money at the levels they had agreed they would. Moreover, it was
becoming increasingly clear to Carrington that NATO would not
take on board the idea that there had to be more collaboration in
building common weapon systems in order that its forces could
operate where necessary together and, coincidentally, place less
reliance on the United States. On the first point, Carrington was
told by his commanders and also by the British members of the
NATO military committee in Brussels that if alliance forces had
to go to war together then fundamental differences would reduce
the effectiveness of the joint force. This joint thinking did not have
to be at mega-budget level. For example, ships of different nations
use different fuel couplings and so could not refuel each other.
German, American and British tanks were all different and could
not even resupply each other with ammunition, never mind spares.
Even the rifles were different, as were the operating procedures.
Most of all, there was little indication among the armies that in
spite of annual joint exercises, field forces would operate efficiently
together even though headquarters had joint commands. Carrington's belief in joint manufacturing was over-enthusiastic: major
joint defence manufacturing projects, when they did occur, were
always hugely expensive and did nothing to improve operational
efficiency.

Despite the difficulties, by 1972 Carrington was already thinking
of the greater European identification of its own defence. He was

beginning to say publicly what Prime Minister Tony Blair would discuss nearly thirty years later. The expansion of community politics had to include some recognition that it needed its own defence policy with – and here Carrington went beyond anything Blair would utter – a nuclear strand.

At the October 1972 conference of the Conservative Party, Carrington announced that he believed that the evolution of European defence must include some kind of nuclear force. Obviously, it would not be on a scale comparable to that of the United States and it would have to be achieved without any weakening of the alliance. To Carrington, Europe had to recognize three important elements that affected its decisions that year: Europe was going through a constitutional transition with increased membership and ambitions; the United States was in the process of presidential changes; and finally, there was also every sign of a new mood in East–West arms control negotiations. As Europe was becoming an economic superpower, it had to consider whether it was willing to pay some of that money towards its own defence and potentially therefore become the third global superpower with all the advantages and dangers that sobriquet brought. 'We have to be realistic,' he told the 1972 Tory Conference.

I cannot see that there would be many people in Europe who would be prepared to advocate an increased defence expenditure of that level [i.e. superpower level]. There would be a distortion of existing economies, and this might be the surest way of opening the door to subversion.

As Defence Secretary, Carrington was also having to take on board developments in arms control. In 1972 the United States and the Soviet Union agreed the Anti-Ballistic Missile (ABM) Treaty. That treaty with its later protocols meant, in broad terms, that both the USA and the USSR had to limit the numbers of missile defence systems (i.e. weapons that could potentially knock out incoming missiles) in order that both nations would remain vulnerable to a nuclear missile attack. The logic of this argument was, that as long as both sides were vulnerable they were less likely to risk going to war. Carrington's contention at the time that the ABM Treaty would be the bedrock of nuclear doctrine for decades to come was to prove correct – certainly until the US administration of President George W. Bush.[1] It was enough for any Defence Secretary to have to think about. It was almost impossible for that same Defence Secretary to give such intricate and important matters his undivided attention while taking on another full-time job. It was an impossible request from Heath that Carrington should become party chairman and carry on as Defence Secretary. Heath argued that much of the Ministry of Defence burden could be carried by junior ministers – effectively declaring that the office, while admittedly not one of the great offices of state, was overrated in its importance. Carrington had his say, then accepted the chairmanship. The senior civil servants and chiefs of staff at the MOD were appalled. Carrington soon found the two political stools too precarious. He fell.

Carrington was criticized in the Defence Ministry for letting his attention wander and not being a good steward. At Central Office he was criticized for spending too much time thinking about the Defence Ministry when he should have been a more active and originating chairman of his own party.

Both sets of critics were right. Carrington was a better Defence Secretary than party chairman. Furthermore, Carrington's vice-chairman at Conservative Central Office, Jim Prior, faced the same problems as Carrington because he was also Minister for Agriculture. At first, the party liked the idea that its chairman was a member of the Prime Minister's inner council and therefore could properly pass on the views of the grassroots. Prior too was

1 One of the most damaging actions by the United States in relations with Russia in the year 2000 was an American proposal to alter that 1972 treaty and its 1974 protocol in order that America could build a more sophisticated missile defence system. The Americans argued that they needed to do so to protect themselves from what they called rogue states, for example, North Korea and Iran. The Russians, however, regarded this as the breaking of one of the most important understandings between the superpowers and diplomatic relations suffered as a consequence.

considered an insider because he had been Heath's Parliamentary Private Secretary (PPS) and was still very much an ally of Heath. Also, as an MP, Prior could bring his experience of the Commons to Carrington's of the Lords. Heath therefore believed he had given the party the ideal double-act at the top. Furthermore, Carrington had Chris Patten, one of the rising young Tory stars, as his personal assistant and both of them had the support of the very clever Sara Morrison at Central Office.[2] On paper it was a very good team. Patten and Morrison provided the young thinking that Carrington demanded. Yet it was Carrington and Heath who carried the image publicly and that image did not look so healthy.

Heath's government had been threatened earlier in the year by the miners and had given in. The miners' industrial muscle tensed, and Heath and his Cabinet, with all the diversions of Bloody Sunday and its consequences, a wobbly economy and increased European involvement, were tested to the full. There may have been public relief because the settlement with the miners removed the immediate consequences of continued confrontation – power cuts and the three-day week – but it did little to bolster the idea of firm government. Carrington believed that the electorate wanted that authority more than anything else from Downing Street. It was as if the people in the castle of Britain needed to know that the lord would protect them from the howling horde beyond the walls: the trade unions bent on the political destruction of Heath rather than the benefit of their members.

As Defence Secretary, Carrington had had, in theory, no part in the way government settled with the miners. Nevertheless, in his own castle, the MOD Main Building, Carrington felt uneasy, and sensed the government was storing up trouble for itself. On reflection, he felt his own colleagues had been weak-kneed. He knew also that the unions would be back for more money, better conditions and more attempts to disgrace and bring down Heath. Heath's was perhaps the last Conservative collegiate government

2 Patten was to be Carrington's personal assistant for two years before going on to direct the Conservative Research Department between 1974 and 1979.

inasmuch as ministers were expected to have views and make contributions during Cabinet debates on other departments. Carrington was asked by Heath's private office to give his views on subjects way beyond Carrington's grasp; state education was a good example of something Carrington never quite understood. He turned for help to his office and in particular to the grammar-school-educated Kevin Tebbit for his views, which Carrington relayed as his own in Cabinet. Once he had taken over as party chairman, Carrington balanced the issues raised by the Tebbits of his department with what he heard talking to local and regional party chairmen.

Constituency associations up and down the country told him that Heath's government had bought its way out of trouble, that it was going back on its tough promises declared during the run-up to the 1970 election, that Heath could not rely on his ministers to work out a firm policy and stick to it in the face of opposition, and furthermore that the government's economic policy lacked vision and fundamental stewardship.

Carrington was trusted at grassroots level to bring about changes and attitudes that would get the Tories re-elected. But he was not trusted at Conservative Central Office: Carrington, the agreeable face of Toryism, was disliked in that place. When it was not criticizing him for spending too much time as Secretary of State for Defence and therefore apparently not caring, Central Office did its best to obstruct many of the innovative ideas that he and his closest advisers – Prior, Morrison and Patten – produced.

By the end of 1972, Carrington was beginning to believe that the best thing might be to close down Conservative Central Office and start again. His charm, diplomacy, energy and long experience went down well in the constituencies, but they counted for very little at Smith Square. Carrington soon gathered that he was not universally admired at Conservative headquarters. Lord Hailsham told the author that he thought at the time Smith Square was something of a 'poisonous place'. Carrington regarded the atmosphere as far more sinister and disruptive than mere backbiting. To him, Conservative Central Office was disloyal to the party and, in particular, to its leader Edward Heath.

It did not take Carrington long to understand that he had no power as party chairman. His continuing task was to whip up enthusiasm among the party workers. In practical measures, his team attempted where it could to improve the pay and conditions of the constituency agents. These were the people that put the local organization together and if they were not happy then the organization faltered and collapsed. Even on such a level as this, Carrington sensed there was no real support at Central Office. In theory his ally was the Chief Whip.

Carrington and the Chief Whip had one thing in common: they sensed the mood of the party. The Chief Whip kept the Cabinet and the Prime Minister informed of what back-benchers were thinking and saying. This political intelligence often reflected what was being said to the back-benchers in their constituencies. Carrington began to understand the moods of their constituencies; his role, like that of the Chief Whip, was to make sure that Cabinet ministers and the Prime Minister understood what people who might vote for them were thinking. The secondary role was to make sure departments of state understood that mood, and if possible alter presentation of policies towards it. Actual policies might not change, but the policy-makers had to be aware of what reactions had been and might be in the future.

It took Carrington less than a year in the job for the impression to be confirmed that his party's back was to the political wall. Two major events would undermine the government's ambitions to get on with running the country uninterrupted. The previous year the government had produced a statutory incomes policy. Its hope was that by doing so, it would show the public that it was determined to keep control over the domestic economy by stemming what was an almost inevitable rise in the inflation figure because of higher wage settlements. There was, it believed, no more sophisticated way of doing this at that time than through an incomes policy. The government was thinking in the long term. The trade unions were sceptical, but in many cases for the moment offered their conditional support. But the miners did not regard themselves as part of any agreement and their leaders had no regard for the incomes policy. When the miners put forward a claim for pay rises far above the government norm, then everyone – the TUC, government and the miners themselves – all understood that confrontation was inevitable and was likely to be drawn out.

A confrontation of another kind drew Carrington's attention back to his ministerial red boxes. The Middle East erupted in conflict – the Yom Kippur War. Carrington's department thought it an inevitable conflict that had been signposted ever since the 1967 June War, at the end of which Israel established new and not always neighbourly borders – from the points of view of the Arab States. The uncertain security considerations within the Middle East had also meant that many Gulf States were rebuilding their armed forces and the British were in the middle of the commercial ruck to get as many short- and long-term contracts as possible. There was more to a signature for a new armoured car, coastal patrol vessel or aircraft than supplying the hardware. At stake were the equally lucrative additions to the main contract in the long-term maintenance agreements. British technicians could easily find themselves spending large parts of their careers working on, for example, a multi-billion-pound military contract with Saudi Arabia. In 1973 Carrington was part of the British political team that sealed that particular contract, a deal that would later be besmirched with accusations of backhanders and commissions passing from British firms to Saudi hands.

Carrington, standing in for Alec Douglas-Home, was in Saudi Arabia during 1973 to seal what was the biggest ever UK–Saudi arms deal. To make sure that nothing should be left to chance, the secretariat at Buckingham Palace was persuaded to send a letter giving the Queen's blessing for the contract. Here was a point of principle to be argued between Heath's government and the Palace: the Queen never signed such letters of endorsement. That would have involved the monarch directly in commerce. Worse still, in such a sensitive subject as the arms trade, the Palace thought

it inconceivable that the Queen should put her name to something
that could so easily turn sour at a later date – as this transaction did.
Carrington knew that the signature was essential to the Saudi royal
family, which would feel insulted if Elizabeth R was omitted. When
he arrived at the official guest house at Jeddah, Carrington took
the letter from the Queen from his briefcase and tried to see inside
it. He had to be certain there was a signature. Because the British
team had been warned that their rooms were bugged, Carrington
and his private secretary Kevin Tebbit went into the bathroom,
turned on the taps and constantly flushed the lavatory to blank out
their conversation. To open a letter from the Palace was an unforgivable act of rudeness. Tebbit and Carrington discussed the
dilemma at some length while water from the shower, taps and lavatory swept down gurgling drains. They agreed that in exceptional
circumstances, the letter could be opened: to check that the translation was correct. The letter was carefully undone. As Carrington
had suspected, the Palace had stood the monarch's ground and the
Queen's signature was missing. The letter had to be handed over
the next day and so Tebbit was sent off to stall proceedings by
organizing entertainment. (One official told me that this involved
Caledonian dancing girls, although in what mode, he did not elaborate.) Encoded telegrams were exchanged between Jeddah and
London with royal officials repeating their insistence that Her
Majesty never signed in these circumstances. At the last possible
moment there was a change of mind and a signature was given
with, as one official remembered, 'some haughty disapproval from
the Palace staff'. Finally the whole affair went off smoothly. The
fulfilment of contracts was a long way off on that day in Jeddah, but
real conflict was close at hand.

On 6 October 1973 the Yom Kippur War broke out between
Israel and the Arab states. Here was the making of a global military
crisis such as had not been witnessed since the confrontation
between the Soviet Union and the United States over Cuba.

The United States believed there to be more at stake than the
future of its client state, Israel. The Gulf States controlled the most
important oil supplies in the world. The Saudis regarded the US

and Western European support for Israel as unacceptable. The US was providing financial, diplomatic and military hardware support, just as the Soviet Union was on Egypt's side. The Saudis used their only available weapon against the US and her allies: on the day the war began, the Saudi Arabian government announced an embargo on oil exports to America and reduced supplies to Britain and some Continental European countries. (Carrington at the time suggested that 'energy security' would be recognized as a major defence issue within a decade. It did not become that until 2003 and the realization that Russia could turn off its gas pipelines into European supplies.)

The Americans had anticipated this action and had decided that, if necessary, they would invade Abu Dhabi, Kuwait and Saudi Arabia to secure the oil fields and thus keep supplies open. Should scholars of contemporary world affairs need to understand the formative years of the leading protagonists in Washington of the war in Iraq, then it might be remembered that the US ambassador to NATO at the time of the Yom Kippur oil crisis was the young Donald Rumsfeld. He decided then that never again would any Arab state hold America oil hostage. In London the Joint Intelligence Committee (JIC) produced an assessment for Prime Minister Heath which concluded that the Americans were quite capable of launching an invasion to protect their strategic interests. At the heart of the US planning was the Secretary of Defense James Schlesinger, considered in Europe to be an abrasive character. Ambassador Rumsfeld was his mouthpiece in Europe.

In 1973, however, the relationship between the US and the UK over Middle East policy could have hardly been more different from that witnessed in 2003. The Heath government was not onside as far as Washington understood the British position. This difference might have had something to do with the fact that British Intelligence and the Foreign Office appear to have misread the political and military situation in the Middle East.

Carrington's ministry had its own Defence Intelligence Staff. What was their input? The answer was, not very much that was good analysis. Carrington thought the DIS unhelpful; he had long ago come to the conclusion that politicians could too easily be swayed by the mystique of the intelligence agencies and that, in truth, most of them were not very good at predictions. It was certainly an impression confirmed by the assessments that came from Defence Intelligence and MI6 prior to the Argentine invasion of the Falklands in 1982.

Now, in 1973, the British position was nowhere near as bullish as America's. US Secretary of State Henry Kissinger was talking to Lord Cromer, the British ambassador to Washington. However, from Cromer's reports, it seems unlikely that Kissinger was telling him very much. Heath could not believe that the Americans cared little for the transatlantic alliance and the security of their allies. For their part, the Americans cared little for Heath's anxieties. Schlesinger's position was made very clear in the JIC briefing paper delivered to Heath. Schlesinger regarded the Middle East states as underdeveloped and underpopulated and quite without the status and power to hold America to ransom. America's problem (and by extension, that of her Western allies) was that these states could do whatever they chose unless the US was prepared to take military action to stop them.

Carrington had not formed much of a relationship with Schlesinger. Socially, they were chalk and cheese but considering the tensions in the Middle East, that seemed no reason not to have a close working relationship, unless of course the Americans little wished it. By contrast, Kissinger came to hold Carrington in the highest regard – indeed, Carrington, on leaving NATO in the 1980s, joined the consultancy firm Kissinger Associates. The Anglo-American relationship, however, in the autumn of 1973, was not nearly so pally.

The US believed that the British had nearly sabotaged any peace effort the Americans were making, and when on 7 November 1973 Schlesinger met Carrington on the eve of a NATO defence ministerial meeting in The Hague, he told him in no uncertain terms that Britain's attitude to US policy during the war had put the so-called special relationship under considerable stress. Schlesinger was referring to the Heath government's refusal to come out on the side of Israel (many State Department people always suspected Carrington of being pro-Arab) and its failure to support a US-sponsored resolution for a ceasefire which went before the UN Security Council on 13 October. The British defence was that the draft resolution could not succeed because President Sadat of Egypt was against it. Did the British government want the Israelis to lose? Carrington denied that he favoured the Arabs.

Schlesinger had little time for Carrington and felt disdain for the British position in the Middle East. A minute of that meeting showed the difference between the two men and their governments.

Mr Schlesinger said that the distinct tendency of British diplomacy in the last few days to work in close collusion with the French [Schlesinger saw this as Suez all over again] had been noticed in Washington. British policies were taking on a quality of 'decaying Gaullism' and this was reflected not only in the discussion about the Middle East conflict but in the Common Market discussions on oil in Brussels on the previous day. When pressed by Lord Carrington to give specific examples of this 'collusion' Mr Schlesinger said that there were reports that the British had actively dissuaded the Egyptians from supporting the ceasefire resolution which the Americans had wanted the British to sponsor in the UN. The inference that was being drawn was that Britain and France had sought to frustrate American efforts to bring about a ceasefire.

Lord Carrington enquired what evidence was available for this accusation which he regarded as offensive. He had been personally involved in the Ministerial discussions in connexion with the ceasefire proposals and our view of its poor prospects had been based on soundings taken in Cairo and Moscow. Dr Kissinger had subsequently agreed with this assessment.[3]

When Foreign Secretary Alec Douglas-Home heard about the tone of the Carrington–Schlesinger meeting he instructed Lord

3 The National Archives, PREM 15/1767.

Cromer to seek out Schlesinger to straighten out the special relationship. Cromer's secret report to Home was not encouraging.

British Embassy, 15 November 1973
I have remarked before that couthness is not Schlesinger's strong point, and he showed it once more. One or two of his remarks bordered on the offensive. I believe our discussion did go some way towards clearing the air, though inevitably it left a lot of questions unanswered. I may say that Schlesinger was clearly somewhat chastened by his session with Peter Carrington. We got off to a not frightfully good start by my remarking that the NPG [Nuclear Planning Group] meeting in The Hague appeared to have been a good one. Schlesinger remarked that he supposed one could say that, given the low standards of the organisation concerned.[4]

How deeply did the American attitude bite into the Anglo-US relationship? A look at some of these secret exchanges suggests the mood could hardly have been grimmer. Carrington's view was that the special relationship existed only when the Americans wanted it to. The concept was something largely imagined by the British public and newspaper editors.

Now, in the autumn of 1973, the JIC had to produce a briefing paper for Heath. The irrefutable assessment in that document was that the US was prepared to take action if the oil fields looked like being taken over, or if Israel were on the brink of defeat. The British believed that the Americans would send in two brigades of marines to secure the major fields in the three states. Once secured, the brigades would be reinforced by two divisions, about 22,000 men. Then they would establish an army of occupation prepared to remain in the Middle East for a decade. Just as the Americans did in the 1991 and 2003 attacks on Iraq, in 1973 they expected the UK government to give them full use of the British Indian Ocean island of Diego Garcia as a jumping-off and logistical supply point for the operation.

4 Ibid.

There was no question of the British government refusing America's request. In practice, it was no more than a formality. Diego Garcia is an Indian Ocean island under British rule. Eight years earlier, on 8 November 1965, an Order in Council established the British Indian Ocean Territory, which included Diego Garcia, one of five coral atolls, the others being Eagle, Egmont, Peros Banhos and Salomon. The territory was established because the Americans wanted a naval base in the Indian Ocean. The islanders were shipped out to Mauritius and the US Navy shipped in. In all but name, Diego Garcia had been given to the Americans for the sake of that special relationship.

The Americans believed the British were not on Israel's side during the conflict, a fight which for some reason none had predicted, in spite of many warnings from the Egyptians, including President Anwar Sadat.[5] The Yom Kippur War began on 6 October and a ceasefire was declared on 24 October.

During the conflict, the two superpowers, the USA and the USSR, went to heightened states of alert. The day following the ceasefire, 25 October, American forces went to what was then called Defcon (defence condition) 3. Both the United States and the Soviet Union saw that the truce could turn out to be nothing more than a military breather, which is why both superpowers were flying in fresh military supplies to their client states at the time.

This high-alert state included US nuclear forces in Britain. Yet extraordinarily neither Ted Heath nor his Foreign Secretary Alec Douglas-Home knew anything about the raised alert state – the Defence Ministry had known about it but had failed to tell Number 10 or the Foreign Office. On 28 October Heath wanted to know how it could have come about that the American forces had raised their nuclear alert state (including those in Britain) but Downing Street had not been told until almost lunchtime. This

5 Mohammed Anwar El-Sadat (1918-81) succeeded Gamel Abdel Nasser (1918-70) as President in 1970. In March 1973 he also assumed the office of Prime Minister, which he relinquished in September 1974.

was even more perplexing to Heath since the Defence Ministry was told at 4 a.m. In Brussels the British ambassador, Sir Edward Peck, had known by 9 a.m. but could not get out of a meeting to tell London. Equally disturbing was the fact that the American President had authorized raising the nuclear weapons level at a time when he was embroiled in the Watergate scandal that would bring him down. Surely such a drastic action as nuclear weapon readiness could not be a political diversionary tactic devised by, perhaps, Kissinger? In a memo to Carrington as Defence Secretary and Alec Douglas-Home as Foreign Secretary and others in the inner circle taking defence decisions, Heath complained,

SECRET

28 October 1973

Surely not even the Russians could believe that the Americans would unleash the whole of their nuclear armoury for such a case. We have to face the fact that the American action has done immense harm, I believe, both in this country and world wide. We must not underestimate the impact on the rest of the world; an American President in the Watergate position apparently prepared to go to such lengths at a moment's notice without consultation with his allies, bound to be directly involved in the consequences, and without any justification in the military situation at the time.[6]

Whatever the strategic implications of raising nuclear weapons levels on transatlantic relations, the practical side of the Yom Kippur War for the British people was the hike in the price of oil. For much of his ministerial life as a junior Defence Minister, as First Lord of the Admiralty and now as Secretary of State for Defence, Carrington had written about and debated the naval case for the protection of the so-called sea lanes. The argument had always seemed simple and even irrefutable.

The United Kingdom needed a large, flexible and multi-faceted surface and sub-surface fleet together with air reconnaissance

6 The National Archives, PREM 1382.

because 70 per cent (or whatever was the agreed figure of the time)
of the foodstuffs and fuel supplies which kept people warm and
industry running came by sea. Anyone who had watched wartime
films understood that those sea lanes had to be kept open whatever
the cost. As the Soviet Union increased the size, the level of sophistication and the area of deployment of its fleet and airforces, then
Carrington's argument became, to his mind, more justified. Thus,
in spite of the moans of the Sea Lords and the armchair pundits,
the Royal Navy was in reasonable shape to protect those supply
lines on Carrington's watch. Few had given much consideration to
what would happen if those supplies, especially of oil, never took
to the high seas in the first place.[7] This was the starting point of
Carrington's concern about energy security.

Now, with the supply cut by the Saudi Arabians, Britain prepared to go into a literally dull and cold winter. Oil stocks and coal
stocks were low and inexorably running down. This meant the
electricity supply was threatened. People were cold and industry
disrupted. If there was no way of keeping industry going, then the
government had no choice but to cut the working week to three
days. The winter of 1973–4 is today remembered for its three-day
week. The economic statistic that was not broadcast at the time
showed that industrial production was not particularly hampered
by the shortened week. Was this due to excellent management in a
crisis? Not according to Carrington, who observed that it indicated something about industrial efficiency and productivity in the
United Kingdom anyway.

Carrington told Heath that the word from the constituencies
was that though the three-day week was unpopular, if the government gave in to the miners yet again, it would lose respect and the
support of its own party members as well as the wider population.
Thus, the ground rules for the General Election were being

7 In fact the less public debate which took place largely in academic and government think tanks did illustrate the need to protect sources as well as highways,
hence (especially after the Yom Kippur War) the rapid response to Saddam Hussein's invasion of Kuwait and the threat he posed to the Gulf States and especially
Saudi Arabia in 1991.

written. It was not a question of whether Conservatives were capable of governing. It was a much bigger question: who governs Britain? The unions or the elected representatives? That was soon to be put to the test. Carrington, still party chairman, was called over to Downing Street by Heath for an emergency meeting. The Prime Minister decided that so serious was the crisis of that winter that he needed to set up a ministry to handle the emergency and the subject. It would be called the Department of Energy, and he wanted Carrington to leave the Defence Ministry and become its first minister. There had been a similar department earlier: in 1942 the Ministry of Fuel and Power was established but was subsumed in the Department of Trade and Industry (DTI) in 1970.

The original department and his new job were not entirely different according to Carrington. Back in 1942 Britain was at war and under siege. In 1974 Carrington sensed the same predicament. Then the severe winter and the dreadful feeling of discontent among Britain's 700,000 mining community in 1947 were not dissimilar to the circumstances of the winter of 1973–4. The new siege had been brought about by the fourfold increase in the price of oil after the Yom Kippur War. At that stage, the DTI, in which sat the minister responsible for energy, was a giant of civil bureaucracy. The chances of the junior minister's case being directly heard in Cabinet were slim. Therefore, the advice to Heath from one or two of his Cabinet colleagues, and especially from Sir John Hunt, the Cabinet Secretary, was that it was time to revert to the status of a single and independent Ministry of Energy.

Thirty or so years on, the shift seems of little interest; another political shuffle of an unremarkable deck of ministers held by Heath. At the time, the setting up of this ministry was considered of the utmost national importance. The consequences of the energy debate, and with it the confrontation with the mineworkers, would bring down the Heath government; easy then to see why Margaret Thatcher, a decade later, would do nothing but confront and be determined to destroy the power of the National Union of Mineworkers.

In Carrington, Heath clearly believed he had the right man

for the task, inasmuch that this was an emergency, needed rapid assessment, identification of resources and the ability to get through bureaucracy to implement plans. As Heath once told me, Carrington's military training (it never abandoned him), coupled with his professional and political experience, suited him for the job. Even so, the ministry was set up with few having any idea how it should run, what its resources would be in the long term, nor what its authority might be without further legislation. Within hours of Heath's announcement, Carrington's doormats in London and at Bledlow were cushioning letters of support. This cheered him, for in spite of Heath's reassurances he had serious doubts about his suitability.

Woodrow Wyatt
19 Cavendish Avenue NW8
9 Jan '74

Dear Peter
You have the determination – and you certainly have the charm – to do a marvellous job for us all. Not a moment too soon. If you can make us self-sufficient by 1978 (not 80) I will write that you should be hereditary Prime Minister.
Good luck,
Yours,
Woodrow

Sunday Express
9.1.74

Dear Peter
. . . all our hopes are with you – and I believe with all my heart that all our hopes will be realized,
Yours,
John [the editor John Junor]

10th January 1974

General Sir Harry Tuzo GCB OBE MC
C-in-C BAOR
My Dear Secretary of State
You will carry with you to your new job the fervent good wishes
of the Army in general and of BAOR in particular. As a house-
holder and ordinary citizen I have every possible selfish reason for
wishing you success; as a soldier I have equally strong reasons for
profound gratitude to you. Your support – and the light-hearted
and stimulating way in which it was applied – will long remain
amongst my happiest memories. All good fortune to you – and
please do not worry to reply.
Yours ever,
Harry

Major-General Pat Howard-Dobson CB
Commandant, Staff College
I think it is true that none of us has ever had more confidence in a
Secretary of State, because we know our problems have been fully
understood and that our needs have been fought for the last ...

Lt Gen Sir David Fraser KCB OBE
VCGS
15 January

My Dear Peter
I do wish you all the luck in the world in your new and intractable
duties. If anybody can manage then you can.
    The sense of personal loss we all feel here is profound ...

In the *Sunday Times*, Muriel Bowen wrote a magazine profile of
Carrington. She'd been sent out to 'do a hatchet job'. She did not,
as she told Carrington in a personal note.

8th January

The only encouraging thing about coming home to a flat without central heating or hot water (all our oil was stolen!) was to turn on the Telly and hear that you have been appointed Energy Minister.

The office does not like the profile too much. They say it is too pro you! I was sent out in search of 'enemies' but after a lot of exhausting effort I wasn't successful . . .

Admiral of the Fleet, Lord Hill-Norton, almost a caricature of a growling sea-dog who assumed all ministers were postmen from the Treasury and should be treated with hostility, believed Carrington's term at the Ministry of Defence had been little short of miraculous.

United Service & Royal Aero Club

Dear Peter

I am sorry that you are leaving Defence, but I (and I suspect very large numbers are) am delighted that you are going to take a grip on Energy.

May I say what countless people are thinking but most too junior to say? We all think that your leadership in the last few years has been an inspiration to all the Services and our equally dedicated Civil oppos. And to those of us at the top your astoundingly successful efforts on our behalf with your colleagues has seemed miraculous. I would not like you to leave without saying from the heart how much we all owe you.

Peter

Carrington regarded his period at the MOD, at least until he was forced to take on the party chairmanship, with pleasure. In theory he was a success. Certainly the likes of Peter Hill-Norton sang his praises. Yet this apparent near adoration of officials and the chiefs of staff throws up a doubt about Carrington's tenure in the ugliest building in Whitehall. Hill-Norton makes the point:

'We all think that your leadership in the last few years has been an inspiration to all the Services and our equally dedicated Civil oppos.' With such a following, from the most junior to the highest levels of military command, why did not Carrington push through the reforms that were crying out to be made? His predecessor Denis Healey had successfully reduced the British commitment east of Suez. True, there had been opposition to Healey's plans, but the military had understood the changed world, the fewer imperial responsibilities and hence the need to rethink its deployment of forces. Healey had not had the time to complete the much needed restructuring of British forces, the ministerial responsibilities and the necessity to take forward Mountbatten's ideas of a decade earlier to make the chiefs of staff more 'purple', that is, less single-service minded. Carrington knew that more radical change was necessary. But instead of pressing on with Healey's reforms – which many chiefs of staff would have supported – Carrington took the decision that the forces had had enough reorganization for the moment and should be allowed a long period as they were. In that, he was probably wrong.

The restructuring that was then needed was at the senior levels. The very concept of separate ministries needed scrapping: all service departments needed to be under one ministry and the command structure streamlined. There was a glaring lack of understanding about what the nearly 160 different major parts of the British defence system were for. There were outposts – even in the British Isles – which no one in the MOD could readily explain and some that no one in Whitehall had even heard of. Carrington's civil servants and military, all enormously loyal to their Secretary of State, could have been persuaded to modernize but they were not asked to. Carrington, though a Whig, was not instinctively a reformer. It was not until nearly a decade later and the appointment of Michael Heseltine as Secretary of State for Defence that this necessary reform was tackled. Having said this, we should also note the goodbye letter from the reformist-minded Chief of the Defence Staff, Field Marshal Michael Carver.

9 January 74

I have been fortunate to have served and worked for many of the
Great and Good; for several Field Marshals including Monty, John
Harding and Gerald Templer to mention the pick of the bunch.

I say with deep sincerity that I have never ever worked for a boss
for whom I had greater admiration than for yourself . . .

However the great and the good sang Carrington's praises at
Defence, nothing could prevent him starting at Energy. He was
tasked to resolve the biggest issue of Heath's day while keeping on
the job of party chairman. It was a formidable commission and one
that Carrington forever believed he should not have been given.

Carrington told Heath that the only possible good outcome
from the energy crisis was that if the new ministry worked and the
miners were contained, then the nation at large, and not just party
activists, would be supportive enough of the government for Heath
to go to the country and ask for another term. But Carrington was
soon to realize that his new job was not so much a department of
state as an office of crisis management.

The Department of Energy compiled a long-term agenda
which, properly attended to, had every chance of bringing some
order to Britain's energy programme. He saw the oil crisis as a
warning that the UK would always be vulnerable to restraint on
oil supplies. The obvious answer to oil, nuclear energy, was uncompromisingly controversial. Carrington believed the long-term
answer to almost all the UK's energy difficulties would be to follow French thinking and embark on a major programme of
building nuclear power stations. He listed the questions that had to
be answered about long-term processing and eventually decommissioning. He understood the debate about balancing nuclear
energy and the concerns it caused with the finite natural resources.
There was also the high cost of building, the unquestionably difficult planning considerations and the political fall-out. On balance,
in his mind, nuclear power made sense.

Within days of taking office Carrington was off to Washington for the International Energy Conference of Foreign and Energy Ministers chaired by the Secretary of State, Henry Kissinger. This was not a routine ministerial meeting. The Yom Kippur War, said Carrington, and the subsequent restriction on oil supplies by the Gulf States, had made many governments understand that oil was so important that it, or the lack of it, could bring about war just as in times past villages, tribes and states had fought over water.

At the Washington meeting, the differences in approach between the Americans and the Europeans were never far below the surface. The French had an open row with Kissinger over what they believed was American arrogance and exacerbation of the oil crisis. It took all the energies of the British Foreign Secretary, Alec Douglas-Home, and Carrington's diplomatic skills to placate, albeit temporarily, the two sides. As a mark of the importance of the conference, President Nixon (himself besieged by the Watergate affair) gave a full banquet at the White House, and it was here that Carrington met for the first time the man who would later refer to him as a 'duplicitous bastard', Alexander Haig, sometime Supreme Allied Commander Europe and US Secretary of State. Nixon's grasp of the consequences of not having an international control of energy sources – by which he meant oil – endorsed Carrington's own belief that an aspect of his new department was not so far removed from those he was more used to, Defence and the Foreign Office. Yet there was no chance then of approaching these subjects in practical terms.

At home, the miners were pushing the Tories to the point where either the government would back down and pay what Heath saw as excessive rises or the whole country would stop functioning as an industrial and service economy. In the third week of January, Carrington went to the House and told the Lords that the TUC had suggested to the Prime Minister that the way to resolve the crisis was to give the miners what they wanted and to publicly call this government back-down (for that is what it would be) a recognition that the miners were to be 'treated as a special case'. The government's contention was that the miners were already treated as a special case. They were being offered more than other industries. Carrington did not doubt the sincerity of the TUC, but he had to accept Heath's judgement that it was not possible for the government to go along with the suggestion, otherwise every other group would agitate for higher pay awards. In fact, the General Secretary of the National Union of Railwaymen, Sidney Greene, had told a meeting of the National Economic Development Council on 9 January that the TUC should promise that the other trade unions, including his own, would not exploit the government's agreement with the NUM. Here was an example of personal chemistry influencing high-level discussions: Heath did not believe Greene. Len Murray, who was the General Secretary of the TUC, then went so far as to give Heath this offer in writing. Carrington's view was that they could go along with the TUC offer, which he considered to be a sincere one, and hope that no other union, such as the NUR, would then claim that it too was a special case. He recognized that some other unions were just as powerful as the miners. For example, the miners could starve the power stations and thus bring the country to a three-day week and eventually a standstill. But the power workers did not even have to control fuel stocks. They could simply throw the switch and black out British industry and homes while they demanded more money – as a special case.

Nonetheless Carrington accepted that ever since the pay settlements of 1972, the miners were indeed a special case, relative to other unions. As the new minister, he wanted to recommend some form of settlement. Yet he also judged that the crisis would not end with a pay agreement. He believed that the militant elements in British trade unionism would never accept that the TUC could come to anything less than confrontation with this, perhaps any, Conservative government. In spite of the soft-handed approach of Len Murray and some of his colleagues, Carrington and Heath saw the energy issue as one that challenged the Conservatives' right to govern.

On 24 January the NUM held a strike ballot, ostensibly to seek member support for the NUM Executive. On 4 February the result of that ballot indicated that at least 80 per cent of those who had voted wanted a walkout. This was winter: the one time the miners believed their strikes would be effective. No coal – no heat. No heat – government loss of popularity. Government falls. The strike was scheduled for 9 February. By then, the NUM was determined to go ahead and there was no longer anything that the TUC could do as an honest broker. During an interview with BBC Radio's *The World This Weekend*, Carrington outlined some of the consequences:

There comes a time when the economy of this country is in such a grave situation that one can't do that [a three-day week] for very long and so it is a question of endurance and of seeing that the things that really matter in this country, the hospitals, the sewage and so on, [have] enough power for them to make life possible in this country. And this is the sort of situation which will arise if people don't understand the gravity of the situation and the economic problems which there are in this country.

Most did understand the gravity. What they wanted was a lead from the government and Carrington was increasingly concerned that Heath was not showing the leadership the country expected. The previous month, Heath had called two private meetings of his Cabinet. Carrington's expressed opinion at both meetings was that although the government had been in power for less than four years there was no point in hanging on in the circumstances. Only William Whitelaw and Francis Pym were willing to speak against an early election. However, by the end of January, when it was clear in which direction the NUM was headed, Whitelaw and Pym raised no further objections and left the timing of the election in Heath's hands. Carrington, as party chairman, was expected to have something of a grip of Conservative opinion and of general opinion throughout the United Kingdom. He told Heath in January 1974 that the longer Heath put off having an election, the more the public would construe his action as indecisiveness. The Queen was in Australia. Heath sent a telegram to the Royal Yacht on 6 February telling her that he was calling an election for three weeks' time. Under constitutional procedure, the Queen had to be in the country in order that her Prime Minister could have access to the monarch on polling day or as soon as the result was declared. The Queen broke off her tour of Australia to return to London.

The issue in Heath's mind was the theme of that General Election: *Who Governs Britain?* Heath's view was that the miners were challenging the British 'democratic way of life'. Here again Carrington and Heath disagreed. Carrington told him that he did not believe that any party, however justified, could sustain over three weeks an election campaign with just one message. It was all very well to be right, but after three weeks of asking who governs Britain, there were going to be many members of the electorate who would come to the conclusion that as the government had raised the question, then very clearly the government did not govern Britain and therefore they had best vote for someone who could.

Carrington's view was that *Who Governs Britain?* would stick in the electorate mind as Who Can Govern Britain?

In the event it was a close-run thing with the Conservatives taking 37.9 per cent of the vote, and Labour 37.1 per cent. Some 200,000 more people voted Conservative than Labour. However, because of the electoral system, the Labour Party won 301 seats, four more than the Conservatives. Heath tried to cling to power by offering the Liberals, under Jeremy Thorpe, some form of power-sharing, but ultimately he was forced to make way for Harold Wilson to return to Downing Street.

The following morning Carrington went over to Downing Street. The results did not make for scintillating conversation, and Heath became gloomier and gloomier. There was a formal front while others were there, but at one point Carrington found himself standing in the lavatory of Downing Street next to the soon-to-be ex-PM. Suddenly, Heath turned to him somewhat alarmingly, and said in obvious anguish, 'Why did they hate me so much?' Carrington recalled that there was nothing he could do to convince Heath that this was not so. He believed that Heath felt rejection more personally than any other politician he had ever known.

Once the ploy to attract the Liberals had failed and the proper course was resumed, Heath accepted it was all finished for him in Number 10. However, he was still party leader and one of the first things he did was sack Carrington as party chairman. Carrington was thankful. He had not liked the job. But he did name one of his dachshunds Ted. In Australia, Bob Menzies watched with some distress as the party he admired went into opposition. His doubts about Heath were apparent in a letter to Carrington:

I am of course tremendously interested in the future of the Conservative Party. Ted Heath presents a problem. He is a very able man but seems to me in some way to lack the power of communication ... He has never quite realized that when he is talking on the Television, he is not talking to millions of people in a rather stilted way, but is talking to Mr and Mrs Brown who have come in to look at the telly with their neighbour. If he could begin to understand that on television he is engaging in conversation, his effectiveness would, I think, be enormously increased.

Carrington agreed, but by then assumed that however accurate Menzies' observation, it was all irrelevant for the party because the Tories were again in the political wilderness and how many days and nights they were to wander was entirely in the hands of the Labour government. Carrington was firmly in the camp that believed governments lose elections rather than oppositions winning them.

11. Wilderness

Carrington was again politically bored in opposition. Shadow Cabinet meetings about early day motions held for him no interest whatsoever. As a peer he had no constituents to look after, no Saturday morning surgeries, no majority to nurse. At Westminster he had no part to play in what he saw as footling manoeuvres to catch out ministers at the despatch box. This certainly did not mean that the House of Lords went to sleep in opposition. As Conservative Leader in the Lords, Carrington had a more difficult job in opposition than in government. In opposition it was often harder to get peers to speak in the House, to vote and maintain pressure on the opposing benches than it had been in government. Their lordships knew that under Salisbury Rules they had room to amend and revise but not block legislation sent from the Commons, particularly when it was law-making promised in the government's election manifesto and perhaps in its parliamentary programme. William Whitelaw, the new party chairman, embarked on the rubber-chicken round to rally the troops, many of whom were despondent and unlikely to put all their efforts into preparing for the autumn election which Carrington was predicting.

Carrington, in conversation twenty-five years on, reflected that given what he, with considerable understatement, called 'adverse comment' over his party chairmanship, few at Tory headquarters at the time were likely to listen to his predictions. He thought that there would be an early election and that quite likely Wilson would win again and therefore Heath would be challenged to step down. Heath could not believe this. Yet he did lose the October 1974 election and the grey-suited political undertakers in the party made ready to remove him. Carrington's view at the time was that Heath should have been re-elected. Carrington told his colleagues and political friends that none likely to challenge Heath had his vision, especially in economic and European affairs, which Carrington believed were to be the main issues of government for the foreseeable future.

However, Carrington was still blamed for his part in failing to get the Tories re-elected in the spring of 1974, and so his opinion counted for nothing. Moreover, he was concerned that the Conservatives would move away from the modern and liberal style of Heath to the right. Not everyone shared his concern and some rather hoped that this would indeed happen. There was a mood in parts of the party that a shift (some thought it was a *return*) to the political right was exactly what the Tories needed to do and the country wanted them to do. When, in 1975, the party leadership election came, Margaret Thatcher beat Heath.

Heath had wondered aloud to Carrington why the electorate hated him so much. He now saw himself utterly let down by his own people. From that moment, Heath felt little but coldness towards Margaret Thatcher: she had taken what was properly his. In fact, the means of taking the leadership had been partly simplified in December 1974 when the Home Committee announced that in future there would be annual elections for the Conservative leadership and that, as in most clubs, a would-be challenger needed no more than a proposer and seconder to stand. To win, he or she would need to get on the first ballot 50 per cent of the parliamentary vote and to have 15 per cent of the party membership vote. This effectively meant that Heath had to be all things to an awfully high percentage of all men and women able to vote. He simply was not that popular in the Commons. Carrington, who once again was not in the country at the time of the election, recognized that Heath had greater support in the countryside than he did at Westminster. He wanted Heath to succeed, for the party's sake as he saw it, but he believed Margaret Thatcher had a much stronger chance than the activists thought.

Most Conservatives thought loyalty rather important and therefore would support Heath. And there were too many who simply thought a woman's place was not in Downing Street unless of course it was in the kitchen. Yet on Tuesday 4 February, Margaret Thatcher got 130 votes, Heath 119 and the second challenger, Hugh Fraser, 16. It was not enough to win outright but the damage was done. Heath did not have the determination to go on: he stood down. William Whitelaw, Jim Prior, John Peyton and Geoffrey Howe put their names forward for the second ballot, but the race was only really between Whitelaw and Thatcher. She picked up 146 votes and he, 79.

Margaret Thatcher was out to change both the party and Britain. She was determined to fight the grandees of her own party. 'I felt no sympathy for them,' she said later. Howe had been the only person she thought might attract votes away from her. She was wrong on that, though of course it was Howe's valedictory speech to the Commons over twenty years later that eventually changed the parliamentary party's mood towards Thatcher and brought about her downfall.

Carrington was later seen as one of Thatcher's two most loyal lieutenants (Whitelaw being the other). However, when Thatcher became Leader of the Conservative Party, Carrington seriously believed that his political career was at an end since he had been one of Heath's closest political allies. Although he had not taken part directly in the leadership campaign (he was in Australia), Carrington had openly supported Heath and had reflected the constituency view that it would be a wise decision to keep Heath as leader. He therefore wrote yet another 'resignation' letter. In it, Carrington pointed out that as he had made it very clear that he thought Heath the more appropriate candidate (clearly not the better, as Heath had lost), he would perfectly understand if she did not require his services as Leader of the Conservatives in the Lords. However, once more it was not the time for the Whig to tend his estate. In fact, Thatcher needed Carrington in the Lords because by then he was elder statesman enough in that House to have considerable influence. Furthermore, he had the ministerial experience in Defence and Foreign Affairs which, for the moment at least, she needed to entrust to someone who, as a peer, could have no political ambitions. She describes her attitude in her memoir:

I asked Peter Carrington to stay on as Leader of the House of Lords ... I
had no illusions about Peter's position in the Tory Party's political spec-
trum: he was not of my way of thinking. He had, of course, been in Ted's
inner circle making the political decisions about the miners' strike and
the February 1974 election. But since we lost office he had proved an
extremely effective Opposition Leader in the Upper House and as a former Defence Minister and an international businessman he had wide
experience of Foreign Affairs. Admittedly, he was likely in Shadow Cabinet to be on the opposite side to me on economic policy. But he never
allowed economic disagreements to get in the way of his more general
responsibilities. He brought style, experience, wit and – politically incor-
rect as the thought may be – a touch of class.[1]

Carrington also had a touch of loyalty. He liked Heath as a
person, he admired him as a politician, and no overture of patronage from his successor would disguise the fact that Carrington
regretted his friend's rejection in the leadership contest. His feelings for Heath's leadership remained for all to see – including
Thatcher.

Until Margaret Thatcher became leader in 1975, Carrington had
not known her at all well. Carrington was hardly isolated from the
Tory leadership because of his position in the Lords, yet they were
not particularly well acquainted. As Carrington remarked to me,
their paths rarely crossed – particularly socially – and in Cabinet
she had 'not taken any great part'. As Secretary of State for Education, she had been criticized by the media when she removed
free milk for children in schools. Thatcher the Milk Snatcher was
not one of her finest hours. She had been deeply upset by the
reaction to it and had relied on Ted Heath's support. He gave
Thatcher that support, willingly and wholeheartedly since it was,
after all, his policy that was being slated. Carrington regarded this
event as an important moment in the tense relationship between
Heath and Thatcher: 'I believe that one of the reasons, though
perhaps not the most important, he took so violently against her

1 Margaret Thatcher, *The Path to Power*, London: HarperCollins, 1995, p. 287.

later on was his perception that he had been poorly rewarded for his support at that time.'

Both Heath and Carrington were surprised at her success in the leadership challenge although Carrington reflected many years on that neither should have been. Thatcherism was really Josephism with Thatcher as Keith Joseph's disciple. When Joseph had understood that he was not a front-runner for the party leadership, he encouraged Thatcher to run. Carrington watched with more than passing interest, as he told me in 2006:

I think the Conservative Party was the most unlikely party to have chosen a woman as its leader and a very untried and comparatively junior minister at that. She quite clearly and sensibly realized that unless she dominated the parliamentary party in the early stages of her leadership, she wouldn't last more than a few weeks. There were a number of those in the party who thought her election a great mistake and would have happily disposed of her. She did, however, two very sensible things. First she incorporated a number of those dissidents in her Shadow Cabinet and she set out to dominate – and dominate she did. I think that was certainly right at the time, but after a bit, the domination became a habit and though she was perfectly normal in a small party of six or eight, anything larger became a public meeting, addressed only by her.[2]

Carrington always thought the Conservatives were lucky to win the 1979 election. His view, not an isolated one, was that the activities of the unions and what he called the 'feebleness of Jim Callaghan' won it for the Tories.

Thatcher inherited a different mood in the country from that of Ted Heath, though his policy had been much the same. Both of them would greatly resent it, but in a way, Ted was John the Baptist to Margaret Thatcher.

Peter Carrington could not be and never was a Thatcher man. He came to like her personally, but her attitude to politics and her

2 This paraphrases Queen Victoria's view of Gladstone.

economic assumptions, together with those who had implanted them, were alien to his way of thinking. Carrington was not an economist. In spite of his banking career while in opposition, he never grasped the concepts that would have made him a Treasury minister. Therefore, he was an incomplete politician. By the mid-1970s, he was becoming a political anachronism, one of those left whose major contribution was a certain amount of wisdom and an enormous sense of duty. He had also the natural desire – and probably instinct – to be at the centre of decision-making. This after all was a career, even for a very well-established peer and landowner. He was a supreme gossip, so being on the fringes of power had no attractions. Consequently there was never any question of his not continuing in the Shadow Cabinet as long as Thatcher wanted him to, even though his acceptance of her offer would lead to the two most miserable periods of his political and personal life.

Carrington came to admire and 'quite like' Margaret Thatcher but he was never happy with her leadership. From their first meeting in her inaugural Shadow Cabinet, Carrington suspected her economic argument, especially her notion that monetarist policies had to be strictly followed to control inflation. At that early stage her political guru Keith Joseph, who at times appeared to be incapable of making clear his considerable intellect and argument, held Thatcher almost spellbound by his political theory. Consequently, Carrington accepted that his new leader was about to do as he feared, and that was to lead the party away from the centre ground. Carrington believed this to be an enormously dangerous policy. To him, it was important that the Conservatives should maintain the middle ground; although he was suspicious of political labels he was an old enough Westminster hand to know that labels could and did win elections, which after all was what the party was there to do.

Once more, he became depressed at the thought of a long period out of government. He had not gone into politics to watch the other side bat. Opposition was to him very boring. Furthermore, of one thing he was sure: the Conservatives had gone through

more than a change of leadership. Soon, it would not be the party
he had joined.

There would be a philosophical change, yet there would be no
debate. Questioning the new leader's values would be seen at the
very least as eccentric and more likely as disloyal. From day one,
Carrington understood that Margaret Thatcher's style was based
on the notion that 'there is no alternative' to her way of thinking –
hence the nickname, Tina, that became widely used in and out of
Cabinet. Carrington felt uneasy. In many ways, he would have
been happier if she had accepted his resignation in February 1975.
He could always have gone anyway. That he did not had something
to do with his persistent predilection for power. Two decades earlier he had been a very young Australian High Commissioner. He
had sat on important boards of large international corporations.
One day he would be Secretary-General of NATO. Carrington
had a need to be close to seats of power. Carrington stayed with a
Thatcher team that he suspected would take the Tories in a direction he mistrusted but back into government.

Margaret Thatcher understood his reservations and she might
have asked Carrington to stay on as leader in the Lords, but
she did not let him get his hands on any other Shadow Cabinet
responsibilities. This suited Carrington. He had returned to business after the February 1974 General Election and began once
more to travel considerably, particularly in Africa. He was back on
the board of Barclays Bank and had also joined Rio Tinto Zinc. It
was his RTZ connection that allowed him to get such a grasp
of African politics without the hamper of political office. His connections in Southern Africa remained with him and his family
for the rest of his life, and he and Iona Carrington were frequent
visitors. They were especially keen to get away from English win-
ters to avoid the potentially fatal consequences of her blood
disorder, chronic cold haemagglutinin, easily exacerbated by cold
weather.

The combination of politics and business meant that Carrington
was talking to the leading industrialists, the opinion formers and
generally to the most important political leaders in every foreign

country he visited. For example, in September 1975 he visited China. That vast country was emerging from its Maoist indignation and Carrington was received as a significant figure. Heath had a similar standing in China as a politician and as a musician and the connection between Heath and Carrington was not lost on the Chinese. Carrington was seen as more than an ex-minister and a director of an international corporation: the Chinese saw him as a man of considerable influence in British political thinking. He had been on the Chinese list of people to watch and cultivate since his time as High Commissioner in Australia and the occasion when one of his first conferences had been a gathering of the South-east Asia Treaty Organization (SEATO). This group was a paper tiger, unless viewed in the 1950s and 1960s from Peking (now Beijing). As a Defence Minister, First Lord of the Admiralty and because Britain still had a naval presence in the Far East, including the Royal Naval HQ HMS *Tamar* in Hong Kong, Carrington's pronouncements were carefully noted in the Chinese capital. Then as Foreign Minister to R. A. Butler, Carrington had returned to Asia for yet another SEATO conference and more importantly for briefings from the Americans, including their commander-in-chief in the region, General Westmoreland, on the war in Vietnam.

Perhaps most of all, the Chinese understood political longevity, and therefore saw this middle-aged aristocrat as an influential Establishment figure who had served with distinction in the Second World War and had been a functionary and minister in every Tory government since Churchill, and also a director of some of the most prestigious companies in the United Kingdom. His membership of the House of Lords was not to be derided but noted as a sign of membership of a lasting establishment. It was therefore hardly surprising that Carrington, a member of a party which had lost an election, but with the most respectable credentials, should be received by the man who was to be the most influential figure for the rest of the century in post-Maoist China, Deng Hsiao Ping.

In November 1978 this same pedigree was acknowledged in the Soviet Union. Carrington was seen there as an important part of

the British *nomenklatura*. He met and talked with the Soviet Foreign Minister, Andrei Gromyko, who told him that he was
convinced that within a year the Callaghan government would fall,
that Margaret Thatcher would be Prime Minister and that he, Carrington, would be Foreign Secretary. That was the political
assessment from the Soviet Embassy in London. The same analysis,
as Gromyko told Carrington, suggested that a Thatcher government would be 'bellicose'. If Carrington believed that the Soviet
analysts were right, he most certainly had doubts about his own
people. When he was Defence Secretary, the intelligence summar-
ies had always presented the Soviet Union as a society governed
with ruthless military efficiency. In late 1978 Carrington's impression, albeit fleetingly, was that the Soviet Union was anything but
efficient. He saw it as an example of just the opposite – slovenly,
introverted, probably corrupt and a land where only the vodka
flowed on time. Carrington's impression would not undo the ma-
trix of the standard British and NATO Threat Lecture. However,
it was an impression he held on to through all his future dealings
with the Soviet Union, first as British Foreign Secretary and then
as Secretary-General of NATO.

There was a sense of pending government change, and crucial to
the Conservative preparation for a coming election was a shadowy
organization called SHIELD. It was made up of Thatcher and just
seven of her closest advisers and a note-taker. The SHIELD
group's secretary was Stephen Hastings, the others were Thatcher
herself, Whitelaw, Sir Keith Joseph, Harry Sporborg, Brian
Crozier, Nicholas Elliott and Carrington. The agendas at the
unpublicized meetings anticipated what they saw as the essential
political and international confrontations facing a new Tory government in the late 1970s. For example, one meeting on 3 May
1978 – exactly a year before the General Election – did not discuss
mundane subjects such as taxation, health, law and order and the
economy. These were issues for Cabinet. The SHIELD members
had more sensitive and secret agendas, as the seven items on the
subject list showed:

1 Reorganization of the Intelligence and Security Services
2 Contingency planning for a Conservative government
3 The Media
4 *The Real Face of Labour* [a Tory anti-government pamphlet]
5 Association of Free Trade Unions
6 Central Office security and course on Marxism/Leninism
7 International terrorism

The restructuring of the Intelligence Services, Carrington believed, was of top priority because in his view their popular image hid the fact that they were not very good and could prove to be a vulnerable element in government decision-making. Yet the services were not reorganized and they did let down the Tory government and others that followed. The Media (in Tory thinking it always had a capital M), according to the group, needed to be better understood, and Media Handling, as it was called, had to be sophisticated and at the same time brutal. Here was a subject that predated the Blair government by a decade. Item 7, on terrorism, was hardly surprising. The group knew all about terrorism in Northern Ireland. Crozier, a celebrated student of world affairs, already saw the potential of terrorism and kidnapping to be an international issue demanding global cooperation for decades to come. Carrington brought a much needed personal experience of foreign affairs to the group. His whole professional life from soldiering, to politics, to business had been largely in world issues and markets. Thatcher understood this and realistically when the time came she had no one on her Commons benches with more experience, as his interventions at the SHIELD group demonstrated.

It was Brian Crozier who set up SHIELD. The purpose was to give Thatcher a continual security brief and to make sure the Tory leader had their view of the world. The meetings were unannounced and rarely minuted. The whole group, with the exceptions of Thatcher and, when he attended, Carrington, were used to the shadowy world of intelligence. Crozier was well known as a journalist but he was far more than that. He first came to

London from Australia to study music and for a time was known as a music critic. His journalistic interests then moved to foreign affairs at Reuters, the *Sydney Morning Herald*, the BBC and in America. He was one of the founders of the Institute for the Study of Conflict, described to the author by the late Frederick Bonnart, the then editor of *Nato's 15 Nations*, as 'the Soviets-are-coming magazine'. SHIELD appeared to have a brief to study and infiltrate what they called subversive organizations which included CND and, where they thought necessary, distribute covert propaganda. Of the other SHIELD members, the Tory MP Sir Stephen Hastings was a former SAS, SOE and MI6 officer; the lawyer and banker Harry Sporborg was a wartime assistant to the head of SOE, Colin Gubbins, and Nicholas Elliott was the MI6 officer sent to bring the traitor Kim Philby back to London from the Middle East in 1963 (Philby 'escaped' to Moscow). They regarded part of their role as to subvert what they deemed the nation's enemies. Thatcher and Carrington were briefed on the intelligence craft of psychological action – part of which was to provide provocative questions for political speeches, thus raising doubts among opposing activists. In July 1978 Thatcher chaired a SHIELD (also called 'The 61') committee that would give her blessing to so-called counter-subversion. Carrington thought the whole matter rather dramatic but he certainly saw the argument for establishing a working group to penetrate, for example, peace fronts through the workings of a Counter-Subversion Executive. This was powerful propaganda and counter-subversive action in preparation for government, yet in later years Carrington always said that he only vaguely remembered its business and the influence of those preparing for administration. Government was not to be for some eighteen months. Carrington's everyday concerns were his business connections, which would at a later stage have political implications because of the contacts he made, especially in Africa.

Carrington's three principal commercial interests were at Cadbury-Schweppes, RTZ and Barclays Bank. Apart from helping consolidate his personal finances, his directorships meant that wherever he travelled during that period in opposition he would lunch and dine at the international top table with many of those who had not moved on since last he visited their countries. There were some who would prove enormously important. People like Henry Kissinger became close personal friends almost from the time they met in the early 1970s.

Carrington's strongest memory of Kissinger's personality was when he arrived in Washington and went to see Kissinger late one evening. It was a time of considerable international instability and many leading personalities were assumed to be under constant threat. As Carrington approached Kissinger's office from the outside, he could see the by then famous profile silhouetted by his desk light. Carrington remarked to Kissinger that he would present a perfect target to a would-be assassin. Kissinger dismissed the danger: 'I am an intellectual. Only another intellectual would want to murder me. Being an intellectual he would never make up his mind to pull the trigger.'

Kissinger took to Carrington right away. When the latter was forced to resign in 1982 Kissinger immediately invited him to join his company that specialized in giving corporate advice on international politics and strategic thinking. Carrington's views reflected Kissinger's belief that too many defence and foreign policy-makers failed to see the world from any other vantage point than Whitehall or Washington. Carrington still did not entirely accept the chestnut that a diplomat was someone who went abroad to lie for his country. Therefore it was his purpose in opposition to use his time to travel and to see Britain from a distance. It was also a reflection on his standing that he could do this, that he could be seen by more or less everyone who mattered and would be listened to on his return to the Shadow Cabinet policy team on defence and foreign affairs.

The most important visits were inevitably to Africa, and in particular to Rhodesia, where he met Ian Smith, Abel Muzorewa and Joshua Nkomo. The one person who refused to talk to Carrington was perhaps the most important person in Rhodesia, Robert Mugabe. Carrington knew that any chance of a lasting settlement – as opposed to the constitutional mockery determined

by the so-called free and fair elections in Rhodesia – would have
to directly involve both leaders of the Patriotic Front, Nkomo and
Mugabe. However, Carrington failed to appreciate that Mugabe
would be eventually the toughest of all the diplomatic and political
nuts that needed cracking. This blind spot was not removed even
when he met the self-styled frontline presidents, particularly Kenneth Kaunda of Zambia.

When they met in Lusaka on 19 February 1977, Kaunda made
it plain to Carrington that Britain's biggest problem in Africa was
Rhodesia. Carrington knew this perfectly well enough for it to
become a distraction from the longer-term task of reviving the
UK relationship with European states. Kaunda's point was that the
United Kingdom was largely to blame for so much that was wrong
in Southern Africa at least. Carrington was not surprised, but certainly impressed.

He maintained that it was all due to Britain that the Rhodesian problem
had got out of hand, and we should not, and had not, behaved similarly
in other situations. As a result of our actions there would be racial war in
Rhodesia which might well spill over into Zambia where 30,000 whites
lived. It was very nearly but not quite too late to do anything about it ...
the only way of averting disaster was the removal of Smith ... almost
anyone but Ian Smith would do. It was imperative for the future of
Southern Africa that this should happen during the current year, if
not there was no prospect or hope for the white man in Rhodesia ...
Neither Nkomo or Mugabe were extreme men, but after a bloody war
either they or their successors would become so. President Kaunda was
both friendly and persuasive. I do not think his analysis of what might
happen in Rhodesia is far wrong.[3]

Each of the African frontline state leaders had similar views to
Kaunda, and they were immediately concerned that any settlement
would have to have the approval of the Commonwealth and
particularly its African members. None of them would be willing

3 Carrington papers, Bledlow.

to make any commitment to resolving the Rhodesian stand-off. The impression they made on Carrington was relayed to Thatcher and the urgency of the Rhodesian crisis explained why it became his immediate priority. The one point on which all the African leaders were agreed was that they expected Carrington to be back in government in the very near future and that therefore he would be expected and encouraged to attend to the Rhodesia File from day one in office.

If Roy Jenkins had had his way, Carrington would not have been available to Thatcher. Jenkins, who had in 1976 become President of the European Commission, had high regard for Carrington's European credentials and asked him to become one of Britain's nominated Commissioners. Carrington, who was wary of the overload of European bureaucracy, was quite certain that he would disappear into a non-job and so said he was flattered but turned down the offer. More immediately, he sensed a Conservative victory at the next election and wanted to be part of it.

12. Thatcher

In May 1979 Carrington became Foreign Secretary. He arrived at the FCO and was surprised to find that one of the first issues presented to him was the question of where he would live. The Foreign Secretary had an official London residence in Carlton Gardens. It was very grand. The Carringtons said that if it was all right with everyone in the department they would prefer to stay in their house off the Brompton Road. Carlton Gardens had just been redecorated at a cost of nearly £100,000 – at 1979 prices. Carrington said that he thought it all very nice but they really did like their cosier Knightsbridge house. He resolved the difficulty of the FCO by suggesting that his deputy, Ian Gilmour, should have the official residence as some form of compensation for not really wanting to be deputy. (He would have liked to have been Secretary of State for the Environment.)

Carrington had succeeded David Owen as Foreign Secretary; the contrast was striking. Both men were highly intelligent and quickly grasped issues. Carrington appeared to do the same amount of work and cover the same ground as quickly as Owen but in a seemingly more relaxed manner. Some thought him *too* relaxed but soon realized that his patrician image did not detract from his understanding of subjects nor the manner he approached them, as his Principal Private Secretary George Walden noted:

His nonchalance, seized on by critics as evidence of a patrician style, was deceptive. Sensitive about any suspicions of lordliness – he was disdainful of peers who performed no public service and was an early believer in the reform of the Upper House – he was a hard worker and a minutely organized man.[1]

1 George Walden, *Lucky George: Memoirs of an Anti-Politician*, London: Allen Lane, 1999, p. 189.

Walden claimed that Carrington's first triumph at the FCO was not diplomatic but gastronomic. He thought the official food horrendous and the decor depressing. It was cheap enough to get a new caterer but the threadbare and tattered Foreign Secretary's room remained untouched. Apart from getting rid of Owen's preferred portrait of Cromwell, there was little to be changed by a government committed to economic stringency.

Margaret Thatcher told me that Carrington was a natural choice. She said he had only to walk into a room to establish his quiet authority. In theory, he was not first choice. The Shadow Foreign Secretary had been Francis Pym. However, Pym did not get on well with Thatcher. Nor did Ian Gilmour, who might have expected to be at least considered. When Carrington got the job he wanted Gilmour with him. It was Gilmour who had followed him to the Defence Ministry, and he had, like Carrington, served in the Grenadiers during the war. Thatcher consented rather than agreed and Gilmour became Lord Privy Seal and a member of the Cabinet. Later, she might not have agreed so readily, as Carrington told me in 2006:

I had particularly asked for him [Gilmour], since he had been in the same position when I was Secretary of Defence and was an old friend. Ian was very good about it, but it must have been particularly galling for him, yet again, not to have his own department. Margaret never liked him, but was in awe of his considerable intellect. She got rid of him as soon as she decently could. Not that Ian minded; he disliked her and her economic policies, though he never put forward an alternative.

Carrington was surprised to get the job. He thought, however, that for the moment he had the advantage over Thatcher of knowing something of foreign affairs. His whole background, from a small child holidaying in France, speaking French, writing long and researched essays at Eton on foreign affairs, fighting through Europe, becoming an Agriculture Minister, High Commissioner, First Lord of the Admiralty, Defence Secretary and the long periods travelling through Africa, China and to Moscow, meant that by the time he became Foreign Secretary, he had an almost perfect grounding in his subject. Thatcher on the other hand knew next to nothing.

I think she had hardly ever been outside the country. From my point of view, this was a considerable advantage, for she could hardly contradict me when I told her where Rhodesia was. Subsequently Geoffrey Howe and Douglas Hurd had a much more difficult passage, for by that time she knew as much as them. Insofar as she thought of Foreign Affairs, instinctively she was on the side of the whites in Africa and on the side of the English-speaking in the rest of the world. Americans, Australians, Canadians were always considered to be a good deal more wholesome than Germans, French or Italians. This predilection did not go unnoticed by her European counterparts.[2]

Carrington's view of the role of Foreign Secretary was to implement foreign policy. But what was British foreign policy? His instinct was to rely on Palmerston's opinion that foreign policy was that which protected British interests at home as well as abroad. The reality test for any Foreign Secretary is that no one starts their given tenure at the FCO with what Carrington called that May, 'a clean sheet: a world with no wars, no long-standing disagreements, all quarrels and differences resolved'. During a lecture at the London School of Economics in October 2003, Carrington observed,

The Foreign Secretary is there to look after Britain's interests and those are not usually a matter of party politics. When I became Foreign Secretary the world was still divided between East and West. The Cold War, though not at its height, was still far and away the most important issue in foreign policy. The threat to our way of life seemed very real and our support for the Atlantic Alliance was crucial. But, surprised though I was as an hereditary peer to become Foreign Secretary, I was not surprised to find so many issues which were fairly familiar and which

2 These and following observations about Margaret Thatcher from Carrington's notes to the author.

occupied a great deal of my time ... Two of them were on my desk in 1979: Zimbabwe and the Falklands.

Yet the most important issue should have been neither of these in 1979. Rhodesia was an entirely secondary problem for Britain and it occupied an inordinate amount of time at the FCO. Carrington should have been concentrating on Europe, but that was a subject that could never attract the full attention of the Prime Minister and certainly not the electorate. The main European issue at the time was the British contribution to the budget, which as Carrington acknowledged was wholly disproportionate to Britain's economic situation and ability to contribute, as compared to that of the French or Germans. Carrington thought that the French and Germans should realize that if they drove the British out of Europe, which at the time was not wholly improbable, they would have to pick up the bill themselves, but they were not prepared to give an inch. In fact, Carrington's judgement was a little wobbly.

Both Helmut Schmidt and Valéry Giscard d'Estaing knew full well that in spite of Thatcher's strong personal feelings she would never have the support to pull out of the EEC (as then it still was) and if she went ahead, then she would certainly risk losing the General Election that would have to follow. Carrington found the subsequent arguments very heated and unpleasant.

Margaret was very shrill, 'I want my money back' repeated over and over again to the disgust of Helmut Schmidt, who at the Dublin Summit lay back in his chair pretending to be asleep, and the haughty disdain of Giscard d'Estaing. It was not Europe at its best.

Carrington and Ian Gilmour were sent off to negotiate a new budget. After an all-day and all-night session they believed that they had wrung out of the foreign ministerial meeting a very good deal for Britain.

Flushed with our success and very tired, we went down to Chequers to inform Margaret of this triumph. We were met not at the front door, but in the middle of the drive by as angry a Prime Minister as it is possible to imagine. 'It's absolutely impossible,' she said. 'You have let me down, you have committed me to something to which I cannot agree. I shall resign,' she cried. No. No. No, we said. We shall resign!

This bizarre scene continued for some time until Carrington pointed out – still in the driveway – that he and Gilmour had been up all night and were tired and hungry. She gave them lunch but not blessings. Thatcher was still threatening resignation and so were they when they drove over to Bledlow, Carrington's estate. On the way, Gilmour hit upon the get-out: 'I'll tell you what we'll do. I will give a press conference in London this evening in which I will emphasize the triumph this settlement has been for the Prime Minister.'

That is the background to the headlines the following day claiming another victory for the Iron Lady. However, Thatcher never forgave Carrington and Gilmour. Apart from her own feelings about Europeanism, there was too, according to Carrington, an animosity among the central players. Her relations with the French President in particular were never harmonious. Carrington went with her on her first visit to Paris to call on Giscard d'Estaing. The French leader made the elementary mistake of trying to patronize her and pat her on the head as a dear little woman. She clearly resented this. At lunch, Thatcher was on Giscard's right, and when a liveried footman approached with a dish, Thatcher held out her hands to help herself. But the dish and the footman moved on to Giscard and left 'her hands hanging in the air'. This may have been the correct protocol (Giscard was head of state, Thatcher a mere PM) but it was hardly tactful. Curiously, Thatcher's relationship with Giscard's successor President Mitterrand was quite different. They got on very well; maybe there was chemistry, maybe they were both wiser, though Carrington remained perplexed by this change of attitude. Giscard was not at all surprised. He told Carrington, 'It's quite simple. Neither has seen anything like the other before and they don't believe it!'

Gradually Carrington became used to Thatcher and they became very good friends. If there was a continuing annoying factor in the relationship, it was because of her son Mark. Carrington could not stand him and thought him of very low character.

Iona and my first encounter with him [Mark Thatcher] was when we gave a lunch party for Margaret and Denis at Bledlow. On the Thatchers' arrival, out of the car stepped Mark, who walked up to Iona and said, 'I had nothing better to do, so I thought I'd come to lunch.' On one occasion she [Thatcher] rang me up from Number 10 to tell me that the Ambassador to Kuwait was no good. I said, 'How do you know, you've never been there?' Oh, she said, 'Mark tells me.' He had got himself a job with a British company, trading on his mother's name, telling the British Ambassador that he must intervene and ensure the British firm got the contract and, incidentally, [he got] his cut. The Ambassador, having politely said that he couldn't intervene between one company and another, was duly reported by Mark Thatcher to his mother. Subsequent events have not improved my opinion of Mark Thatcher.

Although Carrington came to like Mrs Thatcher much more than he imagined he would, there were moments when the relationship was fragile. For example, when Thatcher was deeply unpopular with the public and the party over the Poll Tax, she went to lunch with Carrington at Bledlow to talk privately about what she should be doing. Carrington suggested that she should resign. He told her that she should go while memory of her achievement was fresh in everybody's mind. He then added what to him was obvious: that she would almost certainly dislike her successor, but he (there was no female candidate on the horizon) would naturally keep much of what she had done so she had no need to worry that the best of Thatcherism would be overturned. Carrington believed that the Tories under her leadership would be defeated at the next election and he told her that by resigning she would at least be saved that humiliation.

Thatcher did not regard Carrington's advice as kindly given. She believed that Carrington had become the spokesman of that outwardly anonymous group of Tory grandees – the grey suits. Later, he claimed he was not and that he simply did not want her to 'go out in ignominy'. Equally, he was not unaware of the grey-suit view. Reflecting on this in 2006, he thought his advice had not been entirely sensible.

If things were going right, why should she go? If things were going wrong, she was the last person to give up and throw in the towel. She is still more talked about than any other politician of the twentieth century, save Churchill. As Prime Minister she inherited a country which was demoralized, diminished in its own estimation, economically in trouble. Disillusioned with politics and politicians. In her time, she transformed the country and she did it with courage and absolute commitment.

She was lucky in the sense that the time was ripe, as it was not in Ted Heath's day, but that does not detract from her achievement. For some-one to change things as radically as she did you have to be a little blinkered. This works very well if the objective is sound, but when it comes to such issues as the Poll Tax, the blinkers should come off. She was not a good judge of people. I sometimes thought that she admired nobody from a similar background to hers who had not done as well as her. Equally, she admired nobody from an establishment background, since they were born with a silver spoon in their mouths.

She liked those who were good looking and with sex appeal, though platonic of course, otherwise it is difficult to account for people like [Governor of the Bank of England] Robin Leigh-Pemberton, who came from a background which she most particularly disliked: Eton, Grena-diers and landowner [exactly the same background as Carrington]. She was on the whole rather insensitive to what people were thinking. I remember an occasion, right at the beginning of her time as Prime Min-ister, when she decided to have all Permanent Secretaries and their wives to dinner at Number 10. This was unheard of, never been done before and those involved were extremely gratified. Iona and I were asked to dinner – all went well until she rose to speak. She had them in the palm of her hand, instead of which she told them they were not the sort of people who got things done, she was not going to put up with any obstruction with what she wanted to do and they must get on with it. A wasted opportunity, as indeed was her attitude to her former colleagues after the Falklands.

She was the heroine of the hour and could have dominated the other Heads of Government in the European Union, but her dislike of foreigners wasted that opportunity.

Carrington believed, certainly in the early days of working with Thatcher, that her most important failing was a total lack of a sense of humour. In all the time he knew Thatcher, he only once made her laugh. When foreign leaders came to see her, they would be sat in the Cabinet Room and she would start speaking immediately and never let anyone, however important, get a word in. Carrington would pass notes to her saying, for example, 'He has come five hundred miles, don't you think you could let him say something?' Thatcher would take no notice. One day, Chairman Hua of China arrived and Thatcher made the mistake of asking him, as they were about to sit, what he thought of the world situation. Fifty minutes later the Chairman was still telling her exactly what he thought. Thatcher was extremely irritated and started tapping the table with her ring – a regular sign that she was displeased. The Chairman droned on. Carrington was amused by this and passed her a note which read, 'You're talking too much as usual.' Whereupon she burst out laughing, much to the puzzlement of Chairman Hua who was in the middle of a discourse on the 'nuclear holocaust of Russian hegemony'. In Carrington's opinion Thatcher's lack of humour was in part because she was extremely wary of being laughed at. He and some of his colleagues played on this weakness. Carrington, Hailsham, Whitelaw and Christopher Soames would deliberately pass each other notes in Cabinet meetings knowing full well that Thatcher would be unnerved because she instinctively thought the notes were about her.

This then was the background to the relationship between new Foreign Secretary and new Prime Minister. Both had an enormous sense of public duty, one of them with an utterly unalterable belief in the way it would be exercised. Perhaps because Thatcher's sense of foreign policy was less than sophisticated, instead of having Carrington sweep through European halls of government, she told him to attend to Rhodesia. He did so with enormous foreboding, believing that his nemesis lay in Africa.

In Rhodesia there had been a recent general election. Apart from the South Africans and Ian Smith himself, there were few who regarded those elections as free and fair, particularly since neither Robert Mugabe nor Joshua Nkomo had been allowed to participate. Unfortunately, in his role as Shadow Foreign Secretary Francis Pym had all but committed a Thatcher government to recognizing the result as a democratic outcome. Pym had been guided partly by the report of Alan Lennox-Boyd, who had been sent to judge the conduct of the election. He reported back that it was fair (within the circumstances of some having not taken part). Carrington's first task therefore was to find some method of ridding himself of what he saw as an unnecessary 'embarrassment'. All Britain's European allies regarded the election as spurious. President Carter let Downing Street know that his administration opposed the outcome. There was so much opposition to the British position within the Commonwealth that Carrington judged that the Commonwealth could fragment. Though Thatcher grasped very little of the complications of Rhodesian history and of UDI, she made matters hard for those who did.

Margaret caused all of us difficulties with her instinctive wish for Ian Smith to survive and [Bishop Abel] Muzorewa to remain as Prime Minister. This, in my judgement, would have been disastrous. She always seemed to me to be torn between her instincts and her intelligence. Instinctively, her gut reaction was to support what one might call very right-wing causes, and unless one intervened very quickly, it was too late for her very acute intelligence to take over. Although she went along with the Rhodesian policy which we finally agreed, I was never really convinced that she would not have abandoned it and me if things had gone wrong. It was all hard work trying to persuade her against her instincts that a settlement was essential and I think it hardened her opinion that the Foreign Office was peopled with wets who were not prepared to stick up for British interests. Accommodation, conciliation and compromise were never high on her agenda.

Carrington's assessment was that his political career would be destroyed within perhaps six months of accepting Margaret Thatcher's offer to be Foreign Secretary. A large and influential section of his own party waited to see what he would do about Rhodesia. That same group, he knew, was waiting to claim his head if he attempted to bring about black majority rule, as they believed he would, and as he believed he had to. He would return to his estate by Christmas 1979. As it turned out, Carrington was not crucified but he most certainly was stoned and damned by unforgiving Conservatives and continued to be regarded as a traitor to the Conservative Party by many of its grandees right to the time of his death.

The Rhodesia Affair began in the 1960s during the decolonization of Africa. In February 1960 Macmillan had made his 'wind of change' speech to the South African Parliament. In the same year Togoland, Somaliland and Nigeria became independent. Tanganyika followed in 1961. In 1963 it was the turn of Zanzibar and Kenya and the dissolution of the Federation of Rhodesia and Nyasaland. Northern Rhodesia became Zambia in September 1964, by which time the pressure on Southern Rhodesia, led by Ian Smith, was considerable. The Rhodesians resisted British attempts to bring about independence. The whites had too much investment which they believed vulnerable and, not unconnected with that belief, they did not like what was going on in countries around them which had gained their independence. This was a perfectly understandable view, even though thirty or forty years on it might seem totally irrelevant to the search for independence. The sense of threat, physically and emotionally, felt by white Rhodesians – many of whose families had been in Rhodesia for several generations – should not be underestimated when the Rhodesia Affair is viewed from the quite different times of the twenty-first century.

In November 1965 Ian Smith announced what became known as Rhodesia's UDI – Unilateral Declaration of Independence. Between then and the end of January 1966, world economic sanctions of varying degrees were declared and Britain banned all trade with Rhodesia. The idea was simple: Smith's Rhodesians would be starved into submission.

In December 1966 the then British Prime Minister, Harold Wilson, and Ian Smith held their first negotiations aboard HMS *Tiger*. The talks failed. Britain then tabled and got a United Nations Security Council Resolution to increase the pressure on Smith. Wilson always believed that he came close to success in October 1968 with talks on HMS *Fearless*; and Ted Heath's government edged closer to a settlement when, in November 1971, Britain and Rhodesia produced a draft agreement that Rhodesia could become independent if the majority of the population agreed. Broadly put, the agreement worked out by Smith and Douglas-Home proposed that the UK government would recognize Smith's white-dominated government and that eventually there would be some representation of the 5 million black inhabitants. However, in May 1972, six months later, the Commission of Inquiry led by the jurist Lord Pearce reported that as far as they could tell, the majority of Rhodesians were not happy with the settlement idea. The Smith–Douglas-Home proposal could never have satisfied the majority of Rhodesians. On that evidence, the sanctions continued.

Governments never have the luxury of one crisis at a time. The 1970s were no exception, and the Rhodesia crisis was going on at the same time as the government was trying to resolve its own problem of civil unrest. In Northern Ireland Bloody Sunday and direct rule took place in early 1972, followed in March 1973 by the Ulster Referendum, which produced a clear majority in favour of remaining in the United Kingdom, while a White Paper put forward the idea of an elected Northern Ireland Assembly. This was also the period when the government was equally distracted by the February 1972 declaration of a state of emergency because of winter power cuts and 1.5 million people being sent home from work. In June 1972 the economy was so bad that the Heath government had to float the pound. The following month, Heath lost his Home Secretary, Reginald Maudling, who was forced to resign because of a corruption investigation. The dockers went on strike.

Then in August 1972 President Idi Amin of Uganda expelled 40,000 British Asians. This single act convinced Smith and his many supporters in the United Kingdom that Rhodesians were right to point accusingly at other black African regimes as an example of what might happen to their own country. (Thirty years later those same people had not changed their minds, but this time they were pointing at their own President, Robert Mugabe.)

Rhodesia remained a subject that would not go away from any British government's schedule for four reasons: it had not been resolved and was therefore unfinished business; it threatened the cohesion of the Commonwealth; it was the subject of Anglo-American relations because Washington believed it had a responsibility that was partly tied to Afro-American political sensitivities; and fourthly, the Rhodesia problem got in the way of European affairs.

European governments were uneasy about post-colonial messes. In the British Foreign Office Rhodesia was regarded as an almost silly subject which should and could have been resolved long ago and was now taking up far too much time of the Foreign Secretary, who should really have been concentrating on the future of international arms control and Britain's part in it, and the increasingly complex relations within the European Community.

In 1976 Rhodesians accepted an Anglo-American proposal for majority rule by 1978, but four months later, in January 1977, Smith discarded the proposal. In the autumn of that year the then Foreign Secretary, David Owen, laid out a new proposal. The first real sign that there was a practical movement towards change, and that international pressure both diplomatically and commercially might be working, came when the Smith regime agreed to lift the ban on the two most powerful black groups opposed to white minority rule: ZANU and ZAPU. The Zimbabwe African National Union and the Zimbabwe African People's Union were, between them, the key to the future. In January 1979, Rhodesians voted for a limited form of majority rule. This was the basis of the so-called internal settlement that was handed to Carrington when Thatcher sent him to the Foreign Office in May 1979.

The Conservatives had been as much part of the personal and political anguish that was UDI as any other political group. Strong in their belief that they would win the coming election, the Conservatives had equally strong ideas about what they would do with Rhodesia. In spite of the way he was castigated by the Tory right in the autumn of 1979, Carrington's approach was not unreasonable.

In 1978 Margaret Thatcher had asked for a paper setting out clearly the party's position from her Foreign Affairs spokesman John Davies, prepared in time for that autumn's party conference. She knew that it would be the major platform to demonstrate her leadership on Africa. The issue was unquestionably sensitive and had to balance the right's open support for white Rhodesians with the recognition that a simple solution of white supremacy along with a few token blacks in the administration was no longer viable nor desirable.

The motion for the Rhodesian debate at the autumn conference demonstrated the width of the Tory political tightrope:

This Conference condemns the failure of the Socialist Government to use the opportunity presented by the Salisbury Agreement of 3rd March, 1978 to establish a democratic government in Rhodesia and calls on it to cease giving support to those who use terrorist tactics for despotic ends and to start working constructively with all those Parties prepared to co-operate in the creation of a democratic and multiracial Zimbabwe.

Thatcher chaired what was called the LCC, the Leader's Consultative Committee. John Davies' policy document for the LCC was one which he and Thatcher believed should be the basis for his conference speech outlining Conservative policy. That document (below) was, according to Carrington at the time, intellectually and politically flawed.

It is Britain's responsibility at an appropriate time to make up its mind as to whether any replacement regime in Rhodesia is one which it can regard as legitimate and recognisable ... It is only by the repeal of the Rhodesia Act by Parliament that the formal state of legitimacy [sic] can be removed. No other country has that capacity but Britain alone ... In this very context, I made it abundantly clear to Joshua Nkomo that no Conservative Government I could visualise would ever be prepared to give the imprimatur of legitimacy to him if he had won his way to power in Salisbury through the pursuit of an evil and brutal war ... This critical issue touches very closely that of sanctions. The institution of sanctions [was] certainly not part of the doing of this Conservative Party, and it seems to me entirely at variance [with] its whole philosophy and out-look ... however, Britain having been the sponsoring country for the institution of international sanctions against Rhodesia, even against the views of this Conservative Party, Britain is inevitably involved in their removal. Upon us hangs the whole issue of the maintenance of sanctions against Rhodesia world-wide ... only by an act of the British Parliament can the world-wide strictures on Rhodesia's ability to trade with the world at large be removed ... it is of course open to us as a Party to move for the removal of sanctions against Rhodesia or to refuse to vote for their renewal. Whatever we decide to do in that context we must not abandon the very substantial right to recognise or not to recognise what-ever regime does appear in Rhodesia in the future.

Upon this unrealistic thinking rested the public perception of Margaret Thatcher's Rhodesian policy – Carrington, in a memo to her, said as much: 'If John [Davies] says any of what he proposes in this Paper, we shall be laughed out of court in the informed Press.' Carrington himself prepared a speech for the Conservative Party Conference that year, balancing what he saw as the realities of Rhodesia in the wider context of the whole continent of Africa with the practical ways of moving from a transition period to something approaching democracy.

There are those in this country and the United States who take the view that what happens in Southern Africa does not really matter. Marxism, they say, or an African form of Marxism is inevitable, and that since it is inevitable, we should come to terms with it: and anyway it does not mat-ter because the economic facts of life will oblige the countries of Southern Africa to trade with the West and to sell the minerals which are vital to the Western economy so that they themselves can survive. I do not take that view ... we are vitally concerned with the future of the whole of Southern Africa and therefore we have a double reason to seek these settlements because it is our moral duty to do so and secondly because it is in our interests to do so. It seems to me that there are four essential factors in any settlement.

First there has to be a cease-fire before the transition period takes place ...

Secondly ... a constitution must be devised acceptable to black and white ...

Thirdly there must be a new constitution. Before a new constitution takes place there must be a true and fair internationally supervised election ...

Lastly there must be the reassurance to all races of a security force capable of keeping law and order. Here perhaps is the most difficult problem. It is, to say the least, a bit disquieting that the Government have suggested that the new armies should be based upon the guerrillas and only acceptable elements of the Rhodesian forces included. To suppose that the white Rhodesians, having agreed to majority rule, are then going to put their lives and property in the hands of those who have sought to kill them is stretching the imagination a little far.

A year later, the Tories back in power, Carrington embarked on the diplomatic round that would lead to a controversial settlement. There was a personal aspect to this negotiation. Thatcher had made perfectly clear to him that if he failed, then she would dump him. A successful negotiation would enhance her world standing. An unsuccessful negotiation would be entirely his fault and therefore he would be sacked. It was an uncomfortable position for him in August 1979 as he eyed that year's harvest at his Bledlow estate.

To complicate matters it seemed that none in the party had a middle-of-the-road view. The letters of discontent had started rolling in even before Thatcher got into government. For example, in 1978, following the sanctions continuation debate at Westminster, Conservatives from across the party in Parliament and at grassroots level cursed Thatcher and Carrington. Debates, even the most controversial, usually go unread and unremarked by a general public largely content to leave the government in place for five years or so. Yet the Southern Rhodesia Act 1965 (Continuation) Order 1978, debated in the House in the second week in November, was closely monitored by that enormous rump of Tory traditionalists who feared that the then Labour government and its young Foreign Secretary, David Owen, were not being heavily enough opposed by Margaret Thatcher's front-bench team.

One letter dated 8 November 1978 from Kingsteignton in Devon suggests the atmosphere in the party nationally:

Dear Mrs Thatcher,
You seem to be totally out of touch with the feelings of the Conservatives in this country . . . we had all hoped you would have the courage to lead our Party to vote against those unjust and shameful Rhodesian sanctions. But you are too busy squabbling with that boring Mr. Heath to find out what the people of this country really feel. Down here in Devon many of us are full of admiration for Mr. Smith and his efforts to reach an internal settlement and utterly ashamed of Owen's behaviour as our Foreign Secretary.
    When eventually we have a General Election, the best thing that both you and Mr. Heath could do for the Conservative Party would be to leave it. Then it might have a chance of coming to power once again.

The Conservative Party press (the *Daily Telegraph* and the *Daily Express*) had urged the party to vote against the renewal of sanctions. They did not. Carrington found himself on the end of a writing campaign from *Telegraph* readers reminding him to read the paper and vote accordingly. A distressed party worker wrote to him from Ashtead, Surrey:

When the history of these times comes to be written it will not be about 5% strikes, greed or envy but how we have betrayed Rhodesia. Why not stand up for what all the responsible people have tried to do in

Rhodesia and support their internal statesman-like settlement? It really is a fight for freedom now for them and on Sunday afternoon at 2.10 just after the Salvation Army service we of the Anglo-Rhodesian Society will be at the Cenotaph in Whitehall to give thanks to those young Rhodesians who need not have left their lovely land but came and gave their lives for us when we were in such dire trouble.

This letter was typical of many Carrington received. Thirty years on, the letter writer may appear a sad anachronism. Carrington did not think so then. Without being able to say so, he was probably more in tune with the emotions of the letter writer. Perhaps as a mark of how much Carrington understood and to some extent sympathized with the views of the lady from Ashtead, he kept her letter for the rest of his life. His view on African politics, the development of freedoms and trial democracies, the contradictions of dictators and one-party state leaders demanding democracy in Rhodesia, had not changed during the decade before the Thatcher victory and his move to the Foreign Office. Even his balancing-act over the strength of sanctions was based on the pragmatic assessment of the limited political options rather than the realistic judgement of whether or not they were likely to work.

Carrington was against sanctions. Moreover, he believed that isolation of South Africa would not bring about the changes everyone wished, just as he had never believed that sanctions by themselves would work in Rhodesia. In December 1965 he had told the Lords during a debate on the Southern Rhodesia Petroleum Order, which prohibited British subjects from exporting oil to Rhodesia, that in spite of what the government thought, sanctions would have no effect unless accompanied by a clear statement of the terms on which 'they could begin a new chapter in the history of Rhodesia'. In 1968 he again told the Lords that 'sanctions would not bring Rhodesia to her knees, certainly not while South Africa and Portugal ignored them and other countries tacitly continued trading with Rhodesia'.

By November 1978 Carrington, whilst still believing that sanctions by themselves could not work, had come to believe that

Britain had to support them. By then he had to accept that although some in his own party wanted sanctions abandoned, the consequences to Britain of doing so should not be underestimated. It was simply a question of the rule of international law. Breaking that international law (in this case on sanctions) was an issue that went far beyond Rhodesia. When the Lords once again debated the Southern Rhodesia Act in November 1978, Carrington said that sanctions were the test of whether Britain was serious about a settlement in Rhodesia. Abandonment of that position would bring down universal condemnation. The consequences of that condemnation would again spread far beyond the Rhodesian context. Hostility towards Britain would be so great that it would probably be impossible for it to act as a mediator or catalyst in the settlement of that problem.

Carrington's views in that November debate on applying sanctions to Smith's Rhodesia (see below) reflected many of the concerns of people who honestly believed that it was Britain's duty to support Ian Smith. It was a personal support inasmuch as Smith, the Second World War pilot, really did represent the colonial support for the UK during that conflict. Even thirty-three years after the end of the war the feelings of loyalty and the imperial ties were far stronger than might be imagined now. So that mood that existed across a wide section of the Tory Party inevitably manifested itself in what became a long-running hate campaign against Carrington.

When the Sanctions Renewal Order came up for debate in the Lords, Callaghan's parliamentary business managers tucked it away in a Friday schedule to minimize the opposition. Those Tory MPs against the Order had already voted No in the Commons the previous week.[3] As Carrington saw it, and explained in the Lords,

---

3 Julian Amery, Ronald Bell, Robert Boscawen, Michael Brotherton, Alan Clark, Geoffrey Dodsworth, Anthony Fell, George Gardiner, Alan Glyn, Ian Gow, Stephen Hastings, Toby Jessel, Michael Mates, Roger Moate, Rear Admiral Morgan-Giles, John Page, R. Bonner-Pink, Enoch Powell, William Shelton, T. H. H. Skeet, Jim Spicer, Keith Stainton, R. Taylor, Patrick Wall, Nicholas Winterton. There is no suggestion of course that all the Noes were involved with Julian Amery in the darker side of the anti-Carrington campaign.

the efforts to get a settlement could not be achieved by legislating
for emotions and traditional feelings. In that sense he was speaking
against an influential group within his own party.

There is nobody, wherever they sit in this House, who does not recognise
that Britain has a special responsibility . . . because of the country's history, the fact that many of those that live there are British and that those
of us that know it know it to be a country not just of great natural beauty
but one with a potential unrivalled in that part of Africa.

If the issue of sanctions is largely symbolic, it must be remembered
that sanctions are symbolic to both Parties and not just to the internal
settlement. They are symbolic to the black African world and to the
Third World. They are a test of whether we are serious about a settlement
in Rhodesia which is in accordance with the five principles to which
both Parties in this House have long subscribed . . . If by our actions now
we place ourselves in a position where we cannot play a constructive
role, we are not only making a difficult situation more difficult but
we are in no sense helping the internal settlement upon which we on
this side should like a solution to be built. I think that at this stage
the rejection of the order would be harmful, would polarise the two
sides, would certainly unite the opposition against the internal Government, might very well escalate the fighting and might perhaps remove
the last opportunity that the British Government have for constructive
mediation.

Carrington never saw the task ahead in Southern Rhodesia in political terms. If he had, he could have led a Tory revolt against the
Continuation Order and, because of the arithmetic in the Lords,
the government would have been defeated. This would have been
a very powerful action because the debate was on an Order and the
Parliament Act cannot be invoked against an Order.

Here, then, was more than a political debate over what to do
about Rhodesia. If the Lords had so wanted it, here was a constitutional issue which potentially pre-dated the House of Lords reforms
of the Blair government by twenty years.

Carrington's view was that as two-thirds of Conservative MPs had abstained the previous night in the Commons debate, the large resultant majority in the Lower House meant that the Continuation Order really was a potential constitutional issue and that therefore this was neither the time nor the subject to thrash it out. At the time, late 1978, Carrington believed that the next Labour government would attempt to abolish the House of Lords anyway (the fact that he was right but that Labour would not be in power again until 1997 was immaterial at the time). Far from immaterial was the fact that during that debate Carrington was speaking from the opposition benches but within six months would be Foreign Secretary with the Rhodesia File on top of his Immediate Action tray.

A few weeks before Mrs Thatcher came to power in May 1979 the Rhodesian elections took place. It was estimated that 64 per cent of those eligible to vote did so and the result was that Bishop Abel Muzorewa became the head of a black majority government. A popular view was that if the bishop was not clear where his allegiance and duty lay, then Ian Smith would quickly tell him. The obvious drawback to the whole procedure was that the Patriotic Front groups of Mugabe and Nkomo were not part of the election process. However, a former colonial secretary, Viscount Boyd, had been an observer at the elections and he believed the ballot had been fair and reflected the majority view. Therefore, when Carrington became Foreign Secretary many assumed that the matter of Rhodesia appeared to be resolving itself. It was not.

In the Lords during the previous November, Carrington had proposed, from the opposition benches, a full-scale conference of all the leading political parties in Southern Rhodesia. His original notion was for a summit at Chequers. He wanted the Prime Minister, James Callaghan, to bring all the parties together with the promise that there would be no communiqués, no interviews, no public statements and no media to hassle them. This was highly unlikely to happen since Callaghan had always believed (having watched Harold Wilson fail) that a summit was the last resort. Furthermore, Carrington surely could not believe that such volatile characters attending the conference would not attempt to use the media as and when they thought fit? Nevertheless, with enormous trepidation, he now set out to create that conference.

Smith's supporters in the Conservative Party saw certain elements that had already been satisfied as far as they were concerned and therefore, they believed, as far as their own government ought to be concerned: the elements were contained in the principles that had been laid before the Smith regime before the promise to hold an election had been honoured. Those principles guaranteed the rights of the white minority in Rhodesia; the transition to black majority rule of their own country; an end to racial and economic discrimination, and the establishment of a reasonable code and practice of law. Smith's supporters – and plenty of those with no declared allegiance – saw these elements and principles as leading towards a reasonable form of democracy. Moreover, as the head of government was black and, most important of all, because Alan Lennox-Boyd had told Carrington that the democratic process had been satisfied, the Conservative right wing demanded that their government should immediately recognize Rhodesia and call off the sanctions. Who could possibly reject this view? Carrington could.

His first task was to persuade Margaret Thatcher that it would be wholly wrong to accept the views of her right-of-centre supporters (all of whom adored her, even though many had been against her when she deposed Heath as party leader). Carrington did not dismiss the Boyd report, but recognized its shortcomings. In particular, what would have been the result if the election had included supporters of Mugabe and Nkomo?

Carrington's attitude was informed by the travelling he had done in Africa during his time in opposition. He had talked to every leading politician including those from the so-called front-line states. He knew that Kenneth Kaunda, the President of Zambia, Rhodesia's neighbour, wanted the war to end for three reasons: African stability, economic stability and because Joshua Nkomo's troops had based themselves in Zambia in such numbers that they were bigger than his own security forces – not an acceptable situation for a president of a single-party democracy. Furthermore,

Nkomo's men tended to stay in Zambia rather than fight, unlike Mugabe's troops who were based in Angola. (Mugabe never forgot that it was he and his followers, rather than Nkomo's faction, that had done most of the fighting.) Kaunda consequently felt not a little threatened and wanted a settlement that would mean the withdrawal of all forces into Rhodesia.

Carrington had also met Samora Machel of Angola and understood only too clearly that he wanted proper black majority rule (by which he meant Mugabe) rather than what he saw as an 'Uncle Tom' regime of Muzorewa. Moreover, Carrington had a reasonable knowledge of Nigeria and although many of the main characters had changed, the sentiments towards colonial and puppet colonial rule had not. There was no support in Nigeria for a British government which recognized the Muzorewa/Smith cabal.

This opposition to the election result in Rhodesia went much beyond the frontline states. In fact there was little support anywhere other than London for the Smith-supported Muzorewa government. President Jimmy Carter's administration had made it plain that it was an unacceptable regime. The Commonwealth would be deeply split if Thatcher were to recognize the Rhodesian government. The black African and Caribbean blocs would not tolerate recognition, so much so that in the summer of 1979 Carrington believed the Commonwealth was in real danger of collapsing over Rhodesia. He judged that he had just a few weeks to find a formula, or the basis of one, by the time the Commonwealth heads of government meeting took place in Lusaka during the first week of August. If he found nothing to advance the process of majority rule, then he believed the Commonwealth could indeed break up.

Carrington certainly acknowledged the Commonwealth's frailties – that it had no real powers and offered no alternative solution. Yet he retained a belief in the Commonwealth as an institution. This instinct was based on his own sense of tradition, his imperial genes – and a generous pinch of sentimentalism. Carrington believed very strongly that in spite of what he regarded as perfectly understandable if cynical views, the Commonwealth indeed had three important values. First of all, economically, although not always collectively, its membership was potentially powerful. Nigeria with its oil wealth was an example of this, and that summer flexed its muscle by nationalizing BP (Nigeria) during the August Commonwealth Conference. Second, the Commonwealth could continue to provide a network of links between approximately a quarter of the world's states. Third, Carrington valued the fact that it continued to provide an informal forum in which individuals could anticipate as well as resolve problems.

That summer in Cabinet Carrington underlined the importance of Commonwealth opinion, supported by the reports of two emissaries, Lord Harlech and the diplomat Anthony Duff. He did not believe that the Commonwealth would support the present arrangement in Rhodesia — by now he had convinced Thatcher of this too — and furthermore argued that if she followed Smith's supporters in her party rather than his advice, she was in danger of becoming known as the Prime Minister who brought about the collapse of the institution that was, after the monarchy, closest to the heart of the British people.

There was more at stake than the Commonwealth's refusal to accept the Rhodesian solution as it stood. It may have been convenient to let the Rhodesians get on with their precarious livelihoods, but much larger international opinion would not allow this. Civil war was inevitable because Mugabe for one was not satisfied. Other United Nations members, including the United States, would not ignore the token democracy of the current situation. The United States had to listen to the leaders of Rhodesia's neighbours, even though many of them were themselves running completely undemocratic systems. However, Zambia, led by Kenneth Kaunda, and Tanzania, led by Julius Nyerere, were seen in Washington as examples of countries ruled consistently and largely peaceably within their own versions of common democracy. There was one other potential threat for Carrington and Thatcher to consider: many states, including some from the Commonwealth, might well put a ban on trade with Britain herself.

Thatcher eventually came round to Carrington's way of thinking. That, for her Foreign Secretary, was the easy part. What had to be done next was more difficult.

Carrington returned to his 1978 theme in the Lords and now had to organize a new constitutional conference for the future government of Rhodesia. He had to convince all parties in that country that they should attend that conference and abide by its outcome. Furthermore, he then had to convince all parties that each of the other parties should attend. Smith would have to be there with Mugabe and Nkomo of the Popular Front. Nkomo and Mugabe had to be convinced that they should be there with Smith. Carrington then had to exclude from that conference everyone else, including the Americans, who still believed they had an interest, and most of all the frontline states and the Commonwealth, including its Secretary-General Sir Shridath 'Sonny' Ramphal.

If Carrington could bring the right people together, his next task would be to keep them together. Once at the conference it was up to his diplomatic skills and insistence on following his agenda and not theirs to determine the outcome.

If that conference then reached no agreement but remained intact, Carrington would have failed and have salvaged nothing for Britain. If, however, it broke down because the key players, particularly Mugabe and Nkomo, walked out, at least Carrington could say that as it had all started with an agenda and an aim approved by each faction, he had done his best and Britain could not be blamed for any failure. The way would then be open, if Thatcher so wished, to satisfy her right wing, to recognize the *status quo ante* in Salisbury without reasonably expecting any retribution against the United Kingdom government. This then was the basis upon which Carrington and Thatcher embarked on their search for a constitutional conference.

The first hurdle was to get a general agreement on the aims of that conference and most of all the approval of the Commonwealth heads of government gathering for their meeting in Lusaka on 1 August 1979. The African position was already known: the Organization of African Unity had in July declared that the

Patriotic Front represented the views of Zimbabwe. Africa was thus saying that the Muzorewa government in Salisbury was nothing more than a front for Smith's white minority.

Carrington had made it clear that the previous government's decision to look for a settlement while using the United States as an equal diplomatic partner could no longer continue. This was a British and Commonwealth matter. He regarded the Anglo-American initiative as fruitless, which indeed it had been. He also believed it to be damaging, because many Commonwealth leaders Carrington needed as allies thought America had only domestic political motives for its involvement. To Carrington's mind, President Carter did care that a settlement should be just for the Rhodesian people, but he was being set up by Congress. At some near stage in 1979, when Congress returned from its summer break, Carter would be expected to publicly endorse or denounce the Muzorewa administration. Support could not be based upon Carter's sense of what was right or wrong. Congress had set conditions for recognition. If they were met, Carter would have to explain in some detail the guarantees he offered because recognition would mean that Congress would have to order the lifting of American sanctions. This was a huge step for Carter and Congress considering the power of black opinion in the United States. Carrington's best advice was that Carter would not recommend to Congress that its conditions for recognition had been met. So the White House had unquestionable political interest in what the new British government was about to do.

Thus, Carrington did not want the Americans involved in the process but he knew that he would have to demonstrate to them that his perceptions and his methods were right. He (or, more likely, Thatcher) was going to have to convince the Commonwealth that it did not have exclusive rights of approval. Others had interests and should be listened to. Foremost among these, the position of the Queen, as Head of the Commonwealth, would be particularly important. The meeting was taking place on the front-line of the dispute, and though it was no longer a meeting of the *British* Commonwealth of Nations, there remained, in spite of

28. *Top* With Princess Alexandra – a huge success 'dancing the night away' during her
Australia visit in 1959, shortly before Carrington's time as High Commissioner ended and
he became First Lord of the Admiralty. 29. *Bottom* Since the 1850s the Carringtons have
walked with the British monarchy. Here with the Queen, his very close friend Prince Philip
and then equally close friend Lord Mountbatten (for once at the rear), in the Painted Hall at
Greenwich Naval College.

30. *Right, above* With US Secretary of State John Foster Dulles, a year before his death in 1959, and Sir Alec Douglas-Home, then Commonwealth Relations Secretary, at a South East Asia Treaty Organization (SEATO) meeting. Carrington's time as High Commissioner in Australia taught him to look to Asia at a time when most of his Tory colleagues were thinking Europe. 31. *Right, below* All champagne and smiles with Malta's Prime Minister Dom Mintoff at the 1972 Marlborough House Defence Agreement. But Carrington thought Mintoff an obnoxious character, and the nine months of negotiations had been totally bad-tempered. 32. *Below* With Prince Charles, Robert Mugabe and Joshua Nkomo at independence celebrations in Harare in 1980, with a portrait of Cecil Rhodes watching over the unlikely quartet. Carrington's chairmanship of the Rhodesian negotiations in 1979 led to threats from Tory diehards and hate mail for the rest of his life, yet for others it was his greatest triumph. If he had failed, Thatcher would have sacked him.

33. As short-lived Secretary of State for Energy in 1972 with his ministerial team, Patrick Jenkin, David Howell, Peter Emery. The Energy job was a hopeless task, especially as he was also Tory Party Chairman, yet another example of too many responsibilities meaning neither appointment was quite successful.

34. With Ted Heath during the 1974 'Who Governs Britain?' general election campaign. Carrington warned Heath that it could not be fought on a single subject and there would be questions they had not anticipated. At this news conference neither appears to be sure what question has been broached.

35. *Top* Bonn, November 1980. Yet more humourless European discussions. German Chancellor Helmut Schmidt is on Thatcher's left. 36. *Bottom* After a 'firm' view from Thatcher, Carrington frequently found himself having to say, 'What the Prime Minister means is …' His secret sorrow was that he had not gone into the Foreign Office and become an ambassador – diplomacy was what he did best.

37. *Left* With President Jimmy Carter in 1980.

38. *Below* In 1987 with Ronald Reagan and Caspar Weinberger, two men he much admired and who stood by the UK during the Falklands War – far more than was publicly understood.

39. Two NATO Secretaries not always in alliance. Carrington's Dutch predecessor, Joseph Luns, refused to move out of his office at NATO HQ in Brussels when Carrington was appointed.

40. *Above* Jack Straw, then Labour Foreign Secretary, gave a party for Carrington on his eightieth birthday. Left to right, former Foreign Secretaries Robin Cook, Geoffrey Howe, Carrington, Straw, David Owen, Douglas Hurd and Malcolm Rifkind. 41. *Below* From his time in the Royal Navy Prince Charles had often asked Carrington's advice on international affairs. Carrington's daughter Virginia was part of the Prince's household.

42. *Top left* At Windsor Castle in 1985 for his installation as a Knight of the Garter.

43. *Top right* With daughter Virginia shortly before her wedding to Lord Ashcombe. It was not a happy marriage, just as Carrington had feared.

44. *Bottom* Carrington's only son, Rupert. Virginia Carington said it was a sometimes testing father–son relationship.

45 & 46. Iona and Peter Carrington, the happiest of couples, in the gardens at Bledlow in summer 1988. Who was the gardener? Carrington commanded the operation. Lady Carrington commanded Carrington.

many anti-colonialist sensitivities, a respect for the monarch and her personality.

There was a distinct difference in the approach to the conference between Carrington and his Prime Minister. The reports from Lord Harlech and Anthony Duff, Derek Day of the FCO who shuttled between Salisbury and London, together with all the pre-conference briefings from Britain's high commissioners, suggested to Carrington that they could be in for a very hostile reception. Margaret Thatcher felt that this attitude should be met head on. Carrington, the instinctive diplomat, wished to tread very carefully and regarded the whole meeting as an occasion for – as Thatcher claims he told her – damage limitation. To her this was nonsense. She assumed this would be Carrington's view too by the time they reached Lusaka. Thatcher had not abandoned the thought that Carrington was instinctively Foreign Office Man and, therefore, as a matter of course, on the side of foreigners. This was certainly her view when two and a half years later she was confronted with the crisis over the Falkland Islands. The head of the Diplomatic Service at the time, Sir Michael Palliser, added to the view that Thatcher saw almost every policy decision as needing to reflect Britain's interests above all else. Palliser told me that he, like Carrington, thought that it was her instinct to be anti-black.

The tenseness in the Prime Minister's office prior to the Commonwealth meeting might be illustrated by Carrington's surprise when, on the plane to Lusaka, Thatcher produced a pair of dark glasses because she believed she might be attacked and acid thrown in her face. As the aircraft was due to touch down late at night, the Prime Minister would give every appearance of someone more used to Hollywood receptions than Commonwealth affairs, especially one hosted by the Queen. It took a little time for Carrington to persuade Thatcher that she was in no danger. In fact, he probably did not persuade her, even though she abandoned the dark glasses. Again, Palliser believed that she had an innate fear of the black reception she was to meet. Given the fact that in Lusaka the media had taken the line that she was the bogeywoman in this whole procedure to establish the negotiations with

Rhodesia, then Margaret Thatcher had some justification in being concerned and not altogether trusting in Carrington's soothing words. Iona Carrington describes the journey there:

Monday July 30th 1979
No sooner were the seatbelts unfastened than work began. But any idea that all the faces must be set serious and sober would be quite wrong. Perhaps it is due largely to Peter but Margaret has a sharp wit. Denis [Thatcher] and I were the beneficiaries of all this activity – we retreated with our books to the two sofas. The arrival was chaos in the dark and next morning we read in the Zambian Press of a trembling Mrs T. who had arrived after dark to avoid demonstrators.

Tuesday was all preparation but lunch with Nyerere and dinner with Kaunda cleared the air and raised modest hopes . . .[4]

It was not until the Friday that the round-table talking got under way. Thatcher took the lead. She told the conference that even if there were deficiencies in the present constitutional structure in Rhodesia, there had been advances for all the people. She, and Carrington in his private talks, had conceded that critics would always have the diplomatic advantage because the way things stood the white minority would always have the power to veto any changes in the constitution. More than that, the whites could block key appointments. There really was no argument against the critics. That weekend, the traditional informal gatherings of heads of government were spent drafting an agreement. This was done by a relatively small group which included Thatcher, Carrington, Kaunda, Nyerere, Malcolm Fraser (the Australian Prime Minister) and civil servants including Duff, the actual draughtsman of the agreement.

On the Sunday evening, Fraser, unable to stick to the promise of secrecy (for his own political reasons at home), told the Australian press what had happened. This was diplomatically unethical because the rest of the conference was not due to be told until the

4 Lady Carrington, private diaries, Bledlow archive.

next day. It is a little puzzling how any of the people in the secret session, including Carrington, could have been naive enough to believe their secret would have lasted the night.

That evening, most heads of government trooped into the cathedral for devotions. During the service, Carrington was slipped a note telling him that Fraser had blown the secret. Carrington's reaction was that he really ought to do the same for the British press but this needed the approval of the Secretary-General, Sir Sonny Ramphal. Ramphal thought that following the Australian example was unwise and wrote a suggestion on the back of Thatcher's hymn sheet while she was up at the lectern reading the lesson. It was, thought Ramphal, all a matter of timing. Even Carrington had something to learn from the Secretary-General when it came to diplomacy. The upshot was that at a barbecue that night a formal communiqué was agreed and the whole matter made public. Fraser received a few meaningful looks at the very least, but for Carrington the importance was in the outcome, not in the way it came out.

The British delegation had arrived at the conference with every reason to believe that they would be on the wrong end of disagreement; they left it with considerable praise, plus the agreement to press on immediately with the setting up of a constitutional conference to be held at Lancaster House in London the following month, under Carrington's chairmanship. Carrington wrote the rules, the first of which was that no discussion should be allowed that touched upon the end result. So any ideas of, for example, how proper black majority rule would be implemented would not be aired.

There were a number of difficulties in the run-up to the conference. Ramphal appeared to Carrington to be playing a dangerous, if not a two-timing, game. His wheeling and dealing among the neighbouring states was not altogether helpful.

Then Julian Amery, a Conservative colleague of Carrington's, who was against the way the negotiations were going, seeing the whole thing as a sell-out, made this publicly clear in an attempt to influence the atmosphere.

Carrington certainly believed that it was necessary to get the main players, including Mugabe, Nkomo and Smith, to London and keep them there – away from the African atmosphere. He also had the sense to make sure that when the conference opened there was not too much on the agenda and that what there was, was relatively agreeable to most sides. This was a technique successfully fashioned by Carrington's close friend Kissinger, based on the idea that you start meetings with agenda items that everyone already agrees to and thus build the momentum towards unity. The first point on the agenda, for example, was simply one page of perhaps fifteen lines of constitutional principles.

Yet none of this could dispel the sense of betrayal felt by Smith, Muzorewa and Nkomo, quite apart from the extreme elements of the Conservative Party, who long after Lancaster House would openly regard Carrington with disgust. Nor could it reassure Mugabe that Carrington was not setting a trap for him. At one point in the negotiation, which was an intellectual and physical marathon, Carrington became enormously depressed and even thought that it would all fall apart. Thatcher was watching. Failure would be a disaster and Carrington would have to go. He was not the sort of person who responded well to such pressures. Macmillan was right. During this period, Carrington leant heavily on his team, with the exception of Ian Gilmour who was almost overtly opposed to white Rhodesians, thus confirming Thatcher's original impression that he was wetter than wet.

The conference opened in September 1979. Carrington thought that, given his African visits when in opposition, he had a fair idea of the personalities and their positions. However, he had failed to grasp certain important factors that were to show themselves during the conference. At first he had seen the problem of Rhodesia, as most people had, in terms of characters with deeply opposing views engendered by deeply divisive cultural origins. He had not grasped that the players in this sometimes horrid drama did not think of it in terms of a Chatham House-style think tank, with strategic discussions and briefing papers. They all lived in a relatively small and sparsely populated country. Nkomo and Mugabe, for example, had been prisoners for ten years of the Smith regime. To the Rhodesians, black and white, this was a personal problem and each person at Lancaster House knew the other. These were not enemies eyeing each other for the first time. As Carrington observed, they knew each other very well. Because he had not understood this earlier, Carrington had underestimated how difficult it would be, in personal terms, for people to sit down at the conference table. Once again, logic and scholarly analysis had little part in the chemistry that would make the Lancaster House discussions work.

Carrington began his work away from the conference rooms. He gave a private dinner party for the Ian Smith and Abel Muzorewa contingent and soon learned that the less controllable bitternesses were among this group. Their supporters had suffered at the hands and at the blades of the Patriotic Front guerrillas. There had been much death and, for some who had survived, worse.

To Carrington's mind, the two groups within the Patriotic Front were quite distinct in their tribal and military determination. The Matabele Joshua Nkomo was a large, round, often jovial character whose forces did little of the fighting. Robert Mugabe, a Shona, whose education had started at a Jesuit mission, was quieter, of deeper intellect and a man who had successfully read for a degree while in prison, and whose fighters were the hardest, the most uncompromising and, from the white point of view, the most feared.

While the first group of diners gave Carrington a deeper insight into the bitterness between the two sides, the second group, Nkomo and Mugabe, displayed none of these sensitivities towards individuals that Smith and Muzorewa had expressed. Indeed, it was Mugabe who taught Carrington that their side held no bitterness to individuals – no matter how they might dislike them. It was the *system* that made Mugabe so bitter. In spite of the reasonable facade of his first years in power, Mugabe would never shake off this sense of anger, nor his ability to express that ire in the most deceptively quiet and logical tone.

By this time, Carrington's view of the two leading African opposition leaders was clear. He believed, for example, that the advice of Mugabe's wife kept him on a reasonable and logical course. Nkomo, thought Carrington, was a quite different proposition. Even though he liked Nkomo, Carrington regarded him as 'ruthless, not nearly so intelligent as Mugabe, but with a considerable sense of humour'. He had been the father of the Rhodesian Independence Movement but had lost out to Mugabe, who had a bigger following. Carrington told me that Nkomo

was anxious to come to some kind of settlement since he was getting on in years and felt that time was no longer his ally. The white Rhodesians and South Africans who judged well the dislike between Mugabe and Nkomo hoped in vain that the latter would form an alliance with 'Bishop' Abel Muzorewa.

During the conference, which was to last until December, Carrington had two important dates away from Lancaster House. The first was at the United Nations for the annual meeting of the General Assembly, a session of the UN when foreign ministers and often heads of government were expected to attend and deliver speeches on their views of the world order. As it had been for more than a quarter of a century, the General Assembly seemed preoccupied with Africa. The three main issues of the later 1970s were South Africa itself and apartheid, Namibia and, more immediately in September 1979, Rhodesia. Carrington might have cited the conference as reason for staying in London, but that would have been quite wrong. As he told the UN, 'The talks are now pointing in the right direction, which is why I felt I could leave them to come to the UN. Everyone involved in the war now wants a settlement. There is a wish on all sides for a solution and that's something we haven't had in the past.'

In fact this was diplomatic-speak. Privately Carrington was not at all certain of his ground for optimism.

The importance of that visit to the United Nations was to maintain the support of Third World countries for Britain's position. The African and Asian delegates applauded him, not so much because of what he said about Rhodesia (they remained not unreasonably cynical) but because of his attitude towards the United Nations' public enemy number one, South Africa. This was in line with the majority UN feeling that while Rhodesia was today's subject, the long-term stability of the region depended upon South Africa. His comment was deliberately timed and placed in his speech: 'We share the international communities' distaste of apartheid. It is neither just nor workable.'

The African delegates to the UN knew exactly Carrington's track record over the decade. Hence, the importance of his mid-Lancaster House Conference visit to the General Assembly to keep the other African nations on board.

By the middle of November, Lancaster House was in its tenth week and, for the first time, some in Carrington's office were thinking that a settlement might be possible. Carrington's predecessors as negotiators – Wilson, Douglas-Home, Owen, Goodman and Kissinger – had failed. What distinguished the talks at Lancaster House from those that had gone before, for example aboard the *Tiger* and the *Fearless*, was that there were new economic and political pressures; and Carrington had abandoned the standard format of negotiations. He insisted on dealing with the realities that faced them all. None of the delegates was allowed to pretend that the Muzorewa government did not exist and was not the economic and military power of the country. Carrington therefore worked on the idea that if he could push Muzorewa into accepting a condition that the Mugabe and Nkomo coalition wanted, then the Patriotic Front would find it difficult not to accept it. As one example, Carrington's insistence that step-by-step proposals had to be agreed quickly rather than filibustered seemed to be having some success. Muzorewa (and therefore Smith's people, if not Smith himself) had by now agreed to abandon the blocking power of the white minority in the proposed constitution. Carrington convinced the Salisbury government delegation that after an interim period that would precede the new constitution, they would have to stand down from office.

By themselves these changes were remarkable. Even more remarkable was the way in which both sides (with the exception

of Ian Smith himself) accepted them. Bishop Muzorewa's delegation, but not Smith, accepted Carrington's demands on the
constitution. Nkomo and Mugabe might have been tempted to
reject British ideas as racist, but they could not be seen to be
rejecting something that had been agreed when Ian Smith had
voted against it, and which reflected the guidelines presented at
the Lusaka Commonwealth heads of government conference the
previous August. Carrington's tactic of putting all sides in the
position of being reluctant to walk out of Lancaster House
because of its bad impression on international opinion seemed to
have worked.

The Patriotic Front were persuaded to go to Lancaster House,
not by Carrington, but by people like Kaunda and Nyerere. Once
there, they were on their own. Gradually, they realized that they
were getting a long way towards their goal; by then it was clearer
to Carrington that if it came to a straight fight, Mugabe would
overwhelm Nkomo.

Come November the Lancaster House Conference was
approaching a delicate moment, not at the meeting but three-
quarters of a mile away in the House of Commons. The Sanctions
Renewal Order was once more up for debate. What would the
government do? It had to be clear by then that dismissal of sanctions
could satisfy almost everyone at the conference and in Parliament.
Ironically, it was at this point, when success was a distinct possibility, that Carrington went through one of the most torrid moments
of his career – at the hands of his own party.

In November, he had to go to the Conservative Party Conference at Blackpool. Carrington detested all Conservative
Party Conferences. He thought them, even in uncontentious
times, horrid jamborees. Twenty years on, he deeply disliked the
Conservative Party per se. The origins of this distaste were
perhaps to be found in Blackpool in November 1979. He went
there to explain his Rhodesian policy. From some, he received
congratulations. From many, including very senior people in the
party, he received expressions of hatred. That is not too strong
a phrase.

He had been warned, but was still shocked and deeply hurt when he saw banners saying 'Hang Carrington'. He felt particularly disgusted when he saw one of the most prominent members of the party, Julian Amery, leading a chant of 'Hang Carrington, Hang Carrington'. Amery had been an exact contemporary of Carrington's at Eton, though they were never friends. Carrington found Amery's way of thinking unattractive and thought him a 'rather absurd' man. The bitterness lasted long after the Rhodesian settlement; the morning after Carrington resigned over the Falklands in April 1982, Carrington heard Amery on a BBC Radio 4 programme saying now Carrington had gone, everything would be all right. Others in the Conservative Party were even more hostile, sometimes with fists raised as if they wanted to physically strike him. To need protection from a potential terrorist attack was often part of the Foreign Secretary's lifestyle. To need protection from members of one's own political party was at the very least unnerving. The hate mail was delivered regularly and it continued to come not just that year, but for the rest of Carrington's life. Even before what most saw as a triumphant speech at Lancaster House, Carrington's political enemies were determined that he would never be forgiven for what they continued to see as a sell-out.

During the conference he went, for example, to a meeting of the Tory back-bench Foreign Affairs Committee to explain what progress had been made. Carrington was ambushed by the pro-Ian Smith lobby, who might be called the followers of the Julian Amery school. He received a critical and personal drubbing that he would not again experience until the dreadful (for him) occasion when he would meet the Conservative 1922 Committee during the Falklands crisis of 1982. If Carrington had been an MP and a minister in the Commons, then quite possibly he would not have been so startled. Sensing his distress, there were those at the Blackpool meeting who felt moved to apologize for the treatment.

House of Commons,
London
SW1A OAA
25.X.79

My Dear Peter,
A number of us want to write to you after the meeting of the back-bencher Foreign Affairs Committee last evening. We hope that you will not interpret the criticisms expressed as a true reflection of opinion within the Party or of condemnation of your efforts to reach a cease-fire and find a solution to the Zimbabwe Rhodesian problem.

Certain Members not concerned with the pro-Rhodesian front lobby found that by the time they had caught the eye of the Chairman, their names were too far down the list to be called. Equally, others of us felt that at the meeting it would be damaging to the Party and harmful to your negotiations if a general row developed which would be bound to attract unwelcome newspaper coverage ...
Yours always, Peter [Peter Emery, MP]

Emery's letter was counter-signed by twenty-one other Tory MPs including Kenneth Baker, Michael Ancram, Tristan Garel-Jones and Robert Rhodes James. Robert Banks – whose name was not on that letter – also wrote:

Dear Peter,
I feel so strongly about the appalling way you were treated yesterday in the Foreign Affairs Committee that I believe you should know that other colleagues are speaking in support and admiration for what you have [achieved] and are achieving.

It really is remarkable that when progress is at long last being made, some narrow and I would say stupid views have to be expressed with discourtesy and hostility. I happen to feel very angry about it and I am sure you deserve to be.
Yours ever, Robert

Carrington's facility for understatement was evident in his reply:

> I very much appreciate your letter. It was particularly nice of you
> to write. I did feel a bit sore.

Many years later, Carrington was dining with his friend and
sometime private secretary Sir Nicholas Henderson and his daughter Virginia (who recounted the tale to this author). During the
evening the Conservative MP and political diarist Alan Clark
came in and was shown to the table next to the Carringtons'.
As he reached them, Clark turned to the waiter and in a very
loud voice said, 'Find me another table. I refuse to sit next to a
traitor.'

In November 1979 the 'traitor' was guiding the Conference
towards agreement – but the end was not yet in sight. The progress
was in the mood of the group led by Bishop Abel Muzorewa, Ian
Smith's token prime minister. Carrington had developed a ploy to
entice Muzorewa's delegation even further. The sanctions order
was due to be renewed on 15 November. Carrington could tell
Muzorewa what he wanted to hear, that it would not be renewed,
and that would encourage the bishop to sign up for something in
the future that Carrington might have wanted. Behind this, the
Patriotic Front had to fall in although, as Carrington recognized,
Mugabe did not like doing so. But by then the process had gone
on for too long for them to back off. If they walked out now, it
would have to be back into the bush and they knew that even the
frontline states would not easily condone that tactic. Yet Carrington
had to assume it was possible that the Patriotic Front would leave
if pushed too far on the wrong issue before the groundwork had
been prepared. This was the case in the three stages of the constitutional procedure: the constitution itself; the interim period
between abandoning the existing government and the election;
the ceasefire. Each stage had to be settled before moving to the
next. By the eve of the Sanctions Renewal Order, it appeared that
Carrington had got most of his way. It certainly seemed likely that
the election would happen, yet the important element – whether

or not the Patriotic Front would eventually take part in it – could still bring the whole matter to an unsatisfactory end.

Carrington had made plain his fundamental concerns in a letter to the former Prime Minister and Foreign Secretary Sir Alec Douglas-Home. In that letter he made clear also that he preferred and imagined that the best outcome for the talks and the people of Rhodesia would be the endorsement of Bishop Muzorewa. But he needed Douglas-Home's help.

> I cannot pretend that this conference is being very easy, and the most difficult person is Ian Smith. All the others – David Smith, Cronje [both Smith and Cronje were realists and at the time held ministerial posts in Muzorewa's intermediate government which took office in June 1979] – will go along with twenty white seats, unamendable for a period, plus a Bill of Rights (the essential points of which could not be amended) but Ian Smith has so far dug his toes in. Unless he can be brought along I fear world opinion will think the whites totally unreasonable, and the prospect which I had hoped for of getting world opinion behind the Bishop will recede – as indeed will the prospect of ending the war.
>
> I wonder whether there is anything you can do vis-à-vis Ian Smith. We are using all the pressure we can, but you know what he is! I think it would be a tragedy if once again he wrecked if not an ideal solution to the problem, a way in which survival and success might be possible.[5]

Carrington knew Douglas-Home would not help. He had already told the Rhodesians that 'beyond a platform in the House of Lords, I could not intervene in current events. It would make no sense to try.' The best Douglas-Home felt he could offer was wishes of 'good luck in your awful task'. Carrington sometimes felt that he was alone in the attempt to pull together the parties for a settlement. Smith remained the most difficult person in the

5 Private letter from Carrington to Douglas-Home, 18 September 1979, Carrington papers, Bledlow.

negotiations. He was bolstered by the more traditional-leaning media and especially by Julian Amery and his right-wing Tories, including what one of Carrington's aides described as the 'tightlipped women'. And then Smith walked out, which made everyone else's position easier, even though the Amery group's vitriol towards Carrington became even more personally toxic. But by December 1979 the conference was unstoppable and before Christmas it was a clear success and Rhodesian UDI was at an end.

What were the turning points for Carrington? Smith's going certainly helped, but the success also had a great deal to do with the fact that most of the parties wanted, even needed, a settlement. The Rhodesian government was walking an economic and social tightrope: because so many and so much were diverted to fighting the Patriotic Front, the economy was all but collapsing. Sanctions – often derided as ineffectual – were beginning to do what they had been intended to do, but never on the scale imagined for them. There was also increased regional support for a settlement. The South Africans were finding it harder to support Smith's failing economy. In Zambia, where the majority of Nkomo's men were based – and not fighting in Rhodesia – President Kaunda was weary of his visitors and feared for the instability they could bring to his own side. As for Nkomo himself, he believed that Mugabe's support within Rhodesia was increasing and therefore Mugabe had more chance of being president than he did. Therefore, Mugabe's two main supporters, Mozambique's President Samora Machel and Tanzania's President Julius Nyerere, should have been very pleased with the progress of the war. Yet they were having doubts. They still supported what they saw as the colonial struggle. However, the disruptions and deprivations within Rhodesia had severely affected its agricultural output. Rhodesia was Africa's kitchen garden. The war was stopping food supplies reaching Tanzania and Mozambique. That disruption was causing unrest in both countries. So they wanted a settlement and, once represented at Lancaster House, it was difficult for them to leave until agreement was reached.

Thus, Carrington had his triumph and for the moment he still had his job. He still did not, however, have the thanks of a large part of his own party. The public image of what went on was the moment when the Lancaster House Conference finished in a blaze of cameras shining on dignitaries from the Prime Minister to the Secretary-General of the Commonwealth. The attention in the ornate room beneath the grand fireplace was on Carrington, flanked on one side by Sir Ian Gilmour, Joshua Nkomo and Robert Mugabe and on the other, by the Salisbury government team led by Bishop Muzorewa.

Carrington's speech on the final day made clear his concern for the future of war-weary Rhodesia. Lord Soames, the interim governor, had referred to the winning of a great prize. Carrington wondered what that constitutional trophy suggested.

What is that prize? It is the end of war and enmity? It is the opportunity for all Rhodesians to devote their energies to peaceful activities? It is a chance for the country to renew and strengthen its relations with its neighbours and with the wider international community? It is, in brief, the opportunity for a more normal and settled existence. That is what I believe the people of Rhodesia sought from this conference ... for our part, the British Government intend faithfully to discharge the heavy responsibilities we have undertaken during the period leading to elections ... we have no wish to prolong our role ... the moment, however, for which the people of Rhodesia have been waiting will come at midnight on Friday 28th December [1979]. At that time all hostilities within Rhodesia must cease ... This will be a difficult period ... the subsequent commitments concerning the observance of the cease-fire and the pursuit of the political campaign by peaceful means are of no less importance. The Governor could not undertake his task without the powers and authority which are necessary to enable him to accomplish it ... if, as a result of a negotiated settlement, wounds so deep can be healed in Rhodesia – as I pray they shall be during the months ahead – then the people of that country will have set an example and given hope to others throughout the world.[6]

6 Carrington's corrected speech note in Bledlow archive.

Knowing that Carrington was having something of a hard time from certain colleagues, Ted Heath, who was in the West Indies, wrote to him as the year turned.

New Year's Eve, Barbados

Now that everything at your end concerning Rhodesia is settled, signed and sealed may I offer you my warmest congratulations on your remarkable personal achievement. That the right answer still remains to be delivered does not in any way detract from the well merited tributes paid to your skilful negotiations.
Happy New Year to both you and Iona.
Yrs Ted

Carrington's first patron Alec Douglas-Home had been one who had tried and failed to find a solution. He was now one of the first to write.

The Hirsel,
Coldstream,
Berwickshire.
December 21st.

My Dear Peter,
Just a line of sincere congratulations on a magnificent diplomatic exhibition of patience & skill.
Heaven knows (I doubt that!) what the future holds but you could not have done more to give Rhodesia a chance of peace . . .
Alec

Even one of his most persistent critics, the *Daily Telegraph* journalist and editor Bill Deedes, wrote admiringly in spite of his continuing reservations.

Bill Deedes
December 21

Among all the letters of congratulations to you perhaps I owe one most.

All trivial differences apart, I hand it to you more than any of your predecessors – you deserve a Happy Christmas.

Yours ever Bill

William Whitelaw, then Home Secretary, was full of his usual avuncular enthusiasm and not a little relief.

18 December 1979

May a very old friend write which only very old friends can write without seeming to indulge in false flattery. Of course there are many trials ahead in Rhodesia but your timing and diplomatic skill has been beyond all praise. Whatever happens things will never be the same again and that in itself is a great thing.

Robin Renwick was Carrington's private secretary and later became British Ambassador first to South Africa between 1987 and 1991, then in Washington. He had witnessed more than most the enormous pressure on Carrington, and he knew of the personal animosities set against the Secretary of State.

42 Jubilee Place, SW3

Dear Secretary of State,

It has been an enormous pleasure to have worked for you over the past few months. I have been full of admiration for all the courage you have shown at all the difficult moments and without which we could have got nowhere. I am sorry that Rhodesia has taken up far too much of your time; and we are in for two very difficult months. *I never forget that the whole object must be to put an end to our responsibility, as honourably as possibly* [author's italics]. I am afraid that there will be some more difficult decisions ahead. It is a great relief to know that it is you who will be taking them.

Clearly this was only Part One of the Rhodesian affair. Part Two would take just as long and, as Renwick pointed out, the difficulties ahead would be considerable. There was much to do: the appointment of a governor in old colonial style, the resignation of Muzorewa's government and the elections which Carrington could still only hope would be free and fair.

The first task was to revert to the trappings of colonialism. In the intensity of the negotiations, everyone had agreed that the Muzorewa government would step down. What was to take its place between resignation and the appointment of whichever government might be elected? Constitutionally as far as Britain was concerned, the answer was simple: as the present situation was born out of the illegitimate act of a Unilateral Declaration of Independence, Rhodesia had now to revert to its pre-UDI status. This meant the appointment of a colonial governor. Carrington thought that this would not be accepted and therefore the success thus far achieved would falter. When he put it to a plenary session that the governor would have full powers, there was a long and difficult pause in the conversation. This was not a popular decision, as he recalled to me in 2003:

Blacks and whites regarded a return to colonial rule as outrageous. When I announced that Christopher Soames, who had gallantly accepted the poisoned chalice, was to leave and take up his position of governor, there was a stunned silence, which lasted for what seemed to me to be a very long time. Finally, Joshua Nkomo put up his hand and asked very seriously, 'Will he have plumes and a horse?'

Carrington noted that the tension had been eased by Nkomo and not Mugabe. The appointment of Soames as governor was, according to Carrington, an easy decision. Carrington had known

Soames at Eton. They had remained friends and the Carringtons had been at his wedding to Winston Churchill's daughter Mary. When the Conservatives were back in office, Soames became Churchill's Parliamentary Private Secretary. The political careers of Carrington and Soames were not dissimilar, both having been Ministers of Defence and, perhaps more punishing, of Agriculture. During the negotiations for entry into the European Community, Soames made his reputation as a diplomat, not from negotiations in Brussels, but from the skill he brought to soothing the fears of a large part of Britain's agricultural community, many of whose members were against joining the club of Europe. After losing his seat in the 1966 election, Soames became the British Ambassador to Paris, an appointment which Carrington quite envied. After Paris, Soames went to Brussels as Britain's First Commissioner and then to the House of Lords as Leader. He was full of energy and often bored in Whitehall and seemingly forever telephoning Carrington to see whether or not there might be an interesting and worthwhile job for him to do. At the end of the Rhodesian talks at Lancaster House, Carrington found him just such a job.

Soames died in 1987, and during his address at the memorial service in Westminster Abbey on 29 October, Carrington recalled his decision to make the appointment.

I remember walking over from the Foreign Office across Horse Guards Parade to his office in the Old Admiralty Building – a room twice occupied by Sir Winston Churchill. I had to recommend someone to the Prime Minister and to the Queen to become for a short but vital period, Governor of a Rhodesia, hopefully about to be newly restored to legality. The name that immediately came to my mind was that of Christopher Soames.

He had all the qualities which were required: courage, resolution, political know-how, common-sense and reputation. And also, I may add, the incomparable advantage of having Mary to go with him. Without any preamble I said to him, 'Would you be prepared to go as Governor to Rhodesia?'

'Yes', he said. 'Of course.'

He didn't ask what the job entailed. He didn't speak of its dangers or of the problems which inevitably would arise. It was both his duty to do it and a challenge which should be faced . . .[7]

It was apparently as simple as that: old friends who trust one another, or at least trust others less. Later, in the 1990s, this habit of selecting one's friends for important jobs became known as cronyism but it was a trusted method of appointment that had successfully existed in England since Saxon times. Later George Walden, who was in Carrington's office at the time, suggested that Soames was far from happy.

A cloud passed over his face as if he could see himself plucked of his plumed hat, being eaten by savages. There was no alternative but to agree. Before leaving the building to face the press, Soames asked for another drink.[8]

Holding the diplomatic ring was going to be much harder in what was still Salisbury than in the comfortable surroundings of St James's and Lancaster House. Soames had the stature diplomatically as well as physically to carry off the job. This, however, could not guarantee that the main parties would not succumb to the enormous pressures they would face when they returned to Rhodesia and to their supporters; all the bitterness had not gone away while they had been in London. Moreover, this bitterness, as Carrington believed, would easily turn to violence. So the appointment of governor was no ceremonial bauble.

The intelligence assessments of the personal dangers in Rhodesia were so disturbing that when Carrington said goodbye in London to Christopher Soames and his wife Mary, on their departure for Rhodesia, he feared that they might be assassinated. The letters of goodwill and congratulations were welcome, but Carrington did not open champagne. He may well have been right to be cautious.

7 Carrington's notes for Soames memorial service address, Bledlow papers.
8 Walden, *Lucky George*, p. 198.

In 2006 a former Rhodesian Special Branch officer, Jim Parker, claimed there had been a plan by the South African government to invade Zimbabwe on the eve of its independence. The claim went so far as to suggest the Prince of Wales and Robert Mugabe would have been targets in perhaps a bomb plot and that Soames and Carrington would have been killed as they drove to a reception in Salisbury, or Harare as it was soon to become. The head of the Central Intelligence Organization during the early days of the Mugabe government, Dan Stannard, is quoted as saying,

I don't think Prince Charles was specifically the target. Anybody there would have been fair game. The only specific target was to destroy Zimbabwe before it had a chance to achieve independence.[9]

It never happened, but Carrington daily believed that something similar could go wrong and feared for Christopher and Mary Soames.

Daily, Soames reported by telephone directly to Carrington. He boomed the news from Salisbury. Gradually the machinery of the new constitution and government began to fall into place. The promise of fair elections would be fulfilled. But Carrington's antipathy towards outside interference could have made that task doubly difficult. Fortunately, Carrington's policy was successfully challenged by the Commonwealth Secretary-General Sonny Ramphal. He wanted the Commonwealth to send observers to the election. Carrington thought it would be wrong to do so but Ramphal persisted. Carrington gave way, and the assurances that the observers were able to give proved a great success.

With hindsight, writing at the beginning of the new century, it is proper to note that the worst intimidation and violence came from the followers (and therefore presumably with the authority) of Robert Mugabe. Such was the level of outright intimidation by Mugabe's people during the run-up to the elections that civil servants advised Soames and Carrington that the ZANU-PF leader

9 Jim Parker, *Assignment Selous Scouts: The Inside Story of a Rhodesian Special Branch Officer*, Alberton (Johannesburg): Galago, South Africa, 2006.

had not simply broken the law and the rules, but any future involving him would be bleak and therefore his party should be banned from taking any further part in the election.

Soames's best advice to Carrington was that the civil servants should be ignored and Mugabe allowed to continue. Whatever the shortcomings of the process, banning Mugabe would remove Britain's claim that this was indeed a universal solution and as close to internationally accepted norms of democracy as was possible. Many civil servants continued to advise that Mugabe led a faction which was usurping that democratic process and if he had any form of power by the end of it, he would further corrupt it.

Carrington could not accept this viewpoint. And anyway, privately he did not believe that Mugabe would become Prime Minister. Furthermore, he never believed the thought advanced during the Lancaster House negotiations by many who understood Rhodesia – including his opponents in his own party – that the only reason Mugabe had accepted his terms was that he knew that once he returned to Salisbury he had the physical muscle to determine the outcome of any electoral process. Mugabe's views on intimidation, which were much publicized thirty years on, were no more sophisticated than they were during those first three months of 1980, when he understood clearly the Maoist principle that power comes out of the barrel of a gun in whatever form, real or imagined, that weapon is pointed. Equally, Carrington's view was that in spite of the warnings of what would follow his election, Mugabe's first decade in office did not suggest that which followed in the 1990s and indeed in 2008.

The major threat to the process, once it was decided not to proscribe Mugabe's followers, did not come from black Rhodesians. The Intelligence Services told Carrington that there was a real danger of a right-wing coup d'état encouraged, if not directly supported, by the South African government. There were certainly many in the Rhodesian security services and military who wished to forestall the election. Carrington's confidant was a man who felt he knew what was happening and believed that Mugabe would be successful. This man, General Peter Walls, had given

Carrington good advice during the Lancaster House conference.
He was convinced that a Patriotic Front government would
become a dictatorship and would at the least follow the role model
of surrounding states. He thought the cynical observation 'one
man, one vote, one time' would apply to Rhodesia. Nevertheless,
for all his misgivings and, as Carrington later observed, deep disappointment at the way the country was going, it was Walls who
managed to hold back so many who might have taken the constitutional process into their own hands. In this he was assisted by
one of the few other men Carrington trusted, David Smith (no
relation to Ian Smith). Above all, Carrington's aim was to have a
form of democracy in place in Rhodesia during the summer
of 1980.

Following what was to Carrington the surprise of Mugabe's
election, he told himself that if there had been a better way of
resolving the constitutionally illegal independence of the Ian Smith
and Bishop Abel Muzorewa governments, then he had not discovered it. As for Mugabe, Carrington took some encouragement
from the address to the nation given by the then Prime Minister-
elect on 4 March 1980:

Peace and stability can only be achieved if all of us, first as individuals
and secondly as part of the whole Zimbabwean national community,
feel a definite sense of individual security on the one hand and have an
assurance of national peace and security on the other. It must be realized,
however, that a state of peace and security can only be achieved by our
determination, all of us, to be bound by the explicit requirements of
peace contained in the Lancaster House Agreement, which express the
general desire of the people of Zimbabwe.

In this regard, I wish to assure you that there can never be any return
to the state of armed conflict which existed before our commitment to
peace and the democratic process of election under the Lancaster House
Agreement.

Surely this is now time to beat our swords into ploughshares so we can
attend to the problem of developing our economy and our society ...

I urge you, whether you are black or white, to join me in a new pledge to forget our grim past, forgive others and forget, join hands in a new amity, and together as Zimbabweans, trample upon racialism, tribalism and regionalism, and work hard to reconstruct and rehabilitate our society as we reinvigorate our economic machinery.

This speech in part led to Carrington's own thoughts laid out in his memoirs, written in 1988:

I have been, on the whole, fortified by the magnanimity of Robert Mugabe. There have been disagreeable occurrences in Zimbabwe, and I have never concealed my dislike of them; but when one considers the aftermath of civil war in other African states, when one recalls the long years that Mugabe spent in prison, and when one reflects on his followers' expectations of the spoils of victory, it is not discouraging that at the time of writing there are still white Rhodesian members of Parliament – including until recently Ian Smith – there is still a white minister in Government, there is still a handful of white civil servants, and Ian Smith still has his farm. The truth is that Mugabe, the highly intelligent man, needed the co-operation of all, including whites, to prevent the economy disintegrating. He had no ambition to be Prime Minister of a bankrupt country, and he was prepared to outface, where necessary, his own hard-liners in order to keep his country on something like the rails. He had witnessed follies in other lands not far away, and he had no desire to emulate them.[10]

Carrington wrote those words having returned to what was by then Zimbabwe. This was the only time that he revisited the country. He had the opportunity to go many times again – including a personal invitation from Mugabe's wife, Sally – but did not, sensing the unease of many white Rhodesians. Yet, whatever the outcome almost thirty years on, Carrington continued to believe that he had brought about an end to UDI using the only strategy that had a chance of working. To paraphrase Thatcher's mantra, there was no alternative.

10 Lord Carrington, *Reflect on Things Past*, London: Collins, 1988, p. 305.

There is a tailpiece to Carrington's success (as most people saw it) in bringing a conclusion to the Rhodesian affair. He learned to cope with more than two decades of hate mail. However, there was a lasting hurt caused by comments repeatedly made at the time by Denis Thatcher. Carrington was frequently told that the Prime Minister's husband was saying to anyone who mattered (according to him) that 'the settlement was not Carrington's doing. Margaret was the one that made it happen and should get all the praise.' But not, of course, the poison-pen letters.

From the spring of 1980 to the events of almost two years later, which led to Carrington's resignation from the government, there were few tranquil moments for the Foreign Secretary. He finished the Lancaster House negotiations completely run down. His private office and friends thought him extremely unwell and in need of a long rest. It was not to be. Carrington's nature was never to talk about illness but to press on. True, there were moments to relax during trips to China and Egypt, including a memorable Nile steamer voyage when an attaché from Cairo had to row after the vessel with a red box sent from London. For most of the time, Carrington was split between thinking about Europe, what would happen next in Rhodesia, how British foreign policy would be judged in Washington, and how to deal with Thatcher, who thought far less of President Reagan than the media supposed. This was not an easy period in British government, either at home or abroad.

In January 1980 a three-month steel strike began. This too was the year of the Iranian Embassy siege, which ended in spectacular fashion with the SAS recovering the premises and the hostages during primetime television. It was the year also that the Iran–Iraq War started, with Britain and America supporting the Iraqis under Saddam Hussein in the hope that they could defeat the ambitions of the fundamentalist Iranian regime by proxy. It was the year during which Margaret Thatcher made her famous 'this lady's not for turning' speech at the Conservative Conference at Brighton. The resolve of the Prime Minister could not prevent the worsening situation in Northern Ireland, where the Maze Prison hunger strike started on 27 October. In February 1981 a sure sign that there would be a confrontation with the miners, led by Arthur Scargill, came when the National Coal Board announced a series of pit closures. Little more than a week later, the government had to force the Coal Board to withdraw the list. In April, there were three days of riots in Brixton in south London; in July rioting spread in another London suburb, Southall. And from that came the riots in Toxteth and Moss Side. It was a period of some turmoil at Westminster too, as Margaret Thatcher was forced into two reshuffles of her government. In January she sacked Norman St John-Stevas and Angus Maude. Francis Pym became Leader of the House. This was the time when she appointed two men whom she would later regard as political disasters – John Nott became Defence Secretary and Leon Brittan, who was devoted to her, Chief Secretary to the Treasury. In September Soames was sacked from the government, as was Thatcher's prize wet Ian Gilmour. It was at this September 1981 shuffle that she brought into the Cabinet another man who would later oppose her, and somewhat vehemently – Nigel Lawson.

Carrington's impression was that in spite of all the domestic and foreign difficulties facing the government, including much open criticism of its economic policy, the most important event during those two years was the election on 4 November 1980 of Ronald Reagan as President of the United States. The coming to power of Reagan, and the coincidence of the deeper involvement in the European debate, was the turning point of Margaret Thatcher's inclination to run the foreign policy of the United Kingdom.

For obvious political reasons, most Prime Ministers arrive at Number 10 with no deep knowledge of the big foreign issues. Most of their campaigning years are devoted to domestic issues. (Eden was one of the few Prime Ministers who had spent much time at the Foreign Office.) Certainly this was the case until the 1980s, by which time it was inconceivable that a British politician could assume the highest office without a firm grasp of European Union issues and a political understanding of where they stood in

Britain's relationship with Continental Europe. During these final two years of Carrington's British political life, Thatcher had a strong grasp of her own ideas and even stronger suspicions of those of others. She was learning, as Prime Ministers often do, to mistrust the Foreign Office and its advice, and was beginning to believe – in a suspicion by no means exclusive to Thatcher – that Foreign Secretaries are too influenced by their civil servants. Thatcher was moving towards the not uncommon point for a Prime Minister of having the confidence to want to be her own Foreign Secretary.

It is easy to see why a Prime Minister feels this way. They quite often start a term of office having to put domestic programmes in place, without being quite certain how they might run because most of the Secretaries of State that they appoint to departments are themselves feeling their way. The reality of office is more demanding and often more restricting than opposition for obvious reasons: the overwhelming amount of paperwork, decision-making and meetings that a minister encounters; the reality that, with the exception of the Foreign and Commonwealth Office, the Treasury has considerable control over all departments. Very soon after taking office, a Prime Minister is required to go to large international gatherings and there is something about the trappings and presentations of such meetings that gives Prime Ministers a boost from the drudgery of domestic politics, yet at the same time makes them deeply suspicious of the protocols of inter-national policy forums. By and large, Prime Ministers enjoy the bigger stage and think less and less of the bit players upon it, especially if those players make up the *nomenklatura* of the European Union bureaucracy. In all Carrington's time in government, from Churchill onwards, every Prime Minister aggravated his or her Foreign Secretary in a manner which few other heads of depart-ment suffered – none more so than Margaret Thatcher.

For example, in their first visit together to the United States, Carrington almost resigned as a result of Thatcher's arrogance and what he regarded as downright rudeness. The illusion that they thought as one was quickly shattered. In February 1981 Carrington went with Thatcher to Washington to see the newly inaugurated President Ronald Reagan, who then had been just a month in the White House. Carrington wanted to make sure that the British views on the Middle East were made clear to the Americans. Margaret Thatcher would barely discuss the matter with Carrington, telling him that his views were nothing more than those churned out by 'the camels' of the pro-Arabist Foreign Office. Carrington fumed and waited.

Apparently at Reagan's request, Thatcher was to be the first foreign head of government to visit him as President. Although they had never met apart from a brief moment in London when Reagan was Governor of California, she believed herself to be Reagan's leading advocate among the European members of NATO. Moreover, she had clearly decided by this time that whatever the anomalies and arguments about the so-called special relationship between the United Kingdom and the United States, there would be a special relationship between herself and Reagan.[11] This sense of comradeship did not lessen the enormities of the issues that concerned her. Thatcher understood the impact of American domestic politics on Britain and her allies. For example, the American economy showed an increasing US budget deficit. Reagan, she knew, wanted financial cuts and was still uncertain if Congress would agree to them. A tax-cutting President in normally sound economic times was a good example to follow, but Reagan was bent on tax cuts at a time when the greater effort had to be in controlling the budget deficit. In the worst circumstances this action could weaken the authority of the presidency when Thatcher and the allies needed a strong White House.

At the same time the revolution was beginning in the Soviet

11 Carrington told me that when they first met in London, plain Governor Reagan of California made little impression on Thatcher, but Reagan thought she was impressive. Then when she went to Washington in 1981 to meet him at the White House, she emerged from the Oval Office with a puzzled expression and the comment to Carrington that there was no indication that he had any thoughts never mind understanding of major global issues – including the Middle East – and certainly not the importance of Europe.

Union that would lead to *perestroika* and *glasnost* as expressed in the
political ideas of Mikhail Gorbachev. With Carrington's success in
what was now Zimbabwe, more attention was being paid to the
future of Namibia and the Cuban involvement in Angola. There
were also seemingly endless problems within the Middle East,
together with evidence reported by the intelligence agencies of
Soviet missile deployments in Eastern Europe.

Carrington went with Thatcher to lay his foreign policy views
before President Reagan and Alexander Haig, his Secretary of
State. Thatcher was not so certain they wanted to hear what Carrington had to say, especially on the Middle East, by which most
American politicians meant the electorally sensitive subject of
Israel. The truth was that Thatcher was more and more doubting
Carrington's opinions and those of the Foreign Office he represented. She wondered about Carrington's judgement in his
determination to raise his views with the Reagan administration at
a time when she wanted to establish a firm relationship and not
one that would be tainted by a suspicion that Britain, of all nations,
questioned American foreign policy. Yet Carrington had been dealing with Middle East policies in office and in opposition for a full
decade.

When he was Defence Minister in the Heath administration,
Carrington had been forced to spend considerable time on evaluating Arab–Israeli relations. The Israelis were, at the time, cool to
Britain's idea that it would be better for everyone if it remained
neutral in the Middle East argument. When, for example, Britain's
neutrality during the June 1967 Arab–Israeli War was extended to
putting an embargo on the export of spares for British weapons
already sold to Israel, Britain's policy was heavily criticized in Tel
Aviv. The major problem for the Americans, and therefore
Mrs Thatcher, who tended to support American policy, was that
they were never certain that they were dealing with a united Europe on the Middle East. Some were pro-Arab, some pro-Israeli.
When Europe did speak with one voice it was usually motivated
by self-interest on the question of oil supplies.

Even after leaving Heath's government, Carrington became

involved in Middle East affairs through his commercial interests as well as his membership of the Shadow Cabinet. His contacts at the time included many to whom Britain and America would not normally talk, for example, Yasser Arafat, the leader of the Palestine Liberation Organization. Carrington attempted to balance his understanding of the Arab and Palestinian position against the Israeli belief that it should be uncompromising if its security were to be maintained. This balance was difficult to maintain for the obvious reason, propounded by Margaret Thatcher, that Israel is one country and therefore has one voice only, whereas policy views and intelligence were going back to the Foreign Office in London from a stream of Arab states.

Carrington was at the Foreign Office in the summer of 1980 when the European Foreign Ministers published the so-called Venice Declaration. The Declaration was a European position on Afghanistan (at that time recently invaded by the Soviet Union), Lebanon (in a state of civil war) and, most sensitively, a recognition that the Palestinians had the right to put their case and, equally, had a right case to put. Although the Venice Declaration continued to formally recognize the state of Israel, the reference to the Palestinian position was extremely sensitive.

Carrington went to some lengths to tell people the Foreign Office was not pro-Arab, but that it simply understood the Arab viewpoint. Given the history of the FCO with its almost mythical standing as a home for Arabists, it was little wonder that any pro-Arab or pro-Palestinian statement was treated as confirmation in the minds of others that the Foreign Office must be anti anyone who put the opposing case. Add to this Thatcher's determination to support the Jewish cause and the American viewpoint, and it is easy to see why she did not always agree with her Foreign Secretary.

From all this, Carrington was regarded by some influential people in Whitehall and Washington as anti-Israeli, even anti-Semitic. He helped that impression along by promoting the notion that it was time to get on with developing self-government for the Palestinians on the West Bank of the Jordan and that, when peace talks eventually started, the Palestinians should not be left out.

The British government supported the United Nations Security Council Resolution 242, the internationally famous motion that demanded the Israeli withdrawal from the occupied territories. Even though the Americans also supported Resolution 242, they regarded Carrington as being someone who went beyond the UN position.

Given these sensitive transatlantic positions and suspicions, it is reasonable that Thatcher wanted to tread carefully during her first visit to Reagan. Thatcher believed Reagan to be firm-minded and sure-footed: what she called 'unshakeable'. Thatcher was worried that Carrington would upset the apple cart of UK–US relations. She believed that, for all his experience and wisdom (which is why she had appointed him), Carrington failed to grasp the practical diplomatic principle that there was absolutely no point in telling Reagan what he (Carrington) thought if the argument was not going to be won and the friendship damaged as a result. This then was the atmosphere when Carrington, Thatcher, the Cabinet Secretary Sir Robert Armstrong and the Permanent Under-Secretary at the Foreign Office, Sir Michael Palliser, awoke in Washington on the first morning at the official government guest building, Blair House. Carrington's own memory of the moments before the meeting at the White House remained vivid for the rest of his days. It could so easily have led to the end of his political career. The VIPs had been told by their security people that their rooms at Blair House would be bugged by the Americans. Thatcher and Carrington agreed to meet after breakfast to discuss their position before meeting Reagan. When Carrington arrived, she was with Robert Armstrong and Michael Palliser.

Carrington had hardly got into the room when Thatcher went on the attack. She said she didn't like his Middle East policy, by which she meant his sympathy towards Palestine. Carrington replied that he thought this was government policy.

According to Carrington, Thatcher ignored that, and then said, 'If you go on like that we shall lose the next General Election. Not only will we lose the next election but I shall lose my seat at Finchley [there was a large Jewish vote in her constituency].'

Carrington was disgusted and said, 'If you think British foreign policy should be organized and run on the basis that you might lose your seat at Finchley, you can get another Foreign Secretary.' They glared at one another and Carrington, his famously good temper utterly abandoned, turned and walked out, slamming the door after him.

Later they went to the White House and the Rose Garden.

She was absolutely furious and not speaking at all. Then the sheep in the shape of her and Reagan went off to the Oval Office and the goats in the shape of me and Haig went off. In order to get to the Oval office she had to pass me. She stopped and she said, 'I don't think we did very well this morning, do you?' That was the nearest thing to an apology that anybody has ever got from her.

Thatcher came out of her talk with Reagan totally perplexed. This meeting certainly did not reflect the famous Reagan–Thatcher rapport. She had but one assessment of his intellect: she said to Carrington, 'Peter, there's nothing there!'[12] Almost immediately she had forgotten the confrontation with Carrington that morning. Carrington felt that if he had not been able to argue with her his time as her Foreign Secretary would have been impossible. If Thatcher had not backed down – she did not of course see it like that herself – Carrington would have resigned – he really did mean what he said to her about getting someone else to run foreign policy. Sir Michael Palliser, who witnessed most of these exchanges, thought them inevitable because Carrington was his own man. However, in Palliser's view, Carrington had an important position in her Cabinet that went beyond the Foreign Office. He was the only one of her senior advisers who could not be after her job, as he was safely ensconced in the House of Lords. Later Carrington judged that Thatcher never liked the idea of equals but really had no time for anyone but. He told me that:

12 Author's conversation with Carrington and confirmed by Palliser.

She minds people not rowing. She got rid of all the No men like Jim [Prior] but got bored with all her Yes men like [John] Moore and all those deadly dull Thatcherites who just said yes ma'am no ma'am three bags full.

In the FCO, that was an impossible position. Yet Thatcher did not always appreciate that the Foreign Office was offering realistic advice rather than telling her what she wished to hear. That was certainly true during the rumblings of the approaching Falklands crisis.

13. The Falklands

In spite of being wrapped up in the process to bring about a settlement in Rhodesia, Carrington had been convinced for some time during 1979 that some basic decisions had to be taken over the Falklands. He made it clear in and out of Cabinet that if the UK appeared indifferent to the future of the islands and their roughly 2,000 inhabitants, then the wrong signs could encourage the unstable Argentine leadership to set out on adventures that could only lead to war.

During lunch at Chequers one weekend, he later recalled, Carrington raised the matter of the Falklands. He insisted that Britain had to bring the whole Falklands question to a suitable conclusion because after Rhodesia it was high on the FCO agenda. He suggested that one possibility would be, like Hong Kong, a leaseback arrangement.

Sitting round the table was Willie, Celia [the Whitelaws], Denis & Margaret and Iona and me. There was a thermonuclear explosion and fallout. 'Typical of you and the Foreign Office. You would give the British Empire away to a lot of bloody foreigners,' she fulminated. Finally, Denis said, 'I think you're being a little extravagant, my dear.'

This was not the only time that Carrington and Thatcher confronted each other over the Falklands. During another evening at Chequers, he suggested that the signs were that it really was possible to come to some arrangement with Argentina on the future of the islands. Once more she rounded upon him, accusing him and the Foreign Office of wanting to give away everything that was British. It was only Denis Thatcher's interruption that it was 'time for bed' that tempered yet another disagreeable scene between the two.

There is a hypothesis in foreign policy circles that diplomatic

opportunities and warning signs are missed because most governments find it hard to concentrate on two major events at once. An
example often mentioned is that the British were so preoccupied
with the Ireland debate that they failed to notice the significance
of events that were leading them to the First World War. In
1981 and 1982 Carrington was being pushed more and more by
Thatcher to attend to the Middle East (by which she meant Israel).
The issue of the Falklands, while not ignored, did not have the
department's full attention and certainly not Thatcher's. She continued to have her suspicions about Carrington's feelings towards
Israel. Carrington had been ostracized, denigrated and viciously
treated over his Rhodesian policy by people who were supposed
to be political if not personal friends. The same atmosphere now
clouded him over Middle East policy. He felt shaken and saddened
when in 1981 he was booed while giving a speech at Caxton Hall
in London and people even refused to go through the formality
and courtesy of shaking his hand because of what they saw as his
pro-Arab leanings. Twice, he was supposed to go on official visits
to Israel. On both occasions those visits were cancelled. The Israeli
Foreign Minister Yitzhak Shamir and the Prime Minister Menachem Begin made it clear that he was no friend of Israel and
therefore not welcome.

The tension between Begin and Carrington was evident in the
latter's view that although the Israeli Prime Minister was a former
terrorist with whom diplomacy and politics demanded business
had to be done, Begin was nevertheless a onetime member of a
ruthless gang of killers. In an article in 2003 in the *Jerusalem Post*,
Begin's former adviser Yehuda Avner recorded what he claimed to
have been an accurate description of a confrontation between Carrington and Begin during a Downing Street lunch hosted by
Margaret Thatcher shortly after the 1979 election.[1] Thatcher had
enthused to Begin about her Jewish constituents, who she said
never came to her for hand-outs because Jews looked after their

---

1 Yehuda Avner, 'Why Britain can never be trusted by the Jewish people',
Jerusalem Post, 25 November 2003.

own. Thatcher apparently said that her admiration for Jewish characteristics of sticking to their guns and beliefs and triumphing over adversity was due to her Methodist upbringing. Carrington, sitting opposite Begin, was not caught by this diplomatic enthusiasm. Prompted by Begin, Carrington said he thought the Israelis brought too much baggage to the negotiating tables, and that Begin's settlement policy was really an expansionist policy and so 'a barrier to peace'. Warming to his theme, he said that the settlements were actually built on what he believed to be Arab land and that they 'rob Palestinians of their land. They unnecessarily arouse the animosity of the moderate Arabs. They are contrary to international law – the Geneva Convention. They are inconsistent with British interests.'[2] Thatcher supported him, telling Begin that Carrington was speaking on behalf of the government. Begin chose to fight Carrington, not Thatcher. He leaned forward to focus his fullest attention on him. The two men's eyes traded malevolence. Then he let fly: the settlements were not an obstacle to peace; no Palestinian-Arab sovereignty had ever existed in the biblical provinces of Judaea and Samaria; the Geneva Convention did not apply; the Arabs had refused to make peace before there was a single settlement anywhere; the settlements were built on state-owned, not Arab-owned, land; their construction was an assertion of basic Jewish historic rights; the settlement enterprise was critical to Israel's national security.[3]

The lunch rather lost its way from that point. Was Carrington pro-Arab or, more sensitively, anti-Israel? The latter accusation carried with it a stigma of anti-Semitism. Carrington could never accept the Israeli condition of politics and friendship which dictated that an individual was either for or against Israel. To his mind, nothing was ever so black and white. Yet the Foreign Secretary of the United Kingdom, while understanding the subtleties of shadows, must not walk in them.

Here we have a vision of Carrington not quite in tune with

2 Ibid.
3 Ibid.

the popular view of the ever affable, humorous, honourable and, perhaps above all, wise peer. He was known as a man who brought deep understanding to all his offices, and he was greatly respected by the people of Great Britain and, apparently, throughout the world. Yet here is a case of all these characteristics apparently not ringing quite true. The public image of a generous relationship between Thatcher and Carrington is also disturbed.

When the opportunity finally came for him to go to Israel with the blessing of the Israeli government, he put all other considerations aside and went. Unfortunately he did so during the build-up to one of the biggest crises his office would experience. He was in Israel on that visit when the Argentines invaded the Falklands. Afterwards he deeply regretted going, even though he argued that staying at home would not have prevented the invasion. It is true that the importance of this Israeli visit was such that his private office, and he personally, devoted much time to its preparation. The Foreign Office is a warren of departments preparing briefings that cover the globe. It has access to reports from its own people in overt posts abroad, outside agencies, including the CIA, and all the signals intelligence channelled through the United States and GCHQ as well as the Secret Intelligence Service (MI6). All the reports and analyses are laid before the Joint Intelligence Committee. None of this information covering the Falklands appears to have reached Carrington's private office in any form strong enough for his Israel visit to be postponed. Even though Margaret Thatcher urgently wanted Carrington to go to Israel, it has to be remembered that the leaders of that country had lived in a state of war since 1948. They would have been the first to understand the need to postpone the visit if they had been told that British territory was threatened. As Foreign Secretary, therefore, Carrington was let down. Yet as the fount of foreign policy wisdom in Thatcher's Cabinet, Carrington's judgement was wrong. The invasion could not have been a complete surprise. Thatcher and Carrington did talk about the Falklands during the few hours before his departure. There were ministerial meetings in Brussels that were interrupted to read the latest reports. Yet Carrington read nothing that convinced him to stay and Thatcher believed that nothing could be gained by him staying in London. He did not stay, and he lost his job at the Foreign Office.

He went to Israel on a fruitless diplomatic mission. He wanted to speak to the Palestinians but the Israelis would not let him and one of his staff had to resort to throwing a message of goodwill from Carrington over the wall of the Palestinian mayor's garden.

The hurler of a rock wrapped in that friendly greetings message was Deputy Under-Secretary at the FCO, Sir John Leahy. In his memoir, Leahy described Begin with his gout-ridden foot carefully balanced on a stool giving Carrington a lecture. This was prompted by Carrington's insistence that sooner or later the Israelis would be forced to negotiate with Arabs. Begin's response was to the point: 'It is like asking us to commit suicide.'

When Carrington could get a word in, he said that, during the years of bringing colonial rule to an end, British governments had discovered that they could not choose whom to negotiate with, they had to deal with whoever had the power to deliver an agreement. This often meant people they had once regarded as terrorists, such as Kenyatta in Kenya or Makarios in Cyprus. He was about to add Mugabe's name when Begin broke in and said, with a slight smile, 'Not me, I hope' [in the days of the British Mandate in Palestine Begin had been a member of the Stern Gang who, amongst other acts of violence, blew up the King David Hotel in Jerusalem] ... Notwithstanding Carrington's own assessment, the visit was not a success. The Israelis had long believed that he was anti-Israeli and from the outset they gave him a distinctly chilly public reception; and in the private talks they showed no inclination to moderate their uncompromising views.[4]

During an official dinner on the second day a message came from London asking Carrington to cut short his visit and return. Carrington, distracted and desperately tired, returned to London in time to go straight into an emergency Cabinet meeting on

4 Sir John Leahy, *A Life of Spice*, published privately, 2006.

1 April. Even then he sensed he had made his final ministerial trip.

How did this war that should never have been and which cost more than 1,000 lives come about? Also, why did Carrington, the head of Britain's foreign policy, fail to anticipate the conflict and its consequent tragedies?

Carrington did not discover the Falklands in 1982. He had for a quarter of a century had Falkland briefing notes in his red boxes when he was a junior defence minister, First Lord of the Admiralty, Minister of State at the Foreign Office, Defence Secretary, Leader of the Conservative Party in the Lords and as a member of Thatcher's Cabinet. He had a continuing grasp of Argentine foreign policy where it concerned the islands. He knew the importance that the Malvinas played in the Argentine national and political psyche. He most certainly understood the military limitations for defending the islands, protected as they were by a token land force, occasional ships' visits and the symbolic presence of the Antarctic patrol ship HMS *Endurance*. Moreover, the Foreign Office position did not take much intellectual depth to comprehend: the islanders wanted nothing to do with the Argentines, and Britain would not contemplate surrendering that sovereignty for as long as that remained their wish.

Ideas put forward to ease the tensions that naturally remained between the islanders, the Argentines and the British included nominal ownership by Argentina with the islands being on permanent lease to the United Kingdom. But all potential schemes ended up in the Whitehall pending tray. Most of the negotiations, because of their sensitivities, took place in private and often away from the southern hemisphere. The crux of the debate within successive British Cabinets was always that of sovereignty and therefore any international debate had to recognize that Britain's position was very firm. This was clear in Britain's statement in autumn 1965 to the General Assembly of the United Nations:

We are always ready to discuss these questions [proposal for the future of the islands] in a friendly and constructive spirit, but we must nevertheless apply the principles of consultation and consent.

Even then, the statement to the General Assembly did not come voluntarily. It was prompted by a UN resolution which called on Britain and Argentina to find a peaceful solution to the problem.

It was not as if talks between the British and the Argentines had never taken place. Both Labour and Conservative governments had approved talks at officials level with the Argentines. Officials of both Labour and Conservative governments had often met representatives from Buenos Aires. There had even been discussions about the surrender of some British sovereignty, but only to test the water on both sides. In January 1966 the government once more announced that there was no question that the sovereignty of the Falklands was negotiable. Two years later, Carrington suspected that the Labour government was willing to negotiate away sovereignty, even when Lord Chalfont, the then Minister of State for Foreign and Commonwealth Affairs, on Tuesday 3 December 1968, said that he had been to the islands and that he had made it clear that although Britain was actively seeking some arrangement with Argentina he would not back away from what he regarded as continuing government policy not to 'transfer sovereignty over these islands against the wishes of the islanders'.

Carrington's response in the Lords reflected the deepening suspicion that the islands were in the process of being handed over to Argentina.

There is nothing personal in this, but Lord Chalfont's activities and the motives of Her Majesty's Government are suspect and cause great concern to a large number of people. Does the statement made by the Foreign Secretary [Michael Stewart] in January 1966 – that sovereignty was not negotiable – still stand?

Did Lord Chalfont have discussions on the questions of sovereignty with the Argentine Government and have he or the Government brought any economic pressures to bear on the Falkland Islands.

Has he said, as he is reported to have said, that Britain would no longer be able to continue to defend the islands . . . ?

Chalfont, in that same exchange in the Lords, admitted that sovereignty was being discussed with the Argentine government. His
implication was that it was impossible not to discuss it, but that that
did not mean that the Labour government had changed their
ideas about Britain's legal title to sovereignty. Chalfont tried to
reassure Carrington that he had told the Executive Council of the
Falkland Islands that 'as long as their sovereignty resided with
Britain their defence was our responsibility and that responsibility
should be discharged.'

The debate in December 1968 was the culmination of an important series of developments under the Labour government
during the previous four years. Everyone who knew the islands
understood that they would fall easily to even a modest attack by
an Argentine force. Successive British governments had lacked,
and would continue to lack, the resources and the determination to provide an obvious deterrent to an invasion. While the
Argentines had appeared to have always wanted to negotiate the
islands' sovereignty, they knew, and the British government
knew, that in extreme circumstances a military solution was possible at least in the short term. That short term, with a successful
invasion, would be the moment to force a negotiated settlement
on Argentine terms. This had been the view in Buenos Aires
and understood in Britain for some thirty years before the 1982
invasion. What was different about 1982 was that the circumstances of a threatened Argentine government coinciding with
a number of signs from London (in particular the withdrawal of
the guardship, HMS *Endurance*) made invasion an attractive
proposition.

Not much earlier, the Foreign Office believed (or certainly the
minister responsible, Nicholas Ridley, believed) that a negotiated
settlement was possible. It would be mainly based on the so-called
leaseback scheme. The islands would be Argentine, but leased to
the British for a period to be decided when the stages of an agreement in principle were discussed. Ridley had told Carrington and
Thatcher that he believed he would have the support of the Commons. Carrington at the time doubted that any suggestion of

giving up sovereignty in any form could ever get the backing of the Commons. Ridley's arrogance, and Thatcher's trust in him as a man she so much admired, led to the presentation of that possible settlement to the House of Commons in such a manner that it was rejected by MPs on both sides of the House. If Parliament had agreed, then the Falklands War would not have occurred. Carrington consequently blamed the House of Commons for the invasion of the Falkland Islands in the spring of 1982.

The Argentines had revived their interest in claims on the Falklands in the early 1960s. They had instituted a public holiday called Malvinas Day. In 1964 the Argentine government renewed its political and diplomatic pressure in the United Nations. One result of this pressure was a reference the following year in the report of the UN special committee looking at the granting of independence to colonies: in its introduction, it stated that there should be a 'cherished aim of bringing to an end everywhere colonialism in all its forms, one of which covers the case of the Falkland Islands (Malvinas)'.[5] The follow-up to this was the request of the United Nations that the United Kingdom and Argentine governments should report progress of their negotiations to the UN special committee.

The following spring, in March 1965, the Joint Intelligence Committee (JIC) in Whitehall reported to the Cabinet that it believed that although it was unlikely that Argentina would invade the Falklands, if there should be, for example, some unofficial raiding party, then the Argentine government would probably be prompted to change tack. The following January, as expected, the Argentine Foreign Ministry repeated its claim to the islands when the then British Foreign Secretary, Michael Stewart, visited Buenos Aires. In September 1966 occurred Operation Condor, twenty Argentines landing on the racecourse at Port Stanley. Their government did not support them and was apparently embarrassed when, shortly after, shots were fired at the British Embassy during a visit of Prince Philip to Buenos Aires. The British political response hardly sent a message of resolve. It did no more than

5 UN Resolution 2065, 16 December 1965.

make a modest increase in the size of the Royal Marine detachment in the islands (one officer and five marines).

It was not as if the government underestimated the vulnerability
of the islands. In the autumn of 1966 a Cabinet committee paper
written by George Brown and Fred Lee (the Foreign Secretary and
Colonial Secretary) accepted that if the Argentines chose to do so
they could easily invade and occupy the islands.

By that time, the British position was simple: the question of
Falkland Island sovereignty should be frozen for thirty years, during
which it was hoped that it would be possible to institute normal
relations between the islands and Argentina.

In the spring of 1967 the Argentine government said that it
had considered this proposal but firmly rejected it. The Wilson
government responded by saying that Britain would be willing
under certain conditions to hand over sovereignty to Argentina.
The usual condition was cited: that the wishes of the islanders had
to be respected.

This was the first occasion on which Britain had agreed, even
conditionally, to hand power to Argentina. By early February
1968, the islanders had got wind of this apparent change in policy
and mounted their own campaign at Westminster and in the
British media against what they believed would be a sell-out. The
Memorandum of Understanding between Britain and Argentina
in August 1968 repeated that given that all conditions had been
satisfied – including the interests of the islanders – then 'the
Government of the United Kingdom as part of such a final settlement will recognise Argentina's sovereignty over the islands from
a date to be agreed'.

In June 1970 the Conservatives returned to power and so did
Carrington. The talks that followed between the two countries
produced the 'sovereignty umbrella', which broadly meant that
the talks that were designed to produce better communications
between the islands and the mainland were not seen as a breach of
existing sovereignty.

In May 1972 the Argentines announced they planned to build
a temporary runway in the islands so that the sea-plane service

could be replaced with conventional aircraft. British Defence Intelligence minuted Carrington that a runway could support military operations whereas the existing sea-plane service could not. At the time this was not a major contention between the two governments, but the response indicated that the British in some quarters of Whitehall were deeply suspicious of anything the Argentines planned. Almost inevitably in this atmosphere, bilateral talks were treading diplomatic water and so the whole matter went back to the United Nations. The UN exerted considerable pressure upon the UK government, and it is worth noting that, in spite of the wishy-washy reputation of the UN, the British government took notice of this pressure. Consequently, in January 1974 the Cabinet Defence Committee reported to full Cabinet that UN pressure, together with the military risks to the islanders, made it worthwhile getting the Governor of the Falkland Islands to look at the possibility of persuading the Falklanders that a less sceptical attitude towards sovereignty and cooperation might be encouraged.

In March 1974 Heath was defeated in the General Election. Carrington had been Defence Secretary for much of this period and therefore directly responsible for the security of the islands, including providing the JIC with a regular update from his own Defence Intelligence department on Argentine capabilities and, where at all possible, intentions. The last memorandum by the Defence Committee, cited above, was actually dictated after he had moved from Defence to his short-lived task as Energy Minister.

Harold Wilson's government, with James Callaghan as his Foreign Secretary, continued to press the Falkland islanders to accept that discussions could be opened with Argentina that would, it was hoped, lead to joint control over the islands' affairs – the so-called condominium. They had some success: the islanders did not object, but would not take part in any discussions, thus making it unlikely that those talks would lead very far. It was at this point that Argentine newspapers, including *Cronica*, started to campaign for an invasion. However, in the winter of 1973 and 1974 the JIC assessments continued to suggest that there would be no invasion as long as President Perón's government believed that Whitehall was willing to negotiate sovereignty.

In 1975 Lord Shackleton carried out an official British survey on the future of the islands' economy. This annoyed the Argentine government, partly because it had not been consulted and felt it should have been if there were any chance of condominium, and because Shackleton's survey suggested that Britain saw only a British involvement in the islands. This probably prompted the Argentine statement in the UN General Assembly on 8 December 1975 that 'the limits of our patience and tolerance should not be underestimated'.

The following year there was much diplomatic toing and froing between London and Buenos Aires. Callaghan seemed to think that the increased anti-British feeling in Buenos Aires did not have the backing of its government. Furthermore, Callaghan's opinion was supported by the JIC, which was saying that an invasion was a remote option. The JIC also thought that there was considerable opposition to Perón from the Argentine general staff. They did not want to get involved in any military operation simply to keep him in office.

A curious aspect of the British Intelligence reporting was that they believed that because the Argentines were keen to extend the runway on the Falklands, that meant they were still keen on joint cooperation. That the extension meant also it would be easier for the Argentines to land aircraft apparently never crossed the minds of military planners. Then in February 1976 an Argentine destroyer fired on the British research vessel *Shackleton*. The JIC insisted that this was nothing more than posturing.

The one telling response in Whitehall was that instead of withdrawing HMS *Endurance* from the region – as she was supposed to have been under the 1974 Defence Review – she was kept south by successive Labour defence ministers (Roy Mason and Fred Mulley). The Argentines saw this as a strong military signal: even though *Endurance* was a virtually defenceless vessel, she represented a sure symbol that the United Kingdom would respond with military force should any Argentine attempt be made to usurp

British authority in the islands. Consequently, when John Nott, the Conservative Defence Secretary, announced *Endurance*'s withdrawal in his June 1981 review of military spending, it should have then anticipated that in Buenos Aires this would be seen as a sign of Britain's lack of resolve to defend the islands.

In fact five years earlier, in February 1976, the British Chiefs of Staff had sent a note to the Cabinet Defence Committee outlining what they perceived to be the considerable difficulties of countering an Argentine invasion. The memo, approved by the Chiefs of Staff on 19 February, laid out the brigade group order of battle plus the maritime and long-term logistics that would be necessary to recover the islands. This was the template of the operation they had to mount six years later.

In March 1976 there was the ominous development of a military coup in Argentina. The JIC suggested that the new Argentine military junta had very high hopes of getting back the islands. It continued to believe, however, that if the bilateral talks came to nothing, then the matter would move not to the battlefield, but to the UN in New York, because the Argentines knew they could rely on considerable sympathy there – particularly in the all-important Security Council – for their cause.

For both the Foreign Office and the Defence Ministry, judgement about Argentine intentions was complicated by the difficulty of providing accurate military intelligence of what was going on in the area.

For example, in November, the Argentines landed forces on southern Thule. British Military Intelligence did not discover this until just before Christmas Day. It was not until 5 January 1977 that the British *chargé d'affaires* in Buenos Aires was told by the Foreign Office to ask the Argentine Foreign Affairs Ministry what it thought it was up to. It took at least another week before the Argentines said that the whole thing was a scientific investigation. As this was a British island, Britain felt moved to formally protest. Yet there was not much the British could do about it. The Argentine government had achieved its aims: a claim of sovereignty and a testing of Britain's resolve. It might be noted that although the landing took place in November 1976, the British government did not make any public statement about it until May 1978. In fact, the so-called scientific adventure carried on and was still there at the end of the Falklands War in 1982.

In February 1977 Britain tried again to get some kind of settlement, though it is difficult to see how any of these talks – which took place in London, Buenos Aires, Central America and Rome – could be expected to succeed. Nervous that the Argentines might mount an invasion if the talks got nowhere, plans were made to have a task force in the South Atlantic and to make sure if necessary that the Argentines knew this. The biggest problem, as it always had been, was that talks could get nowhere until the government was convinced that a settlement had the support of the islanders and, equally importantly, of the British electorate.

This then was the atmosphere when in May 1979 Carrington became Foreign and Commonwealth Secretary. He put Nicholas Ridley in charge of the Falklands with three observations: they could call off all negotiations and prepare for the military consequences; they could hand over the islands and give the islanders who wanted them tickets to anywhere in the world; or they could carry on talking.

Throughout his career, from the Second World War to his time in the Balkans at the start of the 1990s, Carrington considered intelligence-gathering a complex and often unreliable craft and intelligence analysis too often inaccurate. Moreover, he had spent ten years since his time at the Defence Ministry and now at the Foreign Office wondering if any government had truly understood what was and what was not possible in seeking some form of settlement with the islanders and Argentina. Accordingly, Carrington now sent Ridley to the Falklands and to Buenos Aires to see for himself. The islanders told Ridley they wanted to go back to the original idea of a long-term freeze on sovereignty. The Argentines, who had never thought much of the Labour government's negotiation strategy, wanted to get on with discussions 'at a more dynamic pace'.

On 20 September 1979 Carrington wrote to Margaret Thatcher.

He wanted her and the Cabinet to agree that they should press ahead on negotiations about sovereignty, with perhaps the best chance of success being a so-called leaseback arrangement – a curious assessment because Ridley, although he agreed with the format, had told Carrington that the islanders did not want leaseback. Carrington wanted a quick answer from Thatcher. He was going to the United Nations the following week and was having a meeting with the Argentine Foreign Minister, Brigadier Carlos Washington Pastor.

Thatcher would not be rushed into a policy decision and wanted the whole matter discussed in the Cabinet Overseas and Defence Committee. Carrington did not like this response. He had little time for this committee and 'disliked bringing FCO business before committee meetings of his colleagues'.[6] Carrington could give an impression that he ran his department in the way he ran his estate: he listened carefully to advice but went to no one to approve his decisions. Later, the inquiry led by Lord Franks into the Falklands conflict would appear to endorse Carrington's view. Carrington's diplomacy at the UN and then directly with the Argentines paid no dividends other than time to come up with a further proposal. But there could be none because, like the unfinished business of what to do about Spanish claims on Gibraltar, the Falklands question continued to return to the simple fact that no government could ever risk the electoral consequences – never mind the moral issues – of handing over a British territory against the wishes of the majority of its inhabitants. In theory, therefore, whatever the level of Cabinet discussion the bottom line was clear: the Falklands were, by the express wishes of the islanders, not for sale.

There arose at this time the matter of personal perceptions of what was likely to happen in the islands. Carrington's thought was very straightforward: the UK had to show every resolve to defend the islanders; the pro-Argentina mood on the UN Security Council had to be countered; the Americans had to give no indication that they would not diplomatically at least support the

6 Peter Hennessy, *Whitehall*, London: Secker & Warburg, 1989, p. 213.

UK in any confrontation; the whole matter could hinge on the stability of the Argentine government.

The last point could only be hoped for. The Argentine navy at least were inclined to use Suez as an example that the United States would not necessarily support the United Kingdom. The mood on the Security Council could easily depend on which states were temporary members at the time of any crisis. The FCO had no control over that and could not easily influence the policies of the four other permanent members – the US, France, Russia and China. There remained the ability of the UK government to convince the Argentines that the islands would, without question, be defended. That was Carrington's difficulty in September 1979 – plus he was about to go into the non-stop effort of trying to resolve the Rhodesian problem. The Falklands went to the simmer-plate of Carrington's foreign policy thinking.

By 1981, with no diplomatic settlement remotely in sight according to Carrington's Foreign Office, there now occurred a reshuffle in Thatcher's Cabinet that was to have a direct influence on Argentine thinking about the Malvinas. Thatcher moved her Trade Secretary John Nott to the MOD as Secretary of State. One admiral told me – in 1981 – that with his background in banking, Nott had a clear ambition to become Chancellor. All three services needed a review of their strategic roles, equipment and deployments. This would mean a radical examination of the financing of Britain's defence capability. To get the defence sums right, as the admiral suggested, would do Nott's ambition to be in Number 11 no harm at all. It is certainly true that the review was necessary and that Nott had the ability to push it through. Two aspects of the preparation for that review published during the summer of 1981 stood out for the Royal Navy and for Carrington. The Navy believed the restructuring of the role of the fleet was wrongly designed. More important for Carrington were the signals coming into the Foreign Office from the MOD that Nott planned to withdraw the Falklands guardship HMS *Endurance*. This would, Carrington believed, send the signal to the Argentines that the UK was tacitly saying that the islanders were undefended. A series of notes to this effect from Lord Carrington to Sir John Nott did not change the former Trade Secretary's mind.

For his part, Nott was never convinced of the likelihood of Argentine action and considering that he was getting the same intelligence briefs as Carrington, that seemed a reasonable conclusion. Nott accepted that Carrington did not want *Endurance* removed but could cite evidence from his own defence staff that the ship was only a token force and therefore unlikely to alter the deterrence factor in the region. There later appeared evidence that the captain of *Endurance*, Nick Barker, had sent warnings of invasion to the MOD. Barker never met Nott but assumed that his urgent report would be relayed to the Secretary of State. Nott told me he never saw it. Most certainly, Barker's signal was fed into the Defence Intelligence mix and that would have been part of the JIC's analysis. But clearly the JIC before April 1982 was incompetent and did not work.[7]

For much of the first three months of 1982 Carrington was grappling with an uncertain diplomatic process that suggested the Intelligence Services were getting a confused picture of Argentine intentions. He made it clear to his staff that in his experience in the army and at the Defence Ministry, Military Intelligence could give an accurate assessment only of the other side's capabilities, not their intentions. In the middle of January, the Argentine Joint Armed Forces Committee met to plan the invasion. Twelve days later, on 24 January, those plans were written up in the Argentine newspaper *La Prensa*. Neither Carrington nor Nott ever saw an intelligence assessment of that article. This could explain to some extent why Carrington, with Nott's assent, thought it safe for Thatcher on 2 February to send a letter to senior Conservative Party officials and members that the best advice was that the token Royal Marine presence in Stanley could stop any Argentine invasion. A week later, so confident were Nott and Thatcher of the defence of the islands that Thatcher, against Carrington's advice, confirmed that the Falklands guard vessel, HMS *Endurance*,

7 Lord Lewin in conversation with author.

would be withdrawn. This was exactly what the Argentine naval planners wanted to hear. Equally, it seems unlikely that the invasion plan would have been swayed by *Endurance*'s presence unless it had been publicly supported by a submarine capable of striking Buenos Aires – which *Endurance* was not. Carrington meanwhile sent one of his ministers, Richard Luce, to New York to start sovereignty talks with his Argentine equivalent, Ernesto Ros. At first all seemed to be well and on 1 March they issued a joint communiqué saying their talks were 'cordial'. Carrington was cautious. He asked what 'cordial' meant. He was told that Luce and Ros got on well. That, thought Carrington, was fine but dangerous. Sure enough, the following day, Ros's ministry rejected the communiqué and as Carrington had predicted then said the Argentines would use any means necessary to gain sovereignty. Even with these warnings, though, Carrington did not press Thatcher or Nott to send a submarine to patrol the Argentine coast. Nott said nothing was available but even the public statement that a vessel had been sent, or the planting of information that one had, may have sent a tougher signal than doing nothing. The Argentines were certainly, with hindsight, signalling their intentions or, at least, probing the islands' defences. On 6 March an Argentine Hercules transport claimed it had a fuel leak during a flight to the Antarctic and landed at Stanley airport. On board were senior military planners who then carried out a reconnaissance of the Falklands capital. This action at least had Carrington's FCO and Nott's MOD dusting off contingency defence plans – but only after Downing Street asked to see them.

The first action was to send the doomed *Endurance* and twenty-four Royal Marines from Stanley to South Georgia to evict the Argentine scrap workers who had set up camp on the island, complete with their national ensign. Yet there was still no announcement of a submarine, no strong words and apparently a policy to do nothing that might exacerbate the situation. Carrington had long been a follower of R. A. Butler's idea that often in a crisis it was better to do nothing. But towards the end of March – and with Butler dead – this did appear to be taking the former Tory Deputy Prime Minister's advice a little too far. On 26 March

British Intelligence in Buenos Aires was telling London that an invasion, codenamed Operation Rosario, looked likely. The MOD and the FCO did not get these reports until too late and then did nothing about them even when Argentina cancelled all military leave – a classic sign of pending conflict. It is also true that the junta did not take the final decision to invade on 2 April (the original date had been 25 May, Argentine's National Day) until 31 March. But twelve hours earlier, Carrington was still saying that all diplomatic efforts were being made to resolve differences. On the day he went to Israel, the Argentine fleet sailed under the cover of taking part in a naval exercise with Uruguay's navy. Only then did the FCO and the MOD seem to believe in the invasion.

Nott had returned from the NATO Nuclear Planning Group meeting in Colorado Springs during the third week in March. There is no evidence that during the NPG any intelligence concerning the Falklands was passed to Nott, nor to the then Chief of the Defence Staff, Admiral of the Fleet Sir Terry Lewin, nor to the First Sea Lord Admiral Sir Henry Leach. During an informal gathering after the meeting had ended, in the lobby of the Colorado Springs resort centre, I asked all three (Nott, Lewin and Leach) what was happening about the Falklands and the apparent preparations for invasion. Nott told me that he thought I was obsessed with the subject. Clearly from that remark, the Secretary of State had not had any urgent intelligence, and confirmed this by allowing Lewin to fly, not back to Britain, but to New Zealand as part of his farewell tour as Chief of the Defence Staff.[8]

After the meeting, Nott returned to London and more or less remained there from 25 March. He says that he was not warned that the Argentines might invade and was never advised to take strong and overt action. A nuclear-powered attack submarine was sent south after a conversation between Carrington and Thatcher, but it was very difficult to deploy or redeploy boats quickly. 'The nuclear submarines were all in the Barents Sea swanning

8 Lord Lewin had come to the end of his career and as Chief of the Defence Staff was spending time visiting his opposite numbers among Britain's allies.

around playing war games against the Soviet fleet,' Nott told me.

Carrington later talked through the events of the 'invasion week' with me and identified the British Intelligence reporting as having been ineffectual during the weeks, not hours, running up to invasion. Even so, the way in which reports were handled in the MOD, the FCO and within the JIC reporting system was at best laid-back and at worst incompetent. The British Intelligence reports to London of an imminent invasion had arrived at the MOD, the FCO and at MI6 headquarters on 26 March. But it took another three days for the Joint Intelligence Committee to report that to the Prime Minister and Nott and Carrington. By that time, Argentine aircraft were flying reconnaissance missions over Stanley for all to see and report back to London. Moreover, the Argentine army and navy were dispersing logistical stores and equipment to the naval bases of Puerto Belgrano and Comodoro Rivadavia. Still there was no tough statement from either Carrington (who had asked Alexander Haig, without much success, to intercede with the Argentines) or Thatcher, although the contingency plans were once more brought out – and found wanting.

Thatcher telephoned Reagan and asked him to warn off the Argentines and then ordered Nott to deploy three nuclear-powered (not armed) submarines to the area. The first submarine to leave was in Gibraltar but Nott said the others would take time to break off from their own exercises and weeks to get into what became the combat zone. HMS *Splendid* managed to leave Faslane on 1 April. The invasion fleet had sailed the previous day. Not until the invasion had almost reached the islands did Carrington's department tell Rex Hunt, the Falklands Governor, that it looked as if an invasion could happen. At 7.15 p.m. Falklands time, Hunt broadcast to the islanders that he had news of an invasion and that the Royal Marines and Falkland Islands Defence Force were on standby. The following morning, Argentine special forces were landed at Mullet Creek and York Bay. At 6 a.m. three of them were killed by the Royal Marines. But at 9.15 Hunt was forced to surrender. President Galtieri immediately told Argentines that the islands were theirs once more, Stanley had been renamed Puerto Argentino and

Brigadier General Mario Menendez was Governor of Islas Malvinas. In London Carrington told Parliament (which sat on a Saturday for the first time since Suez) that all this was indeed true.

Even as late as 31 March, by which time the Argentine force was embarking for the invasion, Nott was still carrying on as normal. He went to the north of England to review the Tornado aircraft building programme with British Aerospace. When he returned to London during the early evening, he was shown details of an Argentine signal intercepted by signals intelligence at GCHQ. This signal was the first time, according to Nott, that he or anyone else had realized the seriousness of the problem.

This is an odd assertion. Carrington was telephoned on Sunday evening, 28 March, at home at Bledlow, by the Prime Minister, who was at Chequers. Thatcher thought it possible that he should have been telephoning her! She told him that she was becoming anxious over the situation. A week earlier, the so-called scrap-metal dealers had made a second landing on South Georgia and had raised the Argentine flag. The Argentine government was not willing to discuss the matter. During that conversation, Carrington told Thatcher that he had asked the US Secretary of State, Alexander Haig, to use American influence on the Argentines. Apart from diplomatic efforts there was not much more that could be done. As we have seen, Carrington was about to go to Israel via a European Council meeting in Brussels. It was on the way to fly to that meeting from RAF Northolt that Carrington and Thatcher agreed to send a nuclear-powered submarine to back up HMS *Endurance*. Thatcher returned from Brussels on Tuesday 30 March and Carrington, with her urging, went off to Israel.

Why did he go during such a crisis? One reason was that he had cancelled a number of proposed visits and the Israeli government was taking the view that the British and particularly Carrington were hostile. That was a straight political assessment and not so unreasonable. But more importantly he had been told by MI6 that there would be no Argentine attack until all diplomatic procedures had been exhausted. Later, Carrington fully accepted that it was a mistake to have gone and that by defying Thatcher's orders and

remaining in the UK, he would have re-emphasized the seriousness of the situation. The MI6 assessment given to Carrington was
wrong in one vital piece of analysis: that there would be no attack
until diplomacy had ended. But who would decide it had ended?
The UK or Argentina? MI6 did not say and Carrington's office
failed to ask them. One MI6 officer told me that in retrospect,
Carrington's visit to Israel was another signal to the Argentines
(along with the plan to withdraw *Endurance*) that the UK did not
care too much about the Falklands. What was needed at that late
stage was an abandonment of quiet diplomacy and a full blast of
megaphone diplomacy from Mrs Thatcher announcing that any
invasion would be met with the fullest retaliation possible. The
view in his office was that the Argentines might have held back if
they had thought a nuclear-powered, or even a Polaris, boat was in
range of their coastline. But Whitehall remained silent and Carrington flew to the Middle East.

As it happens, the Israel tour was far from a success. Carrington
was as affable as ever, but his mind was elsewhere and the Israelis
never really trusted him. Relations were hardly helped in one
exchange during the obligatory visit to the Holocaust Museum,
described to me in later years: 'The display ended with a map of
the concentration camps in Germany and German-occupied
countries. The director said condescendingly to me, "I don't suppose you know anything about that?" I was able to point to one of
the concentration camps [Sandbostel] and say that my Division
and I actually liberated it and dreadful it was.'

In London, on Wednesday 31 March, Nott received the intercepted signal that the Argentine fleet was at sea and within two
days would be invading the islands. It seemed that the Argentines
had come to their own decision about diplomacy.

Nott later asserted that he did not take the matter seriously
until 31 March. That is either a statement of uncharacteristic
incompetence on his part or equally plausibly a failure by his
officials to keep him informed. There is also the possibility of a
lapse of memory or total lack of communication between Downing
Street, the Foreign Office and the MOD on the other side of

Whitehall. Now galvanized, Nott immediately went to see the Prime Minister in her room in the Commons. He took with him Sir Frank Cooper, the Permanent Under-Secretary at the Defence Ministry, and the acting Chief of the Defence Staff, Air Marshal Sir Michael Beetham. Also there with the PM were Sir Antony Acland – in his first week as head of the Diplomatic Service – Humphrey Atkins and Richard Luce, the two Foreign Office Ministers. Atkins was in charge because Carrington was in Israel and Luce was the minister responsible for relations with Argentina.

Nott had been told earlier in the week that any attempt to recapture the Falklands would require a major task force. The army and RAF thought this an almost impossible task, the Royal Navy did not. Nott told me that at the time, 'I did not think it was viable.' That evening in the Commons, Nott, the army and the RAF had not changed their view. It is clear that the First Sea Lord Admiral Sir Henry Leach disagreed. The background to Leach's strong opposition to Nott's thinking was his belief that the Defence Secretary was destroying the overall capability of the Navy. The confrontation between the two men was now coming to a head – in Margaret Thatcher's Commons room. Its origins went back to Nott's June 1981 Defence Review and had involved Carrington as Foreign Secretary. Carrington took Leach's side.

Carrington understood this confrontation for two reasons: his instincts, based on experience with the Defence Ministry since the 1950s, led him to understand that while reform was necessary, Nott's review was, at the Prime Minister's insistence, financially driven and therefore, in Carrington's view, misguided. But the lengths that Leach went to in order to overturn the 1981 review were beyond the normal tactics of the Navy's senior admiral. For example, in November 1981 Leach had had a meeting with Nott. In his forthright manner, the admiral told the Defence Secretary that he was making a mistake. According to Leach, Nott was angry and twitching.[9] Nott cut short the meeting and said he had a train to

9 Conversation with Admiral of the Fleet Sir Henry Leach, Wonston Lea, August 2004.

catch to Cornwall. Leach warned him that he would not be bullied
and fobbed off and that he would follow Nott to Cornwall. Nott
did not believe him. He should have because Leach caught the
next train.

Nott was staying at a friend's castle when at eight o'clock that
night, Leach banged on the door and demanded to see the Secretary
of State. They continued the argument, which Leach lost, and as he
drove in an ageing Hillman to catch the midnight train back to
Paddington, Leach contemplated that only a national emergency
would reverse the Defence Review decisions that, in his view,
neutered the major role of the Navy – defence of the sea lanes.
The plan included selling off the aircraft carrier HMS *Invincible*.

Leach's anxieties were further raised because he had doubts
about the attitude of the British ambassador to Buenos Aires. In
the summer of 2004 Leach confirmed to me that in 1982 there was
an opinion that Anthony Williams, the ambassador, intended to
retire in Argentina and did not want the boat rocked. (See p. 445.)
Equally, Leach believed there was a failure in Intelligence analysis
that was still suggesting that there was nothing untoward in Argentine military preparations. Leach outlined his reservations about
this analysis and sent it to Nott on the Tuesday before the invasion.
The following day, even though he felt apprehensive, Leach went
to inspect the naval shore establishment for anti-submarine research
near Portsmouth. He returned that evening at six o'clock. There
were two piles of briefs on his desk. The naval staff brief suggested
that what was going on in Argentina was simply a repetition of
what had been going on for sixteen years. The Intelligence brief
was, in Leach's words, 'unusually straight': the Argentines did mean
business and planned to invade the lesser islands on 2 April. Leach
went down to Nott's office, which was empty. He was told that the
Secretary of State had gone to see the PM in the Commons. That,
thought Leach, was reasonable. But when he was told that Nott
had taken Beetham with him, Leach became alarmed.

Without an escort and in full admiral's uniform, Leach sped
across to the House of Commons Central Lobby and told the
white-tie-and-tails-wearing staff that he wanted to see Nott

immediately in the PM's room. It is of course curious that an establishment such as the Commons, so used to elaborate livery, was suspicious of this middle-aged man in gold buttons and lace and scrambled-egg peak cap. The tallest policeman in the lobby detained Leach, whose mood was saved by the appearance of Junior Whips who took him into their room and plied him with large whiskies while a note was sent in to Nott that Leach was in the safe custody of the Whips and demanding to see him.

Eventually, he was escorted to the Prime Minister's room. There, as we have seen, he found Thatcher, Nott, Beetham, the ministers Atkins and Luce, together with the Whitehall mandarins Frank Cooper and Antony Acland.

Nott was nervous about the encounter because he knew the First Sea Lord did not trust him. He also knew that Leach had little regard for Beetham. Hardly surprisingly, therefore, Nott believed that Leach had tracked him down to the Commons and wanted to be heard because he thought it likely that Nott would kill a naval response to the invasion. Nott's position was that the other two services had stuck to their earlier assessment and had described the recapturing of the Falklands as virtually impossible. Unless Nott – a former soldier – took the Royal Navy's side, the army and RAF could be right. They said that there was no nearby runway from which to fly in reinforcements and logistics, nor was there a base for ground-attack and air-defence operations. All this was true. The nearest feasible runway was on Ascension Island. Moreover, the army could see nowhere that it might put together the sort of ground force necessary to land, fight, re-enforce that fight and then take the Falklands from what might have become a very entrenched Argentine force – and then defend their positions. Militarily, the RAF and army made sense. But Leach believed they lacked vision. He had runways: aircraft carriers. He had transport ships and re-fuelling vessels and could also charter troop transporters including cruise liners. It was all so simple to Leach but not to Nott and Beetham. However, Leach now had the floor.

According to Leach, in conversation with this author, Thatcher looked a little surprised at his arrival. He found himself sitting opposite her and so he asked if there was anything he could do. It seemed to him that they had already resolved to rely entirely on the diplomatic way forward. Leach said there was an alternative.

Thatcher now looked interested. Leach told her he could assemble a task force, including merchant ships taken up from trade; that could be done with an Order in Council. He was surprised at what he called her most stupid questions. She wanted him to have the *Ark Royal* there. He pointed out she had been scrapped three years earlier. Royal Naval Phantoms and Buccaneers, which she also wanted, had been given to the Royal Air Force.

Thatcher then said to him, 'Can we do it?'

Leach replied, 'Yes, we can and yes, we must ... If we do not, then in a very short time we'll be living in a very different country and our word will count for nothing.'

Leach remembers a long silence and a narrowing of Thatcher's eyes. He sensed he had stolen what would become her best line. He remembers Nott appearing flabbergasted and Thatcher not at all.

Leach then told the Prime Minister what she had not heard from Beetham or Nott. There was a major naval exercise off Gibraltar; he could restructure that exercise and turn it into an operational task force, and have the fleet to sea from the UK – in two days' time. This naturally appealed to Margaret Thatcher. She asked Leach what he needed and he simply said, 'Your permission to get on with it.'

He was quiet, calm and confident: 'I can put together a task force of destroyers, frigates, landing craft, support vessels. It will be led by the aircraft carriers, HMS *Hermes* and HMS *Invincible*. It can be ready to leave in forty-eight hours.' He believed such a force could retake the islands ... Before this, I had been outraged and determined. Now my outrage and determination were matched by a sense of relief and confidence. Henry Leach had shown me that if it came to a fight the courage and professionalism of Britain's armed forces would win through.[10]

10 Margaret Thatcher, *The Downing Street Years*, London: HarperCollins, 1993, p. 179.

On the Sunday, Leach was interrupted at dinner to be told he had the authority of the Prime Minister to sail the task force. The Chief of the Defence Staff Sir Terry Lewin was now back in London from New Zealand and immediately pulled the Chiefs of Staff together. By Monday 5 April, the military machine was back on the rails and Leach kept his promise to Thatcher: the task force sailed from Portsmouth that morning. True, it had few military stores on board and could not have gone into battle. But the public perception was so important to Thatcher and the Navy: the fleet sailed just as it had almost 180 years earlier from Portsmouth, when Nelson boarded *Victory* and sailed south to engage another enemy.

Carrington did not return to London from his trip to Israel until 1 April. By then, the Argentine invasion fleet was standing off the islands. The invasion started on Friday morning, 2 April. An emergency decision was taken to have the House sit on the Saturday. The Prime Minister opened that debate and Nott wound up. Nott endured a withering barrage of questions and comments. He appeared rattled and uncertain. However, he was used to the Commons bear-pit and the behaviour of MPs on both sides of the House. Considering the seriousness of the situation, Nott made a very good job of his replies to questions and his closing speech. Carrington had an altogether easier ride in the House of Lords, but this only angered MPs all the more: they could not get at him (which was one reason that Nott had such a hard time). But they would later, or at least Conservative MPs would.

Many who had never forgiven him for Rhodesia now took their revenge. Nott and Carrington went to a meeting of the Tory back-bench 1922 Committee. Nott, the commoner, was inured to the savage ways of the Commons, and anyway the MPs had had their sport with him that afternoon in the Chamber. But Carrington, even after all his years in politics, was not used to the hurly-burly of Parliament. He was treated with anger and, by some, with open contempt and undisguised scorn at that meeting. As they left the meeting and headed towards the Prime Minister's room in the Commons to report back, Carrington (according to

Nott) told him in the corridor outside the PM's room that he had had enough, that he believed that he should resign after the way he had just been treated by the 1922 Committee. To Nott's mind here was another example of Carrington not having learned his politics in the rough-and-tumble of the House of Commons. Nott told him that he must not resign and assured him that they could get through the whole affair. Nothing more was said and they both went in to see Thatcher and agreed that it had all gone badly.

That Saturday morning before the Falklands debate, Cabinet had been told that a task force was being sent and as far as Nott was concerned, Carrington's remark that he would resign was nothing more than a momentary loss of confidence in someone unused to dealing at that level of politics. For his part, Nott did not contemplate resigning. He did not feel responsible for what he called the drama. Moreover, he was later told by the Prime Minister that he was not responsible. The uncertainty in Carrington's mind persisted. All day he was vexed with the pressure on his position. That evening, he could no longer keep his anxiety to himself. He went to see Thatcher and said that he thought he should resign. She said he should not. Her deputy William Whitelaw agreed. Perhaps most importantly, Carrington's close friend Lord Nugent of Guildford thought he would be happier going. Nugent and Carrington had been the two junior ministers who offered their resignations to Churchill over Crichel Down.

Carrington was openly being criticized at Westminster and in the media for failing to control the Foreign Office and for having failed to anticipate what the Argentines were up to. He continued to contemplate resignation, and yet, in other ways, that weekend, in retrospect, seemed very ordinary for one at this high level of political and public life. On 1 April, as the invasion of the islands was under way, Carrington had to be at the London Coliseum with Lord Harewood and Princess Alexandra. The next day he lunched with the Mayor of Berlin, barely acknowledging the crisis. But beneath his urbane exterior, Carrington was deeply troubled, as he reflected at Bledlow in conversation with me:

It was mostly political. If I hadn't [resigned] and we were going to war people would go on saying here is the Foreign Secretary responsible and [he has] taken his eye off the main chance. Somebody had to cut their throat and I was the obvious person to cut their throat. I think Nott ought to have cut his throat too. But you couldn't have two of us going. She [Mrs Thatcher] didn't want me to at all. We lunched with Willie [Whitelaw] at Dorneywood on the Sunday. He tried to persuade me not to. I wasn't persuadable. It was painful. Lot of abuse. Being Foreign Secretary in the Lords didn't help. Conservative MPs already resented having a peer as Foreign Secretary. It's one of their plum jobs. And a lot of them didn't like me because of Rhodesia. Now we'll get our own back on the bugger. They were really like that. Teddy Taylors of this world. More or less said so.

He went to see his old mentor Alec Douglas-Home. Surely he would support him? 'Alec was rather ambivalent. He said I don't think you ought to.' Stay? Go? That was not so clear but they both knew Douglas-Home quietly thought it was the honourable thing to go.

By Sunday evening, Carrington was drafting his resignation, but had not sent it across to Number 10. While this was happening, Nott went to Portsmouth to see what was being done to get that part of the task force to sea. Publicly it was very impressive, because it included HMS *Hermes*, the aircraft carrier which would be the command and control ship for the seaborne operation.

Carrington awoke on the Monday morning to face a devastating attack in the leader column of *The Times* written by its editor, Charlie Douglas-Home (nephew of Sir Alec). He thundered that the Argentine government had acted in the reasonably held belief that the British had given the impression that they did not care very much for the Falkland islanders. 'It is,' wrote *The Times*, 'late to prove them wrong but not too late. The whole structure of this country's standing in the world, her credibility as an ally, as a guarantor of guarantees, as a protector of her citizens, depends on that willpower existing and being seen to exist.' Its message was simple: Carrington had to go. But it was the column's headline that decided him that the paper's sentiment was correct: *We are all Falklanders now*. Nothing said by colleagues nor family would now stop him resigning. He was, after all, a resigner and had had enough of the vitriol thrown at him by MPs and newspaper editors since his return from Israel.

While Carrington was sending his resignation across to Thatcher, Nott was getting on with the business of going to war. He went to Windsor to get the Queen's signature on the Orders that would allow the operation to proceed to the next point. Neither he nor his very experienced and calm Permanent Under-Secretary Sir Frank Cooper knew that Carrington was resigning. When he found out that Carrington had not changed his mind after that remark in the Commons corridor, Nott was furious. During all this time no one had even hinted to Nott that Carrington was seriously discussing resignation, yet plenty of people knew. Nott's view was simple: there was a crisis and an extremely important job to be done to make the best of it. This was no time to weaken the system or the government by offering resignations.

Nott returned to the Defence Ministry and at 11.30 on the Monday morning he received a telephone call from his junior minister, Jerry Wiggin. Wiggin had gone to RAF Brize Norton with the Foreign Office Minister Richard Luce to greet the Royal Marine detachment that had been evacuated from the Falklands via Montevideo. Wiggin asked John Nott if he knew that all Foreign Office ministers – including Carrington – were going to resign in thirty minutes' time, that is, midday on 5 April. Nott was astonished and immediately rang 10 Downing Street and asked to speak to Thatcher. He wanted to know if the resignation story were true and if it were, then why had he not been informed? He then told her that he would have to think about his own position. Nott said he would ring back in ten minutes. When he did, Nott told Thatcher that he too would resign. Thatcher told him that he could not. He replied that he was in such an impossible position that he had no alternative. If Carrington went and he did not, then publicly, Carrington would appear honourable and he, Nott, would appear cynical. Thatcher disagreed and it was at this point that she told him that it was all the fault of the Foreign and Commonwealth Office and not his Defence Ministry. Once again Nott said that he would call her back.

His private secretary David Ormand, who at the time of the 2003 Iraq War became Cabinet coordinator of security and intelligence, told him to stay, as did Sir Frank Cooper.

Nott then called the Prime Minister and told her that the only circumstance in which he would not go was that his letter of resignation was published and her refusal to accept it was also published. Nott was thoroughly annoyed with the Prime Minister and remained so for ever. He believed that she and Carrington had deliberately kept from him Carrington's proposal to resign. Losing Carrington was bad enough, but to lose all the Foreign Office Ministers and the Defence Secretary would have weakened her authority. Nott was right. He was put in the position of appearing to be dishonourable. While Carrington would always be regarded as a man of great honour, a Whig who would put his duty to Queen and country before personal ambition, Nott believed, wrongly as it turned out, that he would be remembered as a guilty minister who held on to his job. There was an irony in the resignation position of Nott, although he did not realize it – his demand that the price for his staying was publication of his resignation letter and the Prime Minister's rejection was exactly what Peter Carrington had done in 1954. Then he had offered his resignation to Churchill over the Crichel Down Affair. On that occasion the Prime Minister had decided that to lose a second minister was careless. Almost thirty years on nothing much had changed.

Carrington resigned at midday on Monday 5 April.

My Dear Margaret

The Argentine invasion of the Falkland Islands has led to strong criticism in Parliament and in the press of the Government's policy. In my view, much of the criticism is unfounded. But I have been responsible for the conduct of that policy and I think it right that I should resign. As you know, I have given long and careful thought to this. I warmly appreciate the kindness and support which you showed me when we discussed this matter on Saturday. But the fact remains that the invasion of the Falkland Islands has been a humiliating affront to this country.

We must now, as you said in the House of Commons, do every-thing we can to uphold the right of the Islanders to live in peace, to choose their own way of life and to determine their own alle-giance. I am sure that this is the right course, and one which deserves the undivided support of Parliament and of the country. But I have concluded with regret that this support will more easily be maintained if the Foreign Office is entrusted to someone else.

I have been privileged to be a member of this Government and to be associated with its achievements over the past three years. I need hardly say that the Government will continue to have my active support. I am most grateful to you personally for the unfail-ing confidence you have shown in me.

He drove to Windsor for the formality of surrendering his seals of office to the Queen and at 2.30 p.m. he went to Westminster Abbey to give the eulogy at the memorial service for R. A. Butler. 'I could imagine Rab up there somewhere smiling down on the whole affair,' he recalled twenty-five years later. 'Better off out of it.' Carrington had admired Butler all his political life as one of the small group who had restructured the Conservative Party after the disaster of the 1945 election. There is perhaps some irony in the thought that Carrington admired Butler's political philosophy that sometimes the best course of action was to do nothing.

In retrospect, might he have behaved differently? He had tried his best to get Nott to reverse the decision to withdraw *Endurance*, yet he had not pressed Thatcher hard enough to reach a political settlement while it was still possible, and he had relied too much on the Intelligence Services. Such failures can too easily lead to disaster. And that is precisely what happened.

It was not just Tory back-benchers who were after him – the media too gave him no respite. He came face to face with one of his accusers on the very evening of his going, when he agreed to go on the BBC *Panorama* programme to be interviewed by Robert

Kee. Kee accused him of not keeping his eye on the ball. Carrington pointed out that as Foreign Secretary there were a lot of balls to keep an eye on. Moreover, the Falklands Island desk never let their subject out of their sight.

There was something in this argument and yet Carrington was dogged by the truth that ever since January, commentators in the media and analysts in think tanks had been discussing the very real possibility of an invasion of the Falkland Islands. It could hardly be an answer that, as Carrington put it, the Argentine question had been around for twenty or thirty years, during which time the Argentine governments had blown hot and cold. There were also public questions to be answered as to why he was out of the country. The same questions might have been asked of the Defence Secretary, John Nott, as to why he had allowed his Chief of the Defence Staff, Admiral of the Fleet Sir Terence Lewin, to be as far away as New Zealand. Carrington's view, held privately at the time and only expressed to the author in 2004, was that the intelligence reports received by him and by the Defence Secretary were complete failures of analysis.

Carrington was briefed through MI6, after the event, that the Argentines had not made up their minds to invade until as late as 29 March. Every logistical assessment of even the most junior military intelligence officer should have advised Nott and Carrington that this was nonsense. When Carrington asked how it was that the military transports were loaded up if it were such a last-minute decision, he was advised that they were quite often in that state and anyway, they were going off on exercise.

Yet still Carrington had been told before he went to Israel that something was likely to happen. After all, he had made a statement in the House on the Tuesday before the invasion. He had had a meeting with Thatcher on the Thursday. She told him to go to Israel. Though he had five other ministers at the Foreign Office to help handle the situation, he was the boss and, in spite of the telephone, telex and diplomatic cable messages to him in Tel Aviv, he should have been in London.

In the Robert Kee interview, Carrington attempted publicly to defend the intelligence assessment. Yet his claim that, 'I don't think so much the intelligence was lacking. On what we knew, the judgements that I made as Foreign Secretary were sensible and right', sounded, even at the time, lame. Kee went on to lay bare failures in the Foreign Office, right up to the question of whether Carrington's resignation in fact let the Prime Minister down. Did it not undermine the confidence in government just when the country was embarking on a most hazardous exercise?

Carrington could not understand the journalistic logic. Perhaps he never properly understood the media and even the public it represented, or claimed to. How was it that he could be accused of incompetence and in the next breath be asked why he was resigning? If you were incompetent, you resigned. He had tried it before and this time he had succeeded, only to be accused of letting the side down. Thatcher too was in the television studios. In one interview with ITN, she explained why she let Carrington resign, especially when she knew that his successor Francis Pym had no experience of the department.

I had no alternative, I spent a lot of time on Saturday and on Sunday trying to persuade him not to put in his resignation. He felt that he'd been head of the department responsible for the policy, the policy had failed and therefore it was a matter of honour that he should go. If a person says to me, 'It's a matter of honour and I feel I should go,' that's the one ground on which I am not at liberty to refuse because it would make it difficult for him ... Lord Carrington felt that he was in charge of the Foreign Office at the time and there is not much point in going back and seeing whether we could have perceived that this was different from all the previous occasions [the Argentines had threatened to invade], it turned out to be different and there's no point in refuting that fact ... he felt so strongly about the point of honour and after all it is rather a wonderful thing in politics to have people who feel strongly about honour and who [are prepared to] resign.[11]

11 Extract from ITN interview, Thatcher with Glyn Mathias, 5 April 1982.

Who was to succeed him? Thatcher was in a quandary because the obvious candidate was a man she, in Carrington's opinion, detested – Francis Pym. But there was no one in her political entourage with any standing left to become Foreign Secretary.

When I went to see her, I said who are you going to appoint? She was terribly nervous about it. She said, 'I must have Francis Pym.' But I said, you hate Francis Pym. She said, 'Yes. But he's the only one who has political stature who I could make Foreign Secretary.' I said you're going to live to regret it. She did too.

Perhaps that is why Thatcher never again trusted any Foreign Secretary. David Owen, in an address to the London School of Economics, twenty years later, maintained that from that moment 10 Downing Street took over the running of British foreign policy.[12]

That night, Carrington returned from Whitehall a sad and bewildered figure. He knew that he had failed, not so much in diplomacy, but in Cabinet. There was his greatest weakness. In spite of his special position as a senior Cabinet minister and someone especially close to Thatcher, he could not persuade the rest of the Cabinet – not a single member – that they should accept his advice on his own subject. Therefore, the theory that he had resigned because he accepted full responsibility for his department is not fully supported in the evidence in the body of the Franks Report on the Falklands.[13] While it is easy to say that the FCO had many failings during the events that led to the war, it would seem that most of the failures were with the politicians. Franks observed that Carrington's officials warned his ministers that an Argentine attack was quite possible and that he should convince the Cabinet and the Prime Minister that this was not an impossibility, perhaps even a likelihood. Franks also suggested that Carrington had not

12 Lord Owen, *The Ever Growing Dominance of No 10 in British Diplomacy since 5th April 1982.*
13 Command 8787.

followed his officials' advice and asked for an exceptional meeting of the Cabinet Defence Committee to bring the seriousness of the situation to the PM in that manner. One official at the time thought that Carrington had a less than perfect relationship with Thatcher, and because he anticipated that her reaction over the Falklands would be to interfere with other matters too, he did not push the issue. Carrington was the first to admit that mistakes were made and that he made some of them. He was probably right to argue that the Falklands issue in its preventable stage became lost in the pile of political issues that at the time seemed more urgent. Moreover, only a military demonstration against the determination of a teetering dictator could have changed the course of this strand of Britain's history during the opening months of 1982. Making known that armed nuclear-powered submarines were deployed in the South Atlantic – whether or not they were – might have had some influence.

Whether or not the maintenance of the *Endurance* on station would have made much difference will always be open to question, although Leach, in conversation with the author, thought it unlikely. That Carrington was inclined to a partnership with the Argentines over the future of the Falklands would never have been allowed to gather pace in the Thatcher Cabinet.

The theme during that questioning by the Franks Committee[14] centred on the withdrawal of HMS *Endurance* – a decision taken by Nott in his June 1981 Defence Review. Franks told Carrington that while it was appreciated that he had opposed withdrawal,

The view that we have formed is that the decision to withdraw *Endurance* was probably not a wise one and that we think it would have been better if the government, and I suppose that means the Foreign Secretary, had insisted more strongly on the retention of *Endurance* either in his relationship with the Defence Secretary or by taking it to Cabinet.

14 Lord Franks, Chairman, Lord Barber, Lord Lever of Manchester, Sir Patrick Nairne, Mr Merlyn Rees MP and Lord Watkinson.

Carrington's response was one that reflected the reality of the government's position at the time and not one uttered with hindsight.

When I heard – and of course I was not consulted about *Endurance* – that it was proposed to scrap *Endurance* I immediately wrote a letter in June and in June we had a discussion about this. It was quite clear to me that there was no possibility whatever of getting my colleagues to change their mind about this, and this did not have much relationship to the Falkland Islands, it had a relation to the Defence Review, because it was the Defence Review in which the *Endurance* was being scrapped.

The fundamental position on *Endurance* was that Carrington was a political realist. He had been in every Tory government since 1951 and he knew exactly what his late friend R. A. Butler had meant when he noted that politics is the art of the possible. On the question of *Endurance* there was never a chance that he would get the Cabinet to change Nott's decision. In fact the Cabinet was far more sensitive to the overall adverse media response to the 1981 Defence Review and picking on one item was never a political option. Carrington tried to reverse the decision but when he went into Downing Street and spoke against withdrawing the ship he had not one single person on his side.

The collective Royal Navy and Falkland Islands lobby in Parliament tried to get Nott to change his mind but Carrington, in the Lords, had little to do with the lobbies. Franks was not impressed. It did seem that in spite of the apparent impartiality of the Committee, in spite of personal friendships, Franks needed someone to blame. As Carrington had already resigned, he was a reasonable target.

This was certainly Carrington's view when, having given evidence, he found he was the only witness called back in December 1982 to answer more questions.

I understand that I am the only person who is being asked to come back here, so I take it that I am the only person who is being criticised ...

therefore the fact that you intend, unless I persuade you differently today, to criticise me is central to your report, therefore of very great importance to me . . . I hope that you will judge my actions on what I knew and not on what you know now and what I know now, because these two things are very different.

In January 1983 he and his friends felt a counterattack against Franks was needed. A speech was prepared in which he was to say,

In the agitation and frustration of the moment, there were many criticisms, some partisan, others arising from genuine confusion and dismay. There were allegations of incompetence against individuals, against the Foreign and Commonwealth Office, against Government and its agencies; and there were wrangles about what had or had not been done by previous Governments. Some of the debates and Press articles at that time make ugly reading, and are best forgotten.

Carrington was not against the principle of the Franks Inquiry. He made it clear that for the sake of history and above all for the sake of those who had died, it was important to establish what had happened. His conclusion – not recognized by all who read it – was that Franks had decided that the Falklands War was not the result of 'culpable folly by British Ministers or Governments but of the gross irresponsibility of an unstable and unpredictable military dictatorship'. These were not his original sentiments because the author of his speech was not Carrington but George Walden, who had been his Principal Private Secretary and was leaving the FCO to become Conservative MP for Buckingham. He delivered the text with a helpful note:

Foreign and Commonwealth Office,
10 January 1983

Dear Lord Carrington,
The enclosed notes may be of help to you in deciding what you

do *not* want to say; thereby stimulating a brilliant synthetic motion, from which will emerge a splendid speech!

Yours ever,

George

P. S. No one else has seen this.

Walden knew Carrington very well indeed and was not alone in wishing to make sure he was not the scapegoat, even though some, including the former Labour Leader Jim Callaghan, called the report a whitewash. Carrington had anticipated the criticism and would always feel hurt by it.

I have no wish to dwell on my own feelings on reading Lord Franks's conclusions. The gravity of the events he discusses transcends personalities. But only a saint would feel no temptation to clarify his own role now that it is possible to do so openly ... I accept that everything we did could have been done a little better.

It has been suggested that my resignation was an ill-conceived act of personal pique: or, more generously that it was an antiquated act of chivalry. The truth is that it was neither. I resigned for two reasons:

There was an undeniable feeling in this country that Britain's honour and dignity had been seriously affronted ... this widespread sense of impotent outrage understandably sought an outlet. The Foreign and Commonwealth Office is always a convenient target on such occasions and I happened to be at its head. This was not time for self-justificatory explanations, and certainly not to be accused of clinging to office. The honour of the country seemed to me more important than my own.

You do not enter a war amid a welter of recrimination about who was responsible for it. As I said at the time, I did not accept the criticism levelled at me or at the FCO. But I did accept the responsibility of my position at the centre of a controversy which could have been damaging to this country at a time of national emergency. It was my duty to clarify the situation by going: so I went.

There were those who cheered his going long after the event. Many had never forgiven him for what they saw as giving in to the black majority in Rhodesia. Now they wanted him punished over the Falklands. In 1983 Carrington was in no mood to publicly cast blame at anyone. That would have been churlish and unwise. But in 2004 Carrington reflected to me that Thatcher was adamant that there could be no compromise during any negotiations with the Argentine government before April 1982 because she believed that compromise was weakness.

It was the sort of wet thing that everybody but her would do. It was clear as time went on that we would have to be lucky . . . you could really only prolong the thing by tweaking and we had nothing [no real plan] to talk about so it made it that much more difficult. Nick Ridley was hardly a wet and he wanted some form of leaseback. It kept the dialogue going. I thought we could go on for a bit because of the Intelligence assessment that we'd get plenty of warning . . . Then of course that was a mistake, that was an error. Perhaps I should have known it was an error. You relied on the Int. assessment but you had a political problem. Not only Margaret, but the whole House of Commons was violently opposed to any agreement with the Argentines. The right wing of the [Conservative] Party was hostile to the idea of a lot of bloody foreigners and the left wing of the Labour Party was hostile to the idea of any accommodation with a dictatorship. So both parties were united against doing anything. It was the Commons that buggered the whole thing up really as well as Margaret. When it all happened, they turned round and bit. Which I think was a little bit unfair after what they'd done.

How was it that the Cabinet saw Carrington's memo on the consequences of not coming to an agreement with Argentina, but persisted in doing nothing about it? Carrington believed that the Cabinet was far too influenced by the Commons, even when they knew the Commons could not know the true story.

The mistake that I made was to believe that over a period of time, reality would break through. They'd realize they had to do something. That was again on the Intelligence assessment that nothing was going to happen without due warning. That was wrong. In retrospect one ought to have pressed harder for something to be done by government. You could have sent the fleet there with Margaret but that wasn't necessarily such a sensible thing to do. Owen and Callaghan said they sent a submarine down when they faced the same situation and stopped it. It is said that they let it be known they'd sent those vessels. But they didn't.

When I was Secretary [of State] for Defence and also when I was First Lord when people used to talk about the Falklands, the Chiefs of Staff said if the Argentines took the Falklands there was no way we could get them back . . . but we did. They did.

Margaret had to do it; she couldn't have survived otherwise. If only they had listened in the first place. I said we must have a contingency plan. But no one was doing anything. The MOD was retrenching. Nott was removing the ship [*Endurance*] that I kept writing to him and telling him not to do. There was no support for me, not from her and not from anybody else. No Intelligence support, no political support and none from Margaret. The whole thing was probably inevitable. I actually blame Margaret, I think she was too intransigent, and I blame myself. I could have pressed harder. One relied too much on the quality of Intelligence. All sources thought they knew. It was difficult to query it.

Perhaps all my political life I've relied too much on the people round me. On the whole, high-class people. If you go back to all the incidents that never turned out to be wars, there's a limit to what the Foreign Secretary can do in the time available. But there you are. One still wonders what one could have done that was any different. If I had insisted on sending a couple of subs and let it be known. That's the one thing that bothers me.

Clearly, it could be said that Carrington was not tough enough at the Foreign Office. One official in the department mentioned to me that Carrington was always considered relaxed. Yet beneath his easy-going style, there is a very uncompromising character. Very likely the FCO was not very good in its analysis and the presentation of that analysis to its ministers, though one of those ministers, Nick Ridley, seemed to suggest that Carrington had had plenty of ammunition to take to the Cabinet.

Ridley wrote to Carrington on 27 December 1982 that as early as August 1981 he had written to him detailing his views on what should be done.

> Early September 1981. I put a draft paper for O. D. [Overseas & Defence Committee] to you, which suggested the need to 'sweeten' the Islanders as well as do some contingency planning
>
> 7 September 1981. You and I had a meeting to discuss the draft O. D. paper. The minutes are available 'though I do not have them. As a result you put on,
>
> 14 September 1981. A minute to the PM (*not* to the O. D. committee), which may have been slightly different to the O. D. draft paper. Franks didn't ask me about this incident at all.

Many of Ridley's colleagues and friends believed that it was he above all individuals who was to blame for the failure of the government to prevent the invasion. They claimed that Ridley's assertion to the Cabinet that he would have Parliament on his side when he proposed leaseback was due to bad parliamentary footwork and an excess of arrogance. Parliament rejected Ridley's plan. Having done so, that was a public demonstration as far as the Argentines were concerned of Britain's refusal to do anything about the Malvinas.

If three decades on the whole Falklands–Carrington affair seems a piece of arcane political history, there remains one seemingly bizarre story that, if true, suggests an inexplicable lack of authority of the FCO over the British embassy in Buenos Aires. Carrington's private office knew that the British ambassador, Anthony Williams, did not want London's interference. There had been an occasion when the embassy objected most strongly to a suggestion from Carrington that a senior official should be sent from London to assess the situation and report on the efficiency of the embassy's analysis. The embassy gave a point-blank refusal for the visit on the grounds that it would undermine the ambassador's authority. Carrington said that the trip was never made and that there was nothing he could do to override the ambassador. Later, when Carrington was NATO Secretary-General, he talked to the Swiss ambassador to Brussels, Gaspard Bodner, who had been in his own country's embassy in Buenos Aires at the time of the war. The Swiss ran the British interest section for the duration. Bodner confirmed to me in 1997 what Carrington had heard elsewhere but had not wished to believe.

He [Bodner] came to see me and said he was the Swiss chargé d'affaires who was put in charge of British things in Buenos Aires during the Falklands war. The embassy was horrified at what the British ambassador was doing because he was withholding information on the grounds that he wanted to settle and make his career in the Argentine after he retired. He didn't send some of the information to the Foreign Office. My experience of Williams was that when I wanted to send somebody out there to make an assessment of what was going on, he sat on his dignity and he said that he was the man in charge and didn't want anybody interfering. I only met him once when he had subsequently become the ambassador to the disarmament talks in Geneva. I was taking the chair in NATO. He was representing the British government and when he started to speak I very noisily pushed my chair back and walked out of the room.

I did write all this to the FO and to Antony Acland [the Permanent Under-Secretary], but he said let sleeping dogs lie. Can't think what Williams would get out of it unless he was trying to ingratiate himself in a treasonable way, which I find difficult to believe.

Sir Antony Acland told me that he did not remember the incident. Robin Stafford, who would later become Carrington's Press Secretary at NATO, confirmed that he had known Williams for some years and that such action seemed out of character. Carrington and several of his FCO officials believed otherwise. I also spoke to Bodner in Switzerland and he endorsed Carrington's impression and what he believed to be Williams's motive.

If Carrington's people did have problems with the ambassador, whose job was it to make sure the Foreign Secretary's wishes overcame those of the local ambassador? If Carrington was let down by Williams and his own private office, then some might have judged that Carrington was not being firm enough.

14. South Ken to Bruxelles

There were those who continued to believe that Carrington's going produced the result he intended: his resignation satisfied the thirst for political blood; it anticipated and so neutered any future inquiry; it hid the deeper frailties within the Thatcher government's Falklands policy. Whatever the outcome, his departure from the Foreign Office was the lowest point of his political career. He was now an ex-Cabinet minister and for most in his position being an ex-Cabinet minister is rather like being an ex-husband: people take sides, one is portrayed as wretched, the other as a wretch, and conclusively there is no turning back the clock. If Carrington had been an MP he would have had some life on the back-benches in politics. As a peer there was not much for him in the Palace of Westminster other than his interventions and debates in the Upper House. These speeches were usually well attended and well noted.

That he resigned added to the Carrington reputation as a man of considerable honour, and there was always a ready audience in case he let fly his frustrations over the events of March and April 1982. He did not. Given the way of politics towards the end of the twentieth century, ministerial responsibility had become an honourable thing of the past. Resignation was in the 1980s and 1990s a matter for ministers who were in disgrace, avoiding disgrace or simply wishing to spend more time with their families – of whom some ministers seemed to have more than one.

Carrington's anxiety that year was not brought about by the rights and wrongs of his going from the FCO. Deep down, he nursed a greater concern: he did not want to be remembered as nothing more than the Secretary of State who resigned, however honourable a reputation went with that action.

Carrington's ministerial career, which had started in Churchill's administration, had been spent mainly in defence and foreign affairs. Apart from being Leader of the House of Lords, it is very difficult to see what other Cabinet job Carrington might have done if Thatcher or her successors had wanted him back after a suitable period in the political sin-bin. He did not have to think very hard to understand this and it is not surprising that, during those days immediately after resignation, Carrington had few thoughts for politics and none for a political future. He did not wish to think about anything much at all other than family and friends. The Carringtons had been married for forty years that April and the children were determined that they should celebrate. On 5 April, the day he resigned, he gave instructions to stop the newspapers and took few calls. People wanted to see him but understandably he only really wanted to see close friends. His oldest friend David Fraser and his wife drove over to Bledlow for the evening. It was a quiet affair with little deep reflection of what might have been and even less about what the future might hold.

There were immediate offers of jobs, but he was not too enthusiastic. Lord Weinstock wanted to see him, although Carrington did not particularly want to return to GEC, and the Rothschilds came quietly for drinks. On 22 April Margaret Thatcher gave a farewell party for him at Lancaster House. He remembered it as an affair that he would have preferred not to attend. It was much easier to slip away anonymously with the children and Iona for their ruby wedding in the Loire. But that long, quiet weekend was one of the few blanks in the Carrington diary for the rest of his life. He returned to Bledlow without any feelings of rancour and sensing that he had not retired from public life. Indeed, he felt he still had plenty more to offer.

Carrington was now sixty-three. He was at an age where many, even senior, directors of a board might consider retirement if they had been forced out. But leaving Thatcher's board of ministers was no reason to cultivate roses. Such was his popularity that during the next twenty years, Carrington appeared to be as busy if not busier than ever before. Immediately, it was clear that the style of his resignation had not caused many institutions to wonder if his stewardship of the Foreign Office and Britain's interests had indeed been lax. The honours flowed in and so too came very senior appointments. The year that he resigned he became an honorary fellow of St Anthony's College, Oxford, the University of the Philippines awarded him an honorary doctorate of law (both the universities of Leeds and Cambridge had awarded him similar doctorates the previous year) and he became chairman of the Commonwealth Trust. The following year there was another doctorate of law, this time from the University of South Carolina, he became dean of Essex University, an honorary bencher of the Middle Temple, president of the Pilgrims and president of Voluntary Service Overseas. Accepting these honours and appointments showed Carrington's good judgement. But he made the wrong decision when he agreed to join GEC.

Carrington had a miserable time at GEC. He was quite unsuited to the task. After his resignation from the government, his friends had rallied. Two of his oldest chums seemed determined that he should not drift into some institutional sinecure where his talents and sound international reputation would be wasted. A decade earlier, when he was Defence Secretary, Carrington had worked with Arnold Weinstock, the head of GEC. In February 1971 Rolls-Royce, which had traded precariously for some time, went under.

The British military had very much relied on Rolls-Royce engineering and Heath's government's view was that even the name Rolls-Royce was such a distinctive trademark of Britain that the title, if not the company in its existing form, had to be rescued. The car division was set aside and Carrington was given the task to nationalize what was left. He and the then Attorney General Peter Rawlinson devoted practically all their waking moments to the nationalization project. It was complicated because the American aircraft manufacturer Lockheed had designed the Tristar aircraft around the Rolls-Royce 211 engine. If Rolls-Royce could not produce the engine then Lockheed were in trouble and once again there would be more than a dent in the transatlantic relationship that Britain so prized and which the United States promoted when it found it to be useful. Carrington persuaded a handful of his City friends to take part in the rescue operation by becoming members of the board that nationalized Rolls-Royce. It is doubtful if any of those that sat on that board particularly wanted to or enjoyed their task and most of them were probably there because of their friendship with Carrington. Among them was Arnold Weinstock. Forward then to 1982 and Carrington's resignation. Weinstock and Sir Ronald Grierson stood by their old friend in his hour of need.

Ronnie Grierson was then the vice-chairman of GEC, which was run by the autocratic Weinstock. It was Grierson who more than anyone else pressed Carrington to join GEC at a difficult time in his career. Grierson realized much later that Carrington saw it as a non-job. That was not so, but it was not the sort of job Carrington should have been doing. Arnold Weinstock had built GEC singlehandedly. The chairman of GEC really didn't have a job to do. Grierson would see Carrington perhaps three times a week at lunch and although Carrington never said so, it was clear to Grierson that he was unhappy. Carrington had taken over from Lord Nelson of Stafford, who apparently was content with the passive role of chairman.

Much of the task of the chairman was to travel around soothing, reassuring and encouraging people in high places. That sounds a pretty straightforward job where the holder simply gets on an aeroplane, is flown to yet another capital city, attends a function or two, has meaningful talks which will either prompt a contract which the GEC salesman had prepared the way for or, in some cases, save a deal that has started to falter under the weight of international politics and even changes of government policies at home and abroad.

By the nature of the GEC business, quite a bit of this commercial glad-handing was with sensitive governments in sensitive areas. For example, part of the company included Marconi Avionics Limited. This organization was involved in the development of military airborne early-warning systems.

In the spring of 1977 the United Kingdom government, frustrated by its traditional allies' inability to come to a sound decision that would have meant the buying of American AWACS (Airborne Warning and Control System) aircraft, decided to make a British version called Airborne Early Warning Nimrod. This was to be based on the old Comet airliner.

British Aerospace was responsible for the aircraft, including the navigational systems. Marconi Avionics had the radar, the passive listening sensors, the 'sentries' – the system that identified whether another aircraft was friend or foe – and all the data-handling systems which allowed the aircrew to monitor the whole operation. Clearly GEC, Marconi and British Aerospace believed there was huge export business to be had. One of the countries that was targeted by GEC was Iraq. It is necessary to remember that until Saddam Hussein's headstrong excursion into Kuwait in the August of 1990, Iraq was a client state of Britain and the United States.

An Iraqi delegation was brought to the United Kingdom in January 1982. In April of that year the defence sales team of the Ministry of Defence, British Aerospace and Rolls-Royce (the Carrington package to save it had been successful) went to Baghdad. They went back three months later. The key man was the Iraqi Head of Airforce Procurement, Major General Amir Rashid. Rashid was very much an Anglophile and had taken a science degree at Birmingham University. The Defence Secretary, John Nott, strongly supported the Nimrod sale to Iraq even though he had to get Margaret Thatcher's permission to, if necessary, give the Iraqis two Nimrods intended for the Royal Air Force. This she did in November 1982.

In a confidential memo to Carrington in November 1982, P. F. Mariner, GEC's assistant managing director, wrote:

... the achievement of an Iraq agreement to the reopening of the Nimrod production line and the potential deal is ... important to overall UK exports. GEC has, however, further potential outlets ...

There was nothing unusual in Carrington finding himself if not at the centre, then by now wafting as an international *éminence grise* over such sensitive issues. Yet some of the briefings given to him, on what to all intents and purposes were simple goodwill visits, were sometimes hair-raising. For example, when Carrington set off for a Middle East trip in 1982 his briefing notes included 'the Zionist plan for the Middle East'. It had been prepared by Professor Israel Shahak in June 1982 at the Hebrew University. Carrington went on that tour suspecting that the ambitions of Israel had to be countered and that the need to bolster the military significance of her neighbours made political, tactical and strategic as well as of course commercial sense. For example, he was told that an Israel under Ariel Sharon would have a plan for the whole Middle East 'which is based on the division of the whole area into small states and the dissolution of all the existing Arab states ... the idea that all the Arab states should be broken down by Israel, into small units, occurs again and again in Israeli strategic thinking ...'

From Carrington's point of view, commercial dealing in the Middle East was simply fraught with political, military and, to him importantly, moral difficulties. During his time at GEC, Carrington would often wonder about the moral implications of international arms sales. Even non-military commercial directions could, he reasoned, present moral difficulties because of what they would either allow a stressed economy to do where before it could not, or because they could drain resources that were badly needed for the everyday survival of a nation state's people. Carrington reflected that given 75 per cent of the world did not live under what he would call a democracy, any organization such as GEC would always face what the average person might consider a moral dilemma.

Certainly the interests of GEC were, by the simple arrangements of globalization, bound to run up against commercial partners and governments, and inevitably this could lead to criticism that moral issues clashed with simple business arrangements.

For example, in November 1983 Carrington showed up in

Malaysia, where GEC had offices in Penang, Malacca, Kuching and Kuala Lumpur. GEC were having to accept business partnerships in Malaysia which they might otherwise have been reluctant to countenance – GEC preferred to have as few partners as possible. Carrington found himself mixed up in corporate and political discussion which revealed, according to a private company assessment, that 'local equity participation is inevitable if GEC is to continue to prosper in Malaysia. To date the issue has not been too serious, [but] the pressure is increasing . . . we must not allow pressure to build until it is a public issue – that would ruin our good reputation . . .'[1]

Weinstock understood only too well the importance of Carrington in the role of 'international smoothy'. The visit to Malaysia was an example of how the sometimes fickle political hierarchy in that part of the world could frustrate Weinstock's commercial ambitions. Carrington's autumn 1983 visit indeed smoothed what had sometimes been anxious relations between GEC and individuals in the Malaysian government. In a private letter to Weinstock, the senior local director of GEC in Malaysia, Datuk A. P. Arumugam, noted that it was important that Carrington should keep in contact with the Malaysian Prime Minister, who was not always an easy man to do business with. Dr Mahathir was a key figure in relations with GEC. The visit came at a sensitive time because Mahathir's government was right in the middle of what was known as the Bank Bumiputra scandal. It was true also that most of the people that Carrington would have to deal with were caught up in this local difficulty. However, according to the Kuala Lumpur office of GEC, Carrington pulled off what was almost the impossible. Mahathir warmed to him, apparently sensing some chemistry with the English peer. The plum to be pulled from this political pie was a multimillion-pound contract to modernize the local railway system; also, the more sensitive matter of command-and-control and communication systems for the Malaysian armed forces. In later years Dr Mahathir's reputation was such that what-

1 Internal GEC Report, 24 November 1983.

ever chemistry there had been between himself and Carrington had turned to a dark gelatinous precipitate.

Some believed that a further difficulty for GEC operating in the Middle East was the fact that the company was owned by a Jew. This was not true. By and large, international trading is quite capable of ignoring such prejudice. A contract was far more likely to flounder because its terms and conditions were inadequate than because of the ethnic background or religious persuasions of those who operated it. Where GEC at the time did struggle, especially in putting together important deals in Saudi Arabia, was with its association with the American company Monsanto.

It was here that Carrington's diplomatic skills stood him in good stead. Grierson believed that it was largely due to Carrington that GEC did not suffer because of its relationship with Monsanto.

Carrington did not see himself as a long-lasting chairman for Arnold Weinstock, although the latter most definitely wanted him to be. Carrington arranged his own departure and the appointment of his successor, the former Conservative minister Jim Prior, who had been one of the many victims of Margaret Thatcher's political mood changes and suffered from her opinion that he was a Cabinet Wet beyond redemption.

Prior had been, as Northern Ireland Secretary, very much involved in the early stages of the Anglo-Irish Agreement. He had followed Humphrey Atkins to the Northern Ireland Office and had led from the front the support for the government's Northern Ireland White Paper, which was intended to strengthen the hands of so-called moderate nationalists. Margaret Thatcher never believed that to be workable. They did not often see eye to eye. In the late summer of 1984 Carrington resigned as chairman of GEC and Prior quit as Northern Ireland Secretary to take over from Carrington. Weinstock never really liked Prior, but Prior turned the job of chairman into what it really was, that of an international salesman at the highest level. He did particularly well during the political confrontation with Malaysia.

Carrington meanwhile was once more on the move and, apparently having failed to learn the lessons of the early seventies,

was attempting to hold down two jobs. Poisoned chalices came
Carrington's way rather easily.

Carrington now passed through what should have been a thoroughly enjoyable interlude but turned out to be quite disagreeable.
In June 1982 it was necessary to find a chairman for the newly
formed Board of Trustees of the Victoria and Albert Museum. This
was not meant to be a non-job. The V&A was going through a
period of great transition under its sometime brilliant and never
less than interesting director Roy Strong, who had successfully
directed the National Portrait Gallery for six years until 1973.
Strong had promoted a sense of vigour and energy at the gallery
during his fifteen years there, first as assistant keeper and then as
director. During this period the government was still willing to
spend money on the arts and Strong took great advantage of this.
Then on New Year's Day 1974 he moved from Trafalgar Square to
South Kensington to what was, by all accounts, a decrepit institution, the Victoria and Albert Museum. Strong was quite different
from anything seen before in that place. He was, for example, the
first director not to have a private income; he was also a self-
publicist, strongly opinionated and rather good at what he did. He
was never dull. His sometimes difficult traits were to be exacerbated during the commercially oriented 1980s, when there were
alarming suggestions of entry fees and less public funding. The
report into the workings of museums by the chairman of Marks
and Spencer, Lord Rayner, was in Strong's view 'a document of no
great moment, riddled with cost-effectiveness'.

It had been decided that the V&A should have a group of Trustees who would be responsible for its safe keeping while the director,
in theory at least, would implement the wishes of the Trustees.
That was the theory. But who should be chairman of those Trustees? Again the theory was that the chairman would be the most
important person in that he or she (inevitably he) would work
closely with the director, keep the other Trustees in line and be
influential enough to move and shake ministerial opinion. At a
party given by the American ambassador, Roy Strong approached

the vice-chairman of the Trustees of the National Portrait Gallery, Hugh Grafton,[2] and asked him if he would take on the job. Grafton was close to being appalled at the idea. Apart from being at the Portrait Gallery, Grafton was on the Royal Fine Arts Commission, the Cathedrals Advisory Commission and was chairman of the Architectural Heritage Fund. He was too busy and knew exactly all the pitfalls opening up before anyone who took on the new chairmanship at the V&A. Grafton turned down the offer without any hesitation. This was about three months after Carrington's resignation, when his popularity was probably higher than ever before. His reputation as an honourable man was unshakeable, and his influence with the Establishment, from the monarchy, through Whitehall, Westminster and the City, almost without parallel. Strong kept asking Grafton. Grafton kept saying no.

The appointment of Carrington as chairman of the V&A Trustees would hardly be a major political event. Equally, there might be a few sensitivities that would suggest that even though Carrington had done the honourable thing and resigned, his going was the result of his failure to get a proper grip on his department. Certainly there were those who believed that, while there was no doubt that Carrington was an honourable man, he should also be seen as a less than competent one. So why should he be rewarded with the prestigious chairmanship of a national institution?

Against this view, the Establishment held fast. Carrington would get the chairmanship of the V&A and the views of the dissenters were swept aside when in June 1983 the sixth Baron Carrington received the Queen Mother's personal blessing: he was made a Companion of Honour. One of the first people to send congratulations was Queen Elizabeth. This was not a formal letter. It was handwritten and a reflection of the fact that in one way or another the Carringtons – and very much including Peter Carrington's mother Sybil – had been close to the British royal family since the late 1850s. There was clear affection in the letter from Queen Elizabeth.

2 Eleventh Duke of Grafton.

Clarence House
June 17th 1983

Dear Peter

We were all so delighted that you have become a Companion of
Honour, and I am writing to send you my heartfelt congratulations.
I always think that it is one of the nicest honours to have and
no-one deserves it more than you.

So looking forward to seeing you at the Bishop's Beano.

I am, ever yours

Elizabeth R

Congratulations followed from friends and political colleagues
who queued to express their warm regard, and to say that he had
been wrong to resign. Heath's note (and a subsequent conversation
with the author) suggested that Carrington had been offered
another honour by Thatcher but had turned it down.

Dear Peter

Many congratulations on your CH. You deserve at least a Viscountcy but perhaps you rejected that. If so, all credit to you.

Love to Iona

Yrs

Ted

Carrington later said that a viscountcy would not have been appropriate. Robin Fearn, as a member of the FCO South American
department, had been closest to what had gone wrong during
those uncertain days before the 1982 invasion of the Falklands.

Brook House, Egerton, Ashford, Kent
13th June 1983

Dear Peter

Nothing can ever make up – in the eyes of your friends anyway –
for the personal tragedy and the loss to the country and the Party

of last year. I didn't want to bother you at the time but at least this gives an opportunity of saying how deeply we felt for you and how much we admired the dignity and loyalty with which you bore it all. It was a privilege to be allowed to work for you, and I know how many people in the Foreign Office felt the same.

Yours ever, Robin

By the end of 1982 the potential Trustees of the V&A had been lined up and would be appointed by the end of September 1983; Carrington, in the late spring of 1983, much to Strong's delight, accepted the role as the first chairman. Strong's enthusiasm is there for all to read in his diary entry on Carrington:

8 May 1983
Peter Carrington I like enormously and I am thrilled to get him. He's a star, albeit a frustrated one, as being a Lord had deprived him of ever becoming Prime Minister which he should have been.[3]

In a letter to the scholar of seventeenth-century literature, Jan van Dorsten, in August 1983, Strong is once more very cheerful about the new chairman:

Peter Carrington, the incoming Chairman, is, I need hardly say, a sharp cookie and very funny.

Then the following month, again to Jan van Dorsten,

Carrington is marvellous and so funny and indiscreet, wonderful and, more to the point, he's gone down with the staff and one's colleagues.

This was in September. Within a month Strong was having his doubts, not about Carrington's personality, which he hugely enjoyed, but about the former Foreign Secretary's ability as chairman.

3 Sir Roy Strong, *The Roy Strong Diaries, 1967–1987*, London: Weidenfeld & Nicolson, 1997. For this and following extracts see pp. 320–77.

9th October

This is the week that the Trustees take over the V&A. I hope that it will be a success. Peter Carrington seems to read nothing at all and the place is so complex that I wonder how long he can get by with the usual bonhomie and drollery and on the spot response. We shall see.

12th October . . . 1983

The Trustees first meeting was very different, rather a shambles. Carrington didn't stick to the agenda, never once referred to me, and careered his way at juggernaut speed at everything. Nothing mercifully too disastrous happened, but I must give thought as to how to stage-manage these so that he does actually take in and act on what he should.

By the spring of 1985 Strong believed Carrington was losing control of the Trustees, especially Terence Conran and Andrew Knight, who Strong believed were acting like 'Victorian mill owners'.

At that time Strong and his senior staff felt threatened, believing that their jobs were on the line. Strong had produced a paper on his role, targets for achievement and a wiring diagram of various responsibilities, all of which was based upon the mandate laid down for the museum by Parliament. Terence Conran was not impressed. He had, at a private meeting of Trustees at Apsley House in the third week in April 1985, more or less taken over the meeting from Carrington and delivered a long argument denouncing Roy Strong's directorship. It was Strong's view that the Trustees, in whom he had had great hopes, had proved to be inefficient. He had not grasped that most Trustees were too busy in other areas and took on too much. Grafton had understood this and that was one reason he had turned down the offer to become chairman. Strong had failed to take on board such a fundamental truth about the Trustees' diverse interests. By the summer of 1985 the V&A had become a miserable place and Carrington, according to Strong, was in a hopeless position.

13 June 1985

He [Carrington] realized what a failure he'd been. He hardly seems engaged in the place, although too much of a gentleman to make his exit from it as a failure ... in the taxi back from White's [Carrington's club] he said he had been a failure. He has.

20th August

Carrington came to see me today, very mopy, ... we are now at the end of the road. He knows that he has been a flop. He was so good at the start, marvellous at the charm, the up-front, beaming and a-twinkle. But this year it has all been beyond him. He caves in every time to the heavy gang ... he sits there listless and flapping around, with no edge and not an original thought and no help at all. He is a fair-weather prodigy and he wants to get out by Christmas.

Strong's sometimes downright spiteful comments in his memoir were dismissed by Carrington as unimportant. But that was a defensive reaction. In fact, Carrington was deeply hurt.

Much later, he observed to me that what had not been said was the fact that the V&A was in a terrible state when the Trustees arrived: a creaking system from its leaking radiators to appalling administration. Though Strong could hardly be held responsible for the shortcomings of the museum, Carrington believed that the director had had time to do far more than he had done. The whole museums service, especially in London, was at the very best in an indifferent state. He believed it appalling that the different museums' directors were never on the same side and in fact 'hated each other'. At the same time he fully accepted that there were weaknesses among the Trustees.

There was an obvious personal difficulty between Carrington and Strong. Although Strong thought Carrington amusing and a jolly nice man but a bad chairman of Trustees, Carrington never warmed to what he saw as Strong's enormous ego and self-aggrandizing attitude, what Carrington called 'all that long hair and flowing cape business'. On one occasion the Duke of Wellington was to hold a reception at Apsley House, the old Wellington home built at No. 1 London for the Iron Duke. It was now a museum and part of the V&A. The party was to be a grand affair and to be attended by the royal family. The current duke, out of the blue, had a letter from Roy Strong, who as V&A director was responsible for Apsley House. Strong told Wellington that he could not have his reception there. Wellington then rang Carrington and asked him to 'do something about it'.

Carrington rang Strong and explained to him that this was not simply a party, it was a royal affair. Strong told Carrington that as director he was not overly concerned with the quality of the guest list but with the weakness of the floors, which he pointed out had been surveyed and were unlikely to take the pounding of the dancers on that evening, no matter how royal (certainly not dainty) the pumps. Carrington was unimpressed, but Strong stood his ground and said that he would have to order him in writing to give permission. Carrington also believed that Strong was really trying to get revenge for something that had occurred years before. Strong had planned a reception at Apsley House for the Byron Society but the Duke of Wellington had written to him saying that he could not have such a cocktail party because the original duke, the hero of the Peninsular War and Waterloo, had disliked the great poet. Whatever Strong's motives, his warning that the structure was not safe for such a party did have some technical authority, yet Carrington made no effort to seek a second surveyor for an opinion. He was in effect countermanding the advice of his director and risking the delicate fabric of the building when he sent round the required note to Strong.

Carrington did take the precaution on the evening of the party of standing at the entrance to the dance floor and, when he thought it crowded enough, turning away would-be dancers to another room. It was no great consolation to Strong that Carrington did not have an overly enjoyable evening, ever mindful of the consequences of a royal foot disappearing through a hole in the Iron Duke's ballroom.

When Strong's diaries appeared, there was a rumour in the media that Carrington would resign. Instead he said nothing. However, one day the two came face to face at a party given by the magazine *Country Life*, as he recounted to me years later:

I told him that I thought his entries particularly unfair. He looked away and muttered something about it was a long time ago. He then got away as quickly as possible.

Later, I wrote to him and said if he would like to come and have a very private lunch with me I would tell him, to his face, what his staff really thought of him. He never replied.

Carrington did not really want to tell him and Strong did not really want to know. He thought it significant that when Strong announced his resignation to the staff it was received in absolute silence, only the keeper of the Indian department wishing him luck. Carrington and Strong never spoke again and the former made it clear that he did not wish to. As he put it, here was someone else whose memorial service he was unlikely to attend.

There is a footnote. When Strong was to resign from the V&A he wanted to make the announcement to the Trustees himself. Carrington would not let him in the room and made him wait outside on a chair while he told the Trustees. Strong, adding to the silliness of the occasion, organized three despatch riders to take the announcement of his resignation to Fleet Street newspapers in the hope that he would get his version on the news editors' desks before anything came from Carrington and the Minister for the Arts. That was on 26 January 1987. Strong always believed that Carrington tried and failed to nobble the press in order to show the departing director in a bad light. Carrington's sadness about the way in which Strong wrote about him was very much to do with the fact that he made telephone call after telephone call in order to try and secure for Strong a 'big job'.

The relationship was not quite a bureaucratic disaster. Yet clearly nor was it the success that some had hoped for, including Strong and Carrington themselves. They were two hugely different personalities. There was a typically Strong-like example of this difference in 1985 when Carrington was installed as a Knight of the

Garter. In came very sincere letters of congratulations from all over the world, most pointing out what the Queen had already made clear: that Carrington was entirely worthy of the honour. Roy Strong's postcard was quite different.

Peter – Oh, what lovely robes to wear! I am so envious. Homage and congratulations from this loyal monarchist. Roy.

Strong accused Carrington of taking on too many other commitments. That was inevitable for two reasons: the V&A job was not full time and secondly, Carrington once more had yet another major role offered him. He had made the point that he did not like to attempt two jobs at once when he was Secretary of State for Defence and chairman of the Conservative Party. The difficulty he faced as chairman of the V&A Trustees was that it coincided with his appointment as NATO Secretary-General. This was a huge job, so why did he attempt to do both? He had drafted in Sir Michael Butler, who had more recently been British permanent representative to the European Union, as his deputy at the V&A. He had hoped Butler would in fact do the job and leave him simply as a figurehead until he could reasonably bow out. The NATO posting was reason enough to go and not simply an excuse. Carrington, who not unnaturally was to be so disappointed with Strong's published views about him, agreed with the V&A director on one point: he did not feel that he should abandon the chairmanship while the museum was in such a mess. Yet on reflection, it might be thought Carrington was the wrong person for the V&A. As Strong knew perfectly well, the V&A was part of a society littered with score settling, intrigue, waspish humour and above all prima donna principals. Carrington faced as many complications as he would have expected to find in the most Machiavellian government department or international corporation.

After Carrington's resignation from the government in April 1982, there had been the usual suggestions about taking a job in Europe. The Commission was always good for a headline connected with Carrington's future. There were some who believed he would make an attractive Secretary-General to the United Nations. However, the unwritten rule was firm: the UN job should always go to someone from a developing nation. It is frequently said by those who knew Carrington well that he would never have taken a job like the UN because it had no real power. That is only partly true, because he did take the NATO job and that had no power whatsoever. What Carrington liked most of all was the exercising of diplomacy. If he had not joined the army and then gone into politics, he should have liked to have joined the diplomatic service with an ambition to be ambassador to Rome or Paris. After the Falklands inquests had been heard, Mrs Thatcher was able to think what she could next do with him. There were two jobs to be filled: one was that of a political appointee as ambassador to the United States. Yet it seems likely that he would have become frustrated by the determination of successive Prime Ministers to deal directly with the White House.

The other vacancy which was about to be filled was that of Secretary-General of the North Atlantic Treaty Organization. Margaret Thatcher had a twofold interest in this appointment. First, she still felt an obligation to Carrington after the Falklands affair and given his diplomatic and defence pedigree she felt he was the ideal person for the job. Second, Thatcher wanted to make sure that it went to a British candidate. This second concern tied in neatly with Carrington's availability. The Prime Minister saw no great reason to think that Carrington would not get the job, and the round of diplomacy required to ensure the necessary votes from NATO members started even before Carrington himself was approached. The British government instructed its ambassadors and foreign ministers to begin the lobbying process and the first Carrington knew that something was definitely going on was when his name started to appear in the European media as a likely successor to the Dutchman Joseph Luns. Luns had almost refused to move from the post and this made the lobbying even more difficult.

Curiously, the biggest obstacle to Carrington's appointment came not from European members of NATO, but from the United States. It was not that Washington had a candidate of its

own – there was an understanding that an American could not
become Secretary-General. On the other hand, the commander of
the military wing of NATO, the Supreme Allied Commander
Europe, was always an American. The USA made up the bulk
of the effective forces in the alliance and so Washington always
produced, without question, successive SACEURs. It was a diplomatic and military arrangement that worked well.

So why would the Americans have been against Carrington,
who had an enviable international reputation as a politician, a
diplomat and as an honourable man sensitive to the needs of the
European and particularly the transatlantic sinews of the alliance?
The fact was that the Americans did not trust him. Very few people
in Europe, even among the senior echelons of the bureaucracies
and governments, impress Washington. Carrington was not a hero
in the United States and in fact there was a deep suspicion that he
was against American interests.

Carrington had been told that it was suspected that he had an
anti-American position on Israel. Certainly there were those in
Whitehall, including at one time Margaret Thatcher herself, who
suspected Carrington of being pro-Arab and therefore anti-Israeli.
The Americans had been suspicious of Carrington ever since the
summer of 1980, when they saw him as one of the masterminds of
the Venice Declaration. This was a European document which after
enormous diplomatic toing and froing brought together a European foreign policy on three important areas: Afghanistan (the
Soviet Union had invaded the previous year), Lebanon and the
Middle East. It was the section on the Middle East that disturbed
the Americans because, although it declared the importance of
Israel as a state, it went as far as to recognize publicly that Palestinians were entitled to equal and sympathetic rights. In Washington,
with its powerful Jewish lobby, this declaration was not seen as
a reasonable point of view but an unbalanced observation.
Certainly in 1980 any sympathy towards the Palestinians was construed in Washington as being anti-Israeli. This was particularly
difficult that summer because it came right at the height of the
American Presidential Election. The Jewish lobby in the United

States believed that the Europeans had betrayed Jewish interests and were even on the side of terrorism. Therefore both Republicans and Democrats were expected to take some stand on this issue. In Presidential Elections of that period, what a candidate thought about the 'Jewish question' was as politically sensitive as what he thought of an abortion amendment or even gun laws. As it turned out, the man who won that 1980 election, Ronald Reagan, eventually moved towards the sentiment expressed in the Venice Declaration. But the timing had been bad and the grounds for suspicion about Carrington had been laid.

Moreover, when in 1981 the Americans sponsored peace talks between Egypt and Israel and sought to involve European guarantees, it became known that Carrington was quite uncomfortable with the idea. He was, in spite of his protestations of evenhandedness, inclined towards the Arab viewpoint. The Europeans in 1981 supported the Saudi plan for Middle East peace, which included that country's recognition, or at least acknowledgement, of the State of Israel. Once more Carrington was in the firing line. The Israelis saw the Saudi plan as against their interests and although the Americans had initially regarded it as an advancement they quickly buckled to the Jewish lobby. Once more Carrington was singled out, because the plan coincided with Britain's presidency of the European Community, and for that six-month period Carrington chaired the EC Council of Foreign Ministers and thus made the necessary public statements.

Yitzhak Shamir, the Israeli Foreign Minister, and Prime Minister Menachem Begin privately and sometimes publicly denounced Carrington as being anti-Israeli. As we have already seen, this phobia led to the Jewish lobby's setting up claques at public meeting where Carrington spoke and at which he was booed and heckled. Here was the basis, again as we have seen, of the cancellation of two visits planned by Carrington in his role as British Foreign Secretary to Israel. Face to face, Carrington and Begin never got on. At a Downing Street lunch the Israeli Prime Minister, quite inexplicably even to his aides, once accused Margaret Thatcher of being responsible for the death of 2 million Jews at

Auschwitz. It was left to Carrington to try to smooth over the tension stimulated by Begin's passion. He never succeeded in doing this.

Little wonder then that the Americans thought Carrington untrustworthy, especially as he had just made a speech warning against the dangers of megaphone diplomacy – a barely disguised jab at the American style of resolving diplomatic difficulties. Nevertheless the American objections were overcome and Carrington was told that if he wanted the job it was his – as long, of course, as someone could persuade Joseph Luns to quit. The Dutchman had made it clear that he did not think Carrington, or anyone else for that matter, a worthy successor. The alliance always found it difficult to resolve internal, never mind external problems.

Yet if there was ever a time for a fresh look at the way NATO functioned over really big issues such as the Soviet Union and the Warsaw Treaty Organization, that was during the first half of the 1980s. The cruise missile debate was in full flow. It had started out of public earshot in the Pentagon and European defence ministries during the later 1970s. The Soviet Union had developed a series of medium-range surface-to-surface (SS) missiles capable of carrying nuclear warheads, known as SS-20s. Since October 1957 the Soviet Union had publicly demonstrated that intercontinental warfare using missiles was feasible. That demonstration had done what had been so hard to do during the Great and Second World Wars: convince the United States that their security interests lay in Europe and that they too were vulnerable to a threat that might originate in Europe. The resolution of the Cuban missile crisis of the early 1960s had suggested to American strategic thinkers that they had removed the immediate medium-range missile threat to continental United States. In the 1970s Washington began to revise this assessment by including the threat from submarine-launched missiles that could be fired from submerged vessels off the US coast. However, throughout the whole internal debate on threat assessment the East–West balance was argued somewhat predictably. The large Soviet nuclear arsenals and the large American nuclear arsenals made it certain that, however sophisticated their early warning systems, both America and the Soviet Union would suffer terribly if they went to war. The 1972 anti-ballistic missile (ABM) treaty, together with its 1974 protocol, produced the seemingly bizarre agreement that both superpowers were to be restricted in the number of defences against intercontinental weapons, in order that neither side would feel so confident of being able to defend themselves from nuclear attack that they would therefore risk such a conflict. The 1972 ABM Treaty became one of the grand illusions of East–West relations. There was no technology that could embrace a comprehensive defence system. In fact, a core element of all ABM agreements was that only limited defence would be allowed, thus keeping the vulnerability factor that supposedly made both superpowers frightened of war. Even by the year 2000 when the United States wanted to scrap the ABM Treaty in order to legally build a new national missile defence system, the technology was still doubtful yet the debate over the damage to Washington–Moscow relations was furious. To counter the American plan, President Putin of Russia proposed a pan-European missile defence programme. (He did the same in 2007 to counter the American plan for the deployment of ABM systems in the UK, Poland and the Czech Republic.) Looking back and looking forward, here was the context of the debate that was occurring in the early 1980s. Coupled with this was the announcement in April 1983 by President Reagan that he wanted American scientists and technologists to produce what was formally called the Strategic Defence Initiative – more informally known as Star Wars. Even though the concept had long been in development – for example, the Chair Heritage Programme had been working on such ideas as charged particle beam weapons for over twenty years – it was so new to the public, so fantastic to the average mind, that Europeans became alarmed rather than reassured.

By now the fears, especially from the German point of view, of the deployment of SS-20 missiles by the Soviet Union were more widespread. Europe did not have the technology to counter these missiles and was not working on any project that could do so. There were already realistic estimates in defence ministries, including the UK's, that the conventional ground forces deployed by NATO states in Europe had neither the equipment, the force structures nor the political assurances to counter the three categories of readiness of the Soviet ground forces and those of its allies. Thus the European governments saw themselves even more vulnerable to Soviet blackmail, if not direct threat, than at any time in East–West relations. A speech by the West German Defence Minister, Hans Dietrich Genscher, in London in the autumn of 1978 put forward the controversial idea that if the new Soviet missile threat was to be countered, then it would be by the deployment in Europe of similar missile systems. This argument, carefully orchestrated, raised two issues: first, European members of NATO did not have such weapons and no industry to build them. Second, would governments be able to persuade their electorates that the USA, the only source of missiles, should be allowed to deploy them in Western Europe? One public viewpoint held that warheads should not be deployed because that made Europe an even greater target without endangering the United States. The anxiety expressed in this argument was easily spread because the general public in Europe had never been told precisely what American nuclear weapons were on the continent already.

In spring 1979, at a NATO Nuclear Planning Group meeting at Homestead Airforce Base in Florida, it was agreed that the only answer to the SS-20 and similar weapons, American cruise missiles, would be deployed in the very near future in some European countries – the United Kingdom and Italy in particular. This decision was taken by the Labour government of James Callaghan, and quickly endorsed after the May 1979 election by Margaret Thatcher's government, of which Carrington was a member. He was privy to all the debates that took place within the inner sanctum of a handful of Cabinet ministers. With the perceived threat from the Soviet Union, the controversial response by NATO – although this was seen to be largely by the United States, who owned the weapons – and the unprecedented increase in membership of anti-nuclear protest groups such as CND, the need to bring political cohesion to the NATO forum was most urgent. The organization was in need of a Secretary-General who had the confidence of the

United States as well as European members, because Washington was oversensitive to European objections however intelligently offered, while many European members were equally sensitive to the sometimes autocratic style of the United States executive. Because there were some suspicions in Washington about Carrington's credentials, his stock was raised among European members of NATO, even though some member states who were also in the European Union did not care much for Margaret Thatcher.

But Carrington was now an international servant and for the first time in his career had put national considerations behind him. In June 1984, at the age when most would be considering retirement (he was sixty-five on the sixth of that month), he and Iona moved into the official residence of the Secretary-General in Brussels. Iona Carrington kept a note of those first few days.

24.6.84. Brussels.
The sun shines and here I am on the 19th floor of the Hilton Hotel – even the decorated Luns House will be a huge improvement. They [the Luns] have finally left the house and an army of cleaners are attacking the mustard carpets, the pink satin damask sofas, perhaps the mustard damask salon walls; and the aged beds are to be replaced or refurbished. We shall move in next week and I don't think that anyone can mistake it as our own taste. Joseph Luns's bedroom has huge dark red and blue flowers, the inevitable mustard carpet, curtains and bed and the only double room where we must sleep is mustard walls, carpet and curtains and shiny walnut veneer cupboards with fearful brown bathroom en-suite. The light defies belief in its horror and in the dining room with pink velvet chairs there is a Venetian chandelier, blue, pink, mustard and clear! Peter has of course a mustard office at NATO and will find it difficult to make it civilized . . .

We have already felt the dislike for Britain caused by Margaret Thatcher's budget battles. *Now she has settled for far less than Peter could have got for her without rancour nearly three years ago.* [Author's italics.] On the radio she is still talking about we and they . . .[4]

4 Lady Carrington, private diaries, Bledlow archive.

Jo Luns did not go quietly. He rarely did anything quietly. For years he had refused to leave office even though most member states wanted rid of him. Even when Carrington formally took over, Luns kept turning up at NATO headquarters and walking into Carrington's office as if he still owned it. Carrington was firm but courteous, but found it very difficult to disguise the fact that he had little regard for Luns.

A couple of months into Carrington's tenure, when there was enormous need for unity, Luns appeared on German television and said that he had been a fine Secretary-General and that Carrington was thus far an insignificant servant of the alliance.

Carrington's response was to send a transcript of that intervention to Luns with a short note,

> Dear Mr Luns,
> I believe you said this.
> Yours sincerely,
> Carrington.

Luns did not reply. Carrington took it no further. The two men never spoke again. Many years later in a conversation about Luns, Carrington told me that he suspected that the Dutchman was quite old and was probably dead. When told, no, Carrington quietly shook his head and said, 'Oh.'

At NATO Carrington found himself in the same position – albeit on a grander scale – that Roy Strong had at the V&A. As Secretary-General, Carrington had no power, only influence. In theory it was up to him to make sure that the organization was as efficient as it could be, considering that like most international bodies, including the United Nations, the effectiveness of NATO is never more than the sum of the individual wills of its member states. Consequently, NATO is rather like a multinational charity in which each trustee is a government with its own interests to preserve. It recognizes the common aim – in NATO's case, the preservation of peace in Europe. Nevertheless, individual jealousies are exacerbated by the fact that there is an obvious imbalance in the input from member states, both politically and militarily, and the total influence of certainly one and perhaps two other member states.

There is a chestnut from the 1950s which claims that the first Secretary-General, Lord Ismay, announced that NATO's function was to keep the Russians out, the Americans in and the Germans down. The effort not only to engage the American interest and agreement in the transatlantic dream but to do so without jeopardizing the loyalty and effort of other member states is a continuing task for any Secretary-General. When Carrington took over in 1984, NATO's role was certainly to keep the Americans in, to keep the Russians out but not to sit on the Germans. (In fact, Carrington would eventually be succeeded by a German.) He was in the sort of job that he was best fitted for. He understood defence and foreign affairs and he was a far better diplomat than anything else he did, other than farming. He restructured the Secretary-General's office and surrounding desks to give that main part of the Secretariat a more international flavour. Above all, he wanted to have his own people giving their analysis of the focus of the alliance's attention: the present and future capabilities of the Soviet Union. The military had their analysis, but as civilian Secretary-General, Carrington was starved of information rather than overwhelmed by it. He once told me that during visits to London, he had to find a reason to go to the FCO to find out what was going on in the world. Mostly, he needed to know about the Soviet Union in order to anticipate the political climates among member states. Therefore, he made what later seemed a most natural appointment although at the time it was considered radical.

Carrington appointed a Sovietologist to tell him and his staff what the Kremlin and the Soviet General Staff were thinking. His choice was a very strong-minded Russian-speaking north country Englishman called Chris Donnelly, who had been a reserve officer in the Intelligence Corps and a senior member of the Department of Soviet Studies at Sandhurst. Donnelly's post was perhaps the most important Carrington made, especially as NATO did not have (and still does not have at the time of writing) its own intelligence service.

Carrington needed to change the style of the Secretary-General's office. Joseph Luns, one of the more amiable if not always the most logical of international administrators, never lost his belief that the reason for NATO was the Soviet Union and therefore almost everything and everyone that questioned NATO's existence was by definition an inspiration of the Kremlin. Luns's belief and style was on his office walls. They were dressed with photographs of missiles and jets, like the bedroom of a serious but rather worrying small boy. Carrington had them removed. He replaced the photographs with nineteenth-century paintings which might easily have been construed as a reflection of Carrington's colonial and imperial ancestry. Instead of the Secretary-General being an obvious extension of the Supreme Allied Commander Europe, Carrington was determined that he would emphasize the importance of his political role. If NATO had a political and military wing, Carrington most surely represented politics. His view was that it was important to constantly remind the larger public that the military remained servants of the politicians and that all senior council meetings were there for the benefit of defence and foreign ministers, and that the military staffs were, just as they would be in any single capital, subordinate to those political leaders.

In June 1984 the influential Democrat Sam Nunn tabled a motion in the United States Senate for the withdrawal of more than 90,000 American troops from Europe unless European members of NATO put more effort into the conventional forces' order of battle. Nunn's proposal was only narrowly defeated in the Senate. Carrington grasped the importance of what Nunn was doing and immediately set about persuading European governments that they had to make some very public and practical declaration that they would spend more money on facilities for ground forces, including doing something to rectify what all the alliance military saw as the ludicrous shortfall in ammunition stocks. Within the year Sam Nunn recognized Carrington's determination and how within twelve months it had, at least on paper, started a process that would put the numbers if not the efficiency into the European contribution to ground forces. From the very beginning of

NATO, there had been an American suspicion that the Europeans simply wanted the government in Washington to rubber-stamp the military umbrella. Even though strategists in the United States had long recognized that America's frontline was on the River Weser and not the eastern seaboard or the Potomac, there was still a not unreasonable belief on Capitol Hill that American forces should be scaled down in order to force the Europeans to do more for their own defence. As Carrington pointed out, they simply had the same reservations about European contributions as had their predecessors in the 1940s when NATO was first proposed.

Carrington was congratulated for shepherding European defence ministers through the intricate manoeuvre towards drafts and communiqués showing everyone was making the effort that Senator Nunn had demanded. Even he was sufficiently satisfied to propose in the Senate that $200,000 should be set aside by the American government to help finance cooperative arms agreements among the allies. Though he never told the Americans, in truth Carrington was not overly impressed by what had taken place among the European allies. By now he was too old a political hand not to spot the ambiguities of any NATO statement, and also, while the intentions of every defence minister may have been honourable, ultimately it was up to finance ministers to provide the funding.

While this was going on, Carrington had to tackle the controversial issue of the deployment of American cruise missiles in Europe, a task not helped by the public disquiet over Reagan's Strategic Defence Initiative ambitions. Star Wars may have been derided by pundits as fanciful, but it caught the public imagination and sense of unease. Carrington did not think this the best climate to sell the idea of cruise and Pershing missile deployments. Joseph Luns had had an attitude of deep suspicion of all anti-nuclear, indeed anti-military protest, by which he meant almost everything from public discussion to placard-carrying marchers. Carrington's approach was less dogmatic. He had to make the case for five European nations allowing America to base cruise missiles within their borders. There was considerable opposition among even pro-NATO voters as Carrington embarked on a series of speeches reminding audiences throughout Western Europe that the first public initiative for such deployments had in fact come from Europe. He also consistently made the connection between nuclear deployment and conventional (i.e. non-nuclear) improvement. To a military audience the case was very easy to put: there had to be a mix of forces. Missiles would counter missiles, conventional weaponry and manpower would, hopefully, deter groups of Soviet conventional systems. This argument could be argued rationally because the technology existed to show what was and what was not militarily feasible. But when it came to supporting the Strategic Defence Initiative, Carrington could not expect to argue so coherently. There were clear differences about this in Europe at the highest level. For example, SDI became the single most important topic at the annual Wehrkunde Conference in Munich. The conferences were the brainchild of Baron Ewald von Kleist, who as a young officer had taken part in Claus von Stauffenberg's attempted coup against Hitler in 1944. Von Kleist established the Munich conferences as a forum for discussing the bigger issues confronting the alliance. Issues did not get much bigger than the SDI debate. The Americans argued that SDI might be the only hope of achieving stability and, in something of a mood of fantasy, SDI could, according to remarks from the American Secretary of Defense Caspar Weinberger, achieve the ultimate aim of eliminating nuclear weapons. The German Chancellor Helmut Kohl claimed that he had been reassured by the Americans that SDI would protect Western Europe as much as it would the United States, an argument sceptically received in Europe – just as sixteen years later Europeans would be sceptical of claims for President Clinton's National Missile Defence System. Kohl was endorsing SDI because he did not want German industry to miss out on the spin-offs from the technology. At the other end of the scale of scepticism, Charles Hernu, the French Defence Minister, at the same meeting observed that the world had been saved from a cataclysm by the fact that there was not a nuclear weapons defence system. A week later, on 19 February 1985, Carrington was having to make a public statement that he believed that SDI was feasible and that it would be 'extremely imprudent' if the Reagan administration abandoned its research at a time when the Soviet Union was advancing its space weapons technology.

The United States is absolutely right to do this research. If we were to wake up in five years' time and discover that the Soviets had the capacity for some kind of initiative like this, it would be the Europeans who would be quick to say it had been maladroit and foolish of the Americans to have not explored the prospects for a space based defence.[5]

Carrington refrained from expressing his private belief that if America continued with the SDI research programme, then the Soviet Union would do the same. But because the Americans had more military dollars, they would outspend the Soviet Union and so bankrupt a large part of the Soviet economy. Later, this was an acceptable argument. So, why did not Carrington voice it publicly as he did privately? The answer partly lies in his position as Secretary-General: he was not expected to say anything in public that could be construed as controversial, unlikely or partisan. He stuck to the obvious – as one of his aides told me, someone had to. He did, however, tell Reagan what he thought. In October 1985 Carrington went to Washington and after briefings at the British Embassy – where he thought 'the dining room so flowery and Laura Ashley that it makes you feel slightly sick' – he went to the White House for yet another 'one-to-one' briefing with the President.

He had the usual enormous circle around him … he was if anything rather more prepared to listen than he had been on the last occasion. He is as we know inclined to be a little bit anecdotal after ten minutes or so of business, but on this occasion he kept going for well over half an hour and though some of the things he said were somewhat bizarre, I think

5 Carrington statement quoted in NATO press release, Carrington papers, Bledlow.

that those present understood some of the problems that Europeans are having with SDI. In particular the question which they have not yet answered as to how they can expect the Soviet Union to reduce their offensive missiles if they do not know what defences the Americans have, and the worry that the Europeans have that this will mean that the arms talks get nowhere and consequently public opinion in Europe will turn against the United States because an arms race will be the inevitable result.[6]

Carrington, at that point, had not grasped the Reagan belief that the way to bring about the downfall of the Soviet Union was to deploy the American Way — the dollar. Very simply, America would outspend the USSR until the latter was spent. As for Reagan, his impression of that first meeting in 1979 had not much changed: the President was never an intellectual leader, but the American system had made him President and Commander-in-Chief of the Western world and therefore none should under-estimate him.

One cannot help when leaving the White House feel what an extraordinary [*sic*] warm and human and agreeable person Reagan is, and one of the greatest achievements of his Presidency has been to make the Americans feel better.

A visit to the White House does not resolve day-to-day diffi-culties for a NATO Secretary-General. American cruise missiles and Pershing II missiles had been deployed in Italy, the United Kingdom and West Germany. Their arrival had not gone unnoticed.

The agreement in 1979, taken first at the NATO Nuclear Planning Group meeting in Florida and then by the full Council, was that the Americans should have 572 cruise and Pershing II missiles in Europe. The Dutch and Belgian governments were putting off deployment because the final decision was difficult to

6 Notes in Carrington papers, Bledlow.

get through the political process. For example, the Belgian Prime Minister Wilfred Martens was under enormous pressure from his own Christian Democrats not to go ahead with the deployment because there were new East–West arms control talks starting in Geneva, and the hope was that these discussions would actually remove the need for deployment.

Meanwhile, Carrington pressed on with speech after speech, very aware that he had to strike the right balance between supporting what many saw as amazing projects such as SDI, destabilizing deployments such as cruise and Pershing II missiles and demands – not simple requests – for increases in defence spending throughout the alliance at a time when many governments were hard pressed to find sufficient funds from what they regarded as essential domestic projects such as law and order, education and health.

For example, at the end of February 1985 Carrington returned to his praise of SDI during a speech to the German Society for Foreign Policy:

We in Europe, familiar as we are with the homegrown manifestations of anti-nuclear feeling, may be less ready to recognize that similar feelings, and similar fears, may in the United States exert political pressures of a different kind. Are they not one of the political reasons for research into strategic defence? Research, incidentally, which I think that it would be very imprudent of the Americans not to be doing.

It was a very bold speech, especially since in the same month he had gone to Cambridge where he had told an academic audience that he failed to see how 'a system that merely protects can maintain deterrents at the same time'.[7]

A month after that speech, the world witnessed the start of fundamental strategic change in East–West relations, and one that would have almost unimagined consequences for the whole of Eastern and Western Europe. On 11 March 1985 Konstantin Chernenko, the Soviet leader, died. He was replaced officially

7 *Executive Intelligence Review*, 11 February 1985.

by Mikhail Gorbachev, who had effectively been running the Kremlin during the final weeks of Chernenko's life.

By the spring of 1985 Carrington had been working long hours non-stop for almost a year as Secretary-General of NATO, urgently restructuring its office and Secretariat. His was what he called a 'big job' because of the issues and the reason for the alliance. But he was beginning to believe that he was missing opportunities to put across those issues to the widest public audiences and especially to those known as 'opinion formers'.

In spite of his changes that had rid him of the trappings left behind by Luns, Carrington still needed a chief of staff and speech writer he could trust to sum up every opinion but to make sure that his speeches reflected the two that mattered most – those of the United States administration but, most of all, Britain's. In this, Carrington was going back to the principles laid down by his first political boss, Churchill. He had inherited David Brighty as chief of staff, yet good as he was, Brighty could not do exactly what Carrington wanted. But Carrington knew a man who could: Kevin Tebbit, who had worked for him in his private office when he was Secretary of State for Defence.[8] Tebbit knew NATO because he had been first secretary to the UK delegation for three years. He had moved from the MOD to the Foreign Office and was about to go to Washington in a job that marked him out as a future ambassador. Carrington knew all this and telephoned him at home full of apologies for disturbing the packing. He said he knew it was an awful chore, especially as Tebbit was about to leave for Washington, but would he help Carrington enormously (more apologies at this point) and instead of the lively and career-helpful Washington, would he come to dull and rarely inspiring Brussels? Carrington then added that he could not begin to expect Tebbit to agree. Tebbit agreed immediately. Why he did so tells us something about the loyalty Carrington inspired among those who had

8 Later Sir Kevin, Permanent Secretary at the Ministry of Defence, 1998–2005. Author's conversation with Tebbit, May 2006.

worked for him – however long ago. Tebbit, having worked in Brussels, knew exactly what he was letting himself in for. Equally, it was hardly a dull time at NATO and Carrington's *chef de cabinet* was not exactly a bad career move.

One reason for Carrington's plea to Tebbit was the latter's ability as a speech writer. Until Tebbit's arrival, Carrington's private office wrote speeches that reflected his character: there was always a sense of understatement, maybe laconic wit. They started with a small but never offensive joke, and then, while not exactly simply thanking people for coming, were hardly eye-catching. In this sense, Carrington was not at all good in using the role of Secretary-General to promote Western causes publicly, causes in which he believed enormously. Tebbit changed this, with the help of the head of NATO's press office, ex-*Daily Express* foreign correspondent Robin Stafford. Stafford knew exactly how to get a story into a newspaper and to get it on page one. Carrington insisted that he liked to be quietly diplomatic. Tebbit ignored this. He knew what Washington and London wanted to hear from the Secretary-General and so wrote much tougher speeches than Carrington. Stafford taught Tebbit that there had always to be three points in a news story if they wanted headlines. Carrington was not always happy with this, but he trusted his officials – a weakness that had, in April 1982, cost him his job as Foreign Secretary. So he would ask, 'Have I really got to say all this?' then shrug and say it. The result was a headline just when it was needed, a pat on the back from Washington and London, and a definite impression that Carrington was tougher, even harder line, than perhaps he was.

Carrington's instinct for diplomacy – particularly his desire not to upset – was illustrated when Margaret Thatcher visited Brussels to address the NATO Council. Her visit coincided with the debate on the first manoeuvres of the Franco-German Corps. These had taken place as a result of a new pact between France and Germany. Carrington knew that Thatcher thoroughly disliked, even detested, the arrangement. Before Thatcher's address to the Council, Carrington was in a very gloomy mood because he was convinced the British Prime Minister would 'say something', as he put it, about the weakening transatlantic unity and resolve. He asked her, even urged her, to be magnanimous. The Prime Minister fixed the Secretary-General with what she regarded as her best smile. 'I know, Peter, you would be so diplomatic. But I will just have to be my usual brutal self.' The meeting opened with Carrington in an apprehensive mood.

All went well until the German Permanent Representative asked Thatcher what she thought of the Franco-German pact – the Frenchman being much too canny to do that. A note was slipped to her by her private secretary Charles Powell. She glanced at it, then said, 'We [the UK] have just concluded a very successful exercise to reinforce Europe. It was called *Exercise Lionheart*. You have had a similar exercise. You called it *Kecker Spatz* – cheeky sparrow. Enough said.'

With that, she popped the note into her handbag and swept from the room, as one diplomat later remarked, 'like a royal blue galleon under full sail'. Carrington repaired to his office that afternoon, expecting a deluge of complaints from the French and Germans. Instead, there was an avalanche of congratulations – including one from the French ambassador – for a splendid Thatcher performance.

Carrington was always thought to be affable, never liking rows, and a man who would go out of his way to put others at their ease. This was partly true but his NATO staff soon found that the famous smile would disappear when confronted by bad manners. Infuriating protocol and etiquette would be tolerated but rudeness would never be. For example, during the shuttle diplomacy of the Strategic Arms Reduction Talks (START) Carrington walked into his bathroom and found one of the Secret Service men on the staff of US Secretary of State George Shultz snooping in the cistern. He was searching for bugs that might be used during the forthcoming meeting between Carrington and Shultz. Carrington went, in the word of one of his staff, ballistic, and actually did kick him out of the bathroom. He then demanded that the spook be deported before he would see Shultz. The Americans could not believe this was happening. Carrington stood his ground in furious temper. The agent was 'deported' and the meeting went ahead. Carrington's judgement of what was and what was not ill-mannered extended to the protection of his staff, an issue which arose when the Deputy Under-Secretary at the MOD Patrick Nairne criticized Carrington's private office. Carrington liked Nairne immensely and they remained firm friends for the rest of their lives. However, not even Nairne was allowed to criticize Carrington's staff. Carrington strongly upbraided the senior civil servant and personally showed him the door. He regarded that behaviour as ill-mannered and made it clear that in every circumstance he would defend his staff to others while demanding privately their utmost efficiency and effort. Much of that effort during the NATO period was spent putting together a talks programme and a diplomatic campaign to fend off a political move in the US Congress for the withdrawal of most American troops in Europe.

Carrington's office produced a gruelling schedule for him that had him travelling from capital to capital and government to government in an attempt to get reluctant Europeans to show they were pulling their weight in the alliance. Only this European effort, Carrington said, would persuade Congress that what was even then being called 'Old Europe' was an equal partner in the Cold War. He said that the Europeans could get on best terms with the Americans by increasing their defence budgets in real terms and rethinking procurement and development programmes for conventional forces. They could not afford those levels of forces and all the logistics necessary to keep them functioning. But by publicly making the effort the Americans, he argued, would understand better the dilemma of European governments facing increasingly well-organized political and moral opposition to the idea of the deployment of American nuclear missiles in European countries. Carrington pointed out that although deployment was inevitable, that did not mean that much of the public believed that deployment made them increasingly vulnerable to nuclear attack by the Soviet Union. On top of this, Carrington was under pressure from Washington and London to persuade sceptical European members of the alliance not to reject out of hand Reagan's concept

of the Strategic Defence Initiative, the Star Wars research programme. Apart from his own instinct that the sceptics were correct,
Carrington's task was not eased by Washington's hard line on arms
control.

In 1979 the second Strategic Arms Limitation Treaty (SALT-2)
had been agreed between the Soviet Union and the United States
but the US Congress never ratified the treaty. By the late spring of
1985 the White House was almost weekly accusing the Soviet
Union of some misdemeanour that undermined the agreement.
Behind this lay the Americans' decision to put into service more of
their new Trident submarines, which carried ballistic missiles.
At the same time they did not wish to have to take older boats out
of service. This meant that the Americans would be breaching the
treaty by increasing the numbers of submarine-launched ballistic
missile systems. Therefore the accusations against the Soviet Union
enabled the Americans to ignore an agreement which anyway by
the end of 1985 would be out of date. Carrington was being told
by European member states of NATO that Washington should
not abandon SALT-2 because this would increase the rate of the
arms race, introduce a new element of instability in East–West
relations and therefore make it harder for many European countries to convince their electorates that it was right to spend more
on defence. All this was happening at a time when the Americans
wanted Europe to do more for itself on conventional forces; Carrington had put in an enormous amount of energy trying to
convince European defence ministers to take on their respective
treasuries to bring this about. Consequently, Carrington found
himself trying to preserve a transatlantic relationship as well as an
East–West balance. This effort was further complicated: SALT-2
was a bilateral agreement and therefore in theory had nothing to
do with the rest of NATO. Furthermore, this debate was taking
place at the same time as another round of nuclear weapons talks
between Moscow and Washington resumed in Geneva. In the
middle of May 1985 the Dutch government told Carrington that
it would be hard to win public support for the deployment of US
cruise missiles in the Netherlands if Washington were seen to be

tearing up arms control treaties, albeit lapsed ones, which it never ratified.

Consequently, when NATO foreign ministers gathered at Estoril in June 1985 the majority refused the American proposal to publicly endorse Reagan's Strategic Defence Initiative. This opposition was led by France and Denmark and it was enough to show that whatever Carrington's efforts, he could not disguise the deep differences between European members of the alliance and the United States. (Canada was also reluctant to endorse the SDI plan.)

At the same time Carrington was under considerable pressure from some Continental countries to encourage the UK to take a less self-centred position on arms production and joint cooperation. On 12 June 1985 Carrington gave a public speech shortly before European defence ministers were meeting in London to discuss arms cooperation. His message was simple: weapons of the future would be so technically advanced and demanding of resources that it was unlikely that any one country could develop them by itself. But where did that leave national interests and in particular, the politics of jobs and treasury?

It is sensible to look after one's national industries. But looking after national industries does not mean focusing only on the next two or three years. If we don't raise our sights and look much further ahead, there won't be any national industry left to look after at the sophisticated end of the armaments business. Britain is at or pretty near the top of the west European league in the production of high technology armaments. Unfortunately, we are in much the same place when it comes to chauvinism and complacency. How on earth do we think that we are going to stay in the big league without investing big league money in research and development? And where do we think that money will come from, if the Europeans are not willing to get together, to ensure that the funds which we separately have available are combined to avoid duplication and to produce the most efficient return?[9]

9 Carrington, speech at Press Association lunch, Savoy Hotel, London, 12 June 1985.

The sometimes absurd debates over arms control, Strategic Defence Initiative development (so often a euphemism for technological failure), the deployment of cruise and Pershing II missiles and the political in-fighting about, as another example, the basing of US squadrons in Spain constantly proved that the role of Secretary-General in the 1980s was no simple and ceremonial affair. There was hardly a major world issue, certainly no East–West matter, that Carrington could ignore. He was required to have a view on every strategic issue that hit the headlines, but he was not meant to step out of line. The lines were drawn by the Americans, the differing interests of the Continental Europeans (especially the French who had withdrawn from NATO's military wing) and of course the UK. Each nation state expected the Secretary-General to toe their line, or at the very least, make the other lines converge with theirs. Thus it became clear that almost everything Carrington had to do was dependent upon the relationship between European member states and the United States. Yet he had also to contend with the reality that every major issue – from arms control at all levels to the fundamentals of East–West relations – was decided by the current relationship between the US and the USSR. Treaties and agreements did not decide that relationship, they only reflected them. Consequently, Carrington began to see his job as defusing rather than igniting major debates.

When there was political and public feeling against NATO decisions or projects it was therefore often directed solely at the United States. As a result, successive administrations grappled with influential elements on Capitol Hill who publicly cursed what they saw as a European partnership that was utterly ungrateful for American assistance, did nothing to guarantee a reasonable contribution for the common defence of the Western way against Communism, and yet reserved the right to openly criticize and mock the United States.

Carrington was, and always remained, pro-American. He had personal friends in America and, while not always smitten by US foreign and military policies, he dismissed ideas that the United Kingdom and her European allies could ever stand without American support before any major international confrontation. His instincts had been fine-tuned ever since his essays at Eton on foreign policy; these formative years were developed during the Second World War. He had watched as Stalin took Eastern Europe. He had written about and given speech after speech on East–West relations, nuclear power and transatlantic understanding and, finally, had known that Britain would not have been able to recover the Falkland Islands in 1982 if it had not been for the Americans unofficially supplying British forces with satellite intelligence, equipment and, especially, air-to-air missiles. Little wonder that Carrington found himself in the difficult position of being an impartial Secretary-General. He massaged public and political opinions so that American policy and actions would be at least tacitly accepted if not acceptable to the majority of NATO members, particularly when they were surprised by what Macmillan would have called, 'an event, dear boy, an event'.

Such an event took place when Palestinian terrorists killed seventeen people in a coordinated attack on the passenger concourses at Vienna and Rome airports. The terrorists were part of the Abu-Nidal Group. The immediate connection was with Lebanon. However, it was a spokesman for the Libyans, and therefore the President, Colonel Muammar Qaddafi, who publicly described the attacks as heroic actions. The CIA and the SIS told their governments that the Libyans were involved. The United States insisted there should be an oil embargo, but 75 per cent of Libyan output went to European states and so no European government agreed to support America's demands for sanctions. Even Prime Minister Thatcher, Reagan's closest European ally, refused because she had never believed international sanctions worked. If any European was likely to support America it was the French President, François Mitterrand. But that was because the French had their own agenda which included a large migrant population from North Africa. Mitterrand knew also that a public declaration did not sign any dotted line in international diplomacy and there were quite a few Arab customers of France who would look the other way because they too felt uneasy about the Libyans.

Carrington was expected to follow the American position but at that stage there was no direct evidence that they were being targeted and even if they were, the imposition of sanctions would not stop the attacks. Washington once more assumed that Carrington was not always onside – not on their side anyway. But he could be useful, they believed, in another European matter that concerned them: Spain was running a referendum about NATO membership and America had bases in Spain. There had for some time been a question mark over Spain's membership of the alliance. Spain thought it might follow the French model of not being a member of the integrated military group – in other words, having a political but not a military commitment. Carrington anticipated the obvious difficulty: Spain had a bilateral agreement with the United States that allowed the Americans to have some 9,000 military and civilian personnel on four bases in Spain plus aircraft squadrons. This agreement was due to run out in 1988. If the referendum went against military involvement, would it not be unreasonable for the Spanish government to wonder what electoral support it would have for the basing arrangement with the United States? Congress was already flagging up this predicament as a further example of the failure of old Europe – a view and terminology held since Donald Rumsfeld had been the US Permanent Representative to NATO in the 1970s. Carrington was used as the go-between by Madrid and Washington, all the time aware that the White House also wanted European governments to reverse their decision to reject American demands for sanctions against Libya.

As it turned out, the Spanish voted to stay in the alliance and so avoided what would have been the most damaging political reversal for NATO since the French withdrew from its integrated military wing in 1967. But there was no time for the NATO Secretariat to relax, for on 5 April 1986 there was a bomb explosion at a discotheque in West Berlin. Two people died, one of them an American soldier. Two hundred people were wounded, including sixty-four Americans. Once again, the CIA and the British SIS made the connection between the bombing and the Libyan government. The then Supreme Allied Commander Europe, US

General Bernard W. Rogers, confidently believed that the United States had 'indisputable evidence' to support the two intelligence assessments. What he did not immediately say was that before the attack, American Intelligence had been told that the club was a terrorist target. That information was passed up the Washington chain of command but administration officials had been slow to react. Questioned later, Rogers suggested that by the time that intelligence had been sent back across the Atlantic to the European military command the bomb was perhaps already in place or on its way, and that the attempts to warn off American service personnel from going to the club were too late. An internal examination of the intelligence distribution within the American system would follow; more immediately the US wanted harsh retribution.

The pace and structure of international law was, in Washington's eyes, inadequate. Washington ordered two carrier groups to the Mediterranean. This force included full squadrons of reconnaissance, air-defence and ground-attack aircraft and electronic jamming planes. The carriers were supported by destroyer escorts and frigates. Other amphibious assault vessels and submarines were on standby. This was a formidable show of strength and it was aimed at Colonel Qaddafi's Libya. Carrington had lived within the shadow of America's mood and frustration at events 'over there' for almost a year. His own military assessment was not so difficult to come by: he warned his international staff that Washington would take quick and direct action that such a task force could not execute. He was correct. Three days after the bombing President Reagan asked Prime Minister Thatcher to allow him to order American F1-11s based in Britain to be used in air strikes against Libya. This was a politically charged moment.

If Thatcher were to give Reagan permission she would be stretching or even breaking the political accord by which the aircraft were based in the United Kingdom. They were there to support a NATO emergency, usually imagined to be against the Warsaw Pact. They were not based in Britain, on RAF stations, as a jumping-off point for American actions against a third party which posed no threat to the North Atlantic alliance. Thatcher, contrary to general belief, did not immediately give her permission. She wanted assurances that the Reagan reasoning was correct and she wanted to know what targets they were going for.

Carrington observed at the time that the international legitimacy of the request posed a delicate argument as well as a test of Anglo-American friendship. If that had been the only question, then he imagined that the private debate would not have been so difficult. Carrington was very aware of the considerable debt owed by Britain to America for its diplomatic, intelligence and weapons support during the 1982 Falklands confrontation. However, if Britain allowed American Fi-11s to fly from their UK bases to targets in Libya, what would the Libyans do to British personnel there? Carrington also believed that the Thatcher government, which he still supported in spite of his international role, risked enormous political damage should those aircraft be used. He knew from his own experience and the advice of his people at NATO that in its aftermath even a militarily successful bombing raid, unless it were against an entirely inanimate object, would always lose public support once the human casualty list was posted. Carrington's own experiences from Crichel Down to the Falklands had made him extremely wary of the power of the media. He believed that a bombing by American aircraft based in the United Kingdom, supported by a Prime Minister already going through a difficult public relations patch, fell too neatly into the hands of aggressive editors.

Carrington's task was to hold together other NATO nations and the United States. He knew the Americans would do what they wished whatever the political and legal cautions of other member states. His job was to give the impression of unity, which is why on 11 April 1986 the American television networks seized upon what appeared to be Carrington's support. He said that he did not think that Washington could allow terrorist attacks such as the Berlin bombing 'without taking some sort of retaliatory action ... I can tell you there would be a very great deal of sympathy and support for the United States doing something ...'[10]

10 *Washington Post*, 12 April 1986.

Carrington could not stay silent. Nor could he hide behind diplomatic language to avoid expressing some sympathy for the American position. But when Carrington spoke, he spoke for NATO. He did not anticipate that it would be a simple statement quickly disappearing into the ether. Radio Libya immediately broadcast a characteristically belligerent reply:

This means Libya is now facing an imperial alliance which extends from Tel Aviv to Washington via NATO ... in addition to strengthening its existing alliances, Libya might have to go further to confront this imperialist, Zionist, aggressive alliance.

Robin Stafford, Carrington's spokesman in Brussels, tried to publicly emphasize that nothing that Carrington had said could or should be construed as a 'NATO threat to Libya'. Stafford's argument that NATO had not taken an official line was strictly true. But interpretation and perception during such situations establish their own truths. The fact that Carrington and Thatcher had independently been reassured that the United States might be acting in accordance with Article 51 of the United Nations Charter in self-defence of their interests would be of little comfort in trying to sort out the diplomatic and domestic political spaghetti that would almost inevitably follow. On 14 April Thatcher told the Cabinet that it was pay-up time for the Falklands. Within hours of that meeting the aircraft left the United Kingdom bases and bombed targets in Libya. As Carrington had anticipated, the fall-out was not from the weapon systems but from the television cameras. This was not a political success for Thatcher but as Carrington pointed out to the author, 'What else could she have done? It was going to happen.' The consequences of publicly objecting to American use of British bases as launch pads for the F1-11s without having convincing intelligence that the Libyans had not been involved in the club bombing would probably have set back Anglo-American relations for a political generation. Moreover, he believed that in spite of an overt reluctance of certain NATO member states to support the American action, Thatcher's decision probably forestalled Congressional anti-European and therefore anti-alliance actions.

Nevertheless, Carrington had to impress upon the Americans that European disquiet over the bombing was not an Old World instinct that automatically blamed the Americans for faultlines in the transatlantic political and diplomatic bridge. Most of the countries that had objections had domestic agendas that were as politically complicated as any in the United States. Consequently, the permanent NATO Council was called to a meeting chaired by Carrington on 18 April in order that the US Under-Secretary of State, John Whitehead, could talk to these senior officials in some attempt at damage limitation. Britain was in an unenviable diplomatic position because only Canada came out and publicly defended the American action. Downing Street perhaps remembered Churchill's stricture to Lord Ismay that his purpose as Secretary-General was to support America and most of all make sure other states supported the British view. Carrington had been in an impossible position, yet the Alliance was still in one piece whatever the critics wrote. Of the future, Carrington told the NATO Council of Foreign Ministers that there was very little the alliance could do other than establish a common distribution of intelligence that would forewarn and inform sufficiently to forestall the overt differences that surfaced during the Libyan operation. Carrington was never convinced that anything he said on that occasion was acted upon.

In an interview with the American magazine *Newsweek*, which was published a week after the attack, Carrington found himself having to defend his and European perceptions of the way to counteract what some were already calling the Third World War – terrorism. The American argument, encouraged by the reluctance of her European allies to give immediate and unequivocal support for the F1-11 attack, was that most European countries (and therefore, to the Americans, the whole of Europe) were soft when it came to dealing with terrorism. Carrington was appalled at this naivety. To his mind the Americans were entirely forgetting that most European states had suffered terrorism for far longer than the Americans had even known it existed. Moreover, those

European states had suffered from terrorism in their own countries, unlike America.

I don't think it's right that the Europeans have been backward about terrorism. After all, they have suffered from it much longer than anyone else.
It's a question of whether the remedy proposed is exactly the remedy
that each European country feels is the right one ... the terrorism that
has been going on in Europe for the last seventeen to twenty years – in
Germany, France, Belgium, Spain, Italy – has been home grown with the
political aspects of it not relevant, except to the country concerned,
though you could say that the IRA in Northern Ireland was different ...
we are getting terrorism committed by people of, it appears, Middle
Eastern origin, committed mostly on European soil, and that seems to
me to create a much more difficult problem ... consequently when it is
said that various European countries with differing interests in the Middle East and in Libya should take specific action, I think it would be
readily understood if those countries asked for the evidence on which it
is asserted that a particular gang of people was responsible ... that does
raise difficulties about intelligence sources. The American administration
will have to make up its mind about the advantages and disadvantages of
allowing that information to be released.[11]

In London, it was generally accepted that Carrington had made
the best of a bad position and that apart from constitutional and
political historians, the matter of American action over Libya would
soon be forgotten. In other words, it would never be an election
issue and that was all that really mattered.

The previous year it was demonstrated that Carrington was still a
favoured son of the majority within the Tory Establishment. If
there were lingering doubts about his action in resigning three
years earlier, these were publicly ignored when in June 1985 the
Queen conferred upon him the Order of the Garter. At the ceremony at Windsor Carrington wore the insignia of one of the

11 *Newsweek*, 21 April 1986.

Order's late members; by so doing, a new knight metaphorically picks up the shield of a late knight. Carrington took on the insignia of his dear friend R. A. Butler, at whose memorial service he had read the lesson on the day that he had resigned as Foreign Secretary over the Falklands affair.

During all his time as Secretary-General, Carrington continued as chairman of the V&A Trustees. It was never an entirely happy time and yet it went on until 1988. He gave it up more or less at the same time that he stepped down from NATO. The following year the Berlin Wall was torn down and the symbol of the division of Europe was broken in pieces and sold on market stalls. In Carrington's view the very reason for NATO was also breached. The uncertainties of what would follow were not as threatening as those that had existed between the alliance's foundation in April 1949 and November 1989. Nevertheless, the future of Russia's President Gorbachev, who, in October 1986, had almost negotiated an agreement with President Reagan to abandon nuclear weaponry, was without political guarantee.[12] Carrington's view was that NATO had no justifiable role as long as it confined itself to the European politico-military tapestry. This he thought was particularly so as the European Union expanded and developed further political and therefore, inevitably, military functions. He thought the EU too complex an organization to successfully take on the military decision-making process of an international defence pact. NATO was a much simpler organization to run, even though its longer-term deployment decisions were taken by governments who were often also EU members. At a Royal United Services Institute dinner in December 2003, Carrington reflected on his time at NATO and those differences:

Of course we had our difficulties: the deployment of intermediate range nuclear missiles, the perennial problems between Greece and Turkey, the

12 The October 1986 Reykjavik Summit produced a proposal for a so-called zero-zero option for nuclear missiles but this was never going to work once Gorbachev demanded that America abandon its SDI programme.

bombing of Tripoli and so on. But they were blips in an otherwise harmonious scenario and that, of course, is why we finished our business at Evere [NATO HQ] in time for a drink before dinner, whilst up the road our equivalents in the European Union, who had to deal with conflicting national interests, argued into the early hours of the morning about the price of butter, or wine lakes, and the Common Agricultural Policy.

As Carrington came to the end of his time at NATO, there was still a Berlin Wall. Ostensibly, therefore, the fundamental reason for NATO survived. Yet there was every sign that the system that held together the Soviet Union was crumbling. The finality of the change would not occur until 1991 and the political and strategic direction of the new Russia would be unclear for almost two decades after that. Carrington saw himself as a realist; like all who claim that distinction he recognized the sometimes precarious balance of pessimism and optimism expressed by a public figure.

After the demise of the Soviet Union it was quite clear that the threat from the Soviet Union no longer existed and NATO, if it was to continue, had to change ... for an organization to survive, it has to have an identifiable object and it seems to me that the new NATO has two identifiable objects: first, to encompass those countries in Europe which had either hitherto not been members or had been members of the opposing Pact ... Secondly, in my experience, however benign the circumstances at any given moment, the unexpected, almost always disagreeable, invariably happens and it is wise to maintain the capacity to defend yourself and intervene where it is necessary to maintain your own security. The emergence of world terrorism is obviously a case in point.

By 1988 he was not sorry to be gone from Brussels. The future of the NATO alliance was not in doubt but Carrington continued to have doubts about the ability of European governments in particular to understand the commitment needed to maintain it as an effective rather than a paper transatlantic pact. Fifteen years later, the American-led coalition invaded Iraq. This intervention had no role for NATO, but to Carrington, the European reaction to the war and the American view of the 'old' European position illustrated what had been since 1949 the importance of the alliance – the transatlantic relationship which brought Canada and America to the centre of European strategic ambitions. The split between Europe and America was inevitable, he knew, but had to be seen as short term because their interests were similar.

One compelling advantage for the maintenance of NATO, certainly to me who comes from a dying generation, whose participation in the Second World War and its aftermath have lent a particular importance to American involvement in European affairs ... For many years, it has been quite clear, that without US help, there is not much that Europe can do on its own ... the unpalatable fact is that there is a deep suspicion on the part of our American allies, that there is an ulterior motive amongst some Europeans to de-couple Europe from the United States and NATO. Whether this be true or not, it is something for which we should have some regard. NATO is the only organization in which the Europeans and the Americans can exchange views and in which they collaborate. Recent events in Iraq have undoubtedly caused transatlantic differences. Of course I understand the irritation of the Americans at what was said and done by some of us in Europe, understand too, the nervousness of those in Europe, who saw the Iraq war as American unilateralism. What is greatly to be deplored is the attitude and language used on both sides of the Atlantic. Opposition to the war seems to have spilt over into a dislike of Americans or Europeans. But what has been done is done. The time for recrimination is over, on both sides.[13]

Carrington at the age of sixty-nine was not quite out of work, but he was looking, as he always looked, for the next 'big job'. It was time for him to leave the job as chairman of the V&A Trustees. He had been an absentee landlord and found there was little money

13 Extracts from speech at Royal United Services Institute, December 2003. Original in Carrington papers, Bledlow.

going into the V&A (fund-gathering had been part of his brief); he could see little more that he could do at the museum. It was his friend from Eton, Jocelyn Hambro, who suggested to Carrington that he should become chairman of the international fine art auction house, Christie's. He was encouraged even further when Hambro remarked that it was a very agreeable board because every director but one was an Old Etonian. (Carrington's housemaster at Eton, Cyril Butterwick – the renowned social gossip Betty Kenward had been his dame – had recently joined Christie's rival Sotheby's as a silver expert.) Carrington thought the gathering of OEs in St James's to be a plus point in running any auction house; after all, he saw Christie's as a clearing house of paintings and objets d'art for the aristocracy and stately homes of the British Isles. He was not so impressed when, a year into his chairmanship, he suggested someone for the board only to be told that it was an impossible request as the individual was a Jew. He had imagined, wrongly, that such overt anti-Semitism was out of date by the 1990s. Generally, he felt comfortable in his first-floor room which he encouraged all not to pass by. He felt less comfortable when told that he should never meet with directors of Sotheby's as there were growing suspicions of a cartel between the auction houses and that commissions could be fixed. Carrington left Christie's in 1993 and was never implicated in the European Commission's allegations in 2002 that Sotheby's and Christie's – the world's two biggest auction houses – had operated an illegal price-fixing cartel in the UK and Continental Europe for most of the 1990s.

The US Department of Justice had already gathered enough evidence to mount prosecutions even though by the start of the new century the cartel to fix commission fees and 'other trading terms' had allegedly been dissolved – hence the warning that Carrington should have nothing to do with Sotheby's. According to the European Commission, the two chairmen had entered into secret discussions in 1993, the year Carrington departed. As the Commission report asserted, 'These first high-level meetings were followed by regular gatherings and contacts between the companies' chief executive officers.'

The two villains of the story were Sotheby's chairman Alfred
Taubman and, allegedly, Carrington's successor Sir Anthony Tennant. Taubman, in New York anyway, had no option but to go to
court and was found guilty of violating the US anti-trust laws. In
Europe, operating an albeit illegal cartel is not a criminal offence,
but it is in the States. Tennant refused to go to New York and so
never faced trial.

Carrington had no part in any of this. It was Christie's chief
executive Christopher Davidge who told the industry legal regula-
tors in 2000 what was going on. In exchange for whistle-blowing,
Christie's pleaded for leniency – which they got. They escaped a
fine. Sotheby's were fined in Brussels 20 million euros – then about
6 per cent of their turnover. Carrington had left his agreeable but
hardly demanding chairmanship just in time.

Once more, he fidgeted for a big job. It came in 1991 when he
was asked to be chairman of the European Communities Peace
Conference on Yugoslavia. Later, it was his view that events in
Yugoslavia came into the bracket of tragedies that might have been
avoided had international institutions and powerful governments
anticipated the dangers enough to make time to prevent the disaster in the first place.

15. The Former Yugoslavia

The politics of Bosnia had smouldered since the death of Tito in 1980 and they burst into flames at the start of the final decade of the twentieth century. The UN and the European Community turned their attentions to Bosnia and there were hopes early in the conflict of avoiding further bloodshed. Those hopes came to nothing and the Balkans erupted once more into civil war. Diplomacy had failed but the UN and the EC knew that whatever the level of fighting there would come a point when all sides would be willing to negotiate. European governments needed a negotiator with a reputation for balanced diplomacy, which was why in 1991 Carrington once again took it on, albeit reluctantly. His view was that it was very possible to bring the conflict to a peaceful conclusion but he doubted that the differing interests in Europe, at the United Nations and in the United States would let him get on with the job and then trust his conclusion sufficiently to support it. He sought to devise a constructive approach but as he reread the modern history of the Balkans, Carrington wondered whether any wisdom he had once had might have deserted him.

It came close to being the most frustrating job of his career. The story behind Yugoslavia's continuing crisis of regional and ethnic destruction began in 1980 with the death of Josip Broz, known by one of his wartime aliases, Tito. Tito had held together the murderous divisions of what was Yugoslavia. (*Yugo*: south, thus land of the southern Slavs.) Much of West European military thinking during the 1960s and 1970s had been about the hypothesis that when Tito went, Yugoslavia would implode and so the Balkans would be in flames and the rest of Europe and its interests would catch its fire.

As Defence Secretary and periodically as Foreign Secretary, Carrington had been briefed almost daily on the situation in the

former Yugoslavia. As NATO Secretary-General he had an even
deeper interest. So Carrington did not arrive at the new job in
1991 as a Balkans novice; nevertheless, his first task was to read about
the complex recent history of that region. He believed that he had
no chance in bringing differing sides together unless he understood
and, on occasions, displayed a deep understanding of their history.

Twentieth-century military history lessons begin in Sarajevo
with the start of the First World War and the assassination of Arch-
duke Franz Ferdinand on 28 June 1914. Britain, France and Russia
became allied with Serbia. The Bosnians and the Croats were allied
to the forces of the Austro-Hungarian Empire before which the
Serbian army withdrew to the Adriatic from Kosovo. By December 1918 Slovenia, Croatia and Serbia – a mixture of Slavs, Croats,
Serbs, Albanians, Hungarians and pockets of those of Turkish, German and Greek origins – were living in the new kingdom. A
decade later, in 1929, this battery of ethnic-origin religions (Roman
and Serbian Orthodox Christians and Muslims) were officially
called inhabitants of the new European state, Yugoslavia. Any ideas
of democracy were ill-conceived and abandoned in 1929 when for
the next five years King Alexander established his dictatorship. He
was assassinated in 1934 and even then the complex way of the
Balkans was to the fore. He was killed by a Macedonian who had
been contracted for the assassination by the leader of the Croatian
fascists, Ante Pavelic. In 1939 Tito became General Secretary of the
Yugoslav Communist Party.

In April 1941 the Germans invaded Yugoslavia with ground
troops and the carpet bombing of Belgrade. Bulgaria, Romania
and Hungary were given one section of Yugoslavia and Croatia
was established as an independent state, although it was really run
by the Nazis and the Italians.

During this period perhaps some half a million Serbs were killed.
The popular view of the war in that region is that Britain supported the plucky partisans led by Tito. These freedom fighters, who
had the agility and cunning of true mountain men, led a resistance
that successfully tied down thirty German divisions. Like all good
war stories, the truth is somewhat different. There were probably no

more than six German divisions occupied with the partisans. The truth about Yugoslavia was that it was suffering a most terrible civil war. Perhaps some 1.6 million Yugoslavs died during the Second World War. Maybe 60 per cent of them were killed by fellow Yugoslavs. Many died in extermination camps run by the Croatians. The ethnic cleansing of Serbs and Gypsies did not begin with Slobodan Milosevic. It was Tito who ordered the camps to be built. Britain is usually remembered as having supported the brave Tito. That did not happen until 1943. Until then, Churchill had sent public messages in support of the Serbs and their leader Draza Mihailovic.

In 1948 Tito famously broke with Moscow and, for nearly forty years after that, the effective control of the national aspirations of Slovenes, Serbs and Croats removed the Balkan question from Western foreign ministerial test papers. The obvious sign of change came during the 1990 elections in the six republics: Bosnia-Herzegovina, Croatia, Macedonia, Montenegro, Serbia and Slovenia. These elections, the first attempt at apparent democracy for more than sixty years, were a success for the nationalist parties.

A year later the Serbs and Croats were at war. With its ill-coordinated diplomatic reasoning, the largest Western interest group, NATO, did nothing to prevent that war. Most European Union members were also members of NATO and all were, naturally, members of the UN. Common membership does not mean common action. The obvious weakness in the West European case for the prevention of conflict in Yugoslavia was that the only reasonable chance of moderating, deterring and perhaps even stopping war would have been an air campaign. There was no question of deployment of ground troops. This could not be done unless it was led by the United States and that was not on Washington's agenda.

It was into this mess that Carrington slipped reluctantly when in 1991 the six-month presidency of the European Community (later European Union) was held by the Netherlands. Carrington's stock was very high among the Dutch. He was considered to have been a very successful NATO Secretary-General and an admired

British Foreign Secretary and it was not entirely unexpected when the Dutch Foreign Minister Hans van den Broek asked Carrington to chair the projected Peace Conference on Yugoslavia.

Carrington said he did not want to become a travelling peace-maker and that he would take the job if all it meant was chairing a constitutional conference, as the title suggested. But it did not turn out that way. There was fighting in the Balkans and Carrington said that there was no point in having a conference unless there was a ceasefire. Van den Broek replied that unless they promised to have a peace conference, there would never be a cease-fire. It was a classical diplomatic chicken-and-egg affair. Carrington's view, learned at his prep school, was that when there is conflict, in most cases the solution is to let the two sides fight it out. However, in 1991 the European opinion was that the conflict should be stopped before its effects spread into Western Europe.

Moreover, the Americans had their own views on the Balkans. They believed in choosing a side and then with subversive inter-vention supporting that choice; if that failed, then hard bombing of targets would stop the war spreading and make whoever came out on top a client state. Additionally, there were clear signs from Wash-ington that no matter what Carrington succeeded in doing, the United States would disapprove. They did not trust a European solution. The Americans foiled Carrington's attempt at bringing about peace just as they foiled the attempts of his successor, David Owen, who by then was working with the former US Secretary of State, Cyrus Vance.

In July 1991 Carrington had just turned seventy-two. On 13 July the EC Monitor Mission (ECMM) was set up under the first Memorandum of Understanding and was signed by the Yugoslav groups after discussions with the EC negotiators. On 1 September the Monitor Mission extended its work to the ceasefire in Croatia and later to the developing situation in Bosnia and Herzegovina. That autumn of 1991 the Declaration on Yugoslavia was issued, which was intended to outline the ambitions for ceasefires and a peaceful settlement to the internecine war.

On 7 September 1991 Carrington chaired the first session of

The Hague Conference on Yugoslavia. Around the table were representatives of the twelve European Community states, the Serbian President Slobodan Milosevic and the first President of Croatia, Franjo Tudman. Carrington had a mandate that was to satisfy three areas. First, he believed that there was no point in talking until there was a ceasefire – real and not bogus. Second, to hold the political stability together – such as it was – there could be no recognition for any of the six republics of Yugoslavia as independent and sovereign states unless all six agreed on such independence, and even then only as part of an overall settlement. Third, the boundaries had to remain intact unless, again, all six agreed on any state border changes as part of a total settlement. This third point was emphasized by Carrington as being particularly important because nobody should misunderstand that the conference would collapse should there be any sign that those borders might be changed by force. Carrington believed that Tudman and Milosevic wanted to carve up Bosnia.

By 17 September, Milosevic, Tudman and Carrington had signed a ceasefire agreement. It became known as the Igalo Agreement after the small town on the Montenegrin coast. Inevitably the ceasefire did not last. Carrington, reluctantly, opened a second session of talks two days later. On 4 October some form of agreement was reached that would enable them to start negotiations for a Yugoslav settlement. The vexed question of independence was prominent; the aim was a recognition of those republics that wanted independence. On 8 October 1991 the United Nations increased its interests by appointing Cyrus Vance as the Secretary-General's personal envoy for Yugoslavia. By 14 October it was clear that an agreement that would hold would be virtually impossible. For example, the Serbian delegation made it clear that their people wanted a single state and not a number of independent republics. Here was the Milosevic ambition in a nutshell: Serbia wanted to be the new Yugoslavia and expected to be able to annex those regions of Croatia and Bosnia-Herzegovina in which the Serbs were the majority. Although it did not read this way, effectively on 14 October 1991 the template for ethnic cleansing was pasted on that fifth plenary session of the Conference on Yugoslavia.

There was some hope by the next session in a document that was called the Carrington Plan. It demanded that all peoples' human rights and expectations should be protected. This meant autonomous regions and some guarantees to Serbs who lived outside of Serbia. Carrington could see the way towards what he called an à la carte agreement. He felt that those people who wanted independence should have it and have some connection with central government only if they wanted it. The formal phrase within the Carrington Plan, 'recognition of the independence, within the existing borders, unless otherwise agreed, of those republics wishing it', was rejected out of hand by Milosevic. In doing so, Milosevic had rejected the only comprehensive chance of a settlement. The Serb leader would only go as far as accepting the principle of the Carrington Plan – not the detail. On 9 November 1991 Carrington told a meeting of European foreign ministers that the conference could not reach any worthwhile solution without Serbia. In other words, much as the ministers disliked Milosevic and his ambitions, they knew that without him the whole peace process would go into a politically and militarily dramatic freefall. By this time there was an increased agitation for a United Nations peacekeeping operation. Yet all around the negotiators there was fighting. No one could realistically see an end to it. Carrington told the leadership in Belgrade that unless the fighting stopped, he could never recommend a UN intervention on the ground.

Ten days later Cyrus Vance called a UN-sponsored meeting in Geneva with Milosevic, Tudman, the Federal Defence Minister General Veljko Kadijevic and Carrington. The ensuing Geneva Agreement and a supposed ceasefire followed. Here also was the basis for the plan proposed by Cyrus Vance to send in UN peacekeepers in demilitarized zones. Even as they agreed the conditions, Carrington sat at the table with them quietly believing that it stood no chance whatsoever of succeeding because the ceasefire would exist only on paper. On 28 November Carrington was told that the Serbian assembly had passed a declaration to go ahead with the proclamation of Serbian autonomous regions in Bosnia and Herzegovina. Carrington immediately wrote to Hans van den Broek, the EC chairman of foreign ministers. Carrington believed that if Bosnia and Herzegovina demanded independence then there would be a very real possibility of war. He argued strongly that even though independence should not in the long term be denied to individual republics, the EC should withhold any recognition of any individual state until an overall agreement had been reached. On 16 December 1991 a European Summit in Brussels, pushed it would seem thoughtlessly by the German Chancellor Helmut Kohl, ignored Carrington's advice (supported by Vance) and recognized Slovenia and Croatia. Carrington made his view clear that having recognized Slovenia and Croatia, Bosnia would then see no barrier to their own independence, which would mean a civil war in Bosnia.

On 27 December 1991 Alija Izetbegovic wrote to Carrington telling him that he had established an Assembly of the Serbian People in Bosnia and Herzegovina. The political infighting among the different Balkan leaders was obvious to all those who were trying to bring together a formula for preserving the Conference on Yugoslavia. When its ninth session opened in Brussels in January 1992, Milosevic, Tudman and Izetbegovic attended. In Sarajevo, while the conference was taking place, there was a declaration of the Republic of the Serbian People of Bosnia and Herzegovina, claiming the territories of the Serbian autonomous regions and ethnic territories. Moreover, the Assembly of the Serbian People was fixed and Izetbegovic and his colleague Haris Silajdzic were told they no longer had the right to represent their people. There was a broad agreement that Bosnia and Herzegovina would remain within its existing borders. What went on within those borders could not be agreed. The Croats wanted a federal Bosnia and Herzegovina. The Serbs felt safer with a confederation. The Muslims argued for a unitary state.

Throughout December 1991, with no more than a break for Christmas Day, right the way through to the late summer of 1992, there was hardly a day when Carrington was not either in the air travelling to yet another meeting in the Balkans or at EC meetings reporting the view from the brink of civil war. Ceasefires came and went. For example, on 12 April a ceasefire was declared and signed. On the same day the Bosnia and Herzegovina leadership issued a directive declaring war on the Yugoslav National Army and the Serbs. On 5 May another ceasefire was declared. There was supposed to be a routine for the exchange of lists of captured and wounded prisoners, the recovery of the dead, access to food and medical supplies and some effort to restore essential services. Throughout the ceasefire the fighting continued. Izetbegovic told Carrington on 6 May that the Yugoslav National Army, while talking peace, was shelling Mostar and Sarajevo. He said that the Republics of Serbia and Montenegro were the only legitimate successors to the former state of Yugoslavia. Carrington recognized that what Izetbegovic said was true. Equally, he never for one moment trusted him. If Izetbegovic was trying to play the innocent with Carrington he would be disappointed. Izetbegovic pleaded that while talks were going on regarding the future of Bosnia and Herzegovina, Radovan Karadzic with his commander Radko Mladic had continued the fighting without observing a single ceasefire. By this time Carrington was anxious that Milosevic should instruct – 'use influence' was the term actually used – Mladic to stop the siege of Sarajevo. It did not get very far.

Towards the end of June 1992 Carrington failed to persuade the main players, including Milosevic, Tudman and Silajdzic, to move anywhere towards progress. Milosevic swept aside any idea of conciliation with Bosnia and Herzegovina, claiming that Serbia did not want to take over the region. Carrington, in spite of what Tudman had said, was convinced that the latter was determined to bring about the partition of Bosnia and Herzegovina. Tudman refused to withdraw Croatian troops. Silajdzic simply demanded military intervention and claimed that the United Nations was wrong in blaming everybody for continuing the fighting. Silajdzic also was a sworn enemy of Karadzic and he would not sit with him in any conference. Even when Carrington, by this time almost exhausted, finally got to Sarajevo on 3 July 1992 and restarted the so-called peace process, fighting, looting and murdering of civilians continued on the streets.

On 15 July the protagonists came to London. Carrington, who was still chairman of the auction house Christie's, got the Balkan representatives away from the usual negotiating atmosphere. He invited them to Christie's headquarters in St James's in London. Izetbegovic was not swayed by the fine art atmosphere. He refused to talk to Karadzic. He accused him of trying to use these talks to legitimize what he had achieved by violence. 'I will not sit with a child killer,' he told Carrington. After a couple of days Carrington managed to get an agreement that allowed for a two-week cease-fire, some sort of promise to put heavy military equipment under international control and the return of refugees to their homes.

Carrington said that it was really up to the United Nations to provide guarantees that would prevent heavy weapons returning to their dugouts. It was at this point that it was decided that the Conference on the Former Socialist Federal Republic of Yugoslavia would be held in London between 26 and 28 August 1992. There was not much joy in the prospect of this meeting. There had been thirty-eight ceasefires by then. All had been broken. Yet Carrington had started negotiations with the observation that they could not be worthwhile unless they took place without fighting going on. Would there be another ceasefire? Carrington had given up on them. In a report to the EC foreign ministers he included a further observation that:

I don't think there is much object in brokering another ceasefire unless there is a radical change in circumstances ... you would be talking to the same people who ignored what was agreed last time ...

No one was above the accusation that they had failed to honour agreements. There were certain sympathies towards the Muslims, but Carrington pointed out that they had been responsible for the collapse of the latest talks and that they were breaking ceasefires as much as anyone else – perhaps more so. At the beginning of August 1992, reports started circulating that refugees were describing

concentration camps in the Serb-controlled area of northern
Bosnia. Up until this point Carrington had kept the talks moving,
often in the most difficult of circumstances. But when the thir-
teenth session of the conference opened in Brussels on 14 August,
Carrington had a sense of foreboding that the process could too
easily crumble. Milosevic, for the first time in this process, refused
to come to the meeting. Izetbegovic stayed for the opening session
but then walked out and refused Carrington's invitation to go to
the Hilton Hotel in Brussels to talk about the future of Bosnia and
Herzegovina, telling him that it was up to Karadzic to decide
whether to fight or to talk – he could not have it both ways. There
were, therefore, no Bosnians at the talks.

The London Conference, a joint EC and UN gathering, opened
on schedule on 26 August. Carrington's view was that this was the
last diplomatic push to stop the fighting in Bosnia. It was now that
he announced that he was giving up his role in the talks and he
would leave behind his draft agreement that could have led to a
settlement. But he was not walking away until, he hoped, the job
was finished. Hope was not high. Carrington had exhausted his
powers to bring the opposing factions to an understanding. He was
also frustrated by inter-agency differences and by the fact that some
countries, notably the Americans, still had a private agenda to frustrate what he was attempting. Nevertheless, he did not wash his
hands of the conference and became a member of its steering
committee. His final thoughts as he addressed that meeting suggested one frustrated by the inability of those involved to accept
what could have been such a reasonable process towards peace.

It was his view that the European Community should be held
in some large part responsible for the inability of the conference to
succeed and therefore directly for the deaths of so many people in
the region. It was, he believed, the EC's invitation – against his
expressed advice – to invite the Yugoslav republics to apply for
independence that changed the whole nature of the Conference
on Yugoslavia. Equally gloomily, the draft convention that he left
was accepted by all the republics but Serbia. After all this time,
nothing had changed.

There were six unresolved problems: Bosnia, the Serbian Krajina, Vojvodina, Kosovo, Sandjak and Macedonia.

Here, the question of recognition and independence had fouled the flow of the bilateral and trilateral negotiations. Once Bosnia had been recognized officially, fighting had broken out and consequently there had been virtually no chance of progress since April of that year. No one had yet persuaded the Serbs in Krajina to negotiate, nor the Croats there to show any restraint. Carrington was forced to admit that the Krajina Serbs believed themselves to be better off under UN protection than under the authority of the Croatian government as in his plan. Finally he told the British as well as other European governments that the Serbs and Kosovo had to be brought to heel otherwise there would be war. And with that, Carrington handed over his role as EC negotiator to Lord Owen. Carrington's view was that Owen and Vance would work well together and, somewhat cynically, Owen would put all his energies into seeking some solution because there was always the prospect of a Nobel Peace prize.

Carrington became more and more convinced that various nationalities and states within the state that was Yugoslavia would have been better off if they had been left to sort out their own problems. He recognized of course that this policy would have led to considerable bloodshed, but then all the efforts of the so-called NATO allies could not prevent that – indeed, they were responsible for much of it. Particularly, he fell out with Baroness Thatcher, who by 1993 was not only criticizing the way peace programmes had been managed, but was also recommending armed intervention.

In February 1994 Carrington was asked to become a patron, along with the sometime UN Secretary-General Javier Perez de Cuellar, of the European Action Council for Peace in the Balkans. This was one of the many organizations established to find peaceful means for a solution to the problems of that region. The advisory committee of the Council, which was chaired by its founder, Prince Sadruddin Aga Khan, contained some formidable internationally known personalities. They included Simon Wiesenthal, Alexander Langer and Lady Thatcher. This group was supposed to work in conjunction with the American Action Council, which again had a celebrated steering committee from the higher reaches of the Potomac's political elite. They included Zbigniew Brzezinski, the former presidential foreign affairs adviser, the ex-US Secretary of Defense Frank Carlucci, the sometime presidential hopeful Geraldine Ferraro, the arms control negotiator Max Kampelman, former Secretary of State George Shultz, UN ambassador Jeane Kirkpatrick and the international financier George Soros.

On 22 February Prince Sadruddin Aga Khan sent Carrington the mission statement for the Action Council. Apart from stating much of the obvious – very little effort had been made to stop the differences becoming a crisis – the statement urged that the

moral stature [*sic*], political will and perhaps military capacity of the European leadership must be used to stop the horror in the Balkans and preserve a multicultural European state.

Immediately, the Council wanted European powers to deploy a

decisive use of tactical air power to prevent the strangulation and seizure of Sarajevo and other UN safe havens; to lift the seizures; to restore vital services ... and to prevent the re-supply of military forces.

They also wanted the lifting of the arms embargo on Bosnia. Carrington was not impressed. Much as he admired Prince Sadruddin, he was tired of dealing with groups that had little chance of succeeding, but which gained credibility from his reputation. The world was full of non-governmental organizations which had opinions but little real clout and so, while they gathered in fine circumstances to talk but not act, the subject of their discussion waited in misery for someone, somewhere, to do something that would ease their lot. More significantly, Carrington had fallen out with Thatcher's view of the world. It was as if she believed there was a Falklands-type answer to all crises.

A week later, on 28 February 1994, Carrington wrote to the prince:

I have been so intimately concerned over a long period with what is happening in Yugoslavia and deeply upset at some of the decisions of the European Community and of the Americans, that I feel I am not in total sympathy with all those on the Council.

Although, of course, I accept the four main objectives of the Action Council, I do not, for example, share Lady Thatcher's views on what should have been done in the past or what she proposes now. I have increasingly become convinced that international involvement in Yugoslavia has prolonged the suffering of its people, and that all the well meaning attempts to find a political solution have made things worse, though of course I very much support the humanitarian efforts.

I think that my reservations are such that you are better off without me.

Carrington was fed up with the whole process. He thought most of the leading players in the conflict were as devious as each other. He believed that when, as was inevitable, one or the other was indicted for war crimes, then none would be less guilty than another. This was not, he noted, 1945; what would, say, an indictment of Milosevic really achieve? And with that, Carrington packed his diplomatic bag and hoped for a quieter life.

16. A Tale of Two Trees

Few of those who walk for so long on international stages ever really hope for a quieter life, even in their seventies. They may take a cruise, as the Carringtons did, but they long to be at the centre of world affairs and, to a much lesser extent, national affairs. Carrington was no exception to this general rule. He knew almost every individual who was running the bits of the world that interested him. More importantly, those individuals knew him. Carrington had all but disappeared from the British newspaper daily headlines; but departments of state in which many major international issues were decided were still consulting him. The most discreet of global gatherings of the truly powerful took place under the banner Bilderberg. Carrington became one of its most influential members.

Bilderberg is the name given to a regular meeting of some of the most influential people in the world. They include heads of government and sometimes state, international industrialists, bankers, politicians, diplomats and media owners. The meetings are private. The first meeting was held at the Bilderberg Hotel (hence the name) in 1954, at Oosterbeek, Holland. The themes for discussion are world issues; the importance of these annual gatherings is that those attending are in a position to influence those issues. Thus, some outsiders find these meetings sinister and are suspicious that members of Bilderberg are manipulating the way in which the world is run. Carrington's view was that the world would probably be in a much better state if indeed members had such influence.

In May 1998, when Carrington chaired the Bilderberg Group meeting at Turnberry, Scotland, there was hardly a continent without a political or financial crisis that could not justify its inclusion in the Turnberry discussions. Terrorism was not new, but there were those at Turnberry who accepted that the world should be ready to know how to deal with a terrorist-inspired catastrophe. That it would be directed, so they rightly thought, at the United States made emergency and disaster planning even more necessary. The events in New York and Washington DC in September 2001 were not anticipated, but the devasting effects of an assault were. Even Bilderberg could not prevent 9/11. Turnberry and its succeeding meetings brought together those who controlled much of the world in spite of terrorism. Carrington fitted into that grouping because at even just a year short of his eightieth birthday, his international reputation remained sound and his experience valuable. He liked the mix of power. Particularly, he liked the mix of sobriety and flamboyance. One such character at Bilderberg was the Canadian business and media tycoon Conrad Black.

In the early 1980s the British national newspaper industry was on the verge of a printing revolution. This would mean, as Rupert Murdoch and Eddie Shah understood, challenging the authority of the print unions through the introduction of new printing processes. No newspaper could afford to stick to the old ways and even the *Daily Telegraph*, which had a greater circulation than *The Times*, *Financial Times* and *Guardian* added together, was no exception. The *Telegraph* was owned by Lord Hartwell and the Berry family and through their bankers, Rothschild, attempted to raise money to modernize the paper and its plant. It was at this point, in 1984, that Conrad Black became interested in the *Daily Telegraph* and he did so at a meeting of the Bilderberg Group. At the Bilderberg meeting at Westchester in upstate New York, another member of the group quietly told Black that the *Telegraph* was vulnerable, that the search for investors seemed dead in the water and that Black could be well placed to launch a takeover bid. In May 1985 Hartwell agreed to meet Black in New York. Hartwell appears to have been desperate for the money to save the paper and almost immediately agreed to accept Black's £10 million offer for 14 per cent of the business. Crucially, Hartwell also agreed that if there were to be a new issue of shares or if the family sold any

Berry holdings, then Black should have first refusal. This was a financial coup for Black. He had, as one onlooker is said to have remarked, landed an enormous fish with a tiny hook. Six months later, on 28 November 1985, Black, through his holding company Hollinger, took control of the company. He was hardly content with one paper. Hollinger then bought *The Spectator*, the *Jerusalem Post*, the *Chicago Sun-Times* and the *Sydney Morning Herald* as well as regional and local newspapers the length and breadth of North America.

In 1990 Carrington was at a luncheon. One of the other guests was Conrad Black, whom Carrington had seen on a couple of occasions but had never met. After lunch Black cornered him and began a devastating and slanderous character assassination of a former Tory Prime Minister who happened to be Carrington's hero. He let Black go on for some minutes and then cut in with a fierce defence of the Tory leader and with that, turned and left Black standing alone in the middle of a quickly deserting crowd. The next morning, Black telephoned Carrington, not with an apology, but to ask him to lunch. Carrington barked back (in his words) that he would accept, fully expecting to renew battle. They met and Black offered him a seat on the board of Hollinger. Carrington consented and so, in a curious manner, started a very close friendship that was as firm after Black's New York conviction for fraud as it was before the court appearance.

Carrington was on the Hollinger board with international heavyweights such as Henry Kissinger and Richard Perle – the man who had almost single-handedly stopped President Reagan agreeing to scrap US nuclear weapons when he met President Mikhail Gorbachev at the Reykjavik Summit in October 1986. Carrington's direct contact on the Hollinger board did not last much more than a year. But by then, Black wanted Carrington as a symbol of honour in his business dealings. He offered him a seat on the board of the *Daily Telegraph*. Again, Carrington accepted the Canadian's offer. Black's Bilderberg instincts led him to believe that only the great and the good should sit at his boardroom and dining-room tables. Thus Carrington found himself sitting at the *Daily Telegraph* with such Establishment figures as Sir Evelyn de Rothschild, Rupert Hambro and Sir Martin Jacomb. He believed entirely in the idea that it was not just who you knew but also who knew you. Everyone knew Carrington. Nevertheless, Carrington said that few took any notice of what he had to say, including Black, who demonstrated an instinct to do whatever he wished with anything he controlled in the belief that if he had the helm then he owned the vessel. Carrington observed that Black subscribed to this belief no matter how many shareholders there were and whatever the conventions and rules of business in whichever country he operated.

In 1994 Black sold shares to City of London institutions, then cut the price of the *Daily Telegraph*. The company's share price fell from 587p to 350p. His reputation in London financial circles fell as sharply as the shares. It is said that he was told he would 'never lunch in the City again'. But he did because, as one of his board members remarked, money gets a seat at any table. Carrington kept his seat on the board of the *Telegraph* and was still there two years later when Black moved the holding operation to North America.

When it all collapsed because Black was accused of milking the Hollinger assets for his personal gain, Carrington understood the Canadian's failings and certainly his weaknesses. He attributed his friend's downfall to an unquenchable thirst to keep up with billionaires when he was only a millionaire. Even an international millionaire can be in the economy class of the social and financial ratings.

Carrington did not abandon friends. When Black went for trial in New York, Carrington wrote to wish him luck. When Black was convicted, Carrington wrote to say how sorry he was. A few days later, he told me that when Black was released, he would give him lunch at White's. A friend, he said, is a friend.

The extent of the Carrington–Black relationship was seen in October 2001 when Carrington stood robed and caped in ermine to introduce his friend to the House of Lords as Lord Black of

Crossharbour. Margaret Thatcher was Black's other supporter
and the Conservative Leader William Hague proposed him.[1] The
Canadian Prime Minister Jean Chrétien objected to Black's
appointment to the Lords. Black got round this by renouncing his
Canadian citizenship.

A year before joining the *Daily Telegraph*'s board, Carrington,
approaching his seventy-fifth birthday, was once more caught up
in Southern African politics – this time in the dispute between the
African National Congress (ANC) and the Inkatha Freedom
Party (IFP). At the time, the two main parties could not agree on
the drafting of what would be a new constitution for the Republic
of South Africa. The ANC led by Nelson Mandela would not
accept the IFP's wording for the constitution. The issue was
simple: the IFP said that the constitution failed in its objective
of establishing a proper democratic order in South Africa because
it did not provide for the autonomy of the provinces and therefore failed to ensure a federal South Africa. Given the background
and history of Inkatha, the ANC saw this as a desire to be independent within the Republic. Certainly the IFP based a great deal
of their efforts on the need to restore the kingdom of KwaZulu
and the consequent reinstatement of the powers and privileges
of a Zulu monarch. So strongly did the IFP feel on these issues
that it had claimed it would not participate in the April 1994
elections.

The ANC meanwhile believed that the constitution fairly
reflected the intentions of everyone at the first session of the Convention for a Democratic South Africa held in December 1991.
Nelson Mandela and the IFP leader Mangosuthu Buthelezi had
met at the beginning of March 1994. Mandela's view was that if
there should be any international mediation, then it should not get
itself involved in what he regarded as the side issues and internal
politics of South Africa. Mandela wrote to Carrington at the end
of March 1994 in the hope that with his long-term interest in

1 He took the title Crossharbour from the street at Canary Wharf to which the
Daily Telegraph moved from Fleet Street.

African affairs he would become part of the international mediation team. He wanted Carrington to convene this group. Carrington
said yes, but had his doubts. His friend Henry Kissinger, the other
key member of the mediation group, shared them. They believed
the task was almost impossible to resolve, given the complex tangle
of personal, tribal and political interests. Kissinger, working on the
diplomatic principle (expressed firmly during Carrington's attempt
at a Balkans settlement) that there is no point in trying to broker a
peace treaty until there has been a ceasefire, agreed with Carrington that the mediation effort was a non-starter until both sides
had narrowed their differences.

The head of the diplomatic service Sir David Gillmore, who had
been one of Carrington's assistant under-secretaries at the Foreign
Office, wrote to him on 25 March 1994 warning of all the dangers
of accepting the role of convenor but asking him to accept it anyway. At that stage, said Gillmore, there were no terms of reference
agreed. No mediation would be in any way possible in time to
enable Inkatha to participate in the elections. Equally, the real task
and hope was that some agreement on the outstanding constitutional problems was more important than participation in the
elections and could contribute tangibly to reducing violence and
unrest in KwaZulu/Natal. Moreover, Gillmore noted, much to
Carrington's continuing gloom, the South African government
had not yet reached its own view on whether or not mediation
was desirable. Certainly President de Klerk wanted to attempt to
sort out the problems with Mandela and Buthelezi and the Zulu
monarchy. Only if he failed, suggested Gillmore, would de Klerk
consider using international mediation.

If the existence of a mediation effort were effective in reducing levels of
violence and in allowing a free election to proceed peacefully, it will have
been worthwhile. The Prime Minister [Major] and President Clinton
recently sent a joint message to Mandela and Buthelezi offering to help
in any way South Africans thought appropriate. A precipitate rejection of
their approach would lay us open to the charge that we were abandoning South Africa – and in particular Natal/KwaZulu, where there

are 200,000 Britons and substantial British commercial interests – to its fate at a moment of real crisis.[2]

So British interests, not simply the interests of the emerging South African Republic, were very much in the British government's mind when urging Carrington and Kissinger to help out. Clearly Gillmore's encouragement to Carrington was heartfelt if traditionally understated: 'I hope you will be able to give positive consideration to this idea.' Kissinger telephoned Carrington from Washington during the weekend of 26 and 27 March 1994. His general view was that the 'proposed mediation might get nowhere, but it should not be stifled at birth'.

So sensitive were the issues that one of the first problems took ages to resolve: how to find an agreement on the terms of reference for the mediation? The ANC and IFP had different versions and it took until the middle of April before the mediators could start work. Even so, Carrington harboured deep reservations about the mediation exercise. His view was that the ANC and IFP remained miles apart. He thought it wrong that there should be a deadline (22 April) for the team's work to succeed. Also, he could not quite see that Buthelezi would ever be satisfied and therefore any agreement would eventually unravel. He told Baroness Chalker, the Minister of State at the Foreign Office, that he thought the exercise was 'futile', but that neither he nor Kissinger felt able to turn down the South African request flat.

Here was an insight into the way the preamble and indeed some of the international negotiations were conducted. For example, Carrington had many issues which he thought should be clarified. However, he thought it less than constructive if he raised those questions; therefore he arranged for them to be passed through to the South African government to sort out. The mediation team included constitutional experts, but neither Carrington nor Kissinger came into that category – they were there to exercise their

2 Letter from the Permanent Under-Secretary of State at the FCO to Carrington, dated 25 March 1994. Carrington papers, Bledlow.

counselling and negotiating skills. It might be remembered that Kissinger had been involved in the search for a settlement in Rhodesia and that Carrington was still celebrated fourteen years on for having brought that about. Carrington told Chalker that both he and Kissinger thought the proposition that they should work with the five constitutional experts ridiculous. They did not feel able to say this themselves, but a way would have to be found, while saving face among the constitutional experts, for him and Kissinger to be put firmly in the lead.[3]

The truth was that no one could resolve the differences between the factions. All that might be achieved was a form of words that, rather like a truce once the shooting stops, leaves all parties full of hope but at the same time aware that there is much distance to go between truce and treaty. The result of Carrington's involvement was always opposed and consequently futile.

By the mid-1990s Carrington was inclined to bow out of active politics and diplomacy. There were those who thought there would always be a Carrington somewhere doing some important job. Carrington tended to agree. But in August 1996, at the age of seventy-seven, he encountered one of the few moments in his life that frightened him.

Ever since the Carringtons had moved into Bledlow, exactly fifty years earlier, they had tried to be at home for the harvest on the estate. Times had much moved on since those days back in the middle 1940s, especially in the development of farm machinery. Carrington always believed that the tractor revolutionized British agriculture. The combine harvester is the giant member of the tractor family. One afternoon in August one of these monsters became stuck down the lane by the Manor House at Bledlow. A lady had decided to abandon her car opposite the gate to the Lyde garden and so the combine could not be moved. Carrington saw no difficulty in this snag and declared that it was quite a simple task: move the car. He started to lift the car out of the way – not

3 Carrington papers, Bledlow.

something seventy-seven-year-olds often attempt – before anyone bent to help. He felt a twinge. By the late autumn the twinge still twinged. His doctors checked and said that they feared this was not muscular pain. Carrington had a kidney tumour. It had to be removed. Major surgery was arranged at speed. The Carringtons' staff rearranged the diary. Carrington insisted on personal notes, particularly to the Palace.

Lord and Lady Carrington present their compliments to the Lord Chamberlain and much regret that they are now unable to obey Her Majesty's command to attend an evening reception at Buckingham Palace on Tuesday 19 November 1996 owing to Lord Carrington's convalescence from surgery.

Very few were allowed to know of his illness and he dismissed it in one letter replying to an invitation to a Royal Opera House Gala with 'Sorry for this short reply but in hospital for a few days.' On 5 November he wrote to the British ambassador in Washington, Sir John Kerr, who had asked him to come to America:

I think perhaps March [1997] would be the best sort of time to do something in the States. I am off the road for a bit, having been in hospital and anything earlier might be rather too soon. Is that any good? I shall quite understand if it isn't.

On 11 November he wrote to Mollie Butler, Rab's widow: 'I have been to the butcher, who has removed various parts of my anatomy . . . I am so sorry to let you down.' In one month he had to turn down dozens of invitations from all over the world in a similar vein to his reply to Sir Claus Moser on 18 November:

The trouble is that both Iona and I have been to the butcher, though different ones, and neither of us are in much condition at the present time to go anywhere, though we are on the mend.

Recovery was much slower than either of them imagined and Carrington was back in the Lister Hospital towards the end of November. The family rallied round but he was a very difficult person to rally round. Carrington did not like to fuss around others and did not wish others to fuss around him. This applied to family as well as those outside.

Their second daughter, Virginia, was the one who could break these rules.[4] She thought her father her closest friend. They were very alike and Virginia later had very clear thoughts about his character. For example, she believed that he felt guilty about not encouraging her to go to university, something she had very much wanted to do. Coincidentally, of course, one of Carrington's lifelong regrets was that he had gone to Sandhurst rather than Oxford. Virginia had wanted to take a degree and had simply assumed that the matter was never considered; perhaps Carrington needed his children close by him. He had never been close to his father, but then that was not uncommon in those times and at that social level in society. Indeed, Carrington often seemed reluctant to break with a formality of an earlier time in the way children were brought up. He had worshipped his mother and cared very much for his sister Betty. Carrington probably distinguished between being a close family and an open demonstration of sentimental affection, indeed any open demonstration. Virginia thought that he preferred his dachshunds. She certainly had an abiding impression that her brother Rupert's relationship with his father was sometimes strained. She believed Rupert tested his father's patience too much. Not all sisters get it quite right about their brothers.

Looking back on his childhood in late 2007, Rupert remembered a very strict household. For example, he and his sisters were never allowed to use the front door at the Manor House. They were expected to go in and out by the side door. They were not

---

4 Virginia was usually known as Flori. Her father said she was called after floribunda which came from one of her godfathers. Virginia always thought it was her father who started the name after Floribelle, one of the estate cows. They both had a sense of humour.

allowed to use the main staircase. The back stairs would do them fine. When young, they certainly did not eat with their parents. Rupert, Virginia and Alexandra did not have the run of the house. Their place was in the nursery.

Carrington saw family discipline as a matter of course and duty. That did not mean he and Iona were at all uncaring or lacked understanding when it mattered most. For example, when in 1972 Virginia announced that she was to marry Lord Ashcombe, the Carringtons were disturbed.[5] Carrington thought little of Ashcombe. He considered him a drinker and a womanizer as well as being too old for Virginia (Ashcombe was more than twenty years her senior). Ashcombe's previous marriage had ended in failure and his reputation in London society was, according to Carrington, pretty low. Why was there to be a marriage if the groom's reputation was so colourful? Virginia was attracted by Ashcombe's 'experience', as Carrington in a charitable moment described his future son-in-law's background. Shortly before the wedding, Virginia sensed her father's considerable unease as they walked in the garden at Bledlow, yet he understood that she had made up her mind and so he was totally supportive. When the marriage ended just six years later – with Ashcombe heading for wife number three – Carrington simply comforted his daughter and never once said, 'I told you so.' A few years later, Virginia Carington was walking in a London park when she saw her ex-husband. She smiled and greeted him. His response was to ask if he knew her and walked on. Her father, hearing the story, simply shrugged.

Carrington himself was the public image of the family. Yet the strongest person in the family was his wife Iona. Rupert believed that his father's whole life centred on her and that they were totally entwined. To Carrington, Iona came first. One day in the autumn of 2007, Rupert and his sister were in the Bledlow kitchen gardens with their father when Virginia picked a particularly juicy raspberry. Her father was furious. That was for her mother.

Iona Carrington, the daughter of one of the very earliest aviation

5 They were married on New Year's Day, 1973.

pioneers, was sometimes frighteningly shrewd and uncompromising, with a formidable memory. While Carrington chose to pass over the wrongs apparently done him by others, his wife never would. She detested the likes of Julian Amery and John Nott, and said so. It was Iona Carrington who made sure that those who should know were aware of the suspicions of the Swiss diplomat Gaspard Bodner about the actions of the British ambassador to Buenos Aires during 1982. Just as she had no time for charlatans or wrongdoers, she had no patience with those who expected others to share burdens; that included illness – her own or that in others. For years she suffered from a rare blood disease, akin to leukaemia. There were terrible scares when continuous transfusions saved her life. Once out of hospital, she would scarcely acknowledge her illness and thought it bad form for others to ask after her health and worse still to tell her of theirs.

One matter was quite apparent. When Iona Carrington was very ill, her husband was close to utter despair. His family always said that their father was so devoted to their mother, that if 'anything happened to her, then he would go to pieces'. Since 1942 they had never gone through a day without trying to be in contact. When he had perhaps thought he would have a quiet life out of politics and international affairs, it was Iona Carrington who drove him on. She decided which invitations to accept and reject. It was she who said yes to luncheons, dinners and receptions, when he would have liked to stay at home.

Such people tend not to know obscure people. Their Christmas card list not surprisingly read like an international *Who's Who*. They were in demand until the end. When Queen Elizabeth the Queen Mother was celebrating her one-hundredth birthday, it was only natural that she should spend the weekend at Bledlow for a birthday party with the Carringtons. She had a new dress made for the occasion. When she came down for dinner, she asked Iona Carrington how she liked her new frock. At one hundred years old, there was Queen Elizabeth buying new clothes and Iona, twenty years her junior, wondered why she herself should not have more confidence in the future.

They had in April 2002 been inseparable for sixty years. But each winter was becoming a trial for Iona's vulnerability to chills. That winter, she was taken into Stoke Mandeville Hospital's intensive care unit. A flu bug had turned into something more sinister. Carrington's own biannual test for his kidney cancer was clear, yet it was an unpleasant test and there was always a question in the back of his mind as each check-up date approached. It really was a time to slow down. Slow speed was not the experience others might have understood. There was not a week when he did not get a request to speak at some function or attend another dinner, luncheon or reception at the highest social, diplomatic and political level. In the spring of 2002 there was, of course, the twentieth-anniversary examination of the 1982 Falklands War. It was still a bitter memory. He did not want to take part in the media rerun. In a curious way he was a hero of that war. Sir John Nott timed his own memoirs to appear on the eve of the anniversary, thus getting his version of events noticed. Why not? People had made their own judgements long ago, and it was unjust that Nott had never come out of it particularly well. He had been right in thinking that Carrington would remain the honourable fellow who had done the honourable thing. Nott was known as the politically ambitious minister who had stayed on. What was wrong with being politically ambitious? He was an MP, not a peer. He had gone into politics to get on. In different circumstances he might have been Chancellor. A working politician, he would have said, not one with an estate to bugger off to.

Come 2002 the Carrington generation was fading fast and even Ted Heath had given up his seat in the Commons. At Lord Hailsham's memorial service, Carrington was there to give the address. It was a reminder, observed Carrington, that there were few left who had served in the Second World War and had then decided on politics to make the world a better place for those who came after.

More than half a century after he had entered Parliament, Carrington found it hard to trust the political society about him. After the defeat of John Major, he became greatly disillusioned with political parties. He no longer liked the people in the Conservative Party who he felt were totally lacking in any sense of honour and public duty. He still regarded himself as a Conservative but felt totally out of sympathy with the party.

He remained very fond of Margaret Thatcher, although there was an incident in April 1990 that showed how far apart they could be. After dinner the two were sitting in Carrington's London house when she wondered aloud what she should do to counter the anti-Thatcher feeling within her own party. Carrington said that as he was far removed from the politicking of Tory Central Office he could tell her what he believed to be the truth. The general public might have wanted her to stay but he said the Conservative Party wanted her to leave Downing Street. She was taken aback. He then added that she would be allowed to go in her own time 'and with dignity'. At that moment she felt reminded that whatever his age and distance from politics, Carrington remained part of the Tory Establishment that, if it had had its way, would never have allowed her to become Leader and then Prime Minister. She remembered also that Carrington had openly been against her election and had been a prominent ally of Edward Heath. Long after she had left Downing Street, they remained friends and, although he became increasingly bemused by her political eccentricity, they had plenty in common. For example, by 2000 Thatcher had written off William Hague as a hopeless case and so had Carrington. Hague was on occasions not an admirer of Carrington. One day that spring Carrington asked Thatcher if she did not think that the most likely scenario was Hague's defeat in the forthcoming election followed by his replacement as Leader by Michael Portillo. She was appalled at his suggestion. 'Portillo?' she glared. 'Portillo? But he is a foreigner.' In political retirement they were safe from each other but Carrington always believed that even if there had been no Falklands debacle, 'I'd have eventually had a bloody row with Margaret and gone.'

Yet was not Thatcher everything about the Conservative Party the ordinary voter so admired? Did not Tony Blair model himself on Thatcher? Was not therefore Carrington's allegiance not to a

Thatcher figure but to the party that gave him his political platform, its chairmanship and made him into an international celebrity
rather than a backwoodsman peer and of course sponsored him in
his life peerage as Baron Carrington of Upton in 1999?

Yes, but I've always hated the Conservative Party – nothing made me
hate it more than being chairman of it. Individual members all right.
Collective so awful. Look at it now. Going down the plug hole.

In fact, what Carrington never told anyone and what no one ever
seemed to ask about was the fact that this man who had been a
member of every Conservative government from Churchill to
Thatcher claimed he had never been a member of the Conservative Party. He told me he had never paid a single subscription in
his life, even though at one point he had been Treasurer of the
Buckinghamshire Conservative Association. 'I have never thought
it important. After all, I am a Conservative and that should be
enough.'
    Was he really a Conservative? He did not like what the party
had become. In fact, he was sickened by political life. Most of all,
he was saddened by its inability, with all the assets of a wealthy
exchequer and theoretical expertise, to make the nation a happier
as well as a wealthier state. He thought British society and political
machinery of the twenty-first century open to many charges but
the worst was its incompetence and that grieved him more than
anything else in his later years. Carrington did not always understand the society – he would have called it the middle class – that
influenced so much that he had politically represented. He found
it increasingly hard to connect to those middle classes yet perfectly
understood the so-called working classes. An example of this was
during his time as Defence Secretary: Carrington did not find it
easy to understand nor warm to middle-class civil servants but he
had enormous affection for his driver 'Henry' Hall and would have
him down to Bledlow for weekends. They would, said someone
in Carrington's private office, prod sheep together. This was nothing to do with the common touch. It was more to do with an

instinct only to open up to those whom he really liked. Hall had a habit of only polishing the side of the car into which Carrington got ('we only rubs down the side of the 'orse what the officer mounts') and they both saw the joke. It was the sort of very small matter that put all the big issues in perspective. The major moments could so easily be sources of disappointment, regret and uncertainty. So, what mattered a half-rubbed-down 'orse? Carrington thought it funny.

When Fiona Graham-Mackay painted Carrington, she had him sitting on the window seat in the gallery at Bledlow with Edward, his dachshund (named after Heath) on his lap. (Hilda, the other dachshund, named after Thatcher, was excluded from the painting.) Carrington is looking over the garden at two huge trees. 'You know,' he said to the artist, 'I planted those fifty years ago. By the time I realized they were in the wrong place, there was nothing I could do about it. All too late. All too late.' She began to work on the haziness of the trees in the portrait's background and her sitter's eyeline to his past. Through the Georgian panes were those two sturdy images set in a peaceful idyll of an eighteenth-century manor house of aristocrats. They remain there today as the deciduous contradictions to another image: the silver spoon, the privilege of caste, the charmed and very public life that Peter Carrington was so very reluctant to leave.

He had all the trappings and markings of an English Tory aristocrat. But Carrington was not a Tory. He was a Whig, a Whig managing decline.

Epilogue

Carrington had a secret horde of vignettes. They were his very private pen-portraits of people, past and present, whom he had known through decades of public life. Not all were flattering, although none was spiteful. They were in some ways the reports of an international housemaster, and, like the pastime of flicking through end-of-term class notes, the jottings were enlightening.

This was so with the earliest reports on Carrington himself. At his prep school, Sandroyd, it was thought that 'his keenness will carry him a long way . . . enjoys life thoroughly'. When he left in 1932, a note from his final-term report could have been written by a Foreign Office Permanent Secretary fifty years later: 'It is with genuine sorrow that I lose him . . . he has always done his best and that best has been at times, very good.' (This was incidentally almost the exact phrase used to describe Carrington's close friend the Duke of Edinburgh when he left Gordonstoun School.)

Eton was not always so generous with praise for Carrington. At the close of Lent Half 1934, W. R. Colquhoun wrote: 'His most striking failures occurred in the manner in which he did things without any semblance of common sense or determination to apply his knowledge. I think he could have been more attentive and less of a minor bore in the school.' On the other hand, Cyril Butterwick, his housemaster, packed him off to the Royal Military Academy, Sandhurst, with this note to his father: 'He is not very clever but his intelligence is well up to and probably above the average . . . he is a delightful boy, absolutely trustworthy, loyal and good and he is coming on all the time.' Most who knew Carrington would have been surprised at Colquhoun's tetchy view (although the fact that he was a classicist may explain it) and would have said that Butterwick had got it right.

Report-writing is of course part attention to detail and part disguising the tutor's own failure. Carrington was known to overlook detail while remaining an impressive tutor. Few left his company without learning a great deal about the subject and about themselves. But Carrington was rarely scathing, and so perhaps would not have made a good prep-school master. He came to his own conclusions about people, and mostly liked them, as I discovered over lunch on a fine day in 2014. It was inevitable, though, that his feelings towards the people involved in the events at the start of the Falklands War in 1982 should have continued to agitate his sense of fairness. Some could never be forgiven, although he much admired the Chief of the Defence Staff, Admiral of the Fleet Sir Terry Lewin, Admiral Sir Henry Leach and his people in the FCO.

First on his Falklands blacklist was one of those he part blamed for the 1982 war in the South Atlantic that ended his political career – the then British Ambassador to Argentina, Anthony Williams. He believed Williams had never understood Argentina's inability to comprehend British domestic politics and had therefore failed to represent the UK to the Argentine government and equally failed to properly report Argentinian intentions to the FCO. Carrington's view was supported in correspondence between the then head of the FCO, Sir Anthony Acland, and the director of the South American department, Patrick Robin Fearn (later Sir Robin Fearn).

Carrington's view was partly encouraged by his own efforts to stop the then Secretary of Defence, John Nott (later Sir John), decommissioning the ice patrol vessel HMS *Endurance* and selling her off to the Brazilians. In the June 1981 Defence Review *Endurance* was to be withdrawn. Carrington (5 June 1981 and November 1981) objected to the decision. Nott said there was no money and that if Carrington wanted her kept in the Royal Navy, then the FCO should find the funds. Carrington went as far as to suggest funding could come from elsewhere in government. The Brazilians were encouraged to believe they could buy the ship. The idea that she could be sold to Brazil was enough to convince Argentina that the UK was no longer interested in protecting the Falklands, or so Carrington thought. He lodged a strong protest to Nott on 22 January via Robin Fearn. Carrington's frustration was exacerbated by his strong belief that Nott and perhaps even the Prime Minister were more concerned about the political embarrassment of the *Endurance* case rather than the real and practical defence of the Falklands and the islanders.

Carrington saw Anthony Williams's valedictory despatch from Argentina, and its wording was enough for him to believe that Williams had failed and then had attempted to justify his position by stating that the FCO, and by implication Carrington, had ignored his advice.[1] He regarded it as a bitter message. Robin Fearn reported that 'A valedictory despatch would usually be given a wide distribution. After discussion within the Office however, we have concluded that it would not be right in this case.' Williams's despatch was then classified 'Confidential'. Carrington never forgave him and, when they were in the same room at a NATO meeting on some later occasion, publicly snubbed him. Carrington's was a powerful, unforgiving dislike. Perhaps only Mark Thatcher was lower on the Unlikely Bledlow Guest list.

Carrington was never amused by humbug, particularly among the Anglican clergy. Though an enormous admirer of Peter Nott, sometime Bishop of Norwich, and of the late Archbishop Robert Runcie, he was suspicious of Anglican prelates. With some humour he would describe the Athenaeum Club as the haunt of too many bishops. Bishop Harries (once of Oxford) he dismissed as one forgetting his Orders of Christianity and too full of himself. However, by and large he liked the Church of England, regarding it as the purveyor of civilized moral leadership. His was a traditional view – there were spare Books of Common Prayer for house guests who would walk across to the church at Bledlow.

On the pews of Westminster Carrington was less generous. He believed the Lords was a place of poor farce, in total need of reform and increasingly littered with political appointees who knew little and thus made no contribution to the great debate of guiding and even re-thinking society. In the Commons, he liked Margaret

1   The National Archives, File ALA 014/3, Folio 8, Valedictory Despatch OD No. 1/82, particularly paragraphs 9 and 10.

Thatcher very much, even though they often disagreed and even though he thought her totally humourless. He told a good tale about her being given an Old Testament joke to brighten up a speech. When she got to the Commandments, she deleted a reference to the Tablets and inserted Pills. She could never see a joke nor see the point in telling one. He could find her frustrating and insufferably single-minded. He threatened to resign when he believed she was forcing him to adopt a Foreign Office pro-Israel policy that would protect her General Election figures in Finchley. Yet he continued to admire her as a leader. Of Thatcher's son, Carrington could find nothing good to say. He thought him arrogant and rude, giving as an example the occasion described earlier in this book when Mark accompanied his mother, uninvited, to a business lunch at Bledlow.

Of David Cameron, he thought he could not have done much more than he did. In George Osborne, Carrington saw an interesting man and a good Chancellor. He thought that no one else stood out in Cameron's Cabinet. He mourned the Party that could no longer produce Big Beasts, as he called them. Where were the Hailshams, the Macmillans, the Douglas-Homes, the Butlers? Clarke and Heseltine were the last of them, he said.

This mood was not that of a dozing nonagenarian wallowing in political nostalgia. He just supposed that the way of politics had changed so much that there was no place for the kinds of people who went into Parliament during the post-World War II era. Most of all, Carrington mourned what he regarded as the passing of a sense of duty and the responsibility of unearned privilege.

Index